C000024570

CIMA Official
Learning System

CIMA

PUBLISHING

Operational Level

F1 – Financial Operations

Jo Watkins

ELSEVIER

AMSTERDAM   BOSTON   HEIDELBERG   LONDON   NEW YORK   OXFORD
PARIS   SAN DIEGO   SAN FRANCISCO   SINGAPORE   SYDNEY   TOKYO

CIMA Publishing is an imprint of Elsevier
Linacre House, Jordan Hill, Oxford OX2 8DP, UK
30 Corporate Drive, Suite 400, Burlington, MA 01803, USA

Copyright © 2009 Elsevier Ltd. All rights reserved

No part of this publication may be reproduced, stored in a retrieval system
or transmitted in any form or by any means electronic, mechanical, photocopying,
recording or otherwise without the prior written permission of the publisher

Permissions may be sought directly from Elsevier's Science & Technology Rights
Department in Oxford, UK: phone (+44) (0) 1865 843830; fax (+44) (0) 1865 853333;
e-mail: permissions@elsevier.com. Alternatively you can visit the Science and Technology
Books website at www.elsevierdirect.com/rights for further information

Notice
No responsibility is assumed by the publisher for any injury and/or damage to persons
or property as a matter of products liability, negligence or otherwise, or from any use
or operation of any methods, products, instructions or ideas contained in the material
herein.

British Library Cataloguing in Publication Data
A catalogue record for this book is available from the British Library

Library of Congress Cataloguing in Publication Data
A catalogue record for this book is available from the Library of Congress

ISBN: 978-1-85617-791-7

For information on all CIMA publications
visit our website at www.elsevierdirect.com

Typeset by Macmillan Publishing Solutions
(www.macmillansolutions.com)

Printed and bound in Hungary

09 10 11   11 10 9 8 7 6 5 4 3 2 1

Working together to grow
libraries in developing countries
www.elsevier.com | www.bookaid.org | www.sabre.org

ELSEVIER   BOOK AID   Sabre Foundation
            International

Contents

3 Indirect Taxes and Employee Taxation

The CIMA
Learning System

Acknowledgements

Every effort has been made to contact the holders of copyright material, but if any here have been inadvertently overlooked, the publishers will be pleased to make the necessary arrangements at the first opportunity.

We would also like to thank Mike Rogers for his invaluable contribution as the reviewer also Tom Rolfe author of previous editions of this text.

How to use the CIMA *Learning System*

This *Financial Operations Learning System* has been devised as a resource for students attempting to pass their CIMA exams, and provides:

- a detailed explanation of all syllabus areas;
- extensive 'practical' materials, including readings from relevant journals;
- generous question practice, together with full solutions;
- an exam preparation section, complete with exam standard questions and solutions.

This Learning System has been designed with the needs of home-study and distance-learning candidates in mind. Such students require full coverage of the syllabus topics, and also the facility to undertake extensive question practice. However, the Learning System is also ideal for fully taught courses.

The main body of the text is divided into a number of chapters, each of which is organised in the following pattern:

- *Detailed learning outcomes.* These outcomes are expected after your studies of the chapters are complete. You should assimilate these before beginning detailed work on the chapter, so that you can appreciate where your studies are leading.
- *Step-by-step topic coverage.* This is the heart of each chapter, containing detailed explanatory text supported where appropriate by worked examples and exercises. You should work carefully through this section, ensuring that you understand the material being explained and can tackle the examples and exercises successfully. Remember that in many cases knowledge is cumulative: if you fail to digest the earlier material thoroughly, you may struggle to understand later chapters.
- *Readings and activities.* Most chapters are illustrated by more practical elements, such as relevant journal articles or other readings, together with comments and questions designed to stimulate discussion.
- *Question practice.* The test of how well you have learned the material is your ability to tackle exam-standard questions. Make a serious attempt at producing your own answers, but at this stage don't be too concerned about attempting the questions in exam conditions.

In particular, it is more important to absorb the material thoroughly by completing a full solution than to observe the time limits that would apply in the actual exam.

- *Solutions.* Avoid the temptation to merely 'audit' the solutions provided. It is an illusion to think that this provides the same benefits as you would gain from a serious attempt of your own. However, if you are struggling to get started on a question, you should read the introductory guidance provided at the beginning of the solution, and then make your own attempt before referring back to the full solution.

Having worked through the chapters, you are ready to begin your final preparations for the examination. The final section of the CIMA *Learning System* provides you with the guidance you need. It includes the following features:

- A brief guide to revision technique.
- A note on the format of the examination. You should know what to expect when you tackle the real exam, and in particular the number of questions to attempt, which questions are compulsory and which optional, and so on.
- Guidance on how to tackle the examination itself.
- A table mapping revision questions to the syllabus learning outcomes allowing you to quickly identify questions by subject area.
- Revision questions. These are of exam standard and should be tackled in exam conditions, especially as regards the time allocation.
- Solutions to the revision questions. As before, these indicate the length and the quality of solution that would be expected of a well-prepared candidate.

If you work conscientiously through this CIMA *Learning System* according to the guidelines above, you will be giving yourself an excellent chance of exam success. Good luck with your studies!

Guide to the Icons used within this Text

Key term or definition

π Equation to learn

Exam tip to topic likely to appear in the exam

Exercise

? Question

Solution

! Comment or Note

Study technique

Passing exams is partly a matter of intellectual ability, but however accomplished you are in that respect, you can improve your chances significantly by the use of appropriate study and revision techniques. In this section we briefly outline some tips for effective study during the earlier stages of your approach to the exam. Later in the text we mention some techniques that you will find useful at the revision stage.

Planning

To begin with, formal planning is essential to get the best return from the time you spend studying. Estimate how much time you are going to need in total for each subject that you face. Remember that you need to allow time for revision as well as for initial study of the material. The amount of notional study time for any subject is the minimum estimated time that students will need to achieve the specified learning outcomes set out earlier in this chapter. This time includes all appropriate learning activities, for example, face-to-face tuition, private study, directed home study, learning at the workplace, revision time, etc. You may find it helpful to read *Better exam results* by Sam Malone, CIMA Publishing, ISBN: 075066357X. This book will provide you with proven study techniques. Chapter by chapter it covers the building blocks of successful learning and examination techniques.

The notional study time for *Operational Level – Financial Operations* is 200 hours. Note that the standard amount of notional learning hours attributed to one full-time academic year of approximately 30 weeks is 1200 hours.

By way of example, the notional study time might be made up as follows:

	Hours
Face-to-face study: up to	60
Personal study: up to	100
'Other' study – e.g. learning at the workplace, revision, etc.: up to	40
	200

Note that all study and learning-time recommendations should be used only as a guideline and are intended as minimum amounts. The amount of time recommended for face-to-face tuition, personal study and/or additional learning will vary according to the type of course undertaken, prior learning of the student, and the pace at which different students learn.

Now split your total time requirement over the weeks between now and the examination. This will give you an idea of how much time you need to devote to study each week. Remember to allow for holidays or other periods during which you will not be able to study (e.g. because of seasonal workloads).

With your study material before you, decide which chapters you are going to study in each week, and which weeks you will devote to revision and final question practice.

Prepare a written schedule summarising the above – and stick to it!

The amount of space allocated to a topic in the study material is not a very good guide as to how long it will take you. For example, 'Financial accounting and reporting' has a weight of 60 per cent in the syllabus and this is the best guide as to how long you should spend on it. It occupies 60 per cent of the main body of the text.

It is essential to know your syllabus. As your course progresses you will become more familiar with how long it takes to cover topics in sufficient depth. Your timetable may need to be adapted to allocate enough time for the whole syllabus.

Tips for effective studying

(1) Aim to find a quiet and undisturbed location for your study, and plan as far as possible to use the same period of time each day. Getting into a routine helps to avoid wasting time. Make sure that you have all the materials you need before you begin, so as to minimise interruptions.

(2) Store all your materials in one place, so that you don't waste time searching for items around the house. If you have to pack everything away after each study period, keep them in a box, or even a suitcase, which won't be disturbed until the next time.

(3) Limit distractions. To make the most effective use of your study periods, you should be able to apply total concentration, so turn off the TV, set your phones to message mode, and put up your 'do not disturb' sign.

(4) Your timetable will tell you which topic to study. However, before diving in and becoming engrossed in the finer points, make sure you have an overall picture of all the areas that need to be covered by the end of that session. After an hour, allow your-self a short break and move away from your books. With experience, you will learn to assess the pace you need to work at. You should also allow enough time to read rel-evant articles from newspapers and journals, which will supplement your knowledge and demonstrate a wider perspective.

(5) Work carefully through a chapter, making notes as you go. When you have covered a suitable amount of material, vary the pattern by attempting a practice question. Preparing an answer plan is a good habit to get into, while you are both studying and revising, and also in the examination room. It helps to impose a structure on your solutions, and avoids rambling. When you have finished your attempt, make notes of any mistakes you made, or any areas that you failed to cover or covered only skimpily.

(6) Make notes as you study, and discover the techniques that work best for you. Your notes may be in the form of lists, bullet points, diagrams, summaries, 'mind maps', or the written word, but remember that you will need to refer back to them at a later date, so they must be intelligible. If you are on a taught course, make sure you high-light any issues you would like to follow up with your lecturer.

(7) Organise your paperwork. There are now numerous paper storage systems available to ensure that all your notes, calculations and articles can be effectively filed and easily retrieved later.

Paper F1 – Financial Operations

Syllabus Overview

The core objectives of Paper F1 are the preparation of the full financial statements for a single company and the principal consolidated financial statements for a simple group. Coverage of a wide range of international standards is implicit in these objectives, as specified in the paper's content. Similarly, understanding the regulatory and ethical context of financial reporting, covered in the paper, is vital to ensuring that financial statements meet users' needs. Principles of taxation are included, not only to support accounting for taxes in financial statements, but also as a basis for examining the role of tax in financial analysis and decision-making within subsequent papers (Paper F2 Financial Management and Paper F3 Financial Strategy).

Syllabus Structure

The syllabus comprises the following topics and study weightings:

A	Principles of Business Taxation	25%
B	Regulation and Ethics of Financial Reporting	15%
C	Financial Accounting and Reporting	60%

Assessment Strategy

There will be a written examination paper of 3 hours, plus 20 minutes of pre-examination question paper reading time. The examination paper will have the following sections:

Section A – 20 marks
A variety of compulsory objective test questions, each worth between 2 and 4 marks. Mini scenarios may be given, to which a group of questions relate.

Section B – 30 marks
Six compulsory short answer questions, each worth 5 marks. A short scenario may be given, to which some or all questions relate.

Section C – 50 marks
One or two compulsory questions. Short scenarios may be given, to which questions relate.

Learning Outcomes and Indicative Syllabus Content

F1 – A. Principles of Business Taxation (25%)

Learning Outcomes

On completion of their studies students should be able to:

Lead	Component	Indicative Syllabus Content
1. Explain the types of tax that can apply to incorporated businesses, their principles and potential administrative requirements. (2)	(a) identify the principal types of taxation likely to be of relevance to an incorporated business in a particular country; including direct tax on the company's trading profits and capital gains, indirect taxes collected by the company, employee taxation and withholding taxes on international payments;	• Concepts of direct versus indirect taxes, taxable person and competent jurisdiction. (A)
	(b) describe the features of the principal types of taxation likely to be of relevance to an incorporated business in a particular country; (e.g. in terms of who ultimately bears the tax cost, withholding responsibilities, principles of calculating the tax base);	• Types of taxation, including direct tax on the company's trading profits and capital gains, indirect taxes collected by the company, employee taxation and withholding taxes on international payments, and their features (e.g. in terms of who ultimately bears the tax cost, withholding responsibilities, principles of calculating the tax base). (A, B)
	(c) identify and explain key administrative requirements (e.g. record-keeping and record retention rules, filing and tax payment deadlines) and the possible enquiry and investigation powers of taxing authorities associated with the principal types of taxation likely to be of relevance to an incorporated business;	• Sources of tax rules (e.g. domestic primary legislation and court rulings, practice of the relevant taxing authority, supranational bodies, such as the EU in the case of value added/sales tax, and international tax treaties). (A, B)
	(d) explain the difference in principle between tax avoidance and tax evasion;	• Indirect taxes collected by the company: – In the context of indirect taxes, the distinction between unit taxes (e.g. excise duties based on physical measures) and ad valorem taxes (e.g. sales tax based on value).
	(e) illustrate numerically the principles of different types of tax based on provided information.	

– The mechanism of value added/sales taxes, in which businesses are liable for tax on their outputs less credits for tax paid on their inputs, including the concepts of exemption and variation in tax rates depending on the type of output and disallowance of input credits for exempt outputs. (B)

● Employee taxation:

– The employee as a separate taxable person subject to a personal income tax regime.

– Use of employer reporting and withholding to ensure compliance and assist tax collection. (B)

● The need for record-keeping and record retention that may be additional to that required for financial accounting purposes. (C)

● The need for deadlines for reporting (filing returns) and tax payments. (C)

● Types of powers of tax authorities to ensure compliance with tax rules:

– Power to review and query filed returns.

– Power to request special reports or returns.

– Power to examine records (generally extending back some years).

– Powers of entry and search.

– Exchange of information with tax authorities in other jurisdictions. (C)

(Continued)

F1 – A. Principles of Business Taxation (25%) (continued)

Learning Outcomes

On completion of their studies students should be able to:

Lead	Component	Indicative Syllabus Content
		• The distinction between tax avoidance and tax evasion, and how these vary among jurisdictions (including the difference between the use of statutory general anti-avoidance provisions and case law based regimes). (D)
2. Explain fundamental concepts in international taxation of incorporated businesses.	(a) identify situations in which foreign tax obligations (reporting and liability) could arise and methods for relieving foreign tax;	• International taxation:
	(b) describe and explain sources of tax rules and explain the importance of jurisdiction.	– The concept of corporate residence and the variation in rules for its determination across jurisdictions (e.g. place of incorporation versus place of management).
		– Types of payments on which withholding tax may be required (especially interest, dividends, royalties and capital gains accruing to non-residents).
		– Means of establishing a taxable presence in another country (local company and branch).
		– The effect of double tax treaties (based on the OECD Model Convention) on the above (e.g. reduction of withholding tax rates, provisions for defining a permanent establishment). (A, B)
3. Prepare corporate income tax calculations based on a given simple set of rules. (3)	(a) prepare corporate income tax calculations based on a given simple set of rules.	• Direct taxes on company profits and gains:
		– The principle of non-deductibility of dividends and systems of taxation defined according to the treatment of dividends in the hands of the shareholder (e.g. classical, partial imputation and imputation).

– The distinction between accounting and taxable profits in absolute terms (e.g. disallowable expenditure on revenue account, such as entertaining, and on capital account, such as formation and acquisition costs) and in terms of timing (e.g. deduction on a paid basis).

– The concept of tax depreciation replacing book depreciation in the tax computation and its calculation based on the pooling of assets by their classes, including balancing adjustments on the disposal of assets.

– The nature of rules recharacterising interest payments as dividends (e.g. where interest is based on profitability).

– Potential for variation in rules for calculating the tax base dependent on the nature or source of the income (schedular systems).

– The need for rules dealing with the relief of losses.

– Principles of relief for foreign taxes by exemption, deduction and credit.

– The concept of tax consolidation (e.g. for relief of losses and deferral of capital gains on asset transfers within a group).

● Accounting treatment of taxation and disclosure requirements under IAS 12.

4. Explain and apply the accounting rules contained in IAS 12 for current and deferred taxation, including calculation of deferred tax based on a given set of rules. (3)

(a) explain and apply the accounting rules contained in IAS 12 for current and deferred taxation, including calculation of deferred tax based on a given set of rules. (3)

F1 – B. Regulation and Ethics of Financial Reporting (15%)

Learning Outcomes

On completion of their studies students should be able to:

Lead	Component	Indicative Syllabus Content
1. Explain the need for and methods of regulating accounting and financial reporting. (2)	(a) explain the need for regulation of published accounts and the concept that regulatory regimes vary from country to country; (b) explain potential elements that might be expected in a national regulatory framework for published accounts; (c) describe the role and structure of the International Accounting Standards Board (IASB) and the International Organisation of Securities Commissions (IOSCO); (d) describe and explain the meaning of given features or parts of the IASB's *Framework for the Presentation and Preparation of Financial Statements*; (e) describe the process leading to the promulgation of an IFRS;	● The need for regulation of accounts. (A) ● Elements in a regulatory framework for published accounts (e.g. company law, local GAAP, review of accounts by public bodies). (B) ● GAAP based on prescriptive versus principles-based standards. (B) ● The role and structure of the IASB and IOSCO. (C) ● The IASB's *Framework for the Presentation and Preparation of Financial Statements*. (D) ● The process leading to the promulgation of a standard practice. (E) ● Ways in which IFRSs are used: adoption as local GAAP, model for local GAAP, persuasive influence in formulating local GAAP. (F)

(f) describe ways in which IFRSs can interact with local regulatory frameworks;

(g) explain in general terms, the role of the external auditor, the elements of the audit report and types of qualification of that report.

- The powers and duties of the external auditors, the audit report and its qualification for accounting statements not in accordance with best practice. (G)

2. Explain the role of ethics in accounting and financial reporting, and apply the CIMA Code in given hypothetical circumstances (3) apply the provisions of the CIMA Code of Ethics for Professional Accountants, in given hypothetical circumstances.

(a) explain the importance of the exercise of ethical principles in reporting and assessing information;

(b) describe the sources of ethical codes for those involved in the reporting or taxation affairs of an organisation, including the external auditors;

(c) apply the provisions of the CIMA Code of Ethics for Professional Accountants of particular relevance to the information reporting, assurance and tax-related activities of the accountant.

- Ethical requirements of the professional accountant in reporting and assessing information (the fundamental principles). (A)
- Sources of ethical codes (IFAC, professional bodies, employing organisations, social/religious/personal sources). (B)
- Provisions of the CIMA Code of Ethics for Professional Accountants of particular relevance to information reporting, assurance and tax-related activities (especially section 220 and Part C). (C)

F1 – C. Financial Accounting and Reporting (60%)

Learning Outcomes

On completion of their studies students should be able to:

Lead	Component	Indicative Syllabus Content
1. Prepare the full financial statements of a single company and the consolidated statements of financial position and comprehensive income for a group (in relatively straightforward circumstances). (3)	(a) prepare a complete set of financial statements, as specified in IAS 1(revised), in a form suitable for publication for a single company; (b) explain and apply the conditions required for an undertaking to be a subsidiary or an associate of another company; (c) prepare the consolidated statement of financial position (balance sheet) and statement of comprehensive income for a group of companies in a form suitable for publication for a group of companies comprising directly held interests in one or more fully-controlled subsidiaries and associates (such interests having been acquired at the beginning of an accounting period); (d) explain and apply the concepts of fair value at the point of acquisition, identifiability of assets and liabilities, and recognition of goodwill.	• Preparation of the financial statements of a single company, as specified in IAS 1 (revised), including the statement of changes in equity. (IAS 1(revised)) (A) • Preparation of the statement of cash flows (IAS 7). (A) • Preparation of the consolidated statement of financial position (balance sheet) and statement of comprehensive income where: interests are directly held by the acquirer (parent) company; any subsidiary is fully controlled; and all interests were acquired at the beginning of an accounting period. (IFRS 3 and IAS 27, to the extent that their provisions are relevant to the specified learning outcomes). (B, C, D)
2. Explain and apply international standards dealing with a range of matters and items. (3)	(a) explain and apply the accounting rules contained in IFRSs and IASs dealing with reporting performance, non-current assets, including their impairment, and inventories, disclosure of related parties to a business, construction contracts (and related financing costs), post-balance sheet events, provisions, contingencies, and leases (lessee only); (b) explain and apply the accounting rules contained in IFRSs and IASs governing share capital transactions;	• Reporting performance: recognition of revenue, measurement of profit or loss, prior period items, discontinuing operations and segment reporting (IAS 1(revised), 8 & 18, IFRS 5 & 8). (A) • Property, Plant and Equipment (IAS 16): the calculation of depreciation and the effect of revaluations, changes to economic useful life, repairs, improvements and disposals. (A)

explain and apply the principles of the accounting rules contained in IFRSs and IASs dealing with disclosure of related parties to a business, construction contracts (and related financing costs), post-balance sheet events, provisions, contingencies, and leases (lessee only).

- Research and development costs (IAS 38): criteria for capitalisation. (A)
- Intangible Assets (IAS 38) and goodwill: recognition, valuation, amortisation. (A)
- Impairment of Assets (IAS 36) and Non-Current Assets Held for Sale (IFRS 5) and their effects on the above. (A)
- Inventories (IAS 2). (A)
- Issue and redemption of shares, including treatment of share issue and redemption costs (IAS 32 & 39), the share premium account, the accounting for maintenance of capital arising from the purchase by a company of its own shares. (B)
- The disclosure of related parties to a business (IAS 24). (A)
- Construction contracts and related financing costs (IAS 11 & 23): determination of cost, net realisable value, the inclusion of overheads and the measurement of profit on uncompleted contracts. (A)
- Post-balance sheet events (IAS 10). (A)
- Provisions and contingencies (IAS 37). (A)
- Leases (IAS 17) – Distinguishing operating from finance leases and the concept of substance over form (from the *Framework*); accounting for leases in the books of the lessee. (A)
- Issue and redemption of shares, including treatment of share issue and redemption costs (IAS 32 & 39), the share premium account, the accounting for maintenance of capital arising from the purchase by a company of its own shares. (B)

Principles of
Business Taxation –
Introduction

Principles of Business Taxation – Introduction

LEARNING OUTCOMES

After completing this chapter you should be able to:

▶ describe the features of the principal types of taxation likely to be of relevance to an incorporated business in a particular country (e.g. in terms of who ultimately bears the tax cost, withholding responsibilities, and principles of calculating the tax base);

▶ describe sources of tax rules and explain the importance of jurisdiction.

Learning aims

The learning aim of this part of the syllabus is that students should be able to 'describe the types of business taxation rules and requirements likely to affect an entity (in respect of itself and its employees)'.

The topics covered in this chapter are as follows:

- concepts of direct versus indirect taxes, taxable person and competent jurisdiction;
- sources of tax rules.

1.1 Introduction

Principles of business tax account for 25 per cent of the Financial Operations syllabus and therefore 25 per cent of the examination paper. In the first six chapters of this text we will cover general principles of taxation. General principles should apply in most countries and are not specific to any one country. In your studies you can use examples of general principles drawn from a 'benchmark' tax regime (e.g. the UK, the USA, etc.) or an appropriate local tax regime. This text mainly refers to the UK tax system, but any system could be used to illustrate general principles.

> Knowledge of specific tax regimes is NOT REQUIRED and details of any specific tax regime will NOT be examined. The exam paper will include a tax regime of a relevant country. The tax regime will provide all the information, including tax rates, required to prepare the answer for any tax computation questions. An example of a tax regime can be found in Chapter 3.

In the first part of this chapter, we will consider general principles of taxation, basic tax terminology and the classification of taxes. The chapter will then conclude with a consideration of the sources of tax rules in a country.

1.2 Taxation as a source of government revenue

It has been said that 'what the government gives it must first take away'. The economic resources available to society are limited, so an increase in a government's expenditure will mean a reduction in the spending capacity of the private sector. Taxation is the main means by which a government raises revenue to meet its expenditure. Taxation may also be used by a government as a means of influencing economic decisions or controlling the economy; in this way taxation will also reflect prevailing social values and priorities in a country. This characteristic helps explain why no two countries' tax systems will be identical in every respect and it also explains why governments continually change their tax systems.

Revenue raised from taxation is needed to finance government expenditure on items such as the health service, retirement pensions, unemployment benefit and other social benefits, education, financing government borrowing (interest on government stocks), etc.

1.3 Principles of taxation

No tax system is perfect, but an 'ideal' system should conform to certain principles if it is to achieve its objectives without producing negative effects.

1.3.1 Canons of taxation

In 1776 Adam Smith in his book *The Wealth of Nations* proposed that a 'good' tax should have the following characteristics:

- *Equity.* It should be fair to different individuals and should reflect a person's ability to pay.
- *Certainty.* It should not be arbitrary, it should be certain.
- *Convenience.* It should be convenient in terms of timing and payment.
- *Efficiency.* It should be administratively efficient with a relatively small cost of collection as a proportion of the revenue raised. It should not cause economic distortion by affecting the behaviour of taxpayers.

These principles still apply today; in a modern tax system the three major principles of taxation are:

1. *Efficiency.* A tax should be easy and cheap to collect. It is in pursuit of this objective that so much tax is collected 'at source', by deduction from income as it arises. The UK PAYE (pay-as-you-earn) tax on salaries and wages is an example.

2. *Equity.* It is important that tax should be fairly levied as between one taxpayer and another. For example, in the UK, tax legislation is often complex, both to reduce the opportunities to avoid the tax and to promote fairness, although this is not always achieved.
3. *Economic effects must be considered.* The ways in which tax is collected can have profound economic effects which must be taken into account when formulating a tax policy.

Tax reliefs can stimulate one sector, while the imposition of a heavy tax can stifle another. For example, special allowances for capital expenditure may encourage investment in industry, while imposing heavy taxes on cigarettes and alcoholic drink may operate to discourage sales.

1.3.2 The American Institute of Certified Public Accountants' (AICPA) statement – *Guiding Principles of Good Tax Policy: A Framework for Evaluating Tax Proposals*

The AICPA's Guiding Principles of Good Tax Policy: A Framework for Evaluating Tax Proposals lists ten principles for determining if an existing tax or a proposal to modify a tax rule follows good tax policy. The framework also recognises that it is not always possible to incorporate all ten principles into tax systems and that some balancing is needed.

The ten principles are:

1. equity and fairness,
2. transparency and visibility,
3. certainty,
4. convenience of payment,
5. economy in collection,
6. simplicity,
7. appropriate government revenues,
8. minimum tax gap,
9. neutrality,
10. economic growth and efficiency.

Most of these are included in Section 1.3.1; those that need additional explanation are:

- *Appropriate government revenues.* The tax system should enable the government to determine how much tax revenue is likely to be collected and when.
- *Minimum tax gap.* The tax gap is the difference between the amount of tax owed and the amount of tax collected. A tax should be structured to minimise non-compliance.

1.4 Basic tax terminology

This section explains some basic taxation terms that are used in the following chapters and that you need to understand and possibly use to answer questions in the examination.

1.4.1 Direct taxes

A direct tax is one that falls directly on the person or entity who is expected to pay it. For example, the UK corporation tax is a direct tax. The formal incidence and effective incidence of a direct tax are usually the same, although in some situations if it is known in advance that tax will have to be paid, it may be possible to charge a higher rate for the work so that the tax due will be covered.

A direct tax is levied on an individual or entity, so it can be designed to take account of certain individual or entity circumstances, for example, family size, financial commitments, level of investment in non-current assets, etc.

1.4.2 Indirect taxes

An indirect tax is one that is levied on one part of the economy with the intention that it will be passed on to another. For example, in the UK, value-added tax (VAT) is levied on all businesses involved with the production and distribution of a good for a final customer. In most cases the VAT will be added to the final price paid by the customer.

As an indirect tax is not levied on the eventual payer of the tax, it cannot be related to the individual circumstances of that taxpayer.

1.4.3 Incidence

The incidence of tax refers to the distribution of the tax burden. The incidence of a tax is on the person who actually pays it. For example, the incidence of an income tax is on the taxpayer as it is the taxpayer who is assessed and pays the tax.

Incidence can be split into two elements:

1. *Formal incidence.* The person or entity who has direct contact with the tax authorities. For example, the formal incidence of a sales tax (or VAT) will be on the entity making the sale. It is the entity making the sale that must account for the transaction and pay the tax collected to the revenue collection authorities.
2. *Effective (or actual) incidence.* The person or entity who ends up bearing the cost of the tax as they cannot pass it on to someone else. If a sales tax is added to the selling price, it is passed on to the customer and it is actually the customer who ends up paying the tax. The effective incidence is on the customer.

1.4.4 Taxable person

A taxable person is the person accountable for the payment of a tax. Tax is levied on the taxable person who is responsible for its payment. For example, in the UK, traders have to register for VAT as a taxable person; they can then charge VAT to customers and recover the VAT paid to their suppliers (see Chapter 3 for more details on VAT).

1.4.5 Competent jurisdiction

Jurisdiction can be interpreted as meaning power. The tax authority must have the legal power to assess and collect taxes. Taxation is either the sole responsibility of the central government or the combined responsibility of the central government and local authorities within a country. The responsible authorities will pass one or more taxation laws. The primary characteristic of any law is that it is enforceable by sanction (i.e. fine, imprisonment, etc.). An unenforceable law will be ignored. Before a court can order enforcement, it must be competent to hear and determine the alleged non-compliance with the law.

For example, the UK legislation is applicable to UK subjects and non-UK subjects who by entering the UK, whether for a long or short time, have made themselves subject to the UK jurisdiction. UK statutes apply within the UK as jurisdiction is territorial.

For an entity to be subject to tax in a country, it must first be proved to be within that country's legal power to apply its tax rules to the entity. The competent jurisdiction is therefore the country whose tax laws apply to the entity.

The basis of jurisdiction can vary between countries, making it difficult to determine and collect taxes from multinational entities (see Chapter 5 for a discussion of the jurisdiction of multinational entities).

1.4.6 Hypothecation

Hypothecation means that the products of certain taxes are devoted to specific types of expenditures. For example, a tax on motor vehicles could be hypothecated (devoted entirely) to expenditure on building and maintaining roads. Earmarking is an informal hypothecation of taxes. Hypothecation is unpopular with Chancellors/Ministers of Finance as it considerably reduces their choices in public expenditure decisions.

1.4.7 Withholding responsibilities

Persons or entities paying various types of income to persons or entities abroad are usually required by the law of a country to deduct tax from the income before making a payment. The tax deducted is called withholding tax and it is the responsibility of the person or entity making the payment to correctly deduct it. The person or entity making the deduction is responsible for paying the tax deducted to the tax authorities and preparing the correct documents to properly account for it (see Section 5.5 for more detail on withholding taxes).

1.4.8 Tax rate structure

Direct taxes are assessed on individuals, so it is possible to set tax rates that cause marginal and average rates of tax to change according to the size of the individual's tax base. The government's political objectives and current social objectives determine the level of tax and the way rates vary with income. The three possibilities are:

1. progressive taxes, which take an increasing proportion of income as the income rises;
2. proportional taxes, which take the same proportion of income as income rises;
3. regressive taxes, which take a decreasing proportion of income as income rises.

Example of rate structures:

A earns $95,000 profit for the year.
B earns $42,000 profit for the year.

In country 1 the tax on profits is 20 per cent on all earned profits.
In country 2 the tax on profits is 0 per cent on the first $20,000; 10 per cent on amounts between $20,001 and $50,000; and 30 per cent on amounts over $50,001.

How much tax would A and B be subject to in each of the countries?

		Total tax	Effective tax rate	Type
Country 1				
A	$95,000 × 20%	$19,000	20%	Proportional
B	$42,000 × 20%	$8,400	20%	Proportional
Country 2				
A	($30,000 × 10%) + ($45,000 × 30%)	$16,500	17.4%	Progressive
B	$22,000 × 10%	$2,200	5.2%	Progressive

Indirect taxes cannot normally be progressive on the individual as they are either assessed on:

• the number of goods (excise duty) or
• the value (VAT) of the goods.

These taxes can only be progressive or regressive on the individual if different rates of tax are charged on different goods. For example, if higher rates of tax are charged on goods that tend to be bought by those on higher incomes, the indirect tax could be said to be progressive.

1.4.9 The tax gap

The tax gap is the difference between actual tax revenue received and the amount that would have been received had 100 per cent of the amount due been collected. Tax authorities aim to minimise the tax gap by collecting as high a proportion of the tax due as possible.

1.5 Tax bases and classification of taxes

A tax base is something that is liable to tax. Taxes can be classified by tax base, that is, by what is being taxed. Taxes may be based on:

• *income* – for example, income taxes and taxes on an entity's profits;
• *capital or wealth* – for example, taxes on capital gains and taxes on inherited wealth;
• *consumption* – for example, excise duties and sales taxes/VAT.

For example, in the USA, the Federal government taxes income as its main source of revenue. State governments use taxes on income and consumption, while local governments rely almost entirely on taxing property and wealth.

A more detailed classification of taxes is that used by the Organisation for Economic Cooperation and Development (OECD 1976): taxes are grouped into categories similar to those above and then each group is sub-divided into more detailed headings.

The OECD classifications are used to assist when comparing one country with another. For example:

2000	*Taxes on income, profits and capital gains*
2100	Paid by households and institutions
2110	On income and profits
2120	On capital gains
2200	Paid by corporate enterprises
2210	On income and profits
2220	On capital gains

You can access the full OECD classification on the OECD website at http://www.oecd. org/dataoecd/20/39/35589632.pdf the full OECD classification is to be found at annexe 1 of the document.

 You do not need to learn the full OECD classification, but you must know the main categories of tax.

1.6 Sources of tax rules

The nature of tax rules vary considerably from one country to another; however, it is possible to categorise the sources and influences on those rules. Within any country the balance between each source will be different, but in most countries the same elements will be present to a greater or lesser extent. The main sources of tax rules in a country are usually as follows:

- All tax systems are based on domestic primary legislation either at the central government level or at the local authority level or both. In some countries the legislation is very detailed and specific, setting out every possible item of income and expense. In other countries the legislation is less detailed and is supplemented by court rulings or case law.
- The practice of the relevant taxing authority will create precedents which will be followed in the future. Tax authorities sometimes issue guidelines or interpretations which are aimed at clarifying the taxation legislation.
- Supranational bodies may issue directives which the government of a country has to include in the legislation, for example, European Union (EU) directives on VAT.
- International tax treaties signed with other states are also a source of tax rules as the agreements often vary from the country's own tax regulations.

1.7 Summary

This introductory chapter sets out general tax principles, basic terminology, classification models for taxation and sources of tax rules. You need to learn these definitions and be prepared to use them to answer questions in the examination.

Revision Questions

? Question 1

Which of the following is NOT one of Adam Smith's characteristics of a good tax?

(A) Equity
(B) Certainty
(C) Simplicity
(D) Efficiency   **(2 marks)**

? Question 2

In no more than 15 words define 'incidence of tax'.   **(2 marks)**

? Question 3

An indirect tax is a tax that:

(A) is levied directly on an individual
(B) is based on earnings of an individual
(C) is paid indirectly to the tax authorities
(D) is levied on one person with the intention that it is passed on to another   **(2 marks)**

? Question 4

List the three main tax bases used in developed countries.   **(2 marks)**

? Question 5

Which of the following is not usually a source of tax rules in a country?

(A) Domestic primary legislation
(B) International tax treaties
(C) The practice of the tax authorities
(D) International law   **(2 marks)**

Question 6

With reference to an entity paying tax, which of the following is the best definition of 'competent jurisdiction':

(A) The country whose laws apply to the entity
(B) Any country where the entity has operations
(C) Any country where the entity has an office
(D) Any country where the entity has employees   **(2 marks)**

Question 7

The effective incidence of a tax is

(A) the date the tax is actually paid
(B) the person or entity who finally bears the cost of the tax
(C) the date the tax assessment is issued
(D) the person or entity receiving the tax assessment   **(2 marks)**

Question 8

An entity sells furniture and adds a sales tax to the selling price of all products sold.

A customer purchasing furniture from the entity has to pay the cost of the furniture plus the sales tax.

The customer therefore bears the cost of the sales tax.

This is referred to as

(A) formal incidence
(B) indirect incidence
(C) effective incidence
(D) direct incidence   **(2 marks)**

Question 9

BM has a taxable profit of $30,000 and receives a tax assessment of $3,000.

BV has a taxable profit of $60,000 and receives a tax assessment of $7,500.

BM and BV are resident in the same tax jurisdiction.

This tax could be said to be

(A) a progressive tax
(B) a regressive tax
(C) a direct tax
(D) a proportional tax   **(2 marks)**

Solutions to Revision Questions

☑ Solution 1

The correct answer is (C), see Section 1.3.1.

☑ Solution 2

The incidence of a tax is the person who actually pays it. See Section 1.4.3.

☑ Solution 3

The correct answer is (D), see Section 1.4.2.

☑ Solution 4

The tax bases are:

- Income
- Capital or wealth
- Consumption

See Section 1.5.

☑ Solution 5

The correct answer is (D), see Section 1.6.

☑ Solution 6

The correct answer is (A), see Section 1.4.5.

☑ Solution 7

The correct answer is (B), see Section 1.4.3.

Solution 8
The correct answer is (C), see Section 1.4.3.

 ## Solution 9
The correct answer is (A), see Section 1.4.8.

Direct Taxes on Company Profits and Gains

Direct Taxes on Company Profits and Gains

2

LEARNING OUTCOME

After completing this chapter you should be able to:

▶ prepare corporate income tax calculations based on a given simple set of rules.

Note: To fully complete this learning outcome, Chapters 2 and 3 must be completed.

The topics covered in this chapter are as follows:

- Direct taxes on entity profits and gains:
  - the principle of non-deductibility of dividends and systems of taxation defined according to the treatment of dividends in the hands of the shareholder (e.g. classical, partial imputation and imputation);
  - the distinction between accounting and taxable profits in absolute terms (e.g. disallowable expenditure on revenue account, such as entertaining, and on capital account, such as formation and acquisition costs) and in terms of timing (e.g. deduction on a paid basis);
  - the concept of tax depreciation replacing book depreciation in the tax computation based on the pooling of assets by their classes, including balancing adjustments on the disposal of assets;
  - the nature of rules recharacterising interest payments as dividends;
  - potential for variation in rules for calculating the tax base dependent on the nature or source of the income (schedular systems);
  - the need for rules dealing with the relief of losses;
  - the concept of tax consolidation (e.g. for relief of losses and deferral of capital gains on asset transfers.

2.1 Introduction

In the first part of this chapter, we will consider the corporate tax base and some of the general principles applied to the determination of taxable profits. We will examine the concept of trading income and the adjustments to income and expenditure that are required to calculate taxable trading income. We will then discuss capital gains and relief available to entities for their capital gains. This chapter then examines different corporate income tax systems that can be used in a country and then looks at the treatment of losses and their application to groups of entities.

Direct taxation on entities can be referred to using a number of different terms, for example, corporate income tax, income tax and corporation tax are all used. In this chapter, for consistency, we will refer to all these direct taxes on entities as corporate income tax, except examples which directly refer to the UK corporation tax.

2.2 The corporate tax base

Income arising from all sources is usually included in an entity's tax base, whether:

- earnings from trading and other activities;
- gains from disposal of investments and assets;
- other non-business income.

Internationally, there are large differences in the definition of taxable income and therefore large differences in the tax base between countries. In some countries, such as Germany and France, taxable income is closely linked to the accounting profit shown in the income statement. Taxable profit therefore varies with the particular accounting rules used in the country. The accounting rules may also be driven to a large extent by the taxation laws. In countries such as the USA and the UK, there are substantial differences between accounting profits and taxable income, although the nature of the differences varies from country to country or even year to year.

In all countries, income is based on the accounting profit shown in an entity's financial statements, computed using generally accepted accounting practice in a particular country. In order to calculate taxable profit some adjustments are usually required by statute, although the type and number of adjustments will vary by country. These adjustments can give rise to deferred taxation (see Chapter 6 for a discussion on deferred taxation). The following sections cover the revenue and expenditure that can and cannot be included.

2.2.1 Schedular systems of corporate taxation

As stated above, it is common practice for countries to include all of an entity's earnings in their corporate income tax computations. An entity may receive income from several sources:

- trading profit
- capital gains
- interest received
- rent received
- patent royalties
- other sources.

If all earnings are treated in the same way, there is little need to separate them when computing the tax charge for the year. However, some governments want more control over what is and is not taxed and at what rate. This is achieved by using a number of schedules for the tax calculations. Each schedule will relate to a specific type of income and will have specific rules that define how income should be measured and what expenditure will be allowed (if any). There may be a separate rate of tax applicable to each schedule.

In the UK corporation tax system, the main headings are referred to as 'Schedules', and some of the Schedules are divided into 'Cases'. Each schedule/case has its own specific rules for calculating the taxable income. After the taxable income for each schedule/case has been calculated, a total taxable income is prepared by adding all the schedule/case taxable incomes together. The entity's capital gains are then added on to give the total taxable profit for the period. The UK schedules and cases relevant for company taxation are:

UK Corporation tax schedules

Schedule A	Income from land and property
Schedule D	
Case I	Profits of a trade or business
Case III	Interest, etc., receivable
Case V	Dividends received from foreign companies
Case VI	Any income not chargeable under another Schedule or Case

Other items included in an entity's total profit for corporation tax purposes:

Capital gains
Surpluses on disposal of intangible assets

We will first consider income from a trade or business then capital gains.

2.2.2 Classification of income

In computing an entity's corporate income tax liability, the first step is to take the entity's income statement and compute taxable profits. If the tax system uses a schedular system, then separate figures for each category will need to be calculated by examining the entity's income statement and allocating incomes and expenditures to each tax category.

In arriving at the trading profit to be included in the entity's total taxable profit, certain expenses charged in the income statement have to be disallowed because they are not deductible for tax purposes. It is also necessary to remove any non-trading income that is taxable under other categories and capital gains. We need to calculate:

- What moneys received or receivable are taxable as trading income?
- What moneys expended or expendable can be deducted from those receipts?

As stated above, income is generally based on the profit shown in the entity financial statements, computed on generally accepted accounting practice. For example, in the UK, the requirement is that the profit of a trade, profession or vocation must be computed on an accounting basis which gives a true and fair view.

The statement of comprehensive income is then adjusted for tax purposes because not every item received is a taxable receipt of the trade, profession or vocation. Nor is every item of expenditure an allowable deduction for tax purposes. We will first consider receipts then deductions.

Income

Income could be either a profit or gain of the trade. A profit is income, whereas a gain is capital in nature. Most countries make a clear distinction between capital gains and revenue profits for tax purposes with, for example, capital gains tax and income tax. Any item credited to the income statement must be examined to determine if it is revenue or capital in nature. The questions that need to be asked are:

(a) Does the income arise directly from the trade?
(b) Is it a revenue or capital receipt?
(c) Is it a part of the profits of the year under review or of some other year?
(d) Is it taxable under any other category? For example, rents.
  - Non-trading receipts are usually treated separately for tax purposes.
  - Capital receipts will be dealt with under capital gains tax rules.
  - If the receipt relates to other years, it will probably be taxed in that year.
  - Receipts taxable under other categories are deducted from income and dealt with under the rules relating to the other categories.

2.2.3 Expenditure

The starting point for determining the profits or gains of a trade is the profit per financial statements. An item of expenditure or other debit to the income statement will be an allowable deduction in arriving at the trading profit, provided that either:

- it is revenue and not capital expenditure and is not prohibited by any provisions in the tax statute; or
- it is not specifically disallowed by the tax legislation.

We will consider expenditure under the following three sub-headings:

1. depreciation
2. disallowable expenditure
3. allowable expenditure.

Depreciation

Depreciation is by far the most common item of capital debited in the statement of comprehensive income. A deduction in respect of depreciation is a deduction that is related to the capital assets of the business and is therefore never allowable.

Depreciation provided in accounts is replaced by a standard deduction available for most, but generally not all, types of capital expenditure. The reason for this adjustment is that taxpayers can adopt a range of different depreciation rates and accounting policies. A standard deduction common to all taxpayers is fairer for tax purposes, and can also be used to provide investment incentives for businesses; generous allowances can be used to encourage capital expenditure on specific types of asset or in specific areas of the country. The standard deduction is usually referred to as tax depreciation or (as in the UK) capital allowances.

The main categories of expenditure qualifying for tax depreciation are usually:

- plant and machinery (broadly defined to include vehicles, computers, etc.);
- buildings.

Although buildings, plant and machinery are the main types of asset that all countries allow for tax depreciation, any non-current asset could be included, for example, research and development of a capital nature is allowable for capital allowances in the UK.

The way that depreciation is allowed for tax varies from country to country. All countries allow some form of charge to income for the use of assets. Most countries allow the declining balance method of calculating tax depreciation on plant and machinery and the majority use straight-line method for calculating tax depreciation on buildings (see Chapter 13 for an explanation of the methods of depreciation).

In some systems such as the UK, it is not necessary to calculate every asset separately, all assets of a similar type can be 'pooled' and treated as one large asset.

Incentives granted to encourage capital expenditure are usually in the form of accelerated tax depreciation, by allowing depreciation at a higher rate in the early years of the assets useful economic life. This practice is sometimes known as an initial allowance or first-year allowance. For example, in the UK, small companies can claim 100 per cent first-year allowances on some types of asset. Incentives can be used to encourage expenditure on assets generally or to help achieve a government objective, for example, in the UK, expenditure incurred by any business on the purchase of motor cars with low CO_2 emissions will qualify for a 100 per cent first-year allowance.

When an asset qualifying for tax depreciation is disposed of, a balancing charge or balancing allowance may arise. The total claimed for tax depreciation over the life of the asset must equal the original cost less sale proceeds. If there is a difference, a balancing adjustment will be made in the year of disposal.

> ✐ In your examination you will not be tested on any specific country's system of tax depreciation or depreciation rates. If computation questions are set, the details will be given along with all the tax rates needed to answer the question.

The following example illustrates the approach required in questions.

Example 2.A

HL commenced business on 1 June 2001, making up the first accounts for the year to 31 May 2002. The entity's purchases and sales of fixed assets were as follows:

Purchases			$
2001	1 June	Industrial building	260,000
	1 June	Plant	47,000
2004	1 June	Plant	58,000
Sales			
2004	31 May	Plant bought on 1 June 2001	9,500

HL qualifies for accelerated first-year allowance on the plant at the rate of 50% for the first year. The second and subsequent years will be at 25% on the reducing balance method. The industrial building qualifies for an annual tax depreciation allowance of 5% on the straight-line basis.

Calculate HL's tax depreciation for the years ended 31 May 2002, 2003 and 2004.

Solution

		Industrial building $	Plant $	Total tax depreciation for year $
01/06/2001	Purchase	260,000	47,000	
31/05/2002	First-year allowance		(23,500)	}
	Tax depreciation for the year	(13,000)		} 36,500
	Balance at 31/05/2002	247,000	23,500	
31/05/2003	Tax depreciation for the year	(13,000)	(5,875)	18,875
	Balance at 31/05/2003	234,000	17,625	
31/05/2004	Disposal		(9,500)	
	Balancing allowance		(8,125)	}
	Tax depreciation for the year	(13,000)		} 21,125
	Balance at 31/05/2004	221,000	. 0	
01/06/2004	Purchase		58,000	

This means that in the year to 31 May 2002, HL has a tax allowance for $36,500 tax depreciation. This will be deducted from HL's taxable profits before HL's tax liability is calculated.

In the year to 31 May 2003, HL receives an allowance for $18,875 tax depreciation and in the year to 31 May 2004, $21,125. This final amount includes a balancing allowance for the plant disposed of. The plant disposed of during the year cost $47,000 in 2001 and then received tax depreciation allowances of $23,500 and 5,875 leaving a tax written down balance of $17,625. When the plant was sold, $9,500 was received leaving a balance of $8,125 to be written off as a balancing allowance.

Disallowable expenditure

Disallowable expenditure is expenditure that has been incurred and charged to the statement of comprehensive income, but is not allowable for tax purposes. The expenditure therefore has to be added back on to the profit for the year to arrive at taxable profits.

Any expenditure that is deemed to be capital in nature will not usually be allowable expenditure when computing trading profits. For example:

- Losses on sale of non-current assets (also gains on sale).
- Legal, surveyors' and other fees related to capital matters; for example, new buildings, plant, etc.
- Repairs to assets purchased in a run-down condition, only the part attributable to use in the current trade is allowable.

Even if an item of expenditure is revenue expenditure, it may be specifically prohibited as a deduction by the tax legislation, for example, in the UK, expenses incurred in entertaining customers are specifically disallowed. Specifically disallowed items will vary from country to country, they also vary within a country from one year to another. The following items are often specifically disallowed:

- any disbursements or expenses of maintenance of the parties, their families or establishments, or any sums expended for any other domestic or private purposes distinct from the purposes of the trade, profession or vocation;
- any capital withdrawn from the business;
- any capital employed in improvements of the premises;
- any sum recoverable under an insurance;
- any expenditure on entertaining customers;
- any annuity or other annual payment (other than interest);

- donations to political parties;
- expenses that relate to an earlier year and arose in that earlier year.

Allowable expenditure

An item of expenditure or other debit to the income statement can usually be assumed to be an allowable deduction in arriving at the trading profit unless it is specifically disallowed by the tax legislation. Examination questions will specify which items of expenditure need to be disallowed.

2.2.4 Capital gains

Gains arising on the disposal of investments and other assets are not usually covered by income tax rules and are not included in the trading income. Capital gains tax attempts to tax those gains made on disposal of various types of investments and other assets. The assets included in the tax base vary from country to country. For example, in the UK, the most important type of transaction covered by capital gains tax is the sale of listed stocks and shares. The UK also has a large number of assets that are exempted from capital gains tax. The principle is usually that all assets are chargeable unless exempted, but the list of exemptions can be fairly long. In the UK, exemptions include:

- private motor vehicles;
- chattels (tangible movable property) sold for less than £6,000;
- chattels, which are wasting assets (i.e. those with a life of less than 50 years), for example, boats, caravans, animals;
- qualifying corporate bonds.

In addition to exempt *assets,* there can also be exemptions for certain types of *disposals* of assets, for example, in the UK, exempt disposals include:

- gifts to a non-profit-making body of land, buildings, works of art and the like, provided that the gift is for public benefit and public access is allowed;
- sale of works of art and the like to approved UK national or local institutions (e.g. art galleries or museums);
- gifts of any type of asset for charitable purposes to an approved charity.

In principle, the calculation of the gain or loss on a disposal is simply proceeds of sale less cost or value at a date specified in the tax legislation. Additional costs incurred to acquire the asset, improve it or dispose of it may be allowed to be deducted from the gain. When an entity disposes of a depreciable non-current asset, the capital gain or loss is normally calculated as the difference between the net disposal proceeds and the tax base of the asset at the time of disposal. The tax base is the original cost of the asset less accumulated tax depreciation to date.

In some countries the calculation is based on original cost but a few countries such as the UK allow the original cost to be indexed when calculating the gain. During periods of high inflation, a tax on capital gains would be unfair if based on the simple comparison of cost and sale proceeds. Some allowance for the effect of inflation over the period of ownership is needed. For example, in the UK, this is done by allowing the cost to be adjusted to current prices using an index published by the government, the retail price index. The movement in the index over the period of ownership is used to increase the original cost of the asset. Indexation cannot turn a capital gain into a loss, it merely reduces the gain to zero.

Example 2.B   Indexation of the cost of an asset

An asset, which cost $10,000 in February 1988, was sold in April 2003 for $20,000.
Retail price indices were:

February 1988	103.7
April 2003	180.0

The calculation of the chargeable gain will be:

	$	$
Proceeds of sale		20,000
Cost	10,000	
Indexation		
$10,000 × (180.0 − 103.7)/103.7		
i.e. $10,000 × 0.736	7,360	
Total allowable cost		17,360
Chargeable gain		2,640

Rollover relief

When an entity sells a business asset, it may give rise to a chargeable capital gain which, in most countries, will be included in the entity's corporate income tax calculation. In some countries, when an asset is replaced by another business asset, it is possible to defer the charge to tax until the replacement asset is sold. When the replacement asset is sold, any gain arising on that disposal may be deferred. There may be no limit to how often this deferral can take place. For example, in the UK, for an entity with a continuous existence, the deferral can be for an indefinite time, provided that the conditions are fulfilled. This relief from capital gains tax is sometimes known as rollover relief. Rollover relief allows a *deferral* of the payment of the corporate income tax on the gain till a later date, providing a cash flow advantage and allowing the corporate income tax to be paid in depreciated currency at a later date.

In a few countries rollover relief may also apply to intangible assets.

2.3   Nominal corporate tax rates

Corporate income tax rates vary considerably from one country to another. All countries have corporate income taxes at the central government level. Some countries have special lower rates for smaller entities while others have one rate for all entities. In some countries entities also have to pay taxes to other levels of government, for example, the USA and Canada. Any comparison of tax rates between countries is distorted by the range of treatments used for the calculation of tax base.

2.4   The interaction of the corporate tax system with the personal tax system

Dividends are appropriations of profit and are not usually allowed to be deducted from the income when calculating taxable profits. When dividends are paid to individual shareholders, the amount received has already been taxed. If it is then taxed in the hands of the shareholder, it is effectively being taxed twice.

The economic effect of corporate taxes depends on the system of corporate income tax used. The four main systems for taxing entity profits that are discussed below are:

1. classical system
2. imputation system
3. partial imputation system
4. split rate systems.

2.4.1 Classical system

A classical system of corporate income tax does not differentiate between an entity's retained earnings and its distributed earnings and treats the shareholders as completely independent of the entity.

Under a classical system, the entity is liable for corporate income tax on all its taxable income and gains, whether they are distributed or not. The shareholder is liable to income tax on dividends received from the entity and capital gains tax on any taxable gains made on the disposal of their shares.

The classical system is relatively easy to understand and administer, but causes two main problems:

1. Double taxation of dividends, that is, distributed income is subject to corporate income tax and then to personal income tax.
2. A bias against distributing dividends, as distribution causes double taxation; non-distribution will avoid double taxation.

2.4.2 Imputation system

Under imputation systems of corporate income tax, all or a part of the underlying corporate income tax on distributions is imputed to the shareholders as a tax credit, therefore avoiding the problem of double taxation of dividends. With systems using the full imputation system, all of the underlying corporate income tax is passed to the shareholder as a tax credit. A full imputation system is economically neutral between debt and equity finance.

2.4.3 Partial imputation system

With systems using the partial imputation system, only a part of the underlying corporate income tax is passed to the shareholder as a tax credit.

2.4.4 Split rate systems

Split rate systems of corporate income tax distinguish between distributed profits and retained profits and charge a lower rate of corporate income tax on distributed profits so as to avoid the double taxation of dividends. Applying the lower rate for distributed dividends can operate under an imputation or classical system.

2.4.5 Examples to illustrate the difference between traditional and imputation systems

Example 2.C

Country X uses the classical system for corporate income tax. The entity's taxable profits are subject to 15% tax and shareholders are subject to income tax at 25% on all dividends received.

Country Y uses a full imputation system for corporate income tax. Entity taxable profits are subject to 30% tax. Shareholders receive a tax credit for the full amount of tax paid and are not subject to any further tax on dividends.

CT has taxable profits of $100,000 and decides to distribute 50% as dividends.

Calculate the total tax paid by CT and the shareholders, assuming that they are resident first in country X and then in Y.

		$	$
Country X			
Corporate income tax paid by CT	100,000 × 15%	15,000	
Shareholders total income tax on dividends	50,000 × 25%	12,500	
Total tax due if resident in country X			27,500
Country Y			
Corporate income tax paid by CT	100,000 × 30%	30,000	
Shareholders total income tax on dividends	Nil	0	
Total tax due if resident in country Y			30,000

Example 2.D

Country X and Country Y use the same rates of tax as in Example 2.C.

CD has taxable profits of $100,000 and decides to distribute 90% as dividends.

Calculate the total tax paid by CD and the shareholders, assuming again that they are resident in each country.

		$	$
Country X			
Corporate income tax paid by CD	100,000 × 15%	15,000	
Shareholders total income tax on dividends	90,000 × 25%	22,500	
Total tax due if resident in country X			37,500
Country Y			
Total tax due if resident in country Y			30,000
(as Example 1)			

In conclusion, in countries using the classical system, the total amount of tax paid depends on the amount of the profit that is paid as a dividend to shareholders. If less profit is distributed to shareholders, less tax is paid. In countries with a full imputation system, the corporate income tax is imputed to the shareholders receiving the dividend, so the total tax paid is not affected by the level of profits distributed as dividend.

2.5 Rules recharacterising interest as dividends

Interest on high-yield debt can cause otherwise profitable entities to have very low taxable incomes. This has caused some governments to consider limiting the amount of interest that can be charged to profits as an expense. For example, in the USA, certain types of high-yield debt are limited to the amount that can be set against the entity's taxable income. For certain types of debt instrument, where the yield is more than six points above the federal rate, the excess will be treated as a dividend. The result is that the issuing entity does not receive a tax deduction for the excess interest.

2.6 Treatment of losses

Trading and capital losses are usually dealt with separately under the legislation applicable to each.

2.6.1 Trading losses

Trading losses are calculated in the same way as trading profits. During the period when a trading loss occurs, the entity cannot claim a tax refund. The main ways of relieving the loss is by setting it off against profits during other periods or transferring it to another group entity (see Section 2.7 below).

All countries allow the loss to be set off against future profits, some countries limit the time that losses can be carried forward while others, such as the UK have no limit on the time allowed to recover the loss. The methods used to relieve losses can include:

(a) Carry-forward of trading loss to offset against future trading income derived from the same trade.
(b) Offset against other income and chargeable gains of the same accounting period.
(c) Offset against other income and chargeable gains of one or more previous accounting periods.
(d) Group relief (see Section 2.7).

2.6.2 Capital losses

In principle, capital losses are calculated in the same way as capital gains. Capital losses are sometimes allowed to be deducted from trading income but most countries keep capital losses completely separate from trading activities. In most countries, capital losses are off-set against chargeable gains of the same accounting period. Any balance of loss is carried forward to be relieved against the first available chargeable gains. For example, in the UK, capital losses can be carried forward without time limit, they cannot be carried back to previous periods and cannot be set against any other income.

Example 2.E   To illustrate the treatment of losses

Country Z has the following tax regulations:

- Taxable profits are subject to tax at 25%.
- Capital gains are added to profits from trading to give taxable profits.
- Trading losses can be carried forward indefinitely but cannot be carried back to previous years.
- Capital gains/losses cannot be offset against trading gains/losses or vice versa.

LL started trading in 2002 and has the following profits/losses

	Trading profit/(loss) $'000	Capital profit/(loss) $'000
2002	(300)	400
2003	550	0
2004	700	(150)

Calculate the tax payable by LL in each year.

	Trading profit/(loss)	Capital profit/(loss)	Taxable profit	Tax due at 25%
2002		400	400	100
Loss carried forward	(300)			
2003	(550 – 300) = 250	0	250	62.50
Loss carried forward	0	0		
2004	700	(150)	700	175
Loss carried forward	0	(150)		

Note that in 2002 the trading loss cannot be offset against the capital gain and in 2004 the capital loss cannot be offset against the trading profit. This is a common situation that applies in many countries.

2.6.3 Cessation of business

If an entity makes a loss in its last 12 months of operation, its scope for relief under the rules we have considered so far is limited, since there can be no carry-forward. To remedy this most countries have special provisions in the legislation, for example, in the UK, a *terminal loss* relief exists, by which the loss may be carried back for up to 3 years to be set against total profits.

2.7 Principles of relief for foreign taxes

Double taxation treaties can provide for the relief of foreign taxation by one of three possible methods:

1. *Exemption*: The parties to the agreement set out the categories of income that are partially or completely exempt from tax in one country or the other.
2. *Tax credit*: The treaty may allow the tax paid in one country to be allowed as a tax credit in the other country. Tax relief is therefore provided by deducting foreign tax suffered from tax due in the country of residence. This is by far the commonest form of relief. It will be given under a double-tax agreement or, if no such agreement exists some countries, will give it unilaterally. If the foreign tax rate is higher than the country of residence rate, the tax relief will be limited to the tax due using the lower rate. Some tax in high taxation countries may not therefore be fully relieved.
3. *Deduction*: It is almost always better for the taxpayer to claim the reliefs described above so that foreign tax suffered is deducted from tax due in the country of residence. There are a few instances when it will be preferable to make a claim to deduct the foreign tax from the foreign income and bring the net sum into charge to tax in the home country. This could be beneficial if, for example, the entity has a loss in the home country.

2.8 The concept of tax consolidation

The concept of tax consolidation is where for tax purposes a group is recognised so that entities within that group can transfer losses between themselves. If one entity in a group makes a loss while others are making profits, it is possible, subject to conditions, to transfer the benefit of the loss where it can most advantageously be relieved. If a loss is not transferred to another group entity, it could be carried forward for several years before it can be used to offset tax payable on future profits. If it is transferred to another group entity, they can use this year's loss to offset against this year's profits and therefore reduce the total group tax bill for the year.

The tax legislation that sets out the requirements for a group to be recognised varies considerably from country to country. Some countries only allow groups to consist of resident entities while others allow overseas entities to be included to the extent that they have profits/losses within the country. The requirements that need to be met for a tax group to be recognised will be set out in the tax legislation and will usually be different from that required to recognise a group for accounting purposes. For example, the UK requirement for a tax group is that there must be a direct or indirect holding of at least 75 per cent whereas for accounting purposes this will usually be 50 per cent.

Most countries have restrictions on the transfer, or surrender of losses between members of the group, which will limit the time or amount that can be surrendered. For example, in the UK, only losses of the current accounting period may be surrendered, and they may only be offset against the claimant entity's profits for the same period.

Non-trading losses may also be surrendered to other entities in the group.

2.8.1 Capital losses and tax groups

Different rules may apply to tax groups for capital gains. For example, the UK requirement for a capital gains tax group is different to a trading income tax group.

Capital losses are also different from trading and non-trading losses in that capital losses cannot usually be transferred from one entity to another. In the UK, all that is available is the right to transfer assets between members of the same capital gains tax group without triggering off a capital gain or loss. The asset is transferred on a 'no gain, no loss' basis. Where an asset, which will result in a capital loss, is about to be sold to a third party by a group member, and another group member is about to sell an asset to a third party, which would give rise to a chargeable gain, then this rule can be extremely helpful. The asset can be transferred at no loss to the entity making a sale at a profit. When the two assets are in the *same* entity, that entity could sell both assets to third parties and set the loss off against the gain.

2.9 Summary

In this chapter, we have discussed the two main methods of direct taxation that apply to entities, corporate income tax and capital gains tax. We have discussed the alternative systems of corporate income tax and their impact on the double taxation of dividends. We also considered the distinction between accounting and taxable profits, the treatment of losses and the concept of tax consolidation.

Revision Questions

Question 1

A schedular system of corporate income tax means:

(A) A method used to calculate the corporate income tax payable
(B) A system that has a number of schedules which set out how different types of income should be taxed
(C) A system that has a number of schedules which set out when tax returns and tax payments should be made
(D) A system that has a number of schedules which set out the various tax rates   **(2 marks)**

Question 2

Accounting depreciation is replaced by tax depreciation:

(A) To reduce the amount of depreciation allowed for tax
(B) To increase the amount of depreciation allowed for tax
(C) To ensure that standard rates of depreciation are used by all organisations for tax purposes
(D) So that the government can more easily manipulate the amount of tax organisations pay
(2 marks)

Question 3

KM commenced business on 1 June 2002, making up the first accounts for the year to 31 May 2003.

The entity's purchases and sales of fixed assets were as follows:

Purchases			$
2002	1 June	Industrial building	300,000
	1 June	Plant	40,000
2004	1 June	Plant	60,000
Sales			
2004	31 May	Plant bought on 1 June 2001	12,000

KM qualifies for accelerated first-year allowance on the plant at the rate of 50% for the first year. The second and subsequent years will be at 25% on the reducing balance method. No additional charge will result if the asset is disposed of early.

The industrial building qualifies for an annual tax depreciation allowance of 4% on the straight-line basis.

Calculate KM's tax depreciation for the year ended 31 May 2004. **(4 marks)**

? Question 4

The following is a list of payments which an organisation may incur during a year:

(i) capital withdrawn from the business,
(ii) interest paid,
(iii) legal expenses,
(iv) payments for domestic expenses of the directors,
(v) advertising.

Which two of the above items of expenditure will normally be disallowed for corporate income tax purposes?

(A) (i) and (iii)
(B) (i) and (iv)
(C) (ii) and (iv)
(D) (iii) and (v) **(2 marks)**

? Question 5

Rollover relief allows:

(A) Deferral of the payment of corporate income tax on gains arising from the disposal of a business asset
(B) Stock values to be rolled over, replacing cost of purchases with current values
(C) Trading losses to be carried forward or rolled over to future periods
(D) Capital losses to be carried forward or rolled over to future periods **(2 marks)**

? Question 6

An imputation system of corporate income tax means:

(A) All the underlying corporate income tax on the dividend distribution is passed as a credit to the shareholders
(B) The organisation pays corporate income tax on its profits and the shareholder pays income tax on the dividend received
(C) Withholding tax paid on dividends is passed as a credit to shareholders
(D) A percentage of the underlying tax is passed as a credit to shareholders **(2 marks)**

Question 7

Country W has the following tax regulations:

- Taxable profits are subject to tax at 25%
- Capital gains are added to profits from trading to give taxable profits
- Trading losses can be carried forward indefinitely, but cannot be carried back to previous years
- Capital gains/losses cannot be offset against trading gains/losses or vice versa

LN started trading in 2002 and has the following profits/losses

	Trading profit/(loss) $'000	Capital profit/(loss) $'000
2002	(350)	0
2003	200	0
2004	700	(150)

Calculate the amount of tax due for 2004.   **(3 marks)**

Question 8

A full imputation system of corporate income tax is one where an entity is taxable on

(A) All of its income and gains whether they are distributed or not. The shareholder is liable for taxation on all dividends received
(B) All of its income and gains whether they are distributed or not, but all the underlying corporation tax is passed to the shareholder as a tax credit
(C) All of its income and gains whether they are distributed or not, but only part of the underlying corporation tax is passed to the shareholder as a tax credit
(D) Its retained profits at one rate and on its distributed profits at another (usually lower) rate of tax   **(2 marks)**

Question 9

EG purchased a property for $630,000 on 1 September 2000. EG incurred additional costs for the purchase of $3,500 surveyors' fees and $6,500 legal fees. EG then spent $100,000 renovating the property prior to letting it. All of EG's expenditure was classified as capital expenditure according to the local tax regulations.

Indexation of the purchase and renovation costs is allowed on EE's property. The index increased by 50% between September 2000 and October 2007. Assume that acquisition and renovation costs were incurred in September 2000. EG sold the property on 1 October 2007 for $1,250,000, incurring tax allowable costs on disposal of $2,000.

Calculate EG's tax due on disposal assuming a tax rate of 30%.   **(3 marks)**

Solutions to Revision Questions

 Solution 1

The correct answer is (B), see Section 2.2.1.

 Solution 2

The correct answer is (C), see Section 2.2.3.1.

 Solution 3

		Industrial building $	Plant $	Total tax depreciation for year $
01/06/2002	Purchase	300,000	40,000	
31/05/2003	First-year allowance		(20,000)	}
	Tax depreciation for the year	(12,000)		} 32,000
	Balance at 31/05/2004	288,000	20,000	
31/05/2004	Disposal		(12,000)	
	Balancing allowance		(8,000)	}
	Tax depreciation for the year	(12,000)		} 20,000
	Balance at 31/05/2004	276,000	0	
01/06/2004	Purchase		60,000	

The tax depreciation for the year to 31 May 2004 is $20,000.

 Solution 4

The correct answer is (B), see Sections 2.2.3.2 and 2.2.3.3.

 Solution 5

The correct answer is (A), see Section 2.2.4.1.

Solution 6

The correct answer is (A), see Section 2.5.2.

 Solution 7

	Trading profit/(loss) $'000	Capital profit/(loss) $'000	Taxable profit $'000	Tax due at 25% $'000
2002				
Loss carried forward	(350)			0
2003	(200 − 200) = 0	0	0	0
Loss carried forward	(350 − 200) = 150	0		
2004	(700 − 150) = 550	(150)	550	137.50
Loss carried forward	0	(150)		

The tax due in 2004 is $137,500.

 Solution 8

The correct answer is (B), see Section 2.4.2.

 Solution 9

Purchase price	$'000	$'000
Cost	630	
Fees	10	640
Renovation		100
		740
Indexation at 50%		370
		1,110
Selling price	1,250	
Less cost of disposal	2	1,248
Taxable amount		138

Tax at 30% = 5 $41,400

Indirect Taxes and
Employee Taxation

Indirect Taxes and Employee Taxation

3

LEARNING OUTCOMES

After completing this chapter you should be able to:

▸ identify the principal types of taxation likely to be of relevance to an incorporated business in a particular country;

▸ describe the feature on the principal types of taxation likely to be of relevance to an incorporated business in a particular country.

The syllabus topics covered in this chapter are as follows:

- Indirect taxes collected by the entity:
  - In the context of indirect taxes, the distinction between unit taxes (e.g. excise duties based on physical measures) and *ad valorem* taxes (e.g. sales tax based on value).
  - The mechanism of value-added/sales taxes, in which businesses are liable for tax on their outputs less credits for tax paid on their inputs, including the concepts of exemption and variation in tax rates depending on the type of output and disallowance of input credits for exempt outputs.
- Employee taxation:
  - The employee as a separate taxable person subject to a personal income tax regime.
  - Use of employer reporting and withholding to ensure compliance and assist tax collection.

3.1 Introduction

In Chapter 1, we defined an indirect tax as one that is levied on one part of the economy with the intention that it will be passed on to another. In this chapter we are going to examine the types of indirect taxation that an entity may get involved with, either collecting the tax on behalf of government or paying the tax themselves.

In the first part of this chapter we will consider the main type of consumption tax, tax on sales, in its two main forms, sales tax and value-added tax. We then consider other consumption taxes that could effect an entity, including excise duties, property taxes and wealth taxes. In the final part of the chapter, we conclude with a discussion on employee taxation and pay-as-you-earn systems.

3.2 Indirect taxes collected by the entity

3.2.1 Unit taxes and *ad valorem* taxes

Taxes on consumption can be categorised in several ways.

1. Selective or general consumption taxes:
   (a) Selective consumption taxes – those levied on particular products, such as oil products, motor vehicles, alcohol and tobacco.
   (b) General consumption taxes – those levied on a wide range of goods and services, most of which are taxed on a percentage of value basis.
2. Specific or *ad valorem* taxes
   (a) Specific or unit taxes – taxes that are based on the weight or size of the tax base, for example, an excise duty of $5 per bottle of whiskey or $1 per 100 gram of tobacco.
   (b) *Ad valorem* taxes – based on values, these taxes are usually expressed as a percentage of the tax base, for example, a 5 per cent sales tax is calculated as 5 per cent of the selling price before tax.

3.3 Consumption taxes

In theory a general sales tax system could take one of many different forms, in practice there are two main types in use throughout the world, the single-level retail sales tax and value-added tax (VAT) systems. Sales taxes could be single- or multi-stage taxes.

3.3.1 Single-stage sales taxes

Single-stage sales taxes apply at one level of the production/distribution chain only; they can be applied to any one of the following levels:

- the manufacturing level
- the wholesale level
- the retail level.

There are very few countries using single-stage sales taxes, virtually no country uses a single-level sales tax at the manufacturing or wholesale level. The USA is the main example of a country using a retail sales tax, although the USA retail sales tax operates at the individual state government level rather than the federal government level.

3.3.2 Multi-stage sales taxes

A multi-stage sales tax charges tax each time a product or its components is sold in the chain from manufacturer, assembler, wholesaler to retailer. There are two types of multi-stage taxes:

1. A cumulative or cascade tax which does not allow credit for taxes paid on transfers between levels, this means that taxes paid at each stage are not refunded and are therefore treated as a business cost.

2. VAT and similar systems where credit is allowed for tax paid on purchases and traders are reimbursed all of the tax that they have paid. In these systems, the entire tax burden is usually passed on to the consumer.

Almost all countries have adopted VAT systems or are considering its adoption.

Example 3.A Multi-stage cumulative tax

A manufacturer, M produces refrigerators. These are sold first to a wholesaler, W, who sells in turn to a retailer, R. Finally, R sells to the ultimate consumer, C. The prices at which these transactions take place (excluding sales tax) are as follows:

- M sells to W for $ 100
- W sells to R for $ 160
- R sells to C for $300

The country levies a multi-stage cumulative tax at the rate of 5% each time a sale is made.
 Calculate the sales tax due by each entity and in total.

		Tax due
M's sale to W	$100 × 5%	$5
W's sale to R	$160 × 5%	$8
R's sale to C	$300 × 5%	$15
Total tax due		$28

Each entity has to charge tax and then pay it to the tax authorities. The tax paid is not recoverable. The total tax due in this example is $28.

3.4 Value-added tax

VAT is not a tax on profits or gains, and is not even eventually borne by most businesses to a material extent. Nevertheless, it is important to businesses, because its charge and collection enter into many, even most business transactions. Ultimately, VAT falls mainly on the final consumer of goods or services. However, all those involved in the chain of transactions between the manufacturer and the retailer are first charged VAT and then pass it on to the next person in the chain. The standard rate of VAT varies from one country to another; even in Europe where all countries in the EU must have a VAT system, the rates are very varied. Most countries have more than one rate of VAT; sometimes many different rates are used. One rate often used is a 'zero' rate, we will see the significance of this later.

Example 3.B VAT

Use the details in Example 3.A, but instead of a sales tax the country now has a VAT system, with VAT at 17.5%. Calculate the VAT finally due from C and the amount paid by M, W and R.
 The VAT finally due from C is:

$300 × 17.5% = $52.50

This is collected by R who pays it over to the tax authorities, along with the VAT due on other sales. But R first deducts all the VAT suffered on its *inputs*, its purchases. This will include the VAT charged by W on the supply of the refrigerator, and VAT suffered on items such as stationery, telephone and other overhead costs of goods and services. The overall effect on M, W and R is that most of the VAT paid by them on their *inputs* (purchases) is deducted when accounting for VAT on their *outputs* (sales).

Input tax is VAT paid on purchases. Output tax is VAT charged on sales or services provided.

Considering only the VAT relating to the sale and purchase of one refrigerator, the accounting will be as follows:

Entity	Input tax $	Output tax $	VAT paid $
M			
Sale to W		17.50	17.50 paid by M
W			
Purchase from M	17.50		
Sale to R		28.00	10.50 paid by W
R			
Purchase from M	28.00		
Sale to C		52.50	24.50 paid by R
Total suffered by C			52.50

The overall effect on M, W and R is nil. Each has collected VAT on making a sale and paid this over to Customs and Excise, first deducting any VAT paid on purchases and other inputs. C, the ultimate consumer, pays $52.50 and has no-one to pass it on to. He or she thus bears the tax which has been collected by the tax authorities in the three stages shown. This is an oversimplification of the actual process as each registered trader has to submit a return, usually quarterly, showing VAT collected on outputs and VAT suffered on inputs. The difference must be paid to the tax authorities within a specified time after the period end.

3.4.1 Transactions liable to VAT

Most business transactions are within the scope of VAT, which has to be accounted for whenever there is a *taxable supply*. A taxable supply means the supply of goods or services in the course of business, other than supplies that are exempt for one reason or another.

A supply of goods or services in the course of business must be one of the following types of supply:

- *standard-rated* – within the scope of VAT and taxable at the standard rate;
- *subject to a higher or lower rate* – within the scope of VAT and taxable at the appropriate rate;
- *zero-rated* – within the scope of VAT and taxable at 0 per cent;
- *exempt* – an activity on which VAT is not charged.

A further possibility is that the transaction is outside the scope of VAT – examples in the UK include some forms of compensation and the transfer of a business as a going concern.

Exemption and zero-rating

At first sight there appears to be no practical difference between zero-rating and exemption, but there is an important difference. If a trade or business is concerned with transactions that are zero-rated (e.g. in the UK, the supply of most types of food), no VAT is charged on sales, but the supplier may obtain a refund of VAT suffered on input costs to the business.

If, on the other hand, the transaction is exempt, again no VAT is charged on sales but the VAT suffered on costs relating to exempt supplies will not usually be recovered.

The following are examples of UK zero-rated transactions:

- sale of most types of food (but not restaurant meals, etc.);
- printed matter including books, newspapers, etc.;
- children's clothing and footwear;
- transport (by bus, ships, aircraft, but not taxi fares and the like);
- exports;
- drugs and medicines supplied on prescription.

Although the exact list of zero-rated supplies will vary from one country to another, the general principle of zero-rated supplies is fairly universal.

Partially exempt trades

A business could conduct several activities, resulting in some of its sales being standard-rated, some zero-rated, and some 'exempt'.

Such businesses are *partially exempt*. This means that their right to offset input tax is restricted.

Table 3.1 VAT treatment for partially exempt businesses

Input tax category	VAT treatment
(a) Input tax on costs only incurred in making taxable supplies (whether standard-rated or zero-rated)	Reclaimable in full
(b) Input tax on costs only incurred in making exempt supplies or for any other activity (outside scope)	Not reclaimable at all
(c) Other input tax (partly for items used in making taxable supplies – 'unattributable VAT')	Reclaimable pro-rata

To calculate the proportion of input tax which is deductible, a method that is 'practical, accurate and fair' must be agreed. The standard method is to divide input tax into three, as shown in Table 3.1.

The pro-rata calculation to establish the recoverable input VAT is made by apportioning the 'unattributable' input VAT (above) in the same ratio as the value of *all* taxable supplies bears to total supplies.

Entities are required to register for VAT when their *taxable* supplies *(including zero-rated supplies)* exceed the registration threshold. The registration threshold varies from country to country, but is designed to exempt small entities from the problems caused by having to keep VAT records. Exempt sales are generally *excluded* in determining whether a business has reached the registration threshold.

Entities can usually choose to register before their turnover reaches the level for compulsory registration. Only registered entities can charge VAT on sales or recover VAT paid on purchases.

3.5 Indirect taxes paid by the entity

3.5.1 Excise duties

Excise duties are specific taxes on certain commodities. As noted above, 'specific' or 'unit' taxes are based on the weight or size of the tax base.

From the revenue authority's point of view, the characteristics of commodities most suitable for excise duties are:

- few large producers
- inelastic demand with no close substitutes
- large sales volumes
- easy to define products covered by the tax.

The four main product groups, universally subject to excise duties – alcoholic drinks, tobacco and tobacco products, mineral oils and motor vehicles, all share these characteristics.

Special reasons cited for the existence of specific excise duties include:

- to discourage overconsumption of products which may harm the consumer or others, for example, duty on tobacco and alcohol;
- to alter the distribution of income by taxing 'luxuries', for example, in the USA, there are excise duties on heavy tyres, fishing equipment, firearms and airplane tickets;
- to seek to allow for externalities, so that the social and environmental cost of consuming the product is paid for by the consumer, for example, excise duty on tobacco to help pay for the increased cost of healthcare of smokers;
- to place the burden of paying the tax on the consumer of the product/service, for example, excise duty on petrol and diesel is used by some governments to build and maintain roads, bridges and mass transit systems.

Excise duties tend to have high yields and low cost of collection, so they are attractive to governments.

In recent years the number of products covered by specific excise duties has generally decreased in most countries, although the four product groups universally subject to excise duties, listed above, have not been affected.

VAT is usually payable on the goods as well as the excise duty. Excise duties have to be paid by entities and unlike VAT, the amount is not repayable. The duty must therefore be treated as a part of the cost of the item purchased.

3.5.2 Property taxes

Taxes on immovable property exist in many countries. The tax base is usually the capital value of the property although in some countries it is the annual rental value. The tax is usually on land and buildings, but a few countries and some states in the USA also tax other items of personal property such as cars, boats and livestock.

3.5.3 Wealth taxes

The tax base for a wealth tax is usually total wealth. The problem with total wealth is measuring and valuing all of the assets in the tax base. For example, total wealth may be deemed to include rights to a future pension, life insurance policies, etc. These assets are notoriously difficult to value. Problems also occur in areas such as antiques, collections and similar articles, for example, stamp collections.

Despite the difficulties, wealth taxes are levied in a number of countries. Wealth taxes can apply to:

- individuals only
- entities only
- individuals and entities.

In countries where a wealth tax exists for entities, an entity's wealth, that is, a measure of their asset value, will be taxed each year.

3.6 Employee taxation

3.6.1 The employee as a separate taxable person subject to a personal income tax regime

Personal income tax paid by an employee varies from country to country as the result of the interaction of a number of different choices made by governments, for example:

- the way that the assessable earnings are measured, the basis of assessment;
- the way deductible expenses are calculated;
- the schedule of rates used to calculate tax payable.

Basis of assessment

Many countries such as the UK make a distinction between persons employed, earning a wage or salary and subject to tax under the employment income rules and self-employed person taxable under income tax rules. The normal basis of assessment for employed persons can vary from country to country; it could be based on any of the following:

- the amount actually received in the tax year, for example, in the UK;
- the amount earned in the previous year, for example, in France;
- the average of the previous 2 years earnings, for example, in Switzerland.

The assessment will cover basic salary or wage, commissions, fees, gratuities, profit-sharing payments, bonuses and benefits-in-kind. Pensions received after the cessation of employment are also usually taxable. Some expenses may be deductible.

Deductible expenses

There is wide variation of deductible expenses between different countries. In the UK, for expenses to be deductible from income, they must be 'incurred wholly, exclusively and necessarily in the performance of the duties'. Expenses that could meet this definition may include:

- professional subscriptions
- donations to charity and through a payroll deduction scheme
- retirement annuity premiums
- contributions to personal pension plans
- costs of security assets or services included in emoluments.

Benefits-in-kind

Benefits-in-kind are non-cash benefits given by the employer to an employee as part of a remuneration package, often in lieu of further cash payments. In the UK, senior employees and directors often have a remuneration package that includes a number of benefits-in-kind. The tax regulations provide for a number of these benefits to be included in the tax base. The range of benefits-in-kind given to employees varies enormously between countries and their tax treatment varies just as much.

3.6.2 Social security contributions

Social security contributions are not always regarded as taxes. However, they are assessed on individuals and deducted from earnings in the same way as employee taxation is deducted. Social security contributions constitute a significant tax burden on employees and employers, in some countries employee social security contributions may be more than their income tax each month.

Social security rates are progressive but usually less so than income tax, they are based on an employee's monthly earnings, without any adjustments for expenses or family circumstances. The employee pays a percentage of earnings, usually up to a maximum contribution per month.

The employer also has to make a payment; this usually has no maximum and is based on a percentage of the employees pay.

3.6.3 Other payroll taxes

In some countries, governments also impose other payroll taxes, for example, in the USA, in addition to social security contributions, there is a separate unemployment compensation tax.

3.7 Use of employer reporting and withholding to ensure compliance and assist tax collection

The bulk of income tax revenues in developed countries are provided by wage and salary earners. In most countries tax from employment income is collected by the employer using deduction at source; employers withhold tax along with social security contributions from the current earnings of employees.

The deductions are calculated using tables provided by the tax authorities and information about the total allowances to which each employee is entitled is given in the form of a code number. Employers deduct the tax from employees' pay each month and then pay the tax and social security contributions to the tax authorities on a monthly basis. For example, the UK system of tax deducted at source is known as the pay-as-you-earn (PAYE) system.

This arrangement has a number of advantages:

- the tax is collected earlier than systems that assess earnings at the end of the year, this improves the governments cash flow;
- it makes payment of taxes easier for individuals as there is not one large bill to pay, this reduces defaults and late payments;
- most of the administration costs are borne by the employers instead of government.

Other taxes are also withheld by employers or entities making the payment. For example, in the USA property taxes are collected by banks and other entities along with mortgage payments.

3.8 Example of the tax regime information given in the exam

Country X – Tax regime for use through out the examination paper

Relevant Tax Rules for Years Ended 30 April 2007 to 2010

Corporate Profits

Unless otherwise specified, only the following rules for taxation of corporate profits will be relevant, other taxes can be ignored:

- Accounting rules on recognition and measurement are followed for tax purposes.
- All expenses other than depreciation, amortisation, entertaining, taxes paid to other public bodies and donations to political parties are tax deductible.
- Tax depreciation is deductible as follows: 50% of additions to PPE in the accounting period in which they are recorded; 25% p.a. of the written-down value (i.e. cost minus previous allowances) in subsequent accounting periods except that in which the asset is disposed of. No tax depreciation is allowed on land.
- The corporate tax on profits is at a rate of 25%.
- Tax losses can be carried forward to offset against future taxable profits from the same business.

Value Added Tax

Country X has a VAT system which allows entities to reclaim input tax paid.
   In country X the VAT rates are:
   Zero-rated   0%
   Standard-rated   15%

3.9 Summary

This chapter has considered indirect taxes and their impact on entities. We started with a consideration of sales taxes and VAT, then continued with other indirect taxes. The final section considered employee taxation and the operation of advance payment systems.

Revision Questions

? Question 1

Country IDT has a duty that is levied on vehicle fuel oils at 10% of their resale value before sales tax. This duty is a:

(A) *Ad valorem* tax
(B) Specific unit tax
(C) Direct tax
(D) VAT   **(2 marks)**

? Question 2

In no more than 25 words, define 'benefits-in-kind'.   **(2 marks)**

? Question 3

Country IDT has a duty that is levied on all drinks of an alcoholic nature where the alcohol is above 20% by volume. This levy is $2 per 1 litre bottle. This duty could be said to be:

(A) *Ad valorem* tax
(B) Specific unit tax
(C) Direct tax
(D) VAT   **(2 marks)**

? Question 4

List three advantages of requiring employers to deduct employee tax from employees' pay each month.   **(3 marks)**

? Question 5

Country V has a VAT system which allows organisations to reclaim input tax paid. VAT is at 15% of selling price.

B manufactures sports shoes and sells them to C, a wholesaler. C resells them to D, a retailer. D eventually sells them to E for $120. The prices at which transactions take place (excluding VAT) are as follows:

- B sells to C for $50
- C sells to D for $80

Calculate the VAT due from B, C and D. **(3 marks)**

? Question 6

An entity purchases products from a foreign entity. These products cost $21 each and on import are subject to an excise duty of $4 per item and VAT at 20%. If the entity imports 100 items, how much do they pay to the tax authorities?

(A) $400
(B) $420
(C) $500
(D) $900 **(2 marks)**

? Question 7

An entity purchases raw materials for $1,100 and pays VAT at a standard rate on them. The materials are used to produce two products X and Y. The entity sells 200 units of product X at $5 each and 400 units of product Y at $4 each. Product X is zero-rated for VAT purposes and product Y is standard-rated.

Assume that there are no other transactions affecting the VAT payments and that the standard rate of VAT is 20%.

At the end of the period the entity pays the net amount of VAT due to the tax authorities. How much VAT was paid:

(A) $100
(B) $300
(C) $320
(D) $520 **(2 marks)**

? Question 8

If a product is exempt for VAT purposes, it means that an entity:

(A) Can charge VAT on sales at standard rate and cannot reclaim input taxes paid
(B) Cannot charge VAT on sales and can reclaim input taxes paid
(C) Cannot charge VAT on sales and cannot reclaim input taxes paid
(D) Can charge VAT on sales and can reclaim input taxes paid **(2 marks)**

? **Question 9**

Country OS has a VAT system, where VAT is charged on all goods and services. Registered VAT entities are allowed to recover input VAT paid on their purchases. VAT operates at different levels in OS:

Standard rate	10%
Luxury rate	20%
Zero rate	0%

During the last VAT period, an entity, BZ purchased materials and services costing $100,000, excluding VAT. All materials and services were at standard rate VAT.

BZ converted the materials into two products Z and L; product Z is zero-rated and product L is luxury-rated for VAT purposes.

During the VAT period, BZ made the following sales, excluding VAT:

	$
Z	60,000
L	120,000

At the end of the period, BZ paid the net VAT due to the tax authorities. Assuming BZ had no other VAT-related transactions, how much VAT did BZ pay? **(2 marks)**

? **Question 10**

CU manufactures clothing and operates in a country that has a VAT system. This system allows entities to reclaim input tax that they have paid on taxable supplies. VAT is at 15% of the selling price at all stages of the manufacturing and distribution chain.

CU manufactures a batch of clothing and pays expenses (taxable inputs) of $100 plus VAT. CU sells the batch of clothing to a retailer CZ for $250 plus VAT. CZ unpacks the clothing and sells the items separately to various customers for a total of $600 plus VAT. How much VAT do CU and CZ each have to pay in respect of this one batch of clothing?

(2 marks)

? **Question 11**

Country X uses a Pay-As-You-Earn (PAYE) system for collecting taxes from employees. Each employer is provided with information about each employee's tax position and tables showing the amount of tax to deduct each period. Employers are required to deduct tax from employees and pay it to the revenue authorities on a monthly basis.

From the perspective of the government, list THREE advantages of the PAYE system.

(3 marks)

? **Question 12**

Excise duties are deemed to be most suitable for commodities that have certain specific characteristics.

List THREE characteristics of a commodity that, from a revenue authority's point of view, would make that commodity suitable for an excise duty to be imposed. **(3 marks)**

INDIRECT TAXES AND EMPLOYEE TAXATION

 Question 13

Country Y has a VAT system which allows entities to reclaim input tax paid.
In Country Y the VAT rates are:

Zero-rated	0%
Standard-rated	15%

DE runs a small retail store. DE's sales include items that are zero-rated, standard-rated and exempt.

DE's electronic cash register provides an analysis of sales. The figures for the three months to 30 April 2007 were:

	Sales value, excluding VAT
	$
Zero-rated	11,000
Standard-rated	15,000
Exempt	13,000
Total	39,000

DE's analysis of expenditure for the same period provided the following:

	Expenditure, excluding VAT
	$
Zero-rated purchases	5,000
Standard-rated purchases relating to standard rate outputs	9,000
Standard-rated purchases relating to exempt outputs	7,000
Standard-rated purchases relating to zero-rated outputs	3,000
	24,000

Calculate the VAT due to/from DE for the three months ended 30 April 2007. **(2 marks)**

 Question 14

EF is an importer and imports perfumes and similar products in bulk. EF repackages the products and sells them to retailers. EF is registered for Value Added Tax (VAT).

EF imports a consignment of perfume priced at $10,000 (excluding excise duty and VAT) and pays excise duty of 20% and VAT on the total (including duty) at 15%.

EF pays $6,900 repackaging costs, including VAT at 15% and then sells all the perfume for $40,250 including VAT at 15%.

EF has not paid or received any VAT payments to/from the VAT authorities for this consignment.

Requirements
 (i) Calculate EF's net profit on the perfume consignment.
 (ii) Calculate the net VAT due to be paid by EF on the perfume consignment. **(5 marks)**

Solutions to Revision Questions

Solution 1

The correct answer is (A), see Section 3.2.

Solution 2

Benefits-in-kind are non-cash benefits given by the employer to an employee, often in lieu of further cash payments, see Section 3.6.1.

Solution 3

The correct answer is (B), see Section 3.2.1

Solution 4

The advantages are:

- the tax is collected earlier than systems that assess earnings at the end of the year, this improves the governments cash flow;
- it makes payment of taxes easier for individuals as there is not one large bill to pay, this reduces defaults and late payments;
- most of the administration costs are borne by the employers instead of government, see Section 3.7.

Solution 5

Entity	Input tax $	Output tax $	VAT paid $
B			
Sale to C		7.50	7.50 paid by B
C			
Purchase from B	7.50		
Sale to D		12.00	4.50 paid by C
D			
Purchase from C	12.00		
Sale to E		18.00	6.00 paid by D
Total suffered by E			18.00

See Section 3.4.

Solution 6

Excise duty payable is usually added to the cost of the goods, the total being subject to VAT. The correct answer is (D), see Section 3.4.

 ## Solution 7

The entity can reclaim input tax paid and sets this off against VAT charged at the standard rate:

VAT charged at standard rate $(400 \times \$4) \times 20\% = \$320$
Input VAT paid $\quad\quad\quad\quad\quad \$1,100 \times 20\% \quad = \$220$
VAT paid to tax authorities $\quad\quad\quad\quad\quad\quad\quad\quad \$100$

The correct answer is (A), see Section 3.4.

 ## Solution 8

The correct answer is (C), see Section 3.4.1

 ## Solution 9

Input VAT $= 100 \times 10\% = 10$
Output VAT $= (60 \times 0\%) + (120 \times 20\%) = 24$
VAT due $= 24 - 10 = 14$
VAT paid $= \$14,000$

See Section 3.4.

 ## Solution 10

	Cost (Inputs)	Sales	Net	VAT
	$	$	$	$
CU	100	250	150	22.5
CZ	250	600	350	52.5

See Section 3.4.

 ## Solution 11

Three advantages of PAYE are:

- The tax is collected earlier than systems that assess earnings at the end of the year; this improves the government's cash flow.
- It makes payment of taxes easier for individuals as there is not one large bill to pay; this reduces defaults and late payments.
- Most of the administration costs are borne by the employers, instead of government.
- Regular predictable receipts make government budgeting easier.

Note: Any other relevant point would have been acceptable in the exam.

Solution 12

From the revenue authority's point of view, the characteristics of commodities suitable for excise duties are:

- Few large producers/suppliers
- Inelastic demand with no close substitutes
- Large sales volumes
- Easy to define products covered by the tax.

Note: Any **three** of the above would have been acceptable in the exam.

 Solution 13

DE's outputs
$15,000 \times 15\% = 2,250$
Inputs
$[9,000 + 3,000] \times 15\% = 1,800$
Net payment due from DE $= 2,250 - 1,800 = 450$

VAT relating to exempt items cannot be reclaimed and is ignored.

 Solution 14

Perfume consignment income, expenditure and VAT are as follows:

	Total cost (incl VAT) $	VAT $	Net of VAT $
Expenditure			
Cost	10,000		10,000
Excise duty	2,000		2,000
	12,000		12,000
Input VAT @ 15%	1,800	1,800	0
	13,800		12,000
Repackaging costs	6,900	900	6,000
Total costs	20,700		18,000
Sales revenue	(40,250)	(5,250)	(35,000)
Net	19,550	2,550	17,000

(i) Net profit is $17,000
As EF is registered for VAT in its country VAT on expenses can be reclaimed and VAT must be charged on sales. VAT cannot be included in revenue or cost figures, so the revenue and cost must be calculated net of VAT.

(ii) Net VAT due to be paid is $2,550.

4

Administration of Taxation

Administration of Taxation

4

LEARNING OUTCOMES

After completing this chapter you should be able to:

▶ explain key administrative requirements and the possible enquiry and investigation powers of taxing authorities associated with the principal types of taxation lilkely to be of relevance to an incorporated business;

▶ explain the difference in principle between tax avoidance and tax evasion.

The syllabus topics covered in this chapter are as follows:

- The need for record-keeping and record retention that may be additional to that required for financial accounting purposes.
- The need for deadlines for reporting (filing returns) and tax payments.
- Types of powers of tax authorities to ensure compliance with tax rules:
  - power to review and query filed returns
  - power to request special reports or returns
  - power to examine records (generally extending back some years)
  - powers of entry and search
  - exchange of information with tax authorities in other jurisdictions.
- The distinction between tax avoidance and tax evasion, and how these vary among jurisdictions (including the difference between the use of statutory general anti-avoidance provisions and case law based regimes).

4.1 Introduction

In the first part of this chapter, we will consider the need for entities to keep and retain records. Second, we consider the need for deadlines and the various types of powers that tax authorities may enjoy. We conclude the chapter with a discussion on tax avoidance and tax evasion.

ADMINISTRATION OF TAXATION

4.2 The need for record-keeping and record retention

The requirement for entities to keep records is usually included in tax legislation, which will usually set out minimum time limits for the retention of records. Failure to maintain the correct records to support the tax return will usually render the entity liable to a financial penalty.

The range of records required to be kept for tax purposes will frequently be wider than those required to support financial statements as any type of document or record may be needed, for example, copies of contracts. Records need to be kept to support all types of tax that the entity has to pay to the tax authorities, whether the tax has been collected from others or is due from the entity in its own right. In other words, records will usually need to be kept for the following:

- corporate income tax, including capital gains;
- sales tax or VAT;
- excise duties, for example, in relation to sales of fuel oils;
- employee taxes, social security contributions and other payroll taxes deducted at source from employee salaries and wages.

4.2.1 Corporate income tax

All taxpayers need to keep records to enable them to accurately prepare their financial statements in accordance with generally accepted accounting principles. Financial statements are the starting point of the calculation of taxable profits for the period. Entities therefore have to keep all of the records required to support their financial statements and also the additional documents required to support the adjustments made to those statements when completing their tax returns.

4.2.2 Sales tax or Vat

In countries where sales tax or VAT is used, appropriate records need to be kept. For example, in the UK, registered persons are required to keep adequate records and retain them for 6 years. Records must show details of all taxable goods and services received or supplied, and all exempt supplies made.

The records required to be kept include all business documents, such as:

- orders and delivery notes;
- relevant business correspondence;
- purchases and sales books;
- cashbooks and other account books;
- purchase invoices and sales invoices;
- records of daily takings such as till rolls;
- annual accounts, including income statements;
- import and export documents;
- bank statements and paying-in slips;
- VAT account;
- credit or debit notes issued or received.

Records may be computerised or maintained by a computer bureau, provided that they can be made available to the tax authorities when required.

The above list shows how much detail is usually required to be kept to justify tax returns when required to do so by the tax authorities.

4.2.3 Overseas subsidiaries

A further example of the detailed records required is where a resident entity has an overseas subsidiary. In some cases the tax authorities may be concerned about transfer pricing between the subsidiary and its parent. Tax authorities sometimes, for example, in the USA, have powers to require entities to provide them with detailed records providing evidence of the method used to calculate prices used in transactions between the subsidiary and its parent. Entities, therefore, have to keep detailed records of price calculations in case the tax authorities require them to be submitted (note you do not need to know any details about transfer pricing).

4.2.4 Employee taxes and social security

In countries where employee tax and social security contributions are deducted from employees' pay each week or month, the employer will need to keep detailed records of the employees' pay and also the amounts of tax and social security that have been deducted. At the year-end the employer will also need to complete a number of returns for the government that show the total deducted from each employee, the employer's contribution for each employee, and an analysis of the total amounts deducted. The employer will also have to provide details of amounts deducted, usually on standard government forms, to employees.

4.3 The need for deadlines for reporting (filing returns) and tax payments

Tax authorities set deadlines for taxpayers to submit tax returns and pay outstanding tax. There may be different deadlines for income tax and corporate income tax, sales tax and VAT.

There are generally three options available to tax authorities when collecting corporate income tax:

1. The tax authorities prepare an assessment, based on information provided by the entity and notify the entity of the amount of tax due.
2. The entity prepares a tax return and files this along with their computations of tax due.
3. The entity self-assesses the tax due and pays the amount of tax it thinks is due.

In countries where an assessment is raised by the tax authorities, entities will be required to submit tax returns after their accounting year-end. The tax return will usually require a range of information to be provided in addition to the copy of the financial statements. Tax authorities may also require additional information from the entity before raising an assessment on the entity, which will have to be paid within a certain time limit.

Countries using a pay and file type of system, require the corporate income tax to be estimated by the entity and paid by a certain deadline. For example, in the UK, corporation tax for small and medium entities must be paid within 9 months of the end of the accounting period. The corporation tax return, with supporting calculations has to be submitted within 12 months of the end of the accounting period. Upon receipt of the corporation tax return, the tax authorities calculate the tax due and adjust the amount paid by issuing a demand for further payment or making a refund for any amounts overpaid.

In countries using self-assessment, entities have to estimate the amount of corporation tax that they will be due to pay for the year and pay it, often in advance of the year-end. For example, in the UK, large entities have to estimate their corporation tax liability and then pay their corporation tax in four equal instalments, two within the period and two after the end of the tax period. They still have to submit a tax return which must include a self-assessment calculation and be supported by relevant financial accounts.

The deadline for filing returns and paying the tax will vary from country to country, but a deadline is required for the following reasons:

- without any deadline, entities would not know when payment was required;
- it enables the tax authorities to forecast their cash flows more accurately;
- without a deadline, there is no reference point for late payment, it would be difficult to enforce any penalties for entities not paying;
- if tax is deducted from employees at source and not paid to the tax authorities fairly quickly, there is more chance of an entity spending the amount deducted instead of paying it to the tax authorities.

4.4 Types of powers of tax authorities to ensure compliance with tax rules

Revenue authorities generally have powers to inflict penalties for various offences related to corporation tax and sales tax/VAT. For example, late filing of a tax return may attract a fixed penalty and unpaid tax may be subject to interest on the balance due.

4.4.1 Power to review and query filed returns

Tax authorities generally have the power to review and query corporation tax returns that have been filed. The tax legislation will usually specify deadlines limiting the time available for the tax authorities to decide to open an investigation. Tax authorities generally have the power to request any document, etc., relevant to their enquiry. The legislation will specify time limits allowed to comply with the request and will also provide for penalties for non-compliance.

Tax authorities usually have the power to check and query sales tax and VAT returns. There are usually a range of penalties in the legislation which apply to late submission of returns and misdeclaration of tax due.

4.4.2 Power to request special reports or returns

Tax authorities may have the power to request a special report to be made on an entity or to require an entity to complete special returns. They may take this type of action if they believe that the entity is not providing full or accurate information.

4.4.3 Power to examine records (generally extending back some years)

Tax authorities generally have the power to examine any records that support the corporate income tax. As the tax return is based on the financial accounts, this means that they also have the power to examine any documents or records that support the financial accounts.

If the tax authorities suspect fraud or serious understatement of the amount of corporate income tax due, they usually have the power to require the entity to allow them access to their records going back, in some cases as far as the tax authorities wish. For example, in the UK, in cases of fraud, the tax authorities can go back 20 years.

Sales tax and VAT legislation usually includes provisions for officers of the tax authority to visit the premises of registered entities from time to time to confirm that the regulations are being complied with.

4.4.4 Powers of entry and search

Tax authorities do not have the power of entry and search of an entity's premises in all countries. Some countries allow the tax authorities full and free access to an entity's business premises but other countries require a search warrant to be issued first. All countries allow access, with a search warrant if necessary, in fraud cases. In cases where fraud or some other contravention of the tax legislation is suspected, tax authorities also generally have the power to seize documents.

Sales tax and VAT legislation often give officers of the tax authority a statutory right to enter premises at any reasonable time and inspect goods and records to confirm that sales tax or VAT returns are complete and accurate.

4.4.5 Exchange of information with tax authorities in other jurisdictions

Tax authorities generally have the power to pass on information to foreign tax authorities as long as there is a tax treaty with the foreign country. The tax treaty will set out the terms and conditions that need to apply before information will be provided.

4.5 Tax avoidance and tax evasion

The causes of tax avoidance and evasion include high tax rates, imprecise laws, insufficient penalties and apparent inequity. When any of these situations apply, tax avoidance and evasion will tend to increase. For example:

- high tax rates make evasion or avoidance more rewarding and also make it worthwhile spending more on tax advice and using more complex schemes;
- imprecise laws mean that the letter of the law is not tight enough to stop avoidance and the spirit of the law may be unclear. In Chapter 1, we saw that one of the canons of taxation was certainty, imprecise laws lead to uncertainty;
- insufficient penalties mean that it is more rewarding to evade tax and risk getting caught, even if caught the penalty will not be severe;
- apparent inequity can lead to an increased desire to evade tax and also make tax avoidance and evasion more socially acceptable.

4.5.1 Tax evasion

Tax evasion is the illegal manipulation of the tax system to avoid paying taxes. Tax evasion is the intentional disregard of the legislation in order to escape paying taxes; it can include falsifying tax returns and claiming fictitious expenses.

4.5.2 Tax avoidance

Tax avoidance is tax planning to the extent that the affairs of the entity are legally arranged in such a way as to minimise the corporation tax liability. Although tax avoidance is strictly legal and within the letter of the law, it is usually contrary to the spirit of the law. Many tax avoidance schemes exploit loopholes in the legislation, which the tax authorities try to close as soon as the loophole has been identified.

4.5.3 Statutory general anti-avoidance provisions and case law regimes

As mentioned above, one approach to tax avoidance schemes is to try and close loopholes in the tax system as soon as they are identified. This stops others exploiting the loophole, but does not usually apply retrospectively and so those already using the loophole will be able to continue using it. One problem with this approach is that closing loopholes means passing more legislations, thus making the tax system more and more complex; it may also create other (unintended) loopholes which can be exploited. Tax authorities therefore use other administrative methods of minimising both tax avoidance and tax evasion. The methods used can be summarised into four categories:

 (i) reducing opportunity
 (ii) increasing the perceived risk
(iii) reducing the overall gain
(iv) changing social attitudes towards evasion and avoidance.

 (i) Reducing opportunity by:
   - deducting tax at source whenever possible, for example, interest payments and wages and salaries; if not possible, use third party reporting;
   - simplifying the tax structure to minimise opportunities for evasion and false returns. For example, minimising the number of reliefs, allowances, rebates and exemptions within the tax system will reduce the number of false deductions.
 (ii) Increasing the perceived risk by:
   - setting up an efficient system of auditing tax returns and payments to maximise revenue from given resources. This should be well publicised so that it increases the perceived risk of being found out;
   - developing good communications with other tax administrations.
(iii) Reducing the overall gain by:
   - carrying out regular reviews of the penalty structure, with appropriate publicity for increased penalties.
(iv) Changing social attitudes towards evasion and avoidance by:
   - encouraging, developing and maintaining an honest and customer-friendly tax administration;

- creating a tax system which is perceived as equitable to all parties;
- governments trying to encourage an increasing commitment of the population to obey the law.

The overall objective for tax authorities is to reduce the tax gap (see Section 1.4.9).

In countries using a system of common law, case law developed in the courts is important. Over time the cases decided by the courts will interpret and develop the tax legislation. Case law can evolve over time with decisions gradually developing and to some extent even reflecting changing social attitudes. For example, in the UK, anti-avoidance cases have been brought to the courts regularly over the years with the revenue authorities challenging avoidance schemes. The results of the court cases can then be relied upon in future court cases, although they may then be further refined by the court. In this way the case law is developed over time. The UK courts also look at the substance of the transaction instead of the legal form. For example, a UK court case (*Ramsey Ltd v IRC*) found that in a tax avoidance scheme, although each transaction was perfectly legal, they were in total self-cancelling; their only effect was to reduce tax and therefore should be disregarded for tax purposes. Another tax avoidance case (*Furniss v Dawson*) found that steps inserted in a series of transactions that had no commercial purpose other than to avoid tax, should be disregarded. A later tax avoidance case (*Craven v White*) limited this by finding that the series of transactions had to be set up with an intended result that was known at the time the transactions started.

 You do not need to remember any case names for your examination, these cases are here to illustrate the principle of case law, you only need to understand the principle.

4.6 Forum on tax administration

In January 2004, the OECD launched its new Forum on Tax Administration. The Forum is an initiative to promote the dialogue on strategic tax administration issues and to facilitate the exchange of best practices between tax authorities in different countries.

4.7 International tax dialogue

To better discharge their institutions' mandates, the staffs of the IMF, OECD and World Bank proposed to facilitate increased cooperation on tax matters among governments and international organisations through the establishment of a dialogue to share good practices and pursue common objectives in improving the functioning of national tax systems. The International Tax Dialogue (ITD) aims to facilitate such a process. The ITD will not however, at any stage have any power to make, enforce or mediate binding tax rules. The objectives of the ITD are:

- Promote effective international dialogue between governments on taxation, giving all countries a real input into the discussion of tax administration and policy issues.
- Identify and share good practices in taxation.
- Provide a clearer focus for technical assistance.
- Avoid duplication of effort in respect of existing activities.

More information on the ITD can be found at http://www.itdweb.org

4.8 Summary

This chapter has reviewed some of the administrative aspects of taxation. We have looked at the need for records and their retention; the need for deadlines and the general powers that a tax authority would be expected to have. We have also considered the differences between tax avoidance and tax evasion.

Revision Questions

? Question 1

Which of the following taxes is an entity unlikely to need to keep additional detailed records for:

(A) Corporate income tax
(B) VAT
(C) Employee tax deducted from salaries
(D) Property tax   **(2 marks)**

? Question 2

In no more than 30 words, define the meaning of 'tax avoidance'.   **(2 marks)**

? Question 3

List four possible powers that a tax authority may have to help them enforce tax regulations.
                                                                                                     (4 marks)

? Question 4

Which ONE of the following powers is a tax authority least likely to have granted to them?

(A) Power of arrest
(B) Power to examine records
(C) Power of entry and search
(D) Power to give information to other countries' tax authorities   **(2 marks)**

Question 5

Requirements

(i) Explain the difference between tax avoidance and tax evasion. **(2 marks)**

(ii) Briefly explain the methods that governments can use to reduce tax avoidance and tax evasion. **(3 marks)**

(Total marks = 5)

 # Question 6

List THREE possible reasons why governments set deadlines for filing returns and/or paying taxes **(3 marks)**

Solutions to Revision Questions

 Solution 1

The correct answer is (D), see Section 4.2.

 Solution 2

Tax avoidance is tax planning to the extent that the affairs of the entity are legally arranged in such a way as to minimise the corporate income tax liability.

   See Section 4.5.2.

 Solution 3

Any four of the following:

1. power to review and query filed returns;
2. power to request special reports or returns;
3. power to examine records (generally extending back some years);
4. powers of entry and search;
5. power to exchange of information with tax authorities in other jurisdictions.

See Section 4.4.

 Solution 4

The correct answer is (A), see Section 4.4.

 Solution 5

(i) **Tax avoidance** – Tax planning to the extent that the affairs of an entity are legally arranged in such a way as to minimise the tax liability. Although tax avoidance is strictly legal and within the letter of the law, it is usually contrary to the spirit of the law. Many tax avoidance schemes exploit loopholes in the legislation.

   Tax evasion – The illegal manipulation of the tax system so as to avoid paying taxes. Tax evasion is the intentional disregard of the legislation in order to escape paying taxes; it can include falsifying tax returns and claiming fictitious expenses.

   See Sections 4.5.1 and 4.5.2.

ADMINISTRATION OF TAXATION

(ii) A traditional response by governments is often to close loopholes by passing more legislations, but this can create additional opportunities for avoidance. More effective methods are:

Reducing opportunity by:

- deducting tax at source whenever possible;
- simplifying the tax structure to minimise opportunities for evasion and false returns.

Increasing the perceived risk by:

- setting up an efficient system of auditing tax returns and payments to maximise revenue from given resources;
- publicising a system of auditing so that it increases the perceived risk of being found out;
- developing good communications with other tax administrations.

Reducing the overall gain by:

- carrying out regular reviews of the penalty structure, with appropriate publicity for increased penalties.

Changing social attitudes towards evasion and avoidance by:

- encouraging, developing and maintaining an honest and customer-friendly tax administration;
- creating a tax system which is perceived as equitable to all parties;
- trying to encourage an increasing commitment of the population to obey the law.

See Section 4.5.3.

 ## Solution 6

Any three from the following:

1. So that entities know when payment is required;
2. It enables the tax authorities to forecast their cash flows more accurately;
3. Provides a reference point for late payment. It would otherwise be difficult to enforce any penalties for entities not paying;
4. To prevent entities spending tax money deducted from employees. If tax is deducted from employees at source and not paid to the tax authorities fairly quickly, there is more chance of an entity spending the amount deducted, instead of paying it to the tax authorities.

Note: Any other reasonable point would have been acceptable in the examination.

5

International
Taxation

International Taxation

5

LEARNING OUTCOMES

After completing this chapter you should be able to:

▶ identify situations in which foreign tax obligations (reporting and liability) could arise and methods for relieving foreign tax;

▶ explain sources of tax rules and the importance of jurisdiction.

The syllabus topics covered in this chapter are as follows:

● International taxation:
  − the concept of corporate residence and the variation in rules for its determination across jurisdictions (e.g. place of incorporation versus place of management);
  − types of payments on which withholding tax may be required (especially interest, dividends, royalties and capital gains accruing to non-residents);
  − means of establishing a taxable presence in another country (local entity and branch);
  − the effect of double tax treaties (based on the OECD Model Convention) on the above (e.g. reduction of withholding tax rates, provisions for defining a permanent establishment);

5.1 Introduction

This chapter considers aspects of international taxation. We start with a consideration of the term residence; we then consider withholding taxes and different ways of an entity establishing a taxable presence. The chapter concludes with a discussion of double taxation treaties and the methods used to relieve foreign tax.

5.2 The Organisation for Economic Co-operation and Development (OECD) – Model tax convention

The OECD's taxation work covers a broad range of activities, including tax evasion, harmful tax practices, electronic commerce and environmental taxes. In relation to international taxation, the OECD has published a Model tax convention which is a model tax treaty

INTERNATIONAL TAXATION

that can be used by countries when drafting their double tax treaties. We will refer to the OECD model tax convention throughout this chapter.

5.3 The concept of corporate residence

Corporate income tax is usually a residence-based tax, whether corporate income tax will be charged depends on the residence, for tax purposes, of any particular entity.

The test for establishing residence of an entity varies from one country to another, the main types of test are discussed below.

5.3.1 Place of control and central management of an entity

Using this basis, the country from where control of the group is exercised is deemed to be the country of residence for tax purposes. The place where directors' meetings are held is usually an important criterion when examining the exercise of control.

5.3.2 Place of incorporation

The second method is a simple matter of fact as it will be absolutely clear which country an entity has been incorporated in. If a country uses the place of incorporation as a basis, any entity registered in that country will be deemed to be resident in that country for tax purposes, no matter where control is exercised.

5.3.3 Place of control and place of incorporation

Some countries, for example the UK, use both bases to establish whether an entity has residence for tax purposes. In these countries, an entity will be regarded as resident if it meets either of the above criteria. For example, an entity is regarded as resident in the UK:

- if it was incorporated in the UK; or
- if it was incorporated outside the UK, but control and central management is exercised within the UK.

This can lead to problems of double residence for taxation purposes. For instance, if an entity is registered in one country and its place of control and central management is in another country, it could be regarded as resident in both countries, if the first country bases their residence requirement on place of incorporation and the second country uses place of management. The OECD model tax convention sets out a basis for resolving this problem.

5.4 The OECD Articles of the model convention with respect to taxes on income and on capital

The OECD – *Articles of the model convention with respect to taxes on income and on capital* (hereafter referred to as the OECD model) defines the meaning of residence as follows:

'any person who, under the laws of that State, is liable to tax therein by reason of his domicile, residence, place of effective management or any other criterion of a similar nature.'

The OECD model defines person to include:

'an individual, a company and any other body of persons.'

Under the OECD model an entity will have residence in the country of its effective management.

The OECD model provides that its status shall be determined as follows:

(a) it shall be deemed to be a resident only of the State in which its place of effective management is situated;

(b) if the State in which its place of effective management is situated cannot be determined or if its place of effective management is in neither State, it shall be deemed to be a resident only of the State with which its economic relations are closer;

(c) if the State with which its economic relations are closer cannot be determined, it shall be deemed to be a resident of the State from the laws of which it derives its legal status.

From this it should be clear that under an OECD model based tax treaty, residence due to place of incorporation will only apply if effective management and primary economic activity do not resolve the problem. The full text of the OECD model tax convention can be found at http://www.oecd.org/dataoecd/52/34/1914467.pdf

5.5 Withholding tax

In many countries, payments made abroad are subject to a 'withholding tax'. In Chapter 1, we defined a withholding tax as 'a tax deducted from a payment at source before it is made to the recipient abroad'. As countries cannot tax individuals in foreign countries, a withholding tax ensures that the government gains at least some revenue from such payments. The type of payments normally subject to withholding tax include:

- interest
- royalties
- rents
- dividends
- capital gains.

A Country will often have different rates of withholding tax for each of the above categories. Withholding tax is also deducted from payments between entities of the same group established in different countries, thus causing difficulties for business, including time consuming formalities, cash flow losses and sometimes double taxation.

Double taxation treaties between countries aim to reduce or eliminate withholding taxes and double taxation.

5.6 Underlying tax

If an entity receives a dividend from an overseas entity in which it holds at least a minimum percentage of the voting power, relief is also sometimes given for the tax on the profits out of which the dividend was paid. This tax is referred to as the underlying tax. The underlying tax is calculated as the gross amount of dividend received by the entity as a proportion of the after-tax profits of the foreign entity times the tax paid on those profits. This is the proportion of foreign tax paid on the profits that relates to the gross amount of the dividend paid to the entity.

Example 5.A

H owns 30% of the equity shares in S, an entity resident in a foreign country. H receives a dividend of $36,000 from S, the amount received is after deduction of withholding tax of 20%. S had before-tax profits for the year of $400,000 and paid corporate income tax of $100,000. Calculate the underlying tax that H can claim for double taxation relief.

Solution

H receives $36,000 net, this represents 80% of the gross amount, therefore the gross amount is $45,000 ($36,000/0.80).
  The after-tax profits of S are $400,000 − $100,000 = $300,000.
  The underlying tax is then $45,000/$300,000 × $100,000 = $15,000

5.7 Means of establishing a taxable presence in another country

A key decision that entities with trading interests abroad have to make is whether to run an overseas operation as a branch of the entity, which is merely an extension of the entity's business or to incorporate (in the overseas country) a newly formed subsidiary. There are many non-tax factors that influence this decision; however, taxation can also have an impact on the decision. The main taxation considerations in the decision between the two options are considered below.

5.7.1 Subsidiary

- An overseas subsidiary, set up in an overseas country and controlled from abroad may be able to escape tax on its profits, but the holding entity would be liable to tax on dividends received.
- Losses made by the non-resident subsidiary would not be available for a group loss relief. None of the advantages of being in a group can usually be enjoyed by a non-resident entity.
- A non-resident subsidiary cannot claim tax depreciation and any assets transferred to it by the parent may cause the parent to become subject to capital gains tax on the transfer.
- There might be a major problem in establishing that such a newly formed overseas subsidiary was not resident in the country of its parent. The subsidiary would probably be a fully owned subsidiary and would almost certainly be effectively managed by the parent.

- There could be transfer pricing problems. When the parent trades with an overseas subsidiary, the opportunity might be taken to effect the transactions at a price which effectively transfers profit from the home country to the overseas destination or visa-versa, depending on relative tax rates.

5.7.2 Branch

Where a resident entity runs an overseas operation as a branch of the entity, the following taxation implications usually arise:

- Corporate income tax will be payable by the resident entity on any profits earned by the branch. There will usually be relief for any foreign tax paid on these profits.
- Any capital gains made by the branch are also subject to the resident entity's tax whereas an overseas subsidiary will not generally cause the holding entity to be taxed on its capital gains.
- Assets can be transferred to the branch without triggering a capital gain.
- Tax depreciation can usually be claimed on any qualifying assets used in the trade of the branch.
- Losses sustained by the branch are usually immediately deductible against the resident entity's income.
- The specific tax law of the resident entity's country may apply to the specific character of a variety of overseas activities, some may qualify for favourable tax treatment on investment activities.
- Any money transferred from the overseas branch to the resident entity is not normally considered to be a dividend.

5.8 Double taxation treaties

There are two different approaches to taxing entities in a country:

1. The territorial approach to taxation: each country has the right to tax income earned inside its borders.
2. The worldwide approach: a country claims the right to tax income arising outside its border if that income is received by a corporation deemed resident within the country.

The worldwide approach leads to double taxation as income will usually be taxed in the country where it is earned and again in the country where the holding entity is resident. For example, an entity resident in the UK will generally be liable to UK corporate income tax on its income from all sources worldwide. It may also be liable to overseas tax to the extent that its overseas activities fall within the tax net of other countries. Double-tax relief, as its name implies, exists to reduce the heavy tax burden so arising. In essence, its effect is to ensure that the taxpayer finally suffers tax at no more than the higher of the two, home or overseas tax rate.

Most countries applying the worldwide approach grant some form of relief from double taxation. Double tax relief is given according to the terms of double-tax agreements that a country has entered into, for example, the UK has entered into tax treaties with most countries in the world. In this section we are going to consider the principles followed in most double taxation agreements.

5.8.1 The OECD model tax convention

Cross-border investment would be seriously impeded if there was a danger that the returns on such investments were taxed twice. The OECD model and the worldwide network of tax treaties based upon it help to avoid that danger by providing clear consensual rules for taxing income and capital.

The OECD model tax treaty says that business profits of an entity of a contracting state shall be taxable only in that state unless the entity carries on a business in the other contracting state through a permanent establishment in that state. If the entity carries on business in the other state, its business profits may be taxed in the other state to the extent that they are attributable to the permanent establishment.

Provisions for defining a permanent establishment

The OECD model in Article 5 paragraphs 1–3 contains the following definition:

1. For the purposes of this Convention, the term 'permanent establishment' means a fixed place of business through which the business of an entity is wholly or partly carried on.
2. The term 'permanent establishment' includes especially:
   (a) a place of management
   (b) a branch
   (c) an office
   (d) a factory
   (e) a workshop
   (f) a mine, an oil or gas well, a quarry or any other place of extraction of natural resources.
3. A building site or construction or installation project constitutes a permanent establishment only if it lasts more than 12 months.

If an entity has a permanent establishment in a country, it can be taxed in that country, causing a possible problem of double taxation.

5.9 Summary

In this chapter, we have discussed the meaning of residence and permanent establishment. We have considered problems of double taxation and double taxation treaties as well as ways of mitigating double taxation.

Revision Questions

? Question 1

Which of the following could NOT be used to indicate an organisation is resident in a country?

(A) Place of effective management
(B) Buying or selling goods in a country
(C) Place of incorporation
(D) Close economic relations with a country   **(2 marks)**

? Question 2

In no more than 15 words, define the meaning of a 'branch'.   **(2 marks)**

? Question 3

Which of the following would NOT normally be subject to a withholding tax?

(A) Rents
(B) Dividends
(C) Interest
(D) Profits   **(2 marks)**

? Question 4

A double taxation treaty between two countries usually allows relief of foreign tax through a number of methods. Which one of the following is NOT a method of relieving foreign tax?

(A) Refund
(B) Exemption
(C) Tax credits
(D) Deduction   **(2 marks)**

Question 5

The OECD model tax convention defines a permanent establishment to include a number of different types of establishments:

  (i) A place of management
 (ii) A warehouse
(iii) A workshop
 (iv) A quarry
  (v) A building site that was used for 9 months

Which of the above are included in the OECD's list of permanent establishments?

 (A) (i), (ii) and (iii) only
 (B) (i), (iii) and (iv) only
 (C) (ii), (iii) and (iv) only
 (D) (iii), (iv) and (v) only   **(2 marks)**

 Question 6

CW owns 40% of the equity shares in Z, an entity resident in a foreign country.

   CW receives a dividend of $45,000 from Z, the amount received is after deduction of withholding tax of 10%. Z had before tax profits for the year of $500,000 and paid corporate income tax of $100,000.

Requirements

  (i) Explain the meaning of 'withholding tax' and 'underlying tax.'   **(2 marks)**
 (ii) Calculate the amount of withholding tax paid by CW.   **(1 mark)**
(iii) Calculate the amount of underlying tax that relates to CW's dividend.   **(2 marks)**
                                 (Total = 5 marks)

 Question 7

The following details relate to EA:

- Incorporated in Country A.
- Carries out its main business activities in Country B.
- Its senior management operate from Country C and effective control is exercised from Country C.

   Assume countries A, B and C have all signed double tax treaties with each other, based on the OECD model tax convention.

Which country will EA be deemed to be resident in for tax purposes?

 (A) Country A
 (B) Country B
 (C) Country C
 (D) Both Countries B and C   **(2 marks)**

? Question 8

EB has an investment of 25% of the equity shares in XY, an entity resident in a foreign country.

EB receives a dividend of $90,000 from XY, the amount being after the deduction of withholding tax of 10%.

XY had profits before tax for the year of $1,200,000 and paid corporate income tax of $200,000.

How much underlying tax can EB claim for double taxation relief?   **(3 marks)**

Solutions to
Revision Questions

 Solution 1

The correct answer is (B), see Section 5.3.

 Solution 2

A branch of the entity is merely an extension of the entity's business, see Section 5.7.

 Solution 3

The correct answer is (D), see Section 5.5.

 Solution 4

The correct answer is (A), see Section 5.8.

 Solution 5

The correct answer is (B), see Section 5.8.1.1.

 Solution 6

(i) Withholding tax

A withholding tax is a tax deducted from a payment at source before it is made to the recipient. Withholding tax is most frequently used when payments are being made to recipients that are not resident within the same tax jurisdiction, but can also apply to some payments made to resident individuals.

Double taxation treaties between countries aim to reduce or eliminate withholding taxes and double taxation.

Underlying tax

Underlying tax is the tax on the profits out of which a dividend is paid. If an entity receives a dividend from an overseas entity, relief is sometimes given for the tax already deducted from the profits that were used to pay the dividend. This tax is referred to as the underlying tax.

INTERNATIONAL TAXATION

(ii) CW receives $45,000 net, this represents 90% of the gross amount, as withholding tax has been deducted. The gross amount is $50,000 ($45,000/9 × 10) and withholding tax is 5,000.

(iii) After-tax profits of Z are $500,000 − $100,000 = $400,000
Underlying tax is $50,000/$400,000 × $100,000 = $12,500
See Sections 5.5 and 5.6.

 ## Solution 7

The correct answer is (B), see Section 5.4.

 ## Solution 8

	$'000
Gross dividend = 90 × 100/90 =	100
After tax profits	1,000
Underlying tax = 100/1,000 × 200 =	20

See Example 5.A for method.

6

Taxation in Financial Statements

Taxation in Financial Statements

LEARNING OUTCOME

After completing this chapter you should be able to:

▶ apply the accounting rules for current and deferred taxation, including calculation of deferred tax based on a given set of rules.

The syllabus topics covered in this chapter are as follows:

● Accounting treatment of taxation and disclosure requirements under IAS 12.

6.1 Introduction

In this chapter we will discuss the treatment of taxation in financial statements. The taxation system will vary from country to country, so this chapter focuses on the general principles of accounting for tax as prescribed in IAS 12 *Income Taxes*.

> Questions requiring the preparation of financial statements almost always require some calculation or adjustment to tax. The calculation of current tax or deferred tax may also feature as a five-mark question or as an objective test question.

Tax in financial statements may consist of three elements:

1. current tax expense
2. adjustments to tax charges of prior periods (results of over/underprovisions)
3. transfers to or from deferred tax.

We will discuss each of these elements in turn.

> ❗ IAS 12 refers to *Income taxes,* this means any taxes on profits and on profits and gains payable by the entity, including corporate income taxes and capital gains tax.

6.2 Calculation of current tax

IAS 12 includes the following definitions:

- *Current tax.* The amount of income taxes payable (recoverable) in respect of the taxable profit (loss) for a period.
- *Taxable profit (loss).* Profit (loss) for a period, determined in accordance with the local tax authorities rules, upon which income taxes are payable (recoverable).
- *Tax expense.* The total of income tax for the period plus any charge in respect of deferred tax.

As we have seen in earlier chapters, the tax system will vary from country to country. In Chapter 2, we considered types of income and systems of corporate income tax. We also looked at different methods of calculating taxable profits. We will now use this knowledge to move on to discuss taxation in financial statements.

There is one further aspect to consider when calculating current tax, that is, different ways of treating the tax on dividend income received by an entity. IAS 12 does not specifically mention how entities should deal with dividend income, but the general principle is acknowledged.

There are two ways of treating dividends received in the financial statements:

1. The dividend received has already suffered tax and is not usually taxed again in the hands of the receiving entity, so the dividend is ignored when calculating taxable profits. To calculate the current tax, simply apply the income tax rate to the entity's taxable profits.
2. The dividend is grossed up and the recipient of the dividend shows the gross equivalent of the dividend received as a credit in the profit or loss and includes the tax on the dividend as a part of the tax charge for the year.

 Any examination question should specify how tax is to be calculated; if it does not, use the first method.

6.3 Accounting for current tax

Once calculated the income tax payable will be recorded as an expense in the profit or loss. The tax is normally recorded and paid at a later date, the amount which remains unpaid should be shown separately under current liabilities. The income tax charge is recorded as:

Debit   Income tax expense (statement of comprehensive income)
Credit   Income tax liability (statement of financial position)
Being the recording of the income tax expense for the year.

The tax calculated for the current year is estimated by the entity for the period. However, the actual amount that is paid sometime later may be slightly different than the estimate. In this case there will be an over- or underprovision of tax for prior periods. This difference will adjust the current tax charge that is included in the tax expense for the current period.

Example 6.A

The current tax charge for 20X1 is estimated at $36,000. This amount is recorded in the profit or loss for the year ended 31 December 20X1:

Debit	Income tax expense	$36,000
Credit	Income tax liability	$36,000

Being the recording of the income tax expense for the year.

The actual amount paid on 27 March 20X2 is $35,005. The payment is recorded as:

Debit	Income tax liability	$35,005
Credit	Bank	$35,005

Being the payment of the income tax expense for 20X1.

In 20X1, a liability of $36,000 was created and the following period $35,005 was debited against it. This leaves $995 included within the liability account.

This over-provision of income taxes will adjust the income tax expense that is recorded in the 20X2 statement of comprehensive income. Let us assume the tax charge for 20X2 is estimated at $40,000. The liability that must be included in the financial statements is $40,000 because that is what we are expecting to pay in early 20X3. However, there is already a liability amount existing of $995 and so the liability only requires to be increased by a further $39,005.

The current tax charge (including the expense for 20X2 and the adjustment for 20X1) can be recorded as one entry:

Debit	Income tax expense	$39,005
Credit	Income tax liability	$39,005

Being the recording of the income tax expense for 20X2.

Or as two entries:

Debit	Income tax expense	$40,000
Credit	Income tax liability	$40,000

Being the recording of the income tax expense for 20X2.

Debit	Income tax liability	$995
Credit	Income tax expense	$995

Being the reversal of the overprovision from 20X1.

6.4 Calculation of deferred tax

6.4.1 Introduction to deferred tax

Deferred taxation arises from differences between profit calculated for accounting purposes and profit for tax purposes. Differences may arise from temporary or permanent factors.

Permanent difference

Where an expense charged in the statement of comprehensive income is not allowed for income tax purposes, a permanent difference occurs. This difference will not reverse in future periods and need only be accounted for in the tax computation. In the case of a disallowable expense, the amount of the expense will be added back to profits in arriving at taxable profits within the computation (see disallowed expenses in Section 2.2).

Temporary difference

A temporary difference arises when an expense is allowed for both accounting and tax purposes, but there is a difference in the timing of the allowance. Consider the tax relief given for capital expenditure. In many countries, relief for tax purposes is given at a faster rate than most entities chose for accounting for depreciation in the financial statements. In Section 2.2.3.1, we looked at the need for tax depreciation to be used instead of accounting depreciation. The effect of using tax depreciation may be that in the first year the tax depreciation exceeds the accounting depreciation, giving a lower tax charge, since accounting depreciation is added back to accounting profit and tax depreciation is then deducted in arriving at taxable profits for taxation purposes. In subsequent periods, tax depreciation is likely to fall below the accounting depreciation charge and result in future increased taxes payable. It is the likelihood of a future tax liability that drives the need for some provision for this tax that is being deferred to future periods.

Example 6.B

An item of plant and machinery is purchased by U in 20X0 for $300,000. The asset's estimated useful life is 6 years, following which it will have no residual value. Plant and machinery is depreciated on a straight-line basis.
  Tax depreciation for this item is given at 25% on the straight-line basis for the first 4 years.
  Let us first calculate the figures that would appear in the *financial statements* over the six-year life of the asset:

	20X0 $'000	20X1 $'000	20X2 $'000	20X3 $'000	20X4 $'000	20X5 $'000
Financial statements						
Opening carrying value	300	250	200	150	100	50
Accounting depreciation charge	50	50	50	50	50	50
Carrying value (end of the reporting period)	250	200	150	100	50	0

Depreciation is charged at $50,000 per annum ($300,000/6 years).
Now let us look at how this asset would be treated for *tax purposes*:

	20X0 $'000	20X1 $'000	20X02 $'000	20X3 $'000	20X4 $'000	20X5 $'000
Tax computation						
Carrying value	300	225	150	75	0	0
Tax depreciation	75	75	75	75	0	0
(Tax written down value)	225	150	75	0	0	0

  We can see from comparing the above two tables that the carrying value of the asset per accounts differs from the Tax written down value. The annual reduction in the carrying value applied by the entity (that is accounting depreciation) differs from the reduction applied in the tax computation. By the end of the asset's useful life, the two have caught up, as they both show the asset with a carrying value of 0, but the different treatment over 6 years creates the accounting problem that is known as deferred tax.

There are generally two ways to look at the need for deferred tax:

1. The timing difference approach;
2. The temporary difference approach.

6.4.2 Timing difference approach

The timing difference approach focuses on the impact to the statement of comprehensive income by calculating the amount of tax payable on income accounted for to date. Using the data from Example 6.B, we can see that tax depreciation is given in advance of accounting depreciation being charged. In arriving at taxable profit, we add back accounting depreciation and deduct tax depreciation. Let us look at the impact this has on the profit or loss.

Example 6.C

Assume that accounting profit for each of the years is $400,000 and the tax rate is 30%. We would expect to pay $120,000 in tax in each year. However, we have invested in plant and machinery and have been granted tax depreciation in respect of this item, so the calculation of taxable profits for 20X0 is as follows:

	20X0
	$'000
Tax computation	
Accounting profit	400
Add back accounting depreciation charge	50
	450
Less tax depreciation	(75)
Taxable profits	375
Tax at 30%	112.5

We pay $112,500 in tax as opposed to $120,000 because we have capital investment which has earned tax depreciation in the early years. The situation reverses in future years; however, when tax depreciation falls to $0 and accounting depreciation is still being charged to the profit or loss.

Profits of $400,000 in 20X4 and a tax rate of 30%, would result in tax to pay of $120,000. However, the taxable profits would be calculated as:

	20X4
	$'000
Tax computation	
Accounting profit	400
Add back accounting depreciation charge	50
Taxable profits	450
Tax at 30%	135

The tax payable has increased from $120,000 to $135,000 due to the add back of accounting depreciation.

The accounting treatment prudently requires that in the early years when tax depreciation exceeds accounting depreciation and the taxable profits are reduced, we provide for the future increased taxable profits by creating a provision for deferred tax and releasing this provision to cover the increased tax charge when tax depreciation falls below the accounting depreciation charge.

6.4.3 Temporary difference approach

The second approach to deferred tax focuses on the statement of financial position impact of the differences and calculates the tax that would have been paid if the net assets of the entity were realised at book value at the end of the reporting period. A temporary difference is the difference between the carrying amount of an asset or liability in the statement of financial position and its tax base (its value for tax purposes).

It is this approach that is adopted by IAS 12 for the recognition and measurement of deferred tax assets and liabilities and therefore we will concentrate on this approach for the remainder of the chapter.

Example 6.D

Let us use the information from Example 6.B:

An item of plant and machinery is purchased by U in 20X0 for $300,000. The asset's estimated useful life is 6 years, following which it will have no residual value. Plant and machinery is depreciated on a straight-line basis. Tax depreciation for this item is given at 25% on a straight-line basis for the first 4 years.

The figures for accounting and for taxation purposes would be as follows (from Example 6B):

	20X0 $'000	20X1 $'000	20X2 $'000	20X3 $'000	20X4 $'000	20X5 $'000
Financial statements						
Opening carrying value	300	250	200	150	100	50
Accounting depreciation charge	50	50	50	50	50	50
Carrying value (end of the reporting period)	250	200	150	100	50	0
Tax computation						
Carrying value	300	225	150	75	0	0
Tax depreciation	75	75	75	75	0	0
Tax written down value	225	150	75	0	0	0
Taxable temporary differences						
Carrying value (per accounts)	250	200	150	100	50	0
Tax written down value	225	150	75	0	0	0
Temporary difference	25	50	75	100	50	0

The provision for deferred tax under the temporary difference method is based on what tax would become payable if the assets were realised at book value at the end of the reporting period. We compare the carrying value of the item per accounts with the tax base, which is the value of the item for tax purposes (which in the case of fixed assets is usually the tax written down value).

Example 6.E

Using data in Example 6.D to illustrate the deferred tax impact.

The asset purchased above by U is sold at the end of 20X2 for $180,000 when the carrying value of the asset is $150,000 and the tax written down value is $75,000. The taxable profit and resulting tax charge are calculated as follows:

Accounting profit	$'000	Tax computation	$'000
Proceeds	180	Proceeds	180
Carrying value 20X2	150	Tax written down value 20X2	75
Accounting profit	30	Profit per tax computation	105
Tax on profit at 30%	9	Tax on profit at 30%	31.5

Based on the accounting records, we would expect to earn $30,000 profit on sale of the asset. However, due to accelerated tax depreciation, the tax written down value is considerably lower than the book value and so the gain on sale that would be recognised for tax purposes is $31,500. The additional $22,500 ($31,500 − $9,000) tax that would be payable if the asset was sold, must be provided for under the temporary differences method.

The table below shows the movement on the deferred tax liability account in the statement of financial position and the charge/(release) to the profit or loss in each of the 6 years of the asset's useful life.

	20X0 $'000	20X1 $'000	20X2 $'000	20X3 $'000	20X4 $'000	20X5 $'000
Temporary differences						
Carrying value (per accounts)	250	200	150	100	50	0
Tax written down value	225	150	75	0	0	0
Temporary difference	25	50	75	100	50	0
Deferred tax provision required (at a rate of 30%)	7.5	15	22.5	30	15	0

The provision for deferred tax increases in the first 4 years of the asset's life. This is the period that tax depreciation is applied which causes differences between the statement of financial position carrying value and the tax written down value. This taxable temporary difference then reduces in the last 2 years as the book value reduces to the asset's residual value of nil.

The deferred tax provision required is calculated at the tax rate (in this case 30%). This provision represents the additional tax the entity would pay on the gain if the asset was sold any time within its useful life, based on the tax written down value as opposed to the asset's book value.

Tax base

IAS 12 states that a temporary difference is the difference between the carrying value of an asset or liability and its tax base. The tax base is the amount attributed to that asset or liability for tax purposes. Consider the four scenarios below:

1. *Non-current assets.* The detailed illustration above dealt with a tax-deductible non-current asset. Its tax base was the tax written down value at the end of the reporting period. This is normally the case for non-current assets.
2. *Revalued non-current assets.* The temporary difference is defined as the difference between the carrying value of an asset and its tax base. As the tax base will remain the same, an upwards revaluation of a non-current asset will result in an increase in the deferred taxation provision.
3. *Accrued interest.* An entity has recorded accrued interest receivable of $5,000 in its accounts to 31 December 20X1. The interest receivable will only be taxed, however, when it is received. At 31 December 20X1, the asset has a tax base of nil and a carrying value (the value included in receivables in the statement of financial position) of $5,000. At 31 December 20X1, a temporary difference of $5,000 occurs. A deferred tax provision is required in respect of this difference of $1,500 ($5,000 at a rate of 30%).
4. *Pension costs.* In the year ended 30 June 20X3, an entity made provision for unfunded pension costs of $400,000. Tax relief on this item will be given when the retirement benefits are actually paid. The carrying value of the liability is $400,000 at 30 June 20X3; however, the tax base of the liability at that date is nil. It has no amount attributed to it for tax purposes until the liability is settled (when the benefits are actually paid). This creates a deductible temporary difference at 30 June 20X3 and a deferred tax asset must be recognised in the accounts. Assuming a rate of 30%, the deferred tax asset of $120,000 would be included in the statement of financial position.

6.4.4 Deferred tax assets

Deferred tax assets arising from deductible temporary differences should be recognised in the financial statements provided that it is probable that future taxable profits will be available for this asset to be utilised.

A deferred tax asset can arise from the following:

- deductible temporary difference
- unused tax losses
- unused tax credits.

A *deductible* temporary difference is a temporary difference that will result in a deduction from future taxable profits when sold or realised, for example, the pension costs referred to above that will be given tax relief when the benefits are paid. (This is in contrast to the *taxable* temporary difference that was created by the tax depreciation given on the purchase of the fixed asset – which if sold would create an additional tax charge on the increased gain on sale.)

6.4.5 Tax losses

Some tax authorities may permit the tax effect of losses to be carried forward and offset against future taxable profits. IAS 12 requires that these unused tax credits be recognised as assets, where it is probable that the entity will make future profits against which these losses can be offset.

Example 6.F

In 20X1, Delta made losses of $20,000. The associated tax credit on the losses (assuming a rate of 30%) is $6,000. This will be recorded in 20X1 as:

Dr	Income tax deferred asset (statement of financial position)	$6,000
Cr	Tax credit (statement of comprehensive income)	$6,000

Being the recording of the income tax credit for 20X1.

In 20X2, Delta made profits of $24,000. The tax charge for 20X2 is calculated as 30% × $24,000 = $7,200. Delta can offset the tax on the 20X1 losses against the tax on the 20X2 profits. This will be recorded as:

Dr	Income tax expense	$7,200
Cr	Income tax deferred credit	$6,000
Cr	Income tax liability	$1,200

Being the recording of the income tax expense for 20X2.

In summary, the calculation of deferred tax assets and liabilities is as follows:

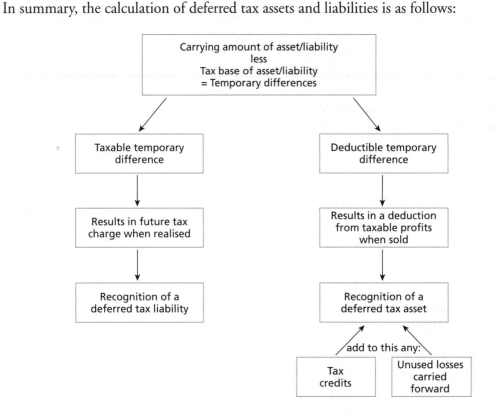

6.5 Accounting for deferred tax

Once the deferred tax position has been calculated, the accounting treatment is relatively straight forward. In the case of a deferred tax liability, the provision is created or increased by:

Dr	Income tax charge (statement of comprehensive income)
Cr	Deferred tax provision (statement of financial position)

Any reduction or release of the provision is recorded as:

| Dr | Deferred tax provision (statement of financial position) |
| Cr | Income tax charge (statement of comprehensive income) |

Consider the deferred tax position created in Example 6.D where temporary differences result from accelerated tax depreciation for the purchase of plant and machinery:

	20X0 $'000	20X1 $'000	20X2 $'000	20X3 $'000	20X4 $'000	20X5 $'000
Temporary difference						
Carrying value (per accounts)	250	200	150	100	50	0
Tax written down value	225	150	75	0	0	0
Temporary difference	25	50	75	100	50	0
Deferred tax provision required						
(at a rate of 30%)	7.5	15	22.5	30	15	0
Charge (credit) to profit or loss in respect of						
changes in the deferred tax provision	7.5	7.5	7.5	7.5	(15)	(15)

The deferred tax provision required in 20X0 is $7,500. This will be recorded as:

| Dr | Income tax charge (statement of comprehensive income) | $7,500 |
| Cr | Deferred tax provision (statement of financial position) | $7,500 |

Being the deferred tax provision in respect of plant and machinery.

From 20X1 to 20X3, the provision requires to be increased by $7,500 in each of these years and so the journal above will occur in 20X1, 20X2 and 20X3.

In 20X4, the required provision at 31 December is $15,000; however, the existing liability in the statement of financial position is $30,000. The reduction of the provision from $30,000 to $15,000 creates a release to the statement of comprehensive income of $15,000. It will be recorded as:

| Dr | Deferred tax provision (statement of financial position) | $15,000 |
| Cr | Income tax charge (statement of comprehensive income) | $15,000 |

The same journal entry will be required in 20X5 as the provision is reduced from $15,000 to nil.

6.6 Income tax charge

The income tax charge that appears in the statement of comprehensive income will include the following:

- the tax charge for the year (estimated based on profits);
- any under/overprovision of income tax from previous year;
- any increase in/release from the provision for deferred tax.

The 'other comprehensive income' section will include the tax implications of other comprehensive income items. The statement of financial position will include a current liability for income tax that will be paid in the following period. The liability will be for the estimated amount. When the tax is actually paid, this will lead to an over/underprovision of income tax, discussed earlier at Section 6.3.

The statement of financial position will also include any deferred tax liabilities or assets.

6.7 Disclosure

IAS 12 disclosure requirements include the following:

- the major components of tax expense should be disclosed separately (for example, current tax expense, adjustments for overprovision, amount for deferred tax expense or release, etc);
- tax expense relating to extraordinary items;
- tax expense relating to discontinuing operations;
- an explanation of the difference between accounting and taxable profits;
- details of temporary differences and the amount of deferred tax assets and liabilities that have been recognised in the financial statements as a result of those differences.

6.8 Summary

Having completed this chapter, we can now account for current tax, including adjustments for over/underprovisions.

We can explain the need for deferred tax, calculate the required provision or asset and account for it in financial statements. We can also explain the main disclosure requirements of IAS 12 in respect of current and deferred tax.

Revision Questions

? Question 1

The corporate income tax estimate for the current year is $420,000. The settlement of corporate income tax due for last year resulted in a credit balance of $10,000 outstanding on the income tax account. Deferred tax was estimated to require an increase of $18,000 in the statement of financial position provision. The corporate income tax charge for the year in the profit or loss and the current liability due in less than 1 year, corporate income tax on the statement of financial position should be:

	Statement of comprehensive income	statement of financial position
(A)	$448,000	$430,000
(B)	$412,000	$410,000
(C)	$428,000	$420,000
(D)	$392,000	$420,000

(3 marks)

? Question 2

Timing differences arise because of:

(A) the timing of the entity's tax payments
(B) the time of year when a transaction occurs
(C) expenses are charged to the profit or loss in one period and to taxable profits in another period
(D) some items of expenditure are disallowed for tax purposes **(2 marks)**

? Question 3

An asset cost $200,000 and had an estimated useful life of 10 years, with no residual value. Accounting depreciation was calculated on the straight-linebasis. Capital allowances were given at 25% on a reducing balance basis. Assume corporate income tax at 30%. At the end of the second year of operation, the deferred tax provision on the statement of financial position should be:

(A) $9,000
(B) $14,250

(C) $18,000

(D) $47,500 **(2 marks)**

[?] Question 4

List the three elements included in the heading 'Income tax expenses' in statement of comprehensive income.

(3 marks)

[?] Question 5

In no more than 30 words, define the meaning of 'permanent difference'. **(2 marks)**

[?] Question 6

WS prepares its financial statements to 30 June. The following profits were recorded from 20X1 to 20X3:

20X1	$100,000
20X2	$120,000
20X3	$110,000

The entity provides for tax at a rate of 30% and incorporates this figure in the year-end accounts. The actual amounts of tax paid in respect of 20X1 and 20X2 were $28,900 and $37,200.

Requirements

(a) Calculate the tax charge for each of the 3 years and prepare the accounting entries to record the tax charge and the subsequent payments of tax.

(b) Prepare extracts from the statement of comprehensive income and statement of financial position of WS for each of the 3 years, showing the tax charge and tax liability.

(5 marks)

[?] Question 7

On 1 January 20X2, C had a credit balance brought forward on its deferred tax account of $1.5m. There was also an opening credit balance of $4,000 on its income taxation account, representing the remaining balance after settling the liability for the year ended 31 December 20X1. The entity has made profits in 20X2 of $3m that are subject to a tax rate of 30%. The deferred tax provision required is estimated at $1.7m at 31 December 20X2.

Requirements

(a) Calculate the income tax charge that will appear in the statement of comprehensive income for 20X2 and prepare the accounting entries to record the current income tax charge and any movement on the deferred tax account.

(b) Prepare the extracts from the statement of financial position for the year ended 31 December 20X2 in respect of income tax and deferred tax. **(5 marks)**

？ **Question 8**

S purchases an item of plant and machinery costing $400,000 in 20X0 which qualifies for 50% capital allowances in the first 2 years. S's policy in respect of plant and machinery is to charge depreciation on a straight-line basis over 4 years.

Requirement

Assuming there are no other capital transactions in the period and a tax rate of 30% over the 4 years, calculate the statement of comprehensive income and statement of financial position impact of deferred tax from 20X0 to 20X3. **(4 marks)**

？ **Question 9**

HW buys an asset in 20X1 costing $80,000 that qualifies for an immediate 100% tax relief on cost. HW plans to depreciate the asset on a straight-line basis over 4 years. HW has accrued $30,000 for tax due for the year ended 31 December 20X1.

In 20X2, HW makes $120,000 profit that is subject to tax at 30%. During the year, $28,600 is paid in respect of tax on profits of 20X1. There were no additions to non-current assets in the year.

Requirements

Calculate the tax charge for 20X2 and any movement in deferred tax for the year.

Draft the extracts from the statement of comprehensive income and statement of financial position in respect of income tax and deferred tax. **(5 marks)**

？ **Question 10**

RS has two accounting adjustments in 20X2 that create temporary differences for deferred tax purposes:

(i) At the year-end, $40,000 of accrued interest receivable has been included in the accounts. It is expected to be received in Spring 20X3 and it will be taxed only on receipt.
(ii) A provision of $80,000 has been made for unfunded pension costs. Tax relief on this will be given only when the retirement benefits are actually paid.

Requirement

Calculate the deferred tax impact of these adjustments for the year-end accounts of RS, assuming an effective tax rate of 30%. **(3 marks)**

Solutions to Revision Questions

 Solution 1

The correct answer is (C), see Section 6.3.

The credit balance on the corporate income tax account means that there was an over-provision last year. The overprovision of $10,000 can be deducted from the current year's estimate. The increase in deferred tax needs to be included under the tax charge for the year. The statement of comprehensive income would show the income tax expense as $428,000, the note to the statement of comprehensive income would show the $428,000 made up as follows:

	$
Estimate of current year's corporation tax charge	420,000
Over-provision previous year	(10,000)
Increase in deferred tax provision	18,000
	428,000

The statement of financial position current liability for corporation tax would be the estimate for the current years tax charge, $420,000.

 Solution 2

The correct answer is (C), see Section 6.4.

Expenses are charged to the statement of comprehensive income in one period and to taxable profits in another period, giving rise to temporary timing differences. Income may also be credited to profit and loss in one period and be taxable in another period.

 Solution 3

The correct answer is (B) see Section 6.4.3.

	$
Cost	200,000
Two years' accounting depreciation at 10% per year is	40,000
Carrying value in accounts	160,000
Cost	200,000
Two years' tax depreciation at 25% is	87,500
Tax written down value	112,500
Temporary difference (160,000 − 112,500)	47,500
Tax at 30%	14,250

Solution 4

The three elements that make up income tax expense (see Section 6.6) are:

1. current tax expense
2. adjustments to tax charges of prior periods (results of over/underprovisions)
3. transfers to or from deferred tax.

 # Solution 5

A permanent difference is where an expense charged in the statement of comprehensive income is not allowed for income tax purposes. A permanent difference will not reverse in future periods, see Section 6.4.1.1.

 # Solution 6

(a) The tax charge for each of the 3 years can be calculated as follows:

Year	Profits	Tax charge based on profits @ 30%	Tax actually paid in respect of previous year	(Over)/ under provision	Statement of comprehensive income charge
20X1	$100,000	$30,000			$30,000
20X2	$120,000	$36,000	$28,900	($1,100)	$34,900
20X3	$110,000	$33,000	$37,200	$1,200	$34,200

The tax charge recorded in 20X1 is $30,000 and $28,900 is then actually paid resulting in an overprovision of $1,100.

The tax charge recorded in 20X2 is $36,000 and $37,200 is then actually paid resulting in an underprovision of $1,200.

The statement of comprehensive income charge is calculated as tax on profits plus any underprovision/less any overprovision.

The amounts will be recorded as follows:

In 20X1

Dr	Tax charge (statement of comprehensive income)	$30,000
Cr	Tax liability (statement of financial position)	$30,000

Being the recording of the estimated tax charge for 20X1.

In 20X2

Dr	Tax liability (statement of financial position)	$28,900
Cr	Bank	$28,900

Being the payment of tax in respect of the year ended 20X1.

Dr	Tax charge (statement of comprehensive income)	$34,900
Cr	Tax liability (statement of financial position)	$34,900

Being the recording of the estimated tax charge for 20X2 ($36,000 estimated tax less the overprovision in 20X1 of $1,100 – estimated $30,000 and paid $28,900).

In 20X3

Dr	Tax liability (statement of financial position)	$37,200
Cr	Bank	$37,200

Being the payment of tax in respect of the year ended 20X2.

Dr	Tax charge (statement of comprehensive income)	$34,200
Cr	Tax liability (statement of financial position)	$34,200

Being the recording of the estimated tax charge for 20X3 ($33,000 estimated tax plus the underprovision in 20X2 of $1,200 – estimated $36,000 and paid $37,200).

(b)

Income Statement extract	20X1	20X2	20X3
Tax charge on profits	$30,000	$36,000	$33,000
(Over)/under provision of tax		($1,100)	$1,200
Tax charge for the year	$30,000	$34,900	$34,200

Statement of financial position extract	20X1	20X2	20X3
Current liabilities			
Income tax liability	$30,000	$36,000	$33,000

See Section 6.5.

 ## Solution 7

(a) Income tax charge

	$'000	$'000
Tax on profits 30% × $3 m	900	
Less over-provision in 20X1	(4)	
Current tax charge		896
Deferred tax provision required	1,700	
Deferred tax provision b/f	1,500	
Increase in provision required		200
Total charge to profit or loss		1096

Accounting entries

Dr	Income tax charge (statement of comprehensive income)	896	
Cr	Income tax liability (statement of financial position)		896

Being the current tax charge for 20X2.

Dr	Income tax charge (statement of comprehensive income)	200	
Cr	Deferred tax provision (statement of financial position)		200

Being the increase required to the deferred tax provision for 20X2.

(b) Statement of financial position extract

Current liabilities	
Income tax ($4,000 + $896,000)	$900,000
Non-current liabilities	
Deferred tax	$1,700,000

See Section 6.5.

 ## Solution 8

	20X0	20X1	20X2	20X3
	$'000	$'000	$'000	$'000
Carrying value	400	300	200	100
Accounting depreciation	(100)	(100)	(100)	(100)
Closing carrying value	300	200	100	0
Opening balance for tax purposes	400	200	0	0
Tax depreciation	(200)	(200)	0	0
Tax written down value (tax base)	200	0	0	0
Temporary difference (carrying value − tax base)	100	200	100	0
Deferred tax provision required at 30%	30	60	30	0
Charge/(release) to profit or loss	30	30	(30)	(30)

TAXATION IN FINANCIAL STATEMENTS

 # Solution 9

Year ended 31 December 20X2

	$	$
Current tax charge $120,000 × 30%		36,000
Less over provision in 20X1 ($30,000 − $28,600)		(1,400)
		34,600

Deferred tax:		
Carrying value of asset ($80,000 − depreciation $40,000, 2 years)	40,000	
Tax base ($80,000 − capital allowances given $80,000)	0	
Temporary difference	40,000	
Deferred tax required @ 30%	12,000	
Release to statement of comprehensive income for reduction in deferred tax (18k − 12k)		(6,000)
Total charge to profit or loss		28,600

31 December 20X1	$
First-year allowance 100%	80,000
Less depreciation	20,000
Timing difference	60,000
Deferred tax @ 30%	18,000

Statement of comprehensive income extract 20X2

Income tax charge	
Tax change on profits	$36,000
Less overprovision in 20X1	($1,400)
Reduction in deferred tax	($6,000)
	$28,600

Statement of financial position extract 20X2

Current liabilities	
Income tax liability	$36,000
Non-current liabilities	
Deferred tax ($18,000 − $6,000)	$12,000

 # Solution 10

	$	$
Deferred tax:		
Carrying value of asset	40,000	
Tax base (value for tax purposes at 31 December 20X2)	0	
Taxable temporary difference	40,000	
Deferred tax liability (at 30%)		12,000
Carrying value of liability − pension costs	80,000	
Tax base (value for tax purposes at 31 December 20X2)	0	
Deductible temporary difference	80,000	
Deferred tax asset (at 30%)		24,000

The IASC and the Standard-Setting Process

The IASC and the Standard-Setting Process

7

LEARNING OUTCOMES

After completing this chapter you should be able to:

▶ explain the need for regulation of published accounts and the concept that regulatory regimes vary from country to country;

▶ explain potential elements that might be expected in a regulatory framework for published accounts;

▶ describe the role and structure of the International Accounting Standards Board (IASB) and the International Organisation of Securities Commissions (IOSCO);

▶ describe the process leading to the promulgation of an international accounting standard (IFRSs);

▶ describe ways in which IFRSs can interact with local regulatory frameworks.

Learning aims

The learning aim of this part of the syllabus is that students should be able to:

'describe and discuss how financial reporting can be regulated and the system of *International Accounting Standards.*'

The syllabus topics covered in this chapter are as follows:

- the need for regulation of accounts;
- elements in a regulatory framework for published accounts (e.g. company law, local GAAP, review of accounts by public bodies);
- GAAP based on prescriptive versus principles-based standards;
- the role and structure of the IASB and IOSCO;
- the process leading to the promulgation of a standard practice;
- ways in which IFRSs are used: adoption as local GAAP, model for local GAAP, persuasive influence in formulating local GAAP.

7.1 The need for regulation of financial statements

Financial statements and reports for shareholders and other users are prepared using principles and rules that can be interpreted in different ways. To provide guidance and try and ensure that they are interpreted in the same way, each time some form of regulation is required.

In Section 2.2, we noted that taxable profits are based on accounting profit and that the number and type of adjustments required to compute taxable profits varies from country to country. Part of this variation was due to the differences in the tax regulations, but a part of it was due to the different approaches to the calculation of accounting profit. In Section 2.2, we noted that in some countries taxable income is closely linked to the accounting profit and that accounting rules are largely driven by taxation laws. These countries are usually known as code law countries, countries where the legal system originated in Roman law. These countries tend to have detailed laws relating to trading entities and accounting standards are usually embodied within the law. Accounting regulation in these countries is usually in the hands of the government and financial reporting is a matter of complying with a set of legal rules.

In other countries the common law system is used, common law is based on case law and tends to have less detailed regulations. In countries with common law systems, the accounting regulation within the legal system is usually kept to a minimum, with detailed accounting regulations produced by professional organisations or other private sector accounting standard-setting bodies.

Whichever system is adopted, there is a need for every country to have a system for regulating the preparation of financial statements and reports.

7.2 Variation from country to country

Accounting and information disclosure practices around the world are influenced by a variety of economic, social and political factors. In addition to the legal system and tax legislation discussed in Section 7.1, a range of other factors that contribute to variations between the accounting regulations of countries are discussed below. The wide range of factors influencing the development of accounting regulations have resulted in a wide range of different systems, this has made it difficult and time consuming to try and harmonise accounting practices around the world. With the growth in international investing, there is a growing need for harmonisation of financial statements between countries.

7.2.1 Sources of finance and capital markets

There is more demand for financial information and disclosure where a higher proportion of capital is raised from external shareholders, rather than from banks or family members. Stock markets rely on published financial information by entities. Banks and family members are usually in a position to demand information directly from the entity, whereas shareholders have to rely on publicly available information.

7.2.2 The political system

The nature of regulation and control exerted on accounting will reflect political philosophies and objectives of the ruling party, for example, environmental concerns.

7.2.3 Entity ownership

The need for public accountability and disclosure will be greater where there is a broad ownership of shares as opposed to family ownership or government ownership.

7.2.4 Cultural differences

The culture within a country can influence societal and national values which can influence accounting regulations.

7.3 Harmonisation versus standardisation

Harmonisation tends to mean the process of increasing the compatibility of accounting practices by setting bounds to their degree of variation.

Standardisation tends to imply the imposition of a rigid and narrower set of rules. Standardisation also implies that one technically correct method can be identified for every aspect of accounting and then this can be imposed on all preparers of accounts.

Due to the variations between countries discussed above in Sections 7.1 and 7.2, full standardisation of accounting practices is unlikely. Harmonisation is more likely, as the agreement of a common conceptual framework of accounting may enable a closer harmonisation of accounting practices. See Section 7.9 for a discussion on some recent harmonisation developments.

7.3.1 The need for harmonisation of accounting standards

Each country has its own accounting regulation, financial statements and reports prepared for shareholders and other uses are based on principles and rules that can vary widely from country to country. Multinational entities may have to prepare reports on activities on several bases for use in different countries, and this can cause unnecessary financial costs. Furthermore, preparation of accounts based on different principles makes it difficult for investors and analysts to interpret financial information. This lack of comparability in financial reporting can affect the credibility of the entity's reporting and the analysts' reports and can have a detrimental effect on financial investment.

The increasing levels of cross-border financing transactions, securities trading and direct foreign investment has resulted in the need for a single set of rules by which assets, liabilities and income are recognised and measured.

The number of foreign listings on major exchanges around the world is continually increasing and many worldwide entities may find that they are preparing accounts using a number of different rules and regulations in order to be listed on various markets.

Exercise

Briefly explain possible benefits that could accrue from the development of a single set of accounting standards that could be applied in all countries.

Solution

Multinational entities could benefit from:

1. access to a wider range of international finance opportunities. If international standards were widely accepted, the international financial markets would be accessible by a wider range of entities. This could have the effect of reducing financing costs;
2. improved management control as all parts of the entity would be reporting using one consistent basis;
3. greater efficiency in accounting departments as they would not have to spend time converting data from one accounting basis to another;
4. easier consolidation of subsidiaries, preparation of group accounts would be simplified.

Investors should benefit by being able to compare the results of different entities more easily and make more informed investment decisions.

It would be easier for international economic groupings such as the EU to function, as the preparation of economic data would be easier.

7.4 Elements that might be expected in a regulatory framework for published accounts

There are several potential elements that might be expected in a regulatory framework within a particular country. The main ones are:

- local law that applies to entities
- locally adopted accounting standards
- local stock exchange requirements
- international body requirements
- international accounting standards
- locally developed or international conceptual framework for accounting.

Every country is different, potentially every one of the above could be different if two countries are compared. Let us briefly consider each of these elements in turn.

7.4.1 Local law that applies to entities

Every country passes its own laws, some that relate to entities in that country. There are two main forms of law:

1. the roman law approach where *everything* is specified in the law directly;
2. the anglo-saxon common law approach where the legislation is more general and the courts interpret the legislation that becomes the case law.

Local legal requirements will have to be followed by entities. In some countries, the legal system embodies the accounting standards that entities are required to follow (see Section 7.1).

7.4.2 Locally adopted accounting standards

Each country will have their own local version of accounting standards. These local standards will be developed using local processes that reflect the social, economic and political factors of the country, or the country could choose to adopt international accounting standards, see Section 7.10.

7.4.3 Local stock exchange requirements

The local stock exchange may have further requirements for listed entities, which are additional to the other legal requirements that apply to all entities in the country.

7.4.4 International body requirements

International bodies can often have a significant influence on the regulatory requirements within a country. For example, EU directives apply to all countries within Europe; however, when they are embodied in local legislation they apply to entities. Another example of an international organisation influencing local regulations is the The International Organisation of Securities Commissions (IOSCO), see Section 7.8.

7.4.5 International accounting standards

International accounting standards are having an increasing influence on local accounting standards. This is discussed in detail in Section 7.11.

7.4.6 Locally developed or international conceptual framework for accounting

Some countries, such as the UK and USA have developed their own conceptual framework of accounting. Countries that have not developed their own conceptual framework may have adopted the IASB's Framework. See Chapter 8 for a discussion on the IASB's Framework.

Where a conceptual framework exists it will assist in the development of accounting standards and generally accepted accounting practice.

7.5 Generally accepted accounting practice (GAAP)

GAAP encompasses the conventions, rules and procedures necessary to define accepted accounting practice at a particular time. It includes not only broad guidelines of general application but also detailed practices and procedures. GAAP includes local legislation requirements, accounting standards and any other locally applicable regulations. GAAP is also dynamic and will change over time as new or different requirements become generally accepted.

GAAP will therefore vary from one country to another as different regulations apply in different countries. The IASB's convergence programme is aimed at reducing these differences over time.

GAAP can be based on legislation and accounting standards that are either:

- prescriptive in nature, setting out in detail every possible permutation that an accountant may come across; or
- principles-based accounting standards, which set out principles but are not specific and do not include many detailed requirements for their application.

 ## Exercise

List the possible advantages of having GAAP based on prescriptive standards versus GAAP based on principles.

 ## Solution

You will probably have a number of points, the following is not intended to be an exhaustive list. Your answer could have included the following:

Advantages of GAAP based on prescriptive standards:

- precise, the requirements will be clear and well understood;
- there will be one 'correct' way of dealing with every item, it does not need professional judgement to be used when deciding how to treat an item;
- it should be more obvious when an entity does not follow GAAP;
- can be taught/learnt more easily;
- it should ensure that similar items are treated in the same way.

Advantages of GAAP on principles:

- It will be harder to construct ways of avoiding the requirements of individual standards, for example, a prescriptive standard may set out definitions or specify values that should be used when applying a standard. If an actual value is specified, it may be possible for some entities to construct various means of avoiding the application of that requirement. Whereas if the standard sets out general principles, it is much harder to avoid the standard's requirements as a principle will apply no matter what value is put on it.
- The requirements in certain situations will need to be applied using professional judgement, which can help ensure that the correct application is used. Whereas a prescriptive standard would require a certain treatment to be used, regardless of the situation, which could lead to similar items being treated the same way even if the circumstances are different.
- Principles-based GAAP should ensure that the spirit of the regulations are adhered to, whereas the prescriptive system is more likely to lead to the letter of the law being followed rather than the spirit.

IFRSs are principle-based standards.

7.6 The International Accounting Standards Committee Foundation (IASC Foundation)

In March 2001, the IASC Foundation was formed as a not-for-profit corporation. The IASC Foundation is the parent entity of the International Accounting Standards Board (IASB).

From 1 April 2001, the IASB assumed the accounting standard-setting responsibilities from its predecessor body, the International Accounting Standards Committee.

The restructuring of the IASC resulted from the recommendations made in the report, *Recommendations on Shaping IASC for the Future.* The overall objectives and principles remain consistent with the original set-up. However, the revised format brings a new committee structure and some changes to the standard-setting process.

7.6.1 Structure of the IASC foundation

The IASC Foundation is an independent organisation having two main bodies: the Trustees and the IASB. The structure also includes the Standards Advisory Council and the International Financial Reporting Interpretations Committee.

A graphical representation of the structure is given in Figure 7.1. The role of each committee will be discussed in turn.

7.6.2 IASC Foundation

The Trustees hold the responsibility for governance and fundraising, and for publishing an annual report on the IASC's activities, including audited financial statements and priorities for the coming year. They will review annually the strategy of the IASC and its effectiveness and approve the annual budget and determine the basis of funding.

The Trustees also appoint the members of the IASB, the Standards Advisory Council and the International Financial Reporting Interpretations Committee. Although the Trustees will decide on the operating procedures of the committees in the IASC family, they will be excluded from involvement in technical matters relating to accounting standards.

The Trustees must have sufficient financial knowledge and experience to allow them to fully appreciate the issues that are relevant to the IASC and the ability to meet the Committee's time commitment. Trustees will normally serve for a term of 3 years, renewable once.

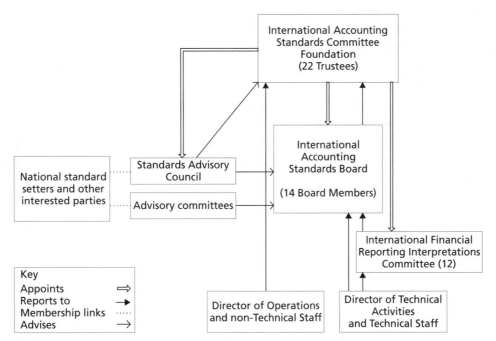

Figure 7.1 Structure of the IASC Foundation

*Source:*http://www.iasb.org/about/structure.asp

Reproduced with permission of the IASC Foundation.

The mix of trustees must be representative of the world's capital markets and therefore are appointed as follows:

- six from North America
- six from Europe
- six from the Asia/Oceania region
- four from other areas giving overall geographic balance.

The IASC also defines the experience required for trustees to be appointed in order to ensure a balance of professional backgrounds. Two of the 22 will usually be senior partners from prominent international accounting firms. Preparers, users and academics should also be represented and the remaining 11 will be selected on the basis that they bring strong public interest backgrounds.

7.6.3 The International Accounting Standards Board (IASB)

The IASB has 14 members, 12 of whom are full-time employees. Appointment of members is primarily based on their having sufficient technical expertise to ensure the IASB has the experience to tackle the relevant business and economic issues.

The Trustees appoint one of the full-time members as chairman of the IASB, who is also the chief executive of the IASC. The current chairman is Gerrit Zalm, former deputy prime minister and finance minister in the Netherlands. Seven of the full-time members of staff are responsible for liaising with national standard-setters in order to promote the convergence of accounting standards.

IASB members are appointed for a term of 5 years, renewable once. The terms are staggered to ensure continuity of members.

The IASB has complete responsibility for all IASC technical matters, including the preparation and publication of international financial reporting standards (IFRS) and exposure drafts; withdrawal of IFRSs and final approval of interpretations by the International Financial Reporting Interpretations Committee.

IASB publishes its standards in a series of pronouncements called IFRSs. The IASB have also adopted all existing pronouncements issued by the IASC referred to as International Accounting Standards (IASs). The two have the same status and existing pronouncements will continue to be referred to as IASs. The manual will follow this format, using the generic term IFRS to apply to all IFRSs and IASs. The term IAS will only be used to refer to specific IASs only.

The standard-setting process is discussed in detail in Section 7.10.

7.6.4 The International Financial Reporting Interpretations Committee (IFRIC)

The IFRIC is a committee of the IASB that assists the IASB in establishing and improving standards of financial accounting and reporting for the benefit of users, preparers and auditors of financial statements.

The IASC Foundation Trustees established the IFRIC in March 2002 when it replaced the previous interpretations committee, the Standing Interpretations Committee (SIC).

The IFRIC provides timely guidance on the application and interpretation of IFRSs, normally dealing with complex accounting issues that could, in the absence of guidance, produce wide-ranging or unacceptable accounting treatments. In this way IFRIC promotes the rigorous and uniform application of IFRSs.

The IFRIC produces draft interpretations, which are open to public comment. If no more than three (of 12) of its voting members have voted against an interpretation, the IFRIC will ask the IASB to approve the final interpretation for issue. Published interpretations are numbered sequentially. Compliance with IFRSs requires compliance with the relevant IFRIC interpretations.

7.6.5 The Standards Advisory Council (SAC)

The Standards Advisory Council comprises 30 members or more, appointed by the trustees for renewable terms of 3 years. This committee is intended to provide a forum for wider participation for those with an interest in the standard-setting process, so its members have diverse geographical and professional backgrounds.

The Standards Advisory Council meets at least three times a year with the objectives of:

- giving advice to the board on agenda decisions and priorities for future work;
- informing the Board of public views on major standard-setting projects;
- giving other advice to the board or the Trustees.

7.7 Objectives of the IASC Foundation

The objectives of the IASC are as follows:

- to develop, in the public interest, a single set of high-quality, understandable and enforceable global accounting standards that require high-quality, transparent and comparable information in financial statements and other financial reporting to help participants in the world's capital markets and other users make economic decisions;
- to promote the use and rigorous application of those standards taking account of the needs of small- and medium-sized entities;
- to bring about convergence of national accounting standards and international accounting standards to high-quality solutions.

The IASC's financial support derives primarily from the professional accountancy bodies, the International Federation of Accountants (IFAC), and from contributions by entities, financial institutions and accounting firms. More than 150 professional accounting bodies in over 100 countries are members of IASC.

7.8 The International Organisation of Securities Commissions (IOSCO)

Securities commissions are the bodies responsible for the regulation of stock markets in their country. IOSCO encourages international investment by making stock market regulations more consistent between countries.

In 1995, IOSCO's Technical Committee agreed the core set of standards that IASC would develop. It was agreed that, should the core standards be acceptable to the IOSCO Technical Committee, IOSCO would recommend endorsement of IFRSs for cross-border capital-raising and listing purposes in all global markets.

The process is now complete, and in May 2000 IOSCO recommended that its members permit incoming multinational issuers to use these standards to prepare their financial statements for cross-border offerings and listings.

7.9 Local regulatory bodies

Worldwide acceptance of IFRSs is to some extent dependent on the promotion by local regulatory bodies. The professional accountancy bodies are well represented on the membership of IASC. The G7 Finance Ministers and Central Bank Governors have also committed themselves to the promotion of IFRSs by ensuring that private sector institutions in their respective countries comply with internationally agreed principles, standards and codes of best practice. Furthermore, they called on all countries that participate in global capital markets similarly to commit to comply with IFRSs.

7.9.1 Convergence activities

IASB must meet with the Standards Advisory Council before it can confirm its technical agenda. Then it works with the chairs of the national accounting standard-setters to co-ordinate their agendas and priorities. The IASB then provides details of how it is co-operating with other key standard-setters and regulatory agencies worldwide towards achieving convergence of accounting standards.

7.9.2 International reaction

Europe

In June 2000, the European Commission issued a Communication proposing that all listed entities in the EU would be required to prepare their consolidated financial statements using IFRSs from 2005. EU Member States may extend this to permit non-publically traded entities to prepare their financial statements in accordance with IFRSs.

In late 2001, the EU published its Fair Value Directive. This formed a part of the process to change the EU's legal framework that allowed EU-listed entities to adopt IFRSs from 1 January 2005.

Many entities already state that their financial statements are prepared in accordance with IFRSs. In 2004 there were around 350 publically listed entities that complied with IFRSs, in 2005 this was approximately 7000 publically listed entities.

USA

The US Securities and Exchange Commission (SEC) is responsible for the regulation of the debt and equity securities markets in the US. In 1996, SEC expressed its support for the IASC's objective of developing accounting standards that could be used for preparing accounts used in cross-border offerings publicly, but the SEC still requires entities to use US GAAP or prepare a detailed reconciliation statement.

In 2002 a Memorandum of Understanding known as the 'Norwalk Agreement' was agreed between the FASB and the IASB. The agreement states that the respective parties agree to:

(a) Make their existing financial reporting standards fully compatible as soon as is practicable, and

(b) Co-ordinate their future work programs to ensure that once achieved, compatibility is maintained.

Since then the FASB and the IASB have been working to increase convergence between US GAAP and IFRSs.

In April 2005 the SEC staff published a 'Roadmap' that set out the steps required to be achieved before the reconciliation statement required from overseas entities could be eliminated. The full article and 'roadmap' can be found at http://www.SEC.gov/news/speech/spch040605dtn.htm

SEC staff have agreed a work plan with the Committee of European Securities Regulators, the main focus being the application by international entities of IFRS and US GAAP in the USA and EU respectively.

Other Countries

Many Countries already endorse IFRSs, and IFRSs are especially useful for developing countries that do not yet have a national standard-setting body.

7.10 The standard-setting process

The IASC Constitution permits the IASB to work in whatever way it considers most effective and cost efficient. The Board may form advisory committees or other specialist technical groups to advise on major projects. The Board may outsource detailed research or other work to national standard-setters.

7.10.1 Development of a standard

The process for the development of a standard involves the following steps:

- During the early stages of a project, IASB may establish an Advisory Committee to advise on the issues arising in the project. Consultation with this committee and the Standards Advisory Council occurs throughout the project.
- IASB may develop and publish *Discussion Documents* for public comment.
- Following receipt and review of comments, IASB develops and publishes an *Exposure Draft* for public comment.
- Following the receipt and review of comments, the IASB may hold a public hearing or carry out field tests. The IASB issues a final IFRS, along with any dissenting view expressed by an IASB member.

When the IASB publishes a standard, it also publishes a *Basis of Conclusions* to explain publicly how it reached its conclusions and to provide background information that may help users apply the standard in practice.

7.10.2 Other aspects of due process

Each IASB member has one vote on technical matters and the publication of a Standard, Exposure Draft, or final IFRIC Interpretation requires approval by eight of the Board's 14 members.

Other decisions, including agenda decisions and the issue of a Discussion Paper, require a simple majority of the Board members present at a meeting, provided the meeting is attended by at least 50 per cent of the members.

Meetings of the IASB, SAC and IFRIC are open to public observation. Where IASB issues Exposure Drafts, Discussion Documents and other documents for public comment, the usual comment period is 90 days. Draft IFRIC Interpretations are exposed for a 60-day comment period.

7.10.3 Co-ordination with national standard-setting

IASB is currently exploring ways in which it can integrate its standard-setting process more closely with those of national standard-setters. The Board is currently investigating the possibility that the procedure for projects that have international implications would include the following:

- IASB and national standard-setters co-ordinating their work plans, so that they can be reviewing an issue at the same time enabling each party to play a full part in developing international consensus.
- National standard-setters could consider this international consensus when voting on their own national standards, although they would not be required to vote for the IASB's preferred solution.
- IASB and national bodies would continue to issue their own exposure drafts, but may consider issuing them at the same time and invite comments on any significant differences in proposed accounting treatments.

7.10.4 Benchmark treatments and allowed alternatives

In some IFRSs, there are alternative treatments for a transaction or event. One is designated the 'benchmark' treatment. This is not necessarily to be taken as the preferred treatment. The term 'benchmark' reflects the Board's intention of identifying a point of reference when making its choice between alternatives.

7.11 Ways in which IFRS's are used by countries

A country chosing to adopt international standards can apply them in a number of ways:

- adoption as local GAAP
- model for local GAAP
- persuasive influence in formulating local GAAP.

Alternatively, local GAAP can be developed with little or no reference to IFRSs.

7.11.1 Adoption as local GAAP

Some countries, particularly countries where the accounting profession is not well developed, take international accounting standards and adopt them as their local standards with very little or no amendments. This approach has the advantage of being quick to implement after the decision is taken. The disadvantage is that it may not take into account any specific local traditions or variations. Examples include Honduras, Armenia, Bangladesh and Bahrain.

There have also been some examples where countries have changed their approach, for example, Malawi used 'IAS's adapted for use in Malawi', then in 2001 they changed to full adoption of IFRSs.

7.11.2 Model for local GAAP

Some countries use international accounting standards, but amend them to reflect local needs and conditions. These countries change some of the IASB standards to suit local needs and may also develop some local standards to cover topics for which there is no international standard. Examples include Tanzania, Egypt and Malaysia.

7.11.3 Persuasive influence in formulating local GAAP

Countries with a track record in setting accounting standards already had standards in place before the original IASC was formed. As these standards pre-dated IFRSs, they often did not conform with them. Many countries in this position have been working for many years to narrow the gap between their local standards and IFRSs. This usually takes the form of all new or revised standards being developed to take account of international standards and comply with them in all material respects. Although most of the standards now comply with IFRSs, they are often different in some way. Examples include Brazil, India, Japan and Australia.

7.11.4 Local GAAP developed with little or no reference to IFRS's

As mentioned in Section 7.11.3, some countries have accounting standards that pre-date IFRSs and whereas most have adjusted their standards in an attempt to converge with IFRSs, some have made no attempt. Others that may not pre-date IFRSs have decided to develop their own standards and make no real attempt to comply with IFRSs. Examples in this category include Jamaica, China and Colombia, although China has now decided to develop new accounting standards that are in harmony with IFRSs.

7.12 Summary

Having completed this chapter, you should be able to discuss briefly the need for the regulation of published accounts and identify the reasons why regulatory regimes vary. You should be able to explain the objectives, role and structure of the IASC Foundation and its various bodies and describe the relationship that IASC has with both IOSCO and the national regulatory bodies. In addition, you can now explain the IASBs standard-setting process and describe different ways that countries use IFRSs.

Revision Questions

? Question 1

A committee of the International Accounting Standards Board (IASB) is known as the IFRIC.

What does IFRIC stand for?

(A) International Financial Reporting Issues Committee
(B) International Financial Recommendations and Interpretations Committee
(C) International Financial Reporting Interpretations Committee
(D) International Financial Reporting Issues Council   (2 marks)

? Question 2

Which of the following is NOT a function of the International Accounting Standards Board?

(A) Issuing accounting standards
(B) Withdrawing accounting standards
(C) Developing accounting standards
(D) Enforcing accounting standards   (2 marks)

? Question 3

The international accounting standards committee foundation (IASC foundation) has two main bodies:

 (i) International Accounting Standards Board
 (ii) International financial reporting interpretations committee
(iii) Standards advisory council
(iv) Trustees

The two committees reporting to the IASC foundation are:

(A) (i) and (ii)
(B) (i) and (iv)
(C) (ii) and (iii)
(D) (iii)and (iv)   (2 marks)

Question 4

Which of the following would not normally be expected to be included in the elements of a regulatory framework for published accounts:

(A) Local law that applies to entities
(B) Local taxation regulations
(C) Local stock exchange regulations
(D) A conceptual framework for accounting   **(2 marks)**

 Question 5

List three ways in which IFRSs can be implemented in a country.   **(3 marks)**

 Question 6

The existing procedures for setting international accounting standards are now well established.

Requirement
(a) Explain the roles of the following in relation to International Accounting Standards:
    (i) The International Accounting Standards Committee (IASC) Foundation;
    (ii) The International Accounting Standards Board (IASB);
    (iii) The International Financial Reporting Interpretations Committee (IFRIC).
                                                                    (5 marks)

 Question 7

Explain how the standard-setting authority approaches the task of producing a standard, with particular reference to the ways in which comment or feedback from interested parties is obtained.   **(5 marks)**

 Question 8

The Technical Committee of the International Organisation of Securities Commissions (IOSCO) and the IASC agree that there is a compelling need for high-quality, comprehensive international accounting standards.

Requirement
Discuss briefly why the development of international accounting standards is considered to be important.   **(5 marks)**

 Question 9

Explain the role that IOSCO has played in the development and promotion of international accounting standards.   **(5 marks)**

？ Question 10

The setting of International Accounting Standards is carried out by co-operation between a number of committees and boards, which include:

  (i) International Accounting Standards Committee Foundation (IASC Foundation)
 (ii) Standards Advisory Council (SAC)
(iii) International Financial Reporting Interpretations Committee (IFRIC)

Which of the above reports to, or advises, the International Accounting Standards Board (IASB)?

  Reports to Advises:

(A) (i) and (iii) (ii)
(B) (i) and (ii) (iii)
(C) (iii) (ii)
(D) (ii) (i)   **(2 marks)**

Solutions to Revision Questions

 Solution 1

The correct answer is (C), see Section 7.6.4.

Solution 2

The correct answer is (D), see Section 7.6.3.

Solution 3

The correct answer is (B), see Section 7.6.1.

Solution 4

The correct answer is (B), see Section 7.4.

Solution 5

Three ways in which IFRSs can be implemented are:

1. adoption as local GAAP
2. model for local GAAP
3. persuasive influence in formulating local GAAP

See Section 7.11.

Solution 6

(i) The IASC Foundation

The IASC Foundation is an independent organisation having two main bodies: the Trustees and the IASB. The Trustees hold the responsibility for governance and fundraising and will publish an annual report on IASC's activities, including audited financial statements and priorities for the coming year. They will review annually the strategy of the IASC and its effectiveness and approve the annual budget and determine the basis of funding.

The Trustees also appoint the members of the IASB, the Standards Advisory Council and the International Financial Reporting Interpretations Committee. Although the Trustees will decide on the operating procedures of the committees in the IASC family, they will be excluded from involvement in technical matters relating to accounting standards.

(ii) The IASB

The Board has complete responsibility for all IASC technical matters, including the preparation and issuing of International Financial Reporting Standards and Exposure Drafts, and final approval of Interpretations by the International Financial Reporting Interpretations Committee. Some of the full-time members of staff are responsible for liaising with national standard-setters in order to promote the convergence of accounting standards.

IASB publishes its standards in a series of pronouncements called International Financial Reporting Standards (IFRSs). It has also adopted the standards issued by the board of the International Accounting Standards Committee.

The Board may form advisory committees or other specialist technical groups to advise on major projects and outsource detailed research or other work to national standard-setters.

(iii) The *International Financial Reporting* Interpretations Committee (IFRIC)

The IFRIC provides timely guidance on the application and interpretation of IFRSs, normally dealing with complex accounting issues that could, in the absence of guidance, produce wide-ranging or unacceptable accounting treatments, see Sections 7.6.2 to 7.6.4.

 ## Solution 7

The process for the development of a standard involves the following steps:

- During the early stages of a project, the IASB may establish an Advisory Committee to advise on the issues arising in the project. Consultation with this committee and the Standards Advisory Council occurs throughout the project.
- The IASB may develop and publish Discussion Documents for public comment.
- Following receipt and review of comments, the IASB develops and publishes an Exposure Draft for public comment.
- Following the receipt and review of comments, the IASB issues a final International Financial Reporting Standard.

When the IASB publishes a standard, it also publishes a Basis of Conclusions to explain publicly how it reached its conclusions and to provide background information that may help users apply the standard in practice.

Each IASB member has one vote on technical matters and the publication of a Standard, Exposure Draft, or final IFRIC Interpretation requires approval by eight of the Board's 14 members. Other decisions including agenda decisions and the issue of a Discussion Paper, require a simple majority of the Board members present at a meeting, provided that the meeting is attended by at least 50 per cent of the members.

Meetings of the IASB, SAC and IFRIC are open to public observation. Where the IASB issues Exposure Drafts, Discussion Documents and other documents for public comment, the usual comment period is 90 days. Draft IFRIC Interpretations are exposed for a 60-day comment period, see Section 7.10.

Solution 8

Investment decisions are largely based on financial information and analysis. Financial reports, which are prepared for shareholders, potential shareholders and other users are, however, based on principles and rules that vary from country to country. This makes comparability and transparency of financial information difficult. Some multinationals may have to prepare reports on activities on several bases for use in different countries and this can cause an unnecessary financial burden and damage the credibility of financial reports.

The increasing levels of cross-border financing transactions and securities trading have highlighted the need for financial information to be based on a single set of rules and principles.

An internationally accepted accounting framework is also beneficial to developing countries that cannot bear the cost of establishing a national standard-setting body, see Section 7.3.1.

 ## Solution 9

Worldwide acceptance of IFRSs will be dependent to some extent on other recognised bodies accepting and promoting their use. IOSCO is looking to the IASC to provide mutually acceptable international accounting standards for use in multinational securities markets.

In 1995, IASC agreed with IOSCO to develop a core set of standards. The standards were identified and, if completed to a satisfactory level, IOSCO would consider endorsing the core standards for cross-border capital-raising and listings in all global markets.

The IASC completed the core standards by 1999 and presented them for technical review by IOSCO. IOSCO had commented on the drafts as they progressed.

In May 2000, IOSCO recommended that its members permit incoming multinational users to use these standards to prepare their financial statements for cross-border trading and listings. There are a number of outstanding issues that are to be addressed by the IASC, but this was considered to be a significant development in gaining acceptance of IFRSs, see Section 7.8.

 ## Solution 10

The correct answer is C, see Section 7.6.3.

8

Regulatory
Framework

Regulatory Framework

8

LEARNING OUTCOME

After completing this chapter you should be able to:

► explain the meaning of given features or parts of the IASB's Framework for the Presentation and Preparation of Financial Statements.

The syllabus topic covered in this chapter is as follows:

● IASBs Framework for the Presentation and Preparation of Financial Statements.

8.1 Introduction

One of the major challenges for those communicating financial information is the enormous range of potential users of that information. In addressing technical problems or developments, it is important to consider the context within which the problem has arisen and how the solution fits in with the objective of providing useful financial information.

The increasing complexity of financial transactions and the need for guidance on suitable and consistent treatment in financial reporting has created a vastly increased workload for standard-setters. As a result, they find themselves dealing with issues that vary in detail, but that have the same underlying technical issues: how should this be recorded? how should this be measured? how should this be presented to users?

As the number of accounting rules and standards increases, it is important that the standard-setters provide a set of rules that are based on principles that can be applied consistently to ensure that the overall objectives of financial reporting are met. Many, including the UK ASB and the US FASB, have developed conceptual Frameworks that establish a broad set of accounting principles on which their standards and accounting rules are based.

The IASB's conceptual Framework is the *Framework for the Preparation and Presentation of Financial Statements* (hereafter referred to as the IASB Framework or the Framework) published by the IASC in 1989. This chapter will discuss the purpose of the Framework, and explain the Framework in detail, including the definitions of assets and liabilities. The chapter concludes with a discussion of the usefulness of the Framework. This is an important chapter as the Framework's concepts underpin all of the IFRSs and will be referred to throughout the following sections.

8.2 The development of the Framework

8.2.1 Purpose of the Framework

According to the *Framework,* its purposes are to:

- assist the Board in the development of future IFRSs and its review of existing IFRSs;
- assist the Board in promoting harmonisation of regulations, accounting standards and procedures relating to the presentation of financial statements by providing a basis for reducing the number of alternative treatments permitted by IFRSs;
- assist national standard-setting bodies in developing national standards;
- assist preparers of financial statements in applying IFRSs and dealing with topics that have yet to be covered in an IFRS;
- assist auditors in forming an opinion as to whether financial statements conform with IFRSs;
- assist users of financial statements that are prepared using IFRSs;
- provide information about how the IASB has formulated its approach to the development of IFRSs.

8.2.2 Status of the Framework

The Framework does not have the status of an accounting standard and does not override any IFRS where conflicts arise. Generally, IFRSs are less prescriptive in nature than other national standards, and so the Framework is referred to more frequently by preparers of financial statements, and particularly where an accounting issue is not dealt with specifically by an IFRS.

Some IFRSs still permit alternative treatments of certain transactions. As the IASB continues to reduce the number of alternative treatments, it is expected that the number of conflicts between standards and the Framework will decrease. The required treatments within the IFRSs will then be consistent with the principles outlined in the Framework.

8.2.3 Scope of the Framework

The Framework applies to the general-purpose financial statements of both private and public entities. A full set of financial statements prepared using IFRSs will normally include a statement of financial position, a statement of comprehensive income, a statement of cash flows and any notes to the accounts which form an integral part of the accounts.

To ensure that the Framework helps to provide useful information, it is important to identify the users of the financial information.

The Framework identifies the following users of financial statements:

- investors
- employees
- lenders
- suppliers
- other trade creditors
- customers
- governments and their agencies
- the public.

The Framework identifies that not all the needs of these users can be met and does not indicate that the needs of one set of users are more important than any other. The Framework does point out, however, that financial statements that meet the needs of investors will generally also meet the needs of other users.

8.3 The Framework

The Framework covers the following main topics:

- the objective of financial statements
- underlying assumptions
- the qualitative characteristics of financial information
- the elements of financial statements
- recognition of the elements of financial statements
- measurement of the elements of financial statements
- concepts of capital maintenance.

8.3.1 The objective of financial statements

The Framework states that 'the objective of financial statements is to provide information about the financial position, performance and changes in financial position of an entity that is useful to a wide range of users in making economic decisions'.

Information about the *financial position* is primarily provided in the *statement of financial position*. The resources the entity controls, its financial structure, liquidity and solvency all affect the financial position.

Information about *performance* is primarily found in the *statement of comprehensive income*. Performance measures, particularly profitability, are required to help assess the entity's ability to generate future cash flows from trading and other activities. It also helps users evaluate how effective the entity is at using its resources.

Information about *changes in financial position* is held primarily in a *statement of cash flows*. This is a useful illustration of the entity's investing, financing and operational activities and how these activities have affected the financial position over the reporting period.

The Framework goes on to say, 'financial statements prepared for this purpose meet the common needs of most users'. Financial statements do not provide all the information that users may need to make economic decisions as they illustrate the financial effects of past transactions. Users are expected to use this reliable historic information to help them evaluate future performance and make their economic decisions.

8.3.2 Underlying assumptions

There are two underlying assumptions outlined in the Framework.

1. *Going concern.* Financial statements are normally prepared on the assumption that an entity is a going concern and will continue in operation for the foreseeable future. Any intention to liquidate or significantly reduce the scale of its operations would require the accounts to be prepared on a different basis and this basis would have to be disclosed.

2. *Accruals basis of accounting.* Financial statements are prepared on the accrual basis of accounting where the effects of transactions are recognised when they occur and are recorded and reported in the accounting periods to which they relate, irrespective of cash flows arising from these transactions.

8.3.3 The qualitative characteristics of financial information

Qualitative characteristics are the attributes that make the information useful to users. The four principal characteristics are:

1. understandability
2. relevance
3. reliability
4. comparability.

Understandability

An essential quality of financial information is that it is readily understandable by users. For this purpose, users are assumed to have a reasonable knowledge of business and economic activities and accounting and a willingness to study the information with reasonable diligence; information on complex issues should be included if relevant and should not be excluded on the grounds that it is too difficult for the average user to understand.

Relevance

To be useful, information must be relevant to the decision-making needs of users. Information is relevant when it influences the economic decisions of users by helping them to evaluate past, present or future economic events, or confirming correcting their past evaluations.

Financial statements do not normally contain information about future activities; however, historical information can be used as the basis for predicting future financial position and performance. The users will then use their predictions as the basis for their decision-making.

An example of this could be where the financial statements show the profitability of a division that has been sold during the year. The users then know to eliminate that division's resources and profitability in evaluating the performance of the total entity for the next year.

Information that helps users assess the future performance and financial position of an entity is likely to be relevant. An item is likely to be relevant by virtue of its nature and materiality. Information is material if its omission or misstatement could influence the decision-making of users.

Information can be relevant because of its nature irrespective of materiality. For example, if an entity has commenced operating activities in a country with an unstable economy, this could change the users' assessment of the overall risk that the entity is exposed to and as a result change the users' assessment of the entity's future results. Irrespective of the materiality of that segment's results, the information may be disclosed.

Information should be released on a timely basis to be relevant to users.

Reliability

To be useful, information must also be reliable. Information is reliable when it is free from material error and bias and can be considered by users to be a faithful representation of the underlying transactions and events.

Faithful representation	To be reliable, the information must faithfully represent the transactions it is intended to represent;
Substance over form	To show a faithful representation, the transactions must be accounted for and presented on the basis of their commercial reality rather than their legal form. Only by applying substance over form will users see the effects of the economic reality of the transactions;
Neutrality	To be reliable, information must be neutral, that is, free from bias;
Prudence	Many estimates are made in the preparation of financial statements, for example, stock valuation, estimated useful lives of assets, recoverability of debts. Being cautious when exercising judgement in arriving at these estimates is known as prudence. This is a generally accepted concept in accounts preparation. The concept does not, however, extend to including excess provisions, overstating liabilities or understating income or assets. This would bias the information and make it unreliable to users;
Completeness	To be reliable, the information must be complete. An omission can cause information to be false or misleading and therefore unreliable.

Comparability

Comparability of financial information is vital to users in their decision-making. The ability to identify trends in performance and financial position and compare those both from year to year and against other entities assists users in their assessments and decision-making.

It is important that users are able to understand the application of accounting policies in order to compare financial information. To achieve comparability, users must be able to identify where an entity has changed its policy from one year to the next and where other entities have used different accounting policies for similar transactions.

The requirement of IFRSs to disclose accounting policies adopted and the inclusion of prior periods' comparative figures helps promote comparability.

8.3.4 The elements of financial statements

The Framework provides definitions of the five elements of financial statements. These definitions, applied together with the recognition criteria, provide guidance as to how and when the financial effect of transactions or events should be recognised in the financial statements.

Asset	An asset is a resource controlled by the entity as a result of past events and from which future economic benefits are expected to flow to the entity;
Liability	A liability is a present obligation of the entity arising from past events, the settlement of which is expected to result in an outflow of resources from the entity;
Equity	The residual interest in the assets of the entity after deducting all its liabilities;

Income   Increases in economic benefits during the accounting period in the form of inflows or enhancements of assets or decreases of liabilities that result in increases in equity, other than those relating to contributions from equity participants;

Expenses   Decreases in economic benefits during the accounting period in the form of outflows or depletions of assets that result in decreases in equity, other than those relating to distributions to equity participants.

8.3.5 Recognition of the elements of financial statements

To be recognised, the item must meet the definition of an element (given above). The Framework then has a further two criteria which must be met for an item to be recognised:

1. it is probable that any future economic benefit associated with the item will flow to or from the entity; and
2. the item has a cost or value that can be measured with reliability.

In the *first criterion,* the idea of *probability* is used regularly in the preparation of financial statements, for example, the probability that your credit customers will pay in order that you can reliably include receivables in the statement of financial position.

The assessment of the degree of uncertainty that an event will take place must be completed using the evidence available when the financial statements are prepared.

Where economic benefits are to arise over time, any related expenses should be systematically recognised over the same periods and matched with the income. Where no future benefits are anticipated, expenses should be recognised immediately.

The *second criterion* requires that a *monetary value* be attached to the item. For some transactions this is straightforward, but often the value we attach to items has to be estimated. This is acceptable, provided that it is a reasonable estimate and does not undermine reliability (a qualitative characteristic noted above).

Where information is relevant to users it should not be excluded from the financial statements because it fails to meet the recognition criteria. For example, where a contingent liability exists at the end of the reporting period but cannot be measured with any degree of certainty, it fails the second recognition criteria; however, due to its nature and existence it should be disclosed to users on the grounds that it is relevant.

8.3.6 Measurement of the elements of financial statements

Once it is decided that an item is to be recognised in the financial statements, it is then necessary to decide on what basis it is to be measured. To be included in the financial statements, the item must have a monetary value attached to it.

The Framework refers to four measurement bases that are often used in reporting, being historic cost, current cost, realisable value and present value. It highlights that historic cost is the most commonly adopted although often within a combination of bases, for example, valuing inventories using the lower of cost and net realisable value.

8.3.7 Concepts of capital and capital maintenance

Concepts of capital

The Framework refers to two concepts of capital: financial concept of capital and physical concept of capital.

Most entities adopt the financial concept of capital which deals with the net assets or equity of the entity. If, instead of being primarily concerned with the invested capital of the entity, the users are concerned with, for example, the operating capability of the entity, then the physical concept of capital should be used.

Determining profit

Under the financial concept of capital, a profit is earned if the financial amount of the net assets at the end of the period is greater than that at the beginning of the period, after deducting any distributions to and contributions from owners.

Under the physical concept of capital, a profit is earned if the physical productive capacity (or operating capacity) of the entity (or the resources or funds needed to achieve that capacity) at the end of the period is greater than that at the beginning of the period, after deducting any distributions to and contributions from owners.

Capital maintenance

In general terms, an entity has maintained its capital if it has as much capital at the end of the period as it had at the beginning of the period. The key in capital maintenance is deciding which concept is being adopted, because this then defines the basis on which profit is calculated.

Financial capital maintenance is measured in either nominal monetary units or units of constant purchasing power.

Physical capital maintenance requires the adoption of the current cost basis of measurement – an appreciation of what it would cost to replace assets at current prices.

The main difference between the two is how they treat the effects of increases in prices of assets and liabilities.

8.4   Usefulness of a conceptual Framework

As was mentioned earlier in this chapter, one of the major challenges for those communicating financial information is the *number and variety of users* of that information. It is difficult to assess its ultimate usefulness when you are unsure how the information is being used and by whom.

It would be almost impossible to address all technical issues in a business context that would meet the needs of every user. It is therefore important that all users appreciate the general principles of financial reporting – if you like, *the theory of how things should be treated.*

A conceptual Framework goes some way to providing this. It gives *guidance on the broad principles* on how items should be recorded, on how they should be measured and how they should be presented.

Where there are no standards specifically covering an issue, a conceptual Framework provides a *point of reference* for preparers of financial information. The Framework can provide guidance on how like items are treated and gives definitions and criteria that can be used in deciding the recognition and measurement of the item.

Where, in general, *accounting standards are less prescriptive,* a conceptual Framework can assist in this way also.

Accounting standards deal with a variety of specific technical issues. The existence of a conceptual Framework can *remove the need to address the underlying issues over and over again.* For example, the Framework gives definitions of assets and liabilities. These definitions must be met for items to be included in financial statements. This is an underlying principle, and as the accounting standards are based on the principles within the Framework, they need not be dealt with fully in each of the standards.

The increasing complexity of the business environment has resulted in a great number of specific accounting standards being developed. It is vital that each standard is developed within the broad Framework of principles. A conceptual Framework will assist standard-setters to develop specific accounting standards that follow a *consistent approach to recognition and measurement.*

The increased complexity of business provides a second challenge – the pace at which technical issues are raised and must be addressed. The process of creating a new accounting standard can be a long one, but where a conceptual Framework exists, the issue can be dealt with temporarily by *providing a short-term solution.* Providing the treatment is consistent with the principles within the Framework, then it will meet the criteria for useful information. This would be an acceptable solution until a specific standard was developed.

8.5 The IASB's Framework and the standard-setting process

We discussed above how a conceptual Framework can be useful in a regulatory environment. Many of the points raised above are true for the Framework and the IASB's standard-setting process. It will provide a reference point for those developing standards and help them provide consistent guidance. It does remove the need to address the underlying principles in each individual standard.

Where new technical issues and problems are raised and not covered specifically by an accounting standard, a short-term solution is provided by the IASB until it can be addressed fully. The International Financial Reporting Interpretations Committee (discussed in Chapter 7) issues such guidance and can use the Framework to ensure that the guidance it provides is consistent with the agreed underlying principles.

8.6 Summary

Having completed this chapter, we can now explain the purpose, status and scope of the Framework. We can identify the main topics included in the Framework and explain briefly what they cover. A number of points have been discussed, illustrating how useful a conceptual Framework can be. We can use these points together with the IASB's objectives of the Framework to evaluate its relationship to the standard-setting process.

Revision Questions

? Question 1

The IASB's *Framework* includes reliability as one of the characteristics that make financial information useful.

(i) Complete
(ii) Predictive value
(iii) Confirmatory value
(iv) Neutrality
(v) Faithful representation.

Which of the characteristics above are listed in the *Framework* as making financial information reliable?

(A) (i), (iv) and (v)
(B) (ii), (iii) and (iv)
(C) (ii) and (iii)
(D) (ii) and (v)   **(2 marks)**

? Question 2

The Framework for the Preparation and Presentation of Financial Statements has a number of purposes, including:

- assisting the Board in the development of future IFRSs and in its review of existing IFRSs;
- assisting the Board in promoting harmonisation of regulations, accounting standards and procedures relating to the presentation of financial statements by providing a basis for reducing the number of alternative treatments permitted by IFRSs;
- assisting preparers of financial statements in applying IFRSs and in dealing with topics that are yet to be covered in an IFRS.

Requirement

Discuss how a conceptual Framework could help IASB achieve these objectives.
                                                            (5 marks)

? Question 3

The IASB's *Framework for the Preparation and Presentation of Financial Statements* (Framework) lists the qualitative characteristics of financial statements.

  (i) Comparability,
 (ii) Relevance,
(iii) Prudence,
 (iv) Reliability,
  (v) Understandability,
 (vi) Matching,
(vii) Consistency.

Which THREE of the above are NOT included in the principal qualitative characteristics listed by the Framework?

(A) (i), (iii) and (vii)
(B) (i), (ii) and (v)
(C) (iii), (vi) and (vii)
(D) (iii), (iv) and (vi)   **(2 marks)**

? Question 4

Relevance and reliability are two of the four main qualitative characteristics of financial information, as set out in the Framework.

Requirements
(a) Briefly discuss what is meant by these terms.   **(5 marks)**
(b) Give an example of when these two attributes could come into conflict and what the outcome is likely to be.   **(5 marks)**
                                                              (Total marks = 10)

? Question 5

The *Framework* includes the following definition:

'an asset is a resource controlled by the entity as a result of past events and from which future economic benefits are expected to flow to the entity.'

Requirement
Explain this definition, using the example of a trade receivable.   **(5 marks)**

? Question 6

The IASB *Framework for the Preparation and Presentation of Financial Statements* (Framework) provides definitions of the elements of financial statement. One of the elements defined by the framework is 'expenses'.

Requirement
In no more than 35 words, give the IASB Framework's definition of expenses. **(2 marks)**

Question 7

The IASB's *Framework for the preparation and presentation of financial statements* (Framework) identifies four principal qualitative characteristics of financial information.

Requirement

Identify and explain EACH of the FOUR principal qualitative characteristics of financial information listed in the IASB's Framework. **(5 marks)**

 Question 8

The International Accounting Standards Board's (IASB) Framework for the Preparation and Presentation of Financial Statements (Framework), sets out four qualitative characteristics of financial information.

Two of the characteristics are relevance and comparability. List the other TWO characteristics. **(2 marks)**

 Question 9

According to the International Accounting Standards Board's Framework for the Preparation and Presentation of Financial Statements, what is the objective of financial statements?

Write your answer in no more than 35 words. **(2 marks)**

 Question 10

The Framework for the Preparation and Presentation of Financial Statements (Framework) was first published in 1989 and was adopted by The International Accounting Standards Board (IASB).

Requirement

Explain the purposes of the Framework. **(5 marks)**

Solutions to Revision Questions

 Solution 1

The correct answer is (A).

Items (ii) and (iii) are included in the *Framework* as characteristics of relevance, see Section 8.3.3.

 Solution 2

A conceptual Framework provides guidance on the broad principles of financial reporting. It highlights how items should be recorded, on how they should be measured and presented. The setting of broad principles could assist in the development of accounting standards, ensuring that the principles are followed consistently as standards and rules are developed.

A conceptual Framework can provide guidance on how similar items are treated. By providing definitions and criteria that can be used in deciding the recognition and measurement of items, conceptual Frameworks can act as a point of reference for those setting standards, those preparing and those using financial information.

The existence of a conceptual Framework can remove the need to address the underlying issues over and over again. Where underlying principles have been established and the accounting standards are based on these principles, there is no need to deal with them fully in each of the standards. This will save the standard-setters time in developing standards and will again ensure consistent treatment of items.

Where a technical issue is raised but is not specifically addressed in an accounting standard, a conceptual Framework can help provide guidance on how such items should be treated. Where a short-term technical solution is provided by the standard-setters, the existence of a conceptual Framework will ensure that the treatment is consistent with the broad set of agreed principles, see Section 8.2.1.

 Solution 3

The correct answer is (C), see Section 8.3.3.

 Solution 4

(a) Information is *relevant* when it influences the economic decisions of users by helping them to evaluate past, present or future economic events, or confirming/correcting their past evaluations.

143

Although financial statements do not normally contain information about future activities, any information that helps users assess the future performance and financial position of an entity is likely to be relevant. An item is likely to be relevant by virtue of its nature and materiality. Information is material if its omission or misstatement could influence the decision-making of users.

Information can also be relevant because of its unusual nature, irrespective of materiality. The directors would have to judge, in this case, if the nature of the information was such that its omission could influence the economic decision-making of users. Information should be released on a timely basis to be relevant to users.

Information is *reliable* when it is free from material error and bias and can be considered by users to be a faithful representation of the underlying transactions and events. To show a faithful representation, the transactions must be accounted for and presented on the basis of their commercial reality rather than their legal form.

In addition, the information must be neutral (free from bias) and complete. An omission can cause information to be false or misleading, as can the overstating of accounting estimates like provisions and valuations.

(b) An example of where relevance and reliability could come into conflict could be the existence of a contingent liability.

If the directors of an entity believe with reasonable certainty that a future liability has been identified they must first consider whether details on it should be included. If they consider that knowledge of it could affect the decision-making of users, then it should be included. However, given it is based on a future event, it cannot be measured with certainty and they may not have sufficient information to make a financial estimate with reasonable certainty. It may be questionable then if the information they could provide would be reliable.

In this case relevance and reliability must be traded off. It is likely that if omission of information on the potential liability would affect users' decision-making then, details should be included even if the financial amount cannot be stated with reasonable certainty. Relevance would override reliability in this case, see Sections 8.3.3.2 and 8.3.3.3.

Solution 5

In the case of a trade receivable, the past event is the making of a credit sale. The goods are transferred and the amount receivable is included in the financial records of the entity making the sale. That entity now has a receivable that is expected to turn into cash on receipt of the payment. The entity can be reasonably certain of payment where the transaction is complete, there is no dispute with the receivables and the receivables is not considered to be a credit risk. In this case, the entity can be reasonably certain that the future economic benefit (cash) will flow to them at the end of the granted credit period and can recognise the receivable as an asset within the financial statements, see Section 8.3.4.

Solution 6

Expenses are decreases in economic benefits during the accounting period in the form of outflows or depletions of assets that result in decreases in equity, other than those relating to distributions to equity participants, see Section 8.3.4.

Solution 7

Understandability

An essential quality of financial information is that it is readily understandable by users. For this purpose, users are assumed to have a reasonable knowledge of business and economic activities and accounting and a willingness to study the information with reasonable diligence. Information on complex issues should be included if relevant and should not be excluded on the ground that it is too difficult for the average user to understand.

Relevance

Information is relevant when it influences the economic decisions of users by helping them to evaluate past, present or future economic events, or confirming/correcting their past evaluations.

An item can be relevant by virtue of its nature or materiality. Information is material if its omission or misstatement could influence the decision-making of users.

Information should be released on a timely basis to be relevant to users.

Reliability

Information is reliable when it is free from material error and bias and can be considered by users to be a faithful representation of the underlying transactions and events.

To be reliable the information must:

- faithfully represent the transactions it is intended to represent;
- be accounted for and presented on the basis of its commercial reality rather than its legal form – substance over form;
- be neutral, free from bias.

Comparability

The ability to identify trends in performance and financial position and compare those both from year to year and against other entities assists users in their assessments and decision-making. To achieve comparability, users must be able to identify where an entity has changed its policy from one year to the next, and where other entities have used different accounting policies for similar transactions, see Section 8.3.3.

 ## Solution 8

Reliability and understandability

See Section 8.3.3.

 ## Solution 9

The objective of financial statements is to provide information about the financial position, performance, and changes in that position, of an entity that is useful to a wide range of users in making economic decisions.

See Section 8.3.1.

Solution 10

According to the *Framework*, its purposes are to:

- assist the Board in the development of future IFRSs and in its review of existing IFRSs;
- assist the Board in promoting harmonisation of regulations, accounting standards and procedures relating to the presentation of financial statements by providing a basis for reducing the number of alternative treatments permitted by IFRSs;
- assist national standard-setting bodies in developing national standards;
- assist preparers of financial statements in applying IFRSs and in dealing with topics that have yet to be covered in an IFRS;
- assist auditors in forming an opinion as to whether financial statements conform with IFRSs;
- assist users of financial statements that are prepared using IFRSs;
- provide information about how the IASB has formulated its approach to the development of IFRSs.

See Section 8.2.1.

The Role of the External Auditor

The Role of the External Auditor

LEARNING OUTCOME

After completing this chapter you should be able to:

▶ explain in general terms, the role of the external auditor, the elements of the audit report and types of qualification of that report.

The syllabus topics covered in this chapter are as follows:

● The powers and duties of the external auditors, the audit report and its qualification for accounting statements not in accordance with best practice.

9.1 External audit

Countries differ widely in their audit requirement. Small entities (variously defined) are often exempt. When an audit is required, the auditor's duty is to express an opinion on the truth and fairness of the entity's published financial statements. Exemptions are usually available for dormant entities (which – by definition – have not traded during the year and so have no transactions to report).

You may work for an entity which requires an external audit and may have encountered members of the audit team. It is, however, impossible to get any real idea of the scale of an audit unless you have actually participated in one. Most of the cost of an audit is staff time charged to the audit. Auditing is a time-consuming and costly activity. It is, therefore, worth spending some time thinking about the reasons why an audit might be carried out.

9.1.1 The purpose of an audit

Managers often feel under pressure to portray their entities in a favourable light when they report to any interested parties. This is one reason why we have a detailed set of accounting standards to regulate the presentation of contentious items in the financial statements. There is, however, an even more fundamental issue that must be addressed in the financial reporting process. It is not enough merely to *publish* rules and regulations governing the financial statements, there has to be some mechanism to *enforce* their implementation. Without enforcement, managers might distort the impression created by the statements in any number of ways. The nature of this distortion could vary from outright fabrication of the figures all the way through to the deliberate exploitation of a loophole in the system of rules.

Auditing is largely about providing the readers of the financial statements with confidence in the figures. This is highlighted by the accountancy profession's definition of an audit.

> Audit of financial statements: an exercise whose objective is to enable auditors to express an opinion as to whether the financial statements give a true and fair view ... of the affairs of the entity at the period end and of its profit or loss ... for the period then ended and have been properly prepared in accordance with the applicable reporting framework (e.g. relevant legislation and applicable accounting standards). *International Standard on Auditing (ISA) 2000 Objective and General Principles Governing an Audit of Financial Statements.*

The logic behind this definition is that the auditor's opinion will add some credibility to the financial statements. The auditor is an independent expert on financial reporting and will have conducted exhaustive checks before signing the audit report.

9.1.2 The auditor's duties

In most countries, the auditor has a statutory duty to make a report to the entity's members on the truth and fairness of the entity's annual accounts. As we have seen in the foregoing section, this report must state the auditor's opinion on whether the statements have been prepared in accordance with the relevant legislation and whether they give a true and fair view of the profit or loss for the year and state of affairs at the year-end. The duty to report on the truth and fairness of the financial statements is the primary duty associated with the external audit.

The auditor has a duty to form an opinion on certain other matters and to report any reservations. The auditor must consider whether:

1. the entity has kept proper accounting records;
2. the entity's statement of financial position and statement of comprehensive income agree with the underlying accounting records;
3. all the information and explanations that the auditor considers necessary for the purposes of the audit have been obtained and whether adequate returns for their audit have been received from branches not visited during the audit;
4. the entity has complied with the relevant legislation's requirements in respect of the necessary disclosures. If the entity has not made all the disclosures required, the audit report should, if possible, contain a statement of the required particulars.

We do not need to elaborate on the above, although it is worth noting that (3) above effectively gives the auditor the right of access to any information or material that seems relevant to checking the financial statements. The entity cannot refuse this request.

The auditor has a limited duty to review the other information issued alongside the audited financial statements. For example, the auditor must consider whether the information in any reports published with the financial statements are consistent with the information in the statement of comprehensive income and statement of financial position. Any inconsistency should be disclosed in the audit report.

The auditor must gather information and evidence in order to support an opinion on the truth and fairness of the financial statements. There is, however, no need to *guarantee* that the statements give a true and fair view. This is partly because the auditor is only required to form an opinion in order to discharge each of the duties described above. It is also because there will always be a limit to the amount of evidence that can be collected. The auditor is required to apply 'reasonable skill and care' in conducting the audit.

Contrary to popular opinion, the auditor does not have a specific duty to search for fraud. The auditor will, however, have to consider the possibility that the truth and fairness of the statements might have been distorted by any irregularity including the concealment of a fraud. In general, auditors rely on control systems within entities to ensure that there has not been any material distortion because of fraud. The auditor would, however, follow up on anything suspicious which came to light during the course of the audit.

Local legal requirements may impose additional duties on auditors.

9.1.3   The powers of auditors

Rights that are designed to ensure that the auditor is able to fulfil their statutory duties are usually given to them under local legislation relating to entities, for example, in the UK, the Companies Act 1985. To be able to carry out their duties, auditors must be independent of the entity that they are auditing. Independence is fundamental to the credibility of the audit process.

The powers granted to the auditor by legislation varies from country to country but typical powers found in many countries are:

- the right of access at all times to the books, records, documents and accounts of the entity;
- the right to be notified of, attend and speak at meetings of owners;
- the right to require officers of the entity to provide them with whatever information and explanations they think necessary for the performance of their duties;
- the right to present a counter-argument to any meeting of owners that is considering the removal of the auditors.

9.1.4   The audit process

The manner in which an audit is conducted is beyond the scope of the syllabus. You should, however, be aware of the broad outline of the manner in which an audit is conducted.

Figure 9.1 illustrates the main steps of an audit. The auditor is usually appointed by the shareholders during the entity's annual general meeting. This appointment is normally effective until the next annual general meeting. It is very common for the same firm to be

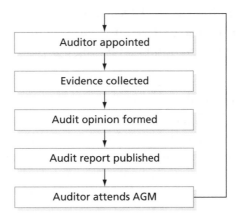

Figure 9.1   Steps in the audit cycle

reappointed annually for many years and so there is normally far more continuity than this annual cycle suggests.

The auditor sets about gathering evidence to support an opinion about the financial statements. There are two aspects to the preparation of the accounts and this means that there are two phases of the audit:

- *Bookkeeping phase.* The auditor must ensure that the transactions and balances recorded in the entity's books and ledgers are sufficiently complete and accurate to form the basis for an acceptable set of financial statements. This aspect of the audit work may be completed in stages, with most of the work undertaken during the year.
- *Accounting phase.* The auditor must review the accounting policies adopted by management in order to ensure that these are acceptable and that the statements give a true and fair view.

The gathering of audit evidence is not a part of our syllabus and so we will not discuss it further. The issues associated with the reporting stage of the audit are examinable. Basically, the auditor is responsible for forming an opinion on the truth and fairness of the financial statements and for reporting this opinion to the shareholders. We will discuss this duty in more detail below. Auditing is governed by a comprehensive set of international standards on auditing (ISAs) issued by the International Auditing and Assurance Standards Board (IAASB). The IAASB is a committee of the International Federation of Accountants (IFAC). Membership of IFAC is open to accountancy bodies worldwide.

9.2 The audit report

The provision of a clear expression of opinion on the financial statements lies at the heart of the external audit. The form and content of the audit report is governed by ISA 700 (Revised) *The Auditor's Report on Financial Statements.* ISA 700 was revised in December 2004, the new form of audit report is effective for auditor's reports dated on or after 31 December 2006. A typical audit report illustrated in ISA 700 is shown below.

Independent auditor's report

Appropriate addressee
We have audited the accompanying financial statements of ABC company, which comprise the statement of financial position as at 31 December 20X1, and the statement of comprehensive income, statement of changes in equity and statement of cash flows for the year then ended, and a summary of significant accounting policies and other explanatory notes.

Management's responsibility for the financial statements
Management is responsible for the preparation and fair presentation of these financial statements in accordance with International Financial Reporting Standards. This responsibility includes: designing, implementing and maintaining internal control relevant to the preparation and fair presentation of financial statements that are free from material misstatement, whether due to fraud or error; selecting and applying appropriate accounting policies; and making accounting estimates that are reasonable in the circumstances.

Auditor's responsibility

Our responsibility is to express an opinion on these financial statements based on our audit. We conducted our audit in accordance with International Standards on Auditing. Those standards require that we comply with ethical requirements and plan and perform the audit to obtain reasonable assurance whether the financial statements are free from material misstatement.

An audit involves performing procedures to obtain audit evidence about the amounts and disclosures in the financial statements. The procedures selected depend on the auditor's judgment, including the assessment of the risks of material misstatement of the financial statements, whether due to fraud or error. In making those risk assessments, the auditor considers internal control relevant to the entity's preparation and fair presentation of the financial statements in order to design audit procedures that are appropriate in the circumstances, but not for the purpose of expressing an opinion on the effectiveness of the entity's internal control. An audit also includes evaluating the appropriateness of accounting policies used and the reasonableness of accounting estimates made by management, as well as evaluating the overall presentation of the financial statements.

We believe that the audit evidence we have obtained is sufficient and appropriate to provide a basis for our audit opinion.

Opinion

In our opinion, the financial statements give a true and fair view of *(or present fairly, in all material respects,)* the financial position of ABC Company as of 31 December 20X1, and of its financial performance and its cash flows for the year then ended in accordance with International Financial Reporting Standards.

[Auditor's signature]
[Date of the auditor's report]
[Auditor's address]

You should look at this report carefully and then think about the following questions. They will help you to appreciate the extent of the auditor's duties.

- To what extent does this report state that the entity is well run?
- To what extent does it assure us that the board has been discharging its duties honestly?
- To what extent does it assure us that there has been no staff fraud?

The answer to each of the foregoing questions is 'not at all'. The audit report will never make any direct reference to the manner in which the entity is run. The financial statements could easily give a true and fair view even though the entity is not doing well. In that case, it would be up to the shareholders to infer that the entity had problems because it was making a loss or had a very poor return on capital employed. Similarly, the auditors do not provide any direct assurances about the stewardship of management or about the honesty of staff. We will return to this issue later, but the auditor's duties for the detection and reporting of fraud and other irregularities are quite severely restricted.

Thus, the only direct benefit to be had from the audit report is that it provides the shareholders with some assurance that the accounts give a true and fair view – in other words, it provides them with some assurance that the accounts provide a credible basis for making decisions.

9.2.1 A closer look at the report

A typical report is analysed in the following sections, to show what the various elements of it mean and why they are required:

Title

The auditor's report should have an appropriate title. It may be appropriate to use the term 'independent auditor' in the title to distinguish the auditor's report from reports that might be issued by others, such as by officers of the entity, the board of directors, or from the reports of other auditors who may not have to abide by the same ethical requirements as the independent auditor.

Addressee

The auditor's report should be appropriately addressed as required by the circumstances of the engagement and local regulations. The report is ordinarily addressed either to the shareholders or the board of directors of the entity whose financial statements are being audited.

Opening or introductory paragraph

The auditor's report should identify the entity whose financial statements have been audited and state that the financial statements have been audited. It should identify the title of each of the financial statements that comprise the complete set of financial statements. It should specify the date of and period covered by the financial statements.

Management's responsibility for the financial statements

The auditor's report should state that management is responsible for the preparation and the fair presentation of financial statements in accordance with the applicable financial reporting framework and that this responsibility includes:

(a) Designing, implementing and maintaining internal control relevant to the preparation and fair presentation of financial statements that are free from material misstatement, whether due to fraud or error;
(b) Selecting and applying appropriate accounting policies; and
(c) Making accounting estimates that are reasonable in the circumstances.

Financial statements are the representations of management. The preparation of such statements requires management to make significant accounting estimates and judgements, as well as to determine the appropriate accounting principles and methods used in preparation of the financial statements. In contrast, the auditor's responsibility is to audit these financial statements in order to express an opinion thereon.

Auditor's responsibility

The auditor's report should state that the responsibility of the auditor is to express an opinion on the financial statements based on the audit.

The auditor's report should state that the audit was conducted in accordance with International Standards on Auditing. The auditor's report should also explain that those standards require that the auditor comply with ethical requirements and that the auditor plan and perform the audit to obtain reasonable assurance whether the financial statements are free from material misstatement.

The auditor's report should describe an audit by stating that:

(a) An audit involves performing procedures to obtain audit evidence about the amounts and disclosures in the financial statements;

(b) The procedures selected depend on the auditor's judgement, including the assessment of the risks of material misstatement of the financial statements, whether due to fraud or error. In making those risk assessments, the auditor considers internal control relevant to the entity's preparation and fair presentation of the financial statements in order to design audit procedures that are appropriate in the circumstances, but not for the purpose of expressing an opinion on the effectiveness of the entity's internal control. In circumstances when the auditor also has a responsibility to express an opinion on the effectiveness of internal control in conjunction with the audit of the financial statements, the auditor should omit the phrase that the auditor's consideration of internal control is not for the purpose of expressing an opinion on the effectiveness of internal control; and

(c) An audit also includes evaluating the appropriateness of the accounting policies used, the reasonableness of accounting estimates made by management, as well as the overall presentation of the financial statements.

The auditor's report should state that the auditor believes that the audit evidence the auditor has obtained is sufficient and appropriate to provide a basis for the auditor's opinion.

Auditor's opinion

An unqualified opinion should be expressed when the auditor concludes that the financial statements give a true and fair view or are presented fairly, in all material respects, in accordance with the applicable financial reporting framework. When expressing an unqualified opinion, the opinion paragraph of the auditor's report should state the auditor's opinion that the financial statements give a true and fair view or present fairly, in all material respects, in accordance with the applicable financial reporting framework (unless the auditor is required by law or regulation to use different wording for the opinion, in which case the prescribed wording should be used).

The terms used to express the auditor's opinion are 'give a true and fair view' or 'present fairly, in all material respects,' and are equivalent. Both terms indicate, among other things, that the auditor considers only those matters that are material to the financial statements.

Date of report

The auditor should date the report as of the completion date of the audit. This informs the reader that the auditor has considered the effect on the financial statements and on the report of events and transactions of which the auditor became aware and that occurred up to that date.

Since the auditor's responsibility is to report on the financial statements as prepared and presented by management, the auditor should not date the report earlier than the date on which the financial statements are signed or approved by management.

Auditor's address

The report should name a specific location, which is ordinarily the city where the auditor maintains the office that has responsibility for the audit.

Auditor's signature

The report should be signed in the name of the audit firm, the personal name of the auditor, or both, as appropriate. The auditor's report is ordinarily signed in the name of the firm because the firm assumes responsibility for the audit.

An example of an audit report is given below.

Extract from the consolidated accounts of the Nestlé Group for the year ended 31 December 2005

Report of the group auditors

To: The General Meeting of Nestlé SA

As Group auditors we have audited the consolidated accounts (statement of financial position, a statement of comprehensive income, statement of cash flows, statement of changes in equity and annex) of the Nestlé Group for the year ended 31 December 2005.

These Consolidated Financial Statements are the responsibility of the Board of Directors. Our responsibility is to express an opinion on these Consolidated Financial Statements based on our audit. We confirm that we meet the legal requirements concerning professional qualification and independence.

Our audit was conducted in accordance with Swiss auditing standards and International Standards on Auditing, which require that an audit be planned and performed to obtain reasonable assurance about whether the Consolidated Financial Statements are free from material misstatement. We have examined on a test basis evidence supporting the amounts and disclosures in the Consolidated Financial Statements. We have also assessed the accounting principles used, significant estimates made and the overall Consolidated Financial Statements presentation. We believe that our audit provides a reasonable basis for our opinion.

In our opinion, the Consolidated Financial Statements give a true and fair view of the financial position, the net profit and cash flows in accordance with International Financial Reporting Standards (IFRS) and comply with Swiss law.

We recommend that the consolidated accounts submitted to you be approved.

KPMG Klynwed Peat Marwick Goerdeler SA

S. R. Cormack   Stéphane Gard

Auditor in charge   London and Zurich

                                             23 February 2006

9.3   Modified audit reports

The auditor will almost always be able to conclude that the statements give a true and fair view, although it might be more difficult to do so in some cases. If an audit involves a particularly difficult problem, then the auditor might have to collect additional evidence before concluding that it has been accounted for correctly. Alternatively, the auditor might decide that the accounting policies chosen by management are unacceptable, in which case it will be necessary to negotiate a change of policy.

Occasionally, the auditor will be unable to conclude that the accounts give a true and fair view and is unable to persuade the directors to change their policy. In those cases, the auditor will have to express some reservation about the statements by giving a 'qualified' opinion. This means that the opinion paragraph of the report is modified to warn the readers that the auditor has some material reservation about the truth and fairness of the statements.

Modified reports are required where there has been a limitation on the scope of the auditor's examination or the auditor disagrees with the treatment or disclosure of a matter in the financial statements. Limitations of scope arise when the auditor is prevented from gathering all the evidence that is necessary in order to complete the audit.

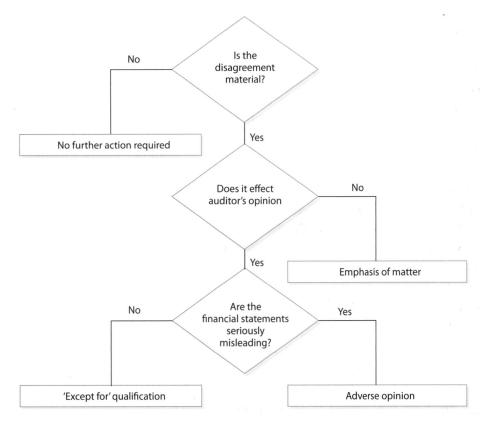

Figure 9.2 Classifying disagreements on the financial statements

While a limitation of scope is a serious problem for the auditor, it is specifically excluded from our syllabus and so we will not discuss it further. Qualifications arising from disagreement are, however, examinable.

The nature of accountancy means that there is always scope for disagreement over the facts, the application of an accounting standard or the amount of disclosure in the financial statements. The auditor would not necessarily treat a difference of opinion about the best possible treatment of a matter as disagreement. The matter would only become a problem if the auditor felt that the treatment adopted by management was unacceptable. Once such disagreement has been identified, the auditor must classify it as shown in Figure 9.2.

9.3.1 Materiality

By definition, a matter is material 'if its omission or misstatement could influence the economic decisions of users taken on the basis of the financial statements' (IASB *Framework)*. This means that there is no real need to report on matters which are not material because they will not affect the behaviour of the readers. In other words, if something is immaterial then – by definition – it does not matter. Indeed, reporting on immaterial matters would be misleading because it would give them unnecessary prominence.

Materiality cannot be measured in terms of any objective criteria. Some audit firms use rules of thumb and treat anything which exceeds, say 5 or 10 per cent of profit or 1.2 or 1 per cent of turnover as material. These benchmarks are not sufficient in themselves because some matters are material by their very nature.

There should be very little doubt about the materiality or otherwise of an item in the exam. If materiality is to be determined by the amounts involved, then these will either be clearly material or immaterial, for example, well in excess of 10 per cent of profit or far less than 5 per cent.

Items which are to be judged in terms of their nature are rather more difficult. It is impossible to be categorical about whether such an item is material or not, but the issues ought either to be reasonably clear-cut or the marks awarded for the quality of arguments – either for or against the matter being material – rather than being for a correct distinction.

Figure 9.2 suggests that there is a second level of material disagreement, one which is so serious that the statements are rendered seriously misleading. The distinction between 'material' and more serious 'fundamental' qualifications is not clear-cut. A disagreement would have to be so serious as to guide readers in the wrong direction altogether before it would be regarded as more than merely material. Thus, this more extreme form of qualification might be reserved for circumstances in which, say the entity was reporting massive profits when the auditor was of the opinion that the entity was making massive losses.

9.3.2 The wording of a modified audit report

International Standard on Auditing 701(revised) *Modifications to the Independent Auditors Report* deals with modified audit reports. ISA 701 classifies modified audit reports into the following categories:

Matters that do not affect the auditor's opinion

(a) *Emphasis of matter* – In certain circumstances, an auditor's report may be modified by adding an emphasis of matter paragraph to highlight a matter affecting the financial statements which is included in a detailed note to the financial statements. The addition of such an emphasis of matter paragraph does not affect the auditor's opinion. The paragraph would usually be included after the paragraph containing the auditor's opinion and states that the auditor's opinion is not qualified in this respect.

An illustration of an emphasis of matter paragraph for a significant uncertainty in an auditor's report: *Without qualifying our opinion we draw attention to Note ... to the financial statements. The entity [brief explanation of circumstances explained in detail in the note].*

Matters that do affect the auditor's opinion

(a) *A qualified opinion* should be expressed when the auditor concludes that an unqualified opinion cannot be expressed but that the effect of any disagreement with management, or limitation on scope is not so material and pervasive as to require an adverse opinion or a disclaimer of opinion. A qualified opinion should be expressed as being 'except for' the effects of the matter to which the qualification relates.
(b) *A disclaimer of opinion* should be expressed when the possible effect of a limitation on scope is so material and pervasive that the auditor has not been able to obtain sufficient appropriate audit evidence and accordingly is unable to express an opinion on the financial statements.
(c) *An adverse opinion* should be expressed when the effect of a disagreement is so material and pervasive to the financial statements that the auditor concludes that a qualification of the report is not adequate to disclose the misleading or incomplete nature of the financial statements.

Whenever the auditor expresses an opinion that is other than unqualified, a clear description of all the substantive reasons should be included in the report and, unless impracticable, a quantification of the possible effect(s) on the financial statements.

9.3.3 Independent auditor's report showing qualified opinion

The most common form of qualified report is as follows. Read this report and compare it with the unqualified report shown above in 9.2.

Independent auditor's report

Appropriate addressee

Disagreement on Accounting Policies – Inappropriate Accounting Method – Qualified Opinion
We have audited the accompanying financial statements of ABC Company, which comprise the statement of financial position as at 31 December 20X1, and the a statement of comprehensive income, statement of changes in equity and statement of cash flows for the year then ended, and a summary of significant accounting policies and other explanatory notes.

Management's responsibility for the financial statements
Management is responsible for the preparation and fair presentation of these financial statements in accordance with International Financial Reporting Standards. This responsibility includes: designing, implementing and maintaining internal control relevant to the preparation and fair presentation of financial statements that are free from material misstatement, whether due to fraud or error; selecting and applying appropriate accounting policies; and making accounting estimates that are reasonable in the circumstances.

Auditor's responsibility
Our responsibility is to express an opinion on these financial statements based on our audit. We conducted our audit in accordance with International Standards on Auditing. Those standards require that we comply with ethical requirements and plan and perform the audit to obtain reasonable assurance whether the financial statements are free from material misstatement.

An audit involves performing procedures to obtain audit evidence about the amounts and disclosures in the financial statements. The procedures selected depend on the auditor's judgment, including the assessment of the risks of material misstatement of the financial statements, whether due to fraud or error. In making those risk assessments, the auditor considers internal control relevant to the entity's preparation and fair presentation of the financial statements in order to design audit procedures that are appropriate in the circumstances, but not for the purpose of expressing an opinion on the effectiveness of the entity's internal control. An audit also includes evaluating the appropriateness of accounting policies used and the reasonableness of accounting estimates made by management, as well as evaluating the overall presentation of financial statements.

We believe that the audit evidence we have obtained is sufficient and appropriate to provide a basis for our audit opinion.

Opinion
As discussed in Note X to the financial statements, no depreciation has been provided in the financial statements which practice, in our opinion, is not in accordance with International

Financial Reporting Standards. The provision for the year ended 31 December 20X1 should be xxx based on the straight-line method of depreciation using annual rates of 5% for the building and 20% for the equipment. Accordingly, the fixed assets should be reduced by accumulated depreciation of xxx and the loss for the year and accumulated deficit should be increased by xxx and xxx, respectively.

In our opinion, *except for the effect on the financial statements of the matter referred to in the preceding paragraph*, the financial statements give a true and fair view of (*or present fairly, in all material respects*,) the financial position of ABC Company as of 31 December 20X1, and of its financial performance and its cash flows for the year then ended in accordance with International Financial Reporting Standards.

[Auditor's signature]
[Date of the auditor's report]
[Auditor's address]

Much of the audit report is unchanged. The two main differences are that there is an additional paragraph which describes the specific area of disagreement between the auditor and the board and the opinion paragraph has been reworded.

The explanatory paragraph spells out the facts clearly and quantifies the matter. The readers of the report can now decide whether they agree with the auditor or the directors. If they support the auditor's opinion, then it is a simple matter to reduce both profit and current assets by the amount in question.

The opinion paragraph is also clear. The readers are left in no doubt that the auditor's only material reservation is in respect of the depreciation charge. This has been disclosed and the accounts otherwise give a true and fair view.

An extract from the more extreme form of qualification is shown below. Again, please read this and compare it with the examples shown above. *Note*: The wording of the first few paragraphs is not affected by the qualification, except that the report would be headed as shown.

9.3.4 Independant auditor's report-adverse opinion

Appropriate addressee
Disagreement on accounting policies – adverse opinion […]

As more fully explained in note 7, no provision has been made for losses expected to arise on certain long-term contracts currently in progress, as the directors consider that such losses should be offset against amounts recoverable on other long-term contracts. In our opinion, provision should be made for foreseeable losses on individual contracts as required by IAS 11 *Construction Contracts*. If losses had been so recognised, the effect would have been to reduce the profit before and after tax for the year and the contract work in progress at 31 December 20X0 by $2.3 million.

In our opinion, in view of the effect of the failure to provide for the losses referred to above, the financial statements do not give a true and fair view of the financial position of ABC as at 31 December 20X0 and its financial performance and its cash flows for the year then ended in accordance with International Financial Reporting Standards and relevant statutes.

Auditor
Date
Address

The report is headed 'adverse opinion'. Again it contains a clear description of a difference of opinion between the directors and the auditor. This time, however, the auditor has concluded that the accounts do not give a true and fair view. Issuing such an opinion is an extreme step to take. Effectively, it suggests that the shareholders should not use the financial statements for decision-making purposes.

> You might be worried about distinguishing between the two types of qualified report. In general, you should decide whether the matter is material. If it is, then the 'except for' form will almost always be appropriate. You do have to be aware of the adverse opinion, but it is unlikely that you will ever use it in answering an examination question. You will not be asked to write out a full audit report in the examination. A question might ask you to decide which type of report is appropriate or to explain what the different types of audit report are, but you do not have to memorise the wording of the reports.

9.4 Summary

The auditor is responsible for forming an opinion on the truth and fairness of the financial statements and expressing this in a report addressed to the shareholders. This is necessary so that the readers of the financial statements can have some confidence that the directors have not manipulated the information in the accounts.

Having completed this chapter, we can now explain the purpose of an audit and the role and duties of the external auditor. We can describe the audit process and explain the contents of an audit report.

We can discuss the circumstances that could result in a qualified opinion being given and how that opinion would be reflected in the audit report.

Revision Questions

? Question 1

What is the objective of an audit?

(A) To check for fraud
(B) To check there are no errors in the accounts
(C) To enable the auditor to express an opinion as to whether the financial statements give a fair presentation of the company affairs
(D) To enable the auditor to approve the accounts **(2 marks)**

? Question 2

Who is responsible for the preparation of the financial statements?

(A) The entity accountant
(B) The auditors
(C) The entity directors
(D) The shareholders **(2 marks)**

? Question 3

What is the external auditor's statutory duty? *(max. 21 words).*
   The auditor has a statutory duty to_____
  (2 marks)

? Question 4

If an auditor disagrees with the treatment of a material item in the financial statements and the directors refuse to change their treatment, the auditor will in most situations:

(A) Issue a qualified audit report using the 'except for' qualification
(B) Issue an unqualified audit report
(C) Issue a qualified audit report using the 'adverse opinion' qualification
(D) Issue a qualified audit report using the 'disagreement of treatment' qualification
  (2 marks)

Question 5

If an external auditor does not agree with the directors' treatment of a material item in the accounts, the first action they should take is to

(A) give a qualified opinion of the financial statements
(B) give an unqualified opinion of the financial statements
(C) force the directors to change the treatment of the item in the accounts
(D) persuade the directors to change the treatment of the item in the accounts

(2 marks)

 Question 6

The external auditor has a duty to report on the truth and fairness of the financial statements and to report any reservations. The auditor is normally given a number of powers by statute to enable the statutory duties to be carried out.

List THREE powers that are usually granted to the auditor by statute.

(3 marks)

Question 7

You are the partner in charge of the audit of G, a major quoted company. You are making a final review of the financial statements before finalising the audit report. The following matters have been marked for your attention:

(i) The draft financial statements indicate a turnover of $500 m and a profit of $50 m.
(ii) The directors have made no provision for the costs that are likely to be incurred as a result of a damages claim for $2.4 m, which is being pursued by one of the company's customers. G's legal department and its lawyers are quite sure that this claim will have to be met in full.
(iii) The directors have not provided for a sum of $2.3 m which ought to be written off in respect of debts that are almost certainly irrecoverable.

Requirements

(a) Explain the implications for your audit report of the matters described in (ii) and (iii) above.

Your answer should make a clear statement of the type of report which you consider appropriate, although a full audit report is *not* required. **(5 marks)**

(b) It has been suggested that the quality of audit reporting could be improved enormously if accounting standards were clearer and auditors had more explicit guidance on issues such as materiality.

Discuss this suggestion, making it clear how improved guidance on financial reporting might support the auditor. **(5 marks)**

(Total marks = 10)

Question 8

You are the partner in charge of the audit of K. The following matter has been brought to your attention in the audit working papers.

The entity has refused to write the closing inventory down to the lower of cost and net realisable value, despite the requirements to do so in IAS 2. The audit senior estimates that closing inventory has been overstated by $500,000 because of this.

The draft financial statements show turnover of $40 million and profit of $4.5 million.

Requirements

(a) Explain what is meant by the term 'materiality'. Explain whether the matter highlighted above is material, giving reasons. **(5 marks)**
(b) Assuming that the directors refuse to amend the financial statements, explain what type of audit report would be appropriate to the above statements. **(5 marks)**

(Total marks = 10)

Question 9

An external auditor gives a qualified audit report that is a "disclaimer of opinion".
This means that the auditor:

(A) has been unable to agree with an accounting treatment used by the directors in relation to a material item.
(B) has been prevented from obtaining sufficient appropriate audit evidence.
(C) has found extensive errors in the financial statements and concludes that they do not show a true and fair view.
(D) has discovered a few immaterial differences that do not affect the auditor's opinion.

(2 marks)

Question 10

The International Standard on Auditing 701 Modifications to the Independent Auditor's Report, classifies modified audit reports into "matters that do not affect the auditor's opinion" and "matters that do affect the auditor's opinion". This latter category is further subdivided into three categories.

List these THREE categories. **(3 marks)**

Solutions to Revision Questions

In the real world, it is usually difficult to tell whether a problem is material or even if there is a serious disagreement. The nature of examination questions suggests that matters will always be more clear-cut.

 ## Solution 1

The correct answer is (C).

The auditor does not check for fraud or errors specifically. The auditor does not 'approve' the accounts, see Section 9.1.1.

 ## Solution 2

The correct answer is (C), see Section 9.1.2.

 ## Solution 3

The auditor has a statutory duty to make a report to the company's members, expressing an opinion on the truth and fairness of the company's published financial statements, see Section 9.1.2

 ## Solution 4

The correct answer is (A), see Section 9.3.

 ## Solution 5

The correct answer is (D), see Section 9.1.2.

Solution 6

Powers of the auditor can include:

- Right of access at all times to the books, records, documents and accounts;
- Right to be notified, and attend meetings, of owners;

- Right to require officers of the entity to provide them with information and explanations;
- Right to speak at owners' meetings.

Note: Any three of the above would have gained the marks available.

 ## Solution 7

(a) The first question to be resolved is whether these amounts are material. If they are not then it would not matter whether the auditor disagreed or not.

Bear in mind that either item might be immaterial when taken on its own but the combined effect could be material. Both items tend to overstate profits and so we should consider whether their total value is misleading.

One half of 1 per cent of turnover = $2.5 million, as does 5 per cent of profit. This suggests that neither item is material in itself, but that the two taken together lead to a material overstatement of profits. If the directors refuse to alter their treatment of them, then the auditor will have to qualify the audit report.

IAS 37 requires that item (ii) should be accrued. This is on the grounds that the payment is probable and the amount can be estimated with reasonable accuracy. This accrual would reduce profits by $2.4 million and would create a current liability of the same amount.

The bad debt should be written off because of the need for prudence in the valuation of assets and recognition of losses. There is also a need to match the loss to the same period as the loss arose. This means that both profits and receivables should be decreased by $2.3 million.

In the absence of any change by the directors, we will need to qualify the financial statements on the grounds of disagreement. The extent of our disagreement is not so serious as to warrant an adverse opinion and so we will use the 'except for' form of words, see Section 9.3.

(b) The ambiguity of accounting standards is a major problem for the auditor. It is possible to create a slightly misleading impression without breaching any of the formal standards. It can be difficult for the auditor to justify a change to the financial statements if the directors argue that their treatment falls within the requirements of local company law and accounting standards. These same directors can, of course, seek out the loopholes and ambiguities in the standards in order to achieve the desired effect on the statements.

If accounting standards could be made clearer and less ambiguous, then the auditor could find it easier to demonstrate that a particular treatment was unacceptable. On the other hand, the statements might not be any more useful because the greater clarity might be arrived at by making the requirements more rigid – thereby reducing the scope for deciding on the most realistic treatment.

The other major problem facing the auditor is over the determination of materiality. It is never clear where the precise cut-off between material and immaterial actually lies. The danger is that the directors are aware of this and could bias the figures until just before the point at which the auditor would be forced to treat the matter as a material disagreement.

Greater clarity over materiality might help, but it could also provide management with a better idea of exactly how far they could push the figures. This suggests that it might not improve the overall quality of financial reporting and auditing.

Solution 8

(a) A matter is material if knowledge of it could influence users' decisions taken on the basis of the financial statements.

In strictly numerical terms, 0.5 per cent of turnover is $200,000 and 5 per cent of profit is $225,000.

The disagreement over inventory appears to be material because of its numerical significance. There is little point in considering the nature of the matter because it would be material by virtue of its effect on profit.

(b) This is a material disagreement and so the auditor must qualify the audit report in respect of the overstatement of stock.

The disagreement is material, but not fundamental and so the adverse opinion is not required.

The auditor would state that the accounts gave a true and fair view except for the overstatement of closing inventory and profits by $500,000, see Section 9.3.

 Solution 9

The correct answer is B, see Section 9.3.2.

 Solution 10

Qualified opinion
Adverse opinion
Disclaimer of opinion, see Section 9.3.2.

10

CIMA Code of Ethics for Professional Accountants

CIMA Code of Ethics for Professional Accountants

10

LEARNING OUTCOMES

After completing this chapter you should be able to:

- explain the importance of the exercise of ethical principles in reporting and assessing information;
- describe the sources of ethical codes from those involved in the reporting or taxation affairs of an organisation, including external auditors;
- apply the provisions of the CIMA Code of Ethics for Professional Accountants of particular relevance to the information reporting, assurance and tax-related activities of the accountant.

10.1 Fundamental principles of the code

A professional accountant is required to comply with the following fundamental principles:

(a) *Integrity*
(b) *Objectivity*
(c) *Professional competence and due care*
(d) *Confidentiality*

10.1.1 Integrity

A professional accountant should be straightforward and honest in all professional and business relationships.

The principle of integrity imposes an obligation on all professional accountants to be straightforward and honest in professional and business relationships. Integrity also implies fair dealing and truthfulness.

A professional accountant should not be associated with reports, returns, communications or other information where they believe that the information:

(a) contains a materially false or misleading statement;
(b) contains statements or information furnished recklessly; or
(c) omits or obscures information required to be included where such omission or obscurity would be misleading.

10.1.2 Objectivity

A professional accountant should not allow bias, conflict of interest or undue influence of others to override professional or business judgements.

The principle of objectivity imposes an obligation on all professional accountants not to compromise their professional or business judgement because of bias, conflict of interest or the undue influence of others.

A professional accountant may be exposed to situations that may impair objectivity. It is impracticable to define and prescribe all such situations. Relationships that bias or unduly influence the professional judgement of the professional accountant should be avoided.

10.1.3 Professional competence and due care

A professional accountant has a continuing duty to maintain professional knowledge and skill at the level required to ensure that a client or employer receives competent professional service based on current developments in practice, legislation and techniques. A professional accountant should act diligently and in accordance with applicable technical and professional standards when providing professional services.

The principle of professional competence and due care imposes the following obligations on professional accountants:

(a) To maintain professional knowledge and skill at the level required to ensure that clients or employers receive competent professional service.
(b) To act diligently in accordance with applicable technical and professional standards when providing professional services.

Competent professional service requires the exercise of sound judgment in applying professional knowledge and skill in the performance of such service. Professional competence may be divided into two separate phases:

(a) Attainment of professional competence; and
(b) Maintenance of professional competence.

The maintenance of professional competence requires a continuing awareness and an understanding of relevant technical professional and business developments. Continuing professional development develops and maintains the capabilities to enable a professional accountant to perform competently within the professional environments.

Diligence encompasses the responsibility to act in accordance with the requirements of an assignment, carefully, thoroughly and on a timely basis.

A professional accountant should take steps to ensure that those working under the professional accountant's authority in a professional capacity have appropriate training and supervision.

Where appropriate, a professional accountant should make clients, employers or other users of the professional services aware of limitations inherent in the services to avoid the misinterpretation of an expression of opinion as an assertion of fact.

10.1.4 Confidentiality

A professional accountant should respect the confidentiality of information acquired as a result of professional and business relationships and should not disclose any such information to third parties without proper and specific authority unless there is a legal or professional right or duty to disclose.

The principle of confidentiality imposes an obligation on professional accountants to refrain from:

(a) Disclosing outside the firm or employing organisation confidential information acquired as a result of professional and business relationships without proper and specific authority or unless there is a legal or professional right or duty to disclose.
(b) Using confidential information acquired as a result of professional and business relationships to their personal advantage or the advantage of third parties.

A professional accountant should maintain confidentiality even in a social environment. The professional accountant should be alert to the possibility of inadvertent disclosure, particularly in circumstances involving long association with a business associate or a close or immediate family member.

A professional accountant should also maintain confidentiality of information disclosed by a prospective client or employer.

A professional accountant should also consider the need to maintain confidentiality of information within the firm or employing organisation.

A professional accountant should take all reasonable steps to ensure that staff under the professional accountant's control and persons from whom advice and assistance is obtained respect the professional accountant's duty of confidentiality.

The need to comply with the principle of confidentiality continues even after the end of relationships between a professional accountant and a client or employer. When a professional accountant changes employment or acquires a new client, the professional accountant is entitled to use prior experience. The professional accountant should not, however, use or disclose any confidential information either acquired or received as a result of a professional or business relationship.

The following are circumstances where professional accountants are or may be required to disclose confidential information or when such disclosure may be appropriate:

(a) Disclosure is permitted by law and is authorised by the client or the employer.
(b) Disclosure is required by law, for example:
   (i) Production of documents or other provision of evidence in the course of legal proceedings; or
   (ii) Disclosure to the appropriate public authorities of infringements of the law that come to light.
(c) There is a professional duty or right to disclose, when not prohibited by law:
   (i) To comply with the quality review of a member body or professional body;
   (ii) To respond to an inquiry or investigation by a member body or regulatory body;
   (iii) To protect the professional interests of a professional accountant in legal proceedings; or
   (iv) To comply with technical standards and ethics requirements. In deciding whether to disclose confidential information, professional accountants should consider the following points:

(a) Whether the interests of all parties, including third parties whose interests may be affected, could be harmed if the client or employer consents to the disclosure of information by the professional accountant.

(b) Whether all the relevant information is known and substantiated, to the extent it is practicable; when the situation involves unsubstantiated facts, incomplete information or unsubstantiated conclusions, professional judgment should be used in determining the type of disclosure to be made, if any.

(c) The type of communication that is expected and to whom it is addressed; in particular, professional accountants should be satisfied that the parties to whom the communication is addressed are appropriate recipients.

10.2 Section 220 of CIMA's Code of conduct Preparation and Reporting of Information

Professional accountants in business are often involved in the preparation and reporting of information that may either be made public or used by others inside or outside the employing organisation. Such information may include financial or management information, for example, forecasts and budgets, financial statements, management discussion and analysis, and the management letter of representation provided to the auditors as part of an audit of financial statements. A professional accountant in business should prepare or present such information fairly, honestly and in accordance with relevant professional standards so that the information will be understood in its context.

A professional accountant in business who has responsibility for the preparation or approval of the general purpose financial statements of an employing organisation should ensure that those financial statements are presented in accordance with the applicable financial reporting standards.

A professional accountant in business should maintain information for which the professional accountant in business is responsible in a manner that:

(a) Describes clearly the true nature of business transactions, assets or liabilities
(b) Classifies and records information in a timely and proper manner
(c) Represents the facts accurately and completely in all material respects.

Threats to compliance with the fundamental principles, for example self-interest or intimidation threats to objectivity or professional competence and due care, may be created where a professional accountant in business may be pressured (either externally or by the possibility of personal gain) to become associated with misleading information or to become associated with misleading information through the actions of others.

The significance of such threats will depend on factors such as the source of the pressure and the degree to which the information is, or may be, misleading. The significance of the threats should be evaluated and, if they are other than clearly insignificant, safeguards should be considered and applied as necessary to eliminate them or reduce them to an acceptable level. Such safeguards may include consultation with superiors within the employing organisation, for example, the audit committee or other body responsible for governance, or with a relevant professional body.

Where it is not possible to reduce the threat to an acceptable level, a professional accountant in business should refuse to remain associated with information they consider is or may be misleading. Should the professional accountant in business be aware that the issuance of misleading information is either significant or persistent, the professional accountant in business should consider informing appropriate authorities in line with the guidance in Section 140 of the code. The professional accountant in business may also wish to seek legal advice or resign.

More information on code of ethics can be found on the CIMA website. http://www1.cimaglobal.com/cps/rde/xbcr/SID-0AE7C4D1-04D0658E/live/CodeofEthics_October07.pdf

Published Financial Statements

Published Financial Statements

11

LEARNING OUTCOME

On completion of their studies students should be able to:

► prepare a complete set of financial statements in a form suitable for publication for a single company.

Learning aims

The learning aims of this part of the syllabus are that students should be able to: 'prepare statutory accounts in appropriate form for a single company'.

With this chapter we commence the third section of the syllabus, section C. This section is a very important part of your studies and accounts for 60 per cent of your syllabus. Questions based on this section will appear in all three sections of the examination paper. The third section of the examination paper will comprise questions entirely from this section of the syllabus.

This text is based on IFRSs in force at January 2009. It includes all revisions made to IFRSs within the syllabus, during 2008.

The syllabus topics covered in this chapter are as follows:

• Preparation of the financial statements of a single company, as specified in IAS 1 (revised), including the statement of changes in equity.

11.1 Introduction

You will have prepared financial statements for sole traders and been introduced to the elements found in entity financial statements, either in the certificate level or in the examinations giving exemption from *Financial Accounting Fundamentals*. The work we will do at the operational level builds on that knowledge, so it would be advisable to refresh your knowledge of these areas before proceeding (The accounts of limited companies are covered in the CIMA study text for *Fundamentals of Financial Accounting*.)

The focus of the preparation of financial statements at this level is on entity financial statements that are prepared in a form suitable for publication. To ensure consistency and comparability of the information provided, the IASB prescribes the content for the main statements included in published financial statements.

IAS 1 was revised in 2007, the new version applies to financial statements beginning on or after 1 January 2009. The revised IAS 1 has made a number of changes to the terminology used in financial statements and changed the title of some of the statements and their content. The new terminology applies to all other IFRSs, these are changed by IAS 1 where appropriate.

Summary of the main changes made to terminology by IAS 1 revised 2007:

- 'On the face of' is amended to 'in'.
- 'Income statement' is amended to 'statement of comprehensive income'.
- 'Balance sheet' is amended to 'statement of financial position'.
- 'Cash flow statement' is amended to 'statement of cash flows'.
- 'Balance sheet date' is amended to 'end of the reporting period'.
- 'Equity holders' is amended to 'owners'.
- 'Removed from equity and recognized in profit or loss' and 'removed from equity and included in profit or loss' are amended to 'reclassified from equity to profit or loss as a reclassification adjustment'.
- 'Standard or Interpretation' is amended 'IFRS'.
- 'Standards and Interpretations' is amended to 'IFRSs'.
- References to the current version of IAS 7 Statement of Cash Flows.
- References to the current version of IAS 10 Events after the Balance Sheet Date are amended to IAS 10 Events after the Reporting Period.

This text has been written using the new IAS 1 terminology, the IFRSs are referred to by the new titles and the financial statements are referred to by the new titles through out the text, questions and answers.

This chapter will first discuss the general requirements for published financial statements and will then concentrate on the formats for the statement of financial position and the statement of comprehensive income, identifying the items to be presented in these statements and those to be included in the notes to the accounts.

The chapter focuses on the presentation aspects of the accounts, specifically addressed in IAS 1 (revised 2007) *Presentation of Financial Statements*. Accounting for and disclosing the effects of individual transactions will be covered in later chapters; however, the presentation requirements covered in this chapter will still apply.

Extracts from actual entity accounts cannot be included for the new formats as they are not mandatory until 2009 and entities have not published any financial statements using the new terminology and formats at the date of writing.

11.2 General requirements

11.2.1 Purpose of financial statements

IAS 1 states that financial statements are a structured financial representation of the financial position of an entity, showing the effect of the transactions it has undertaken.

We know from Chapter 8 that the objective of financial statements is to provide information about the financial position, performance and cash flows of an entity that is useful to a wide range of users in making economic decisions.

To meet this objective, financial statements provide information about an entity's

- assets
- liabilities
- equity
- income and expenses, including gains and losses
- contributions by and distributions to owners in their capacity as owners
- cash flows.

This information, together with information contained in accompanying notes, assists users in evaluating the entity's future cash flows.

11.2.2 Responsibility for financial statements

The board of directors (and/or other governing body) of an entity is responsible for the preparation and presentation of its financial statements.

11.2.3 Components of financial statements

A complete set of financial statements normally includes:

- statement of financial position at the end of the period
- statement of comprehensive income for the period
- a statement of changes in equity for the period
- statement of cash flow for the period
- notes comprising a summary of significant accounting policies and other explanatory information.
- statement of financial position as at the start of the earliest comparative period, if the entity applies a change in accounting policy retrospectively or restates items in earlier periods or reclassifies items in its financial statements.

Entities are encouraged (but not required) to also present a financial review by management describing and explaining the main features of the entities' financial performance and financial position and the principal uncertainties it faces. This review may include:

- a description of the environment in which the entity operates
- changes in the environment and how management has responded to them
- resources not recognised in the balance sheet in accordance with IFRSs
- management policies on investment and dividends.

11.2.4 Fair presentation and compliance with IFRSs

Financial statements should present fairly the financial position, financial performance and cash flows of an entity. Fair presentation requires the faithful representation of the effects of transactions, other events and conditions in accordance with the definitions and recognition criteria for assets, liabilities, income and expenses set out in the Framework. The application of IFRSs, with additional disclosure when necessary, is presumed to result in financial statements that achieve a fair presentation. In virtually all circumstances, a fair presentation is achieved by compliance with applicable IFRSs. A fair presentation also requires an entity:

(a) to select and apply accounting policies in accordance with IAS 8 *Accounting Policies, Changes in Accounting Estimates and Errors*. IAS 8 sets out a hierarchy of authoritative guidance that management considers in the absence of a Standard or an Interpretation that specifically applies to an item;

(b) to present information, including accounting policies, in a manner that provides relevant, reliable, comparable and understandable information; and

(c) to provide additional disclosures when compliance with the specific requirements in IFRSs is insufficient to enable users to understand the impact of particular transactions, other events and conditions on the entity's financial position and financial performance.

Inappropriate accounting policies are not rectified either by disclosure of the accounting policies used or by notes or explanatory material.

Compliance with IFRSs requires that all relevant standards are complied with. IFRSs refer to international standards and IFRIC/SIC interpretations adopted by the IASB. When this text refers to IFRSs, it is referring to:

- IFRSs
- IASs
- IFRIC interpretations
- SIC interpretations.

Entities should disclose the fact that they comply with IFRSs in the financial statements. This compliance statement is often included in the accounting policies and is usually the first stated policy.

Departure from requirements

In the unlikely event that the management decides that compliance with a particular requirement would result in misleading information, which would conflict with the objective of financial statements set out in the framework, they can *depart from that requirement in order to achieve fair presentation*. In this event, the entity should disclose:

- that management has concluded that the financial statements present fairly the entity's financial position, financial performance and cash flows;
- that it has complied with all relevant IFRSs except that it has departed from a standard to achieve fair presentation;
- the IFRS that it has departed from and details of the required treatment, why it was misleading and the treatment that has been adopted; and
- the financial impact of the departure for each period presented.

11.2.5 Other requirements affecting the preparation of financial statements

IAS 1 also outlines the following requirements for the preparation of financial statements. (Most of these you will be already familiar with, but are included for completeness.)

- *Accounting policies* should be selected so that financial statements will comply with IFRSs.
- Management should make an assessment of the entity's ability to continue as a going concern. Financial statements should then be prepared on a *going concern* basis, unless there are plans to liquidate or cease trading.

- The financial statements should be prepared under the *accruals basis* of accounting, with the exception of the cash flow information.
- The financial statements should retain a *consistent approach to presentation* and classification of items year-on-year.
- *Material amounts* should be *presented separately* in the financial statements. Immaterial amounts should be aggregated with other like items.
- *Assets and liabilities should not be offset,* except where required or permitted by another IFRS.
- *Income and expenses* should not be offset except where it is required or permitted by another IFRS.
- *Comparative information* should be disclosed for the previous period for all numerical information. Where presentation or classification of an item has changed, the comparative figures should be restated using the new treatment, if possible.
- Financial statements should be *presented at least annually* and should be issued on a timely basis (within 6 months of the end of the reporting period) to be useful to users.

IAS 1 does not specify the format of financial statements, but it does provide an appendix which sets out illustrative formats for the statements to be included in financial statements. In addition, it provides guidance on the items that should be disclosed in these statements and those that can be relegated to the notes that accompany the statements.

11.3   The statement of financial position

11.3.1   Specimen statement of financial position

A specimen statement of financial position (based on that provided in IAS 1) is set out below, this shows the minimum requirements for disclosure in the statement of financial position.

Take a moment to study the statement of financial position headings. The statement has two main sections – Assets and Equities and Liabilities. Most of the headings within the statement will be familiar to you, for example, property, plant and equipment, inventories, issued capital, reserves, trade and other payables. Most entities will have amounts that relate to these headings that are sufficiently material that they appear in the statement of financial position. Some of the other headings may not be so familiar, for example, goodwill. These amounts will only appear in the statement of financial position if the reporting entity has relevant amounts relating to these account categories.

IAS 1 (revised 2007) Specimen Format

Statement of financial position as at 31 December 20X8

	$'000	$'000
Assets		
Non-current assets		
Property, plant and equipment	X	
Goodwill	X	
Other intangible assets	X	
Available for sale investments	X̲	X
		X
Current assets		
Inventories	X	
Trade receivables	X	
Other current assets	X	
Cash and cash equivalents	X̲	
		X̲
Total assets		X̲
Equity and liabilities		
Equity		
Share capital	X	
Other components of equity	X	
Retained earnings	X̲	
Total equity		X
Non-current liabilities		
Long-term borrowings	X	
Deferred tax	X	
Long term provisions	X̲	
Total non-current liabilities		X
Current liabilities		
Trade and other payables	X	
Short-term borrowings	X	
Current portion of long-term borrowings	X	
Current tax payable	X	
Short term provisions	X̲	
Total current liabilities		X̲
Total liabilities		X̲
Total equity and liabilities		X̲

The format requires comparative figures for the previous year, these have been omitted as you will not need to prepare comparatives in questions.

11.3.2 Information to be presented in the statement of financial position

IAS 1 requires that, as a minimum, the following line items appear in the statement of financial position (where there are amounts to be classified within these categories):

(a) property, plant and equipment;
(b) investment property;
(c) intangible assets;
(d) financial assets (excluding amounts shown under (e), (h) and (i));
(e) investments accounted for using the equity method;**

(f) biological assets;

(g) inventories;

(h) trade and other receivables;

(i) cash and cash equivalents;

(j) the total of assets classified as held for sale in accordance with IFRS 5 *Non-current assets held for sale and discontinued operations*;

(k) trade and other payables;

(l) provisions;

(m) financial liabilities (excluding amounts shown under (k) or (l));

(n) liabilities and assets for current tax as defined in IAS 12, *Income Taxes*;

(o) deferred tax liabilities and deferred tax assets, as defined in IAS 12, *Income Taxes*;

(p) liabilities included in disposal groups classified as held for sale in accordance with IFRS 5;

(q) minority interest, presented within equity;**

(r) issued capital and reserves attributable to owners of the parent.

** These items relate to group accounts and are beyond the scope of this syllabus.

The above list includes items that the IASB believes are so different in nature or function that they should be separately disclosed, but *does not require them to appear in a fixed order or format*.

Additional line items, headings and subtotals should be shown in the statement of financial position if another IFRS requires it or where it is necessary to show a fair presentation of the financial position.

In deciding whether *additional items* should be separately presented, management should consider:

- the *nature and liquidity of assets* and their materiality (e.g. the separate disclosure of monetary and non-monetary amounts and current and non-current assets);
- their *function* within the entity (e.g. the separate disclosure of operating assets and financial assets, inventories and cash); and
- the *amounts, nature and timing of liabilities* (e.g. the separate disclosure of interest-bearing and non-interest-bearing liabilities and provisions and current and non-current liabilities).

Assets and liabilities that have a different nature or function within an entity are sometimes subject to different measurement bases, for example, plant and equipment may be carried at cost or held at a revalued amount (in accordance with IAS 16). The use of these different measurement bases for different classes of items suggests separate presentation is necessary for users to fully understand the accounts.

11.3.3 Information to be presented either in the statement of financial position or in the notes

Further subclassifications of the line items should be presented either in the statement of financial position or in the notes. The *size, nature and function* of the amounts involved, or the *requirements of another IFRS* will normally determine whether the disclosure is in the statement of financial position or in the notes.

The disclosures will vary for each item, but IAS 1 gives the following examples:

(a) *tangible assets* are analysed (IAS 16) by class: property, plant and equipment;
(b) *receivables* are analysed between:
   • amounts receivable from trade customers
   • receivables from related parties
   • prepayments
   • other amounts;
(c) *inventories* are classified (IAS 2) into merchandise, production supplies, materials, work in progress and finished goods;
(d) *provisions* are analysed showing provisions for employee benefits separate from any other provisions;
(e) *equity capital and reserves* are analysed showing separately the various classes of paid-in capital, share premium and reserves.

11.3.4 Share capital and reserves disclosures

IAS 1 also requires that the following information on share capital and reserves be made *either in the statement of financial position or in the notes*:

(a) *for each class of share capital*:
   • the *number* of shares *authorised*,
   • the number of shares *issued and fully paid*, and issued but not fully paid,
   • *par value* per share, or that the shares have no par value,
   • *a reconciliation* of the number of shares outstanding at the beginning and at the end of the year,
   • the *rights, preferences and restrictions* attaching to that class, including restrictions on the distribution of dividends and the repayment of capital,
   • *shares* in the entity *held by the entity itself* or by subsidiaries or associates of the entity, and
   • shares reserved for issuance under *options and sales contracts*, including the terms and amounts;
(b) a description of the *nature and purpose of each reserve* within owners' equity;
   IAS 1 requires the following to be disclosed in the notes:
   • the amount of *dividends* that were proposed or declared after the reporting period but before the financial statements were authorised for issue;
   • the amount of any *cumulative preference dividends* not recognised.

Note: IAS 1 and IAS 10 do not allow proposed dividends to be included as a liability in the statement of financial position, unless the dividend was declared before the end of the reporting period.

11.3.5 The current/non-current distinction

An entity shall present current and non-current assets and current and non-current liabilities as separate classifications in the statement of financial position except when a presentation based on liquidity provides information that is reliable and more relevant.

Where an entity chooses not to classify by current and non-current, assets and liabilities should be presented broadly in order of their liquidity.

Whichever method of presentation is adopted, an entity should disclose, for each asset and liability, the amount that is expected to be recovered or settled *after more than 12 months.*

Most entities will show both current and non-current liabilities in the statement of financial position. However, say, for example, an entity does not normally have non-current trade liabilities but as a result of one particular transaction has a payable due 20 months from the end of the reporting period. The entity may, in this case, classify the entire amount as a trade payable under current liabilities and then show separately a one-off amount that is due in 20 months' time (i.e. in more than 12 months from the end of the reporting period).

In judging the most suitable presentation, management should consider the usefulness of the information they are providing. Information about the financial position of an entity is often used to predict the expected future cash flows and the timing of those cash flows. Information about the expected date of recovery and settlement of items is likely to be useful and therefore worth disclosing.

11.3.6 Current assets

An asset should be classified as a current asset when it is any of the following:

(a) is expected to be realised in, or is intended for sale or consumption in the entity's normal operating cycle;
(b) is held primarily for trading purposes;
(c) is expected to be realised within 12 months of the end of the reporting period; or
(d) is cash or cash equivalent.

All other assets should be classified as non-current assets.

11.3.7 Current liabilities

A liability should be classified as a current liability when it:

(a) is expected to be settled in the entity's normal operating cycle;
(b) is due to be settled within 12 months of the end of the reporting period;
(c) is held primarily for the purpose of being traded; or
(d) the entity does not have an unconditional right to defer settlement of the liability for at least 12 months after the end of the reporting period;

All other liabilities should be classified as non-current liabilities.

11.4 The statement of comprehensive income

IAS 1 (2007) requires an entity to present all items of income and expense recognised in the period, whether realised or unrealised, either:

(a) in a single statement of comprehensive income
(b) in two statements;
  (i) an income statement covering components of profit or loss;
  (ii) a statement comprehensive income that begins with profit or loss from the income statement and then adds/subtracts components of other comprehensive income.

11.4.1 Information to be presented in the statement of comprehensive income

IAS 1 requires that certain information (as a minimum) is presented in the statement of comprehensive income, including:

(a) revenue;
(b) finance costs;
(c) share of profits and losses of associates and joint ventures accounted for using the equity method (beyond the scope of this syllabus);
(d) tax expense;
(e) the total of the post tax profit or loss of discontinued operations and the post tax gain or loss recognised on the remeasurement to fair value less cost to sell, or on the disposal of the assets or disposal group constituting the discontinued operation;
(f) profit or loss;
(g) each component of other comprehensive income classified by nature (excluding amounts in (h));
(h) share of other comprehensive income of associates and joint ventures
(i) total comprehensive income.

Additional line items, headings and subtotals should be shown in the statement of comprehensive income if another IFRS requires it or where it is necessary to show a fair presentation of the financial position.

Materiality, the nature and function of the item are likely to be the main considerations when deciding whether to include an additional line item in the statement of comprehensive income.

11.4.2 Specimen statements of comprehensive income

Specimen statements of comprehensive income (based on those provided in IAS 1) are given below. Headings relating to items outside the scope of the syllabus have been omitted.

Statement of comprehensive income illustrating the presentation of comprehensive income in one statement

This first part illustrates the presentation of comprehensive income in one statement and the classification of expenses within profit by function.

Statement of comprehensive income for the year ended 31 December 20X8

	$'000
Revenue	X
Cost of sales	X
Gross profit	X
Other income	X
Distribution costs	(X)
Administrative expenses	(X)
Other expenses	(X)
Finance costs	(X)
Profit before tax	X
Income tax expense	(X)
Profit for the year from continuing operations	X
Loss for the year from discontinued operations	(X)
PROFIT FOR THE YEAR	X
Other comprehensive income:	
Available-for-sale financial assets	X
Gains on property revaluation	
Income tax relating to components of other comprehensive income	(X)
Other comprehensive income for the year, net of tax	X
TOTAL COMPREHENSIVE INCOME FOR THE YEAR	XX

Note that as an alternative the components of comprehensive income can be presented net of tax.

Statement of comprehensive income illustrating the presentation of comprehensive income in two statements

An entity may present two statements instead of one; a separate income statement and a statement of comprehensive income. In this case the statement of comprehensive income starts with the profit or loss from the income statement and includes components of other comprehensive income (items g to h above).

This second part illustrates the presentation of comprehensive income in two statements and classification of expenses within profit by function.

Income Statement for the year ended 31 December 20X8

	$'000
Revenue	X
Cost of sales	X
Gross profit	X
Other income	X
Distribution costs	(X)
Administrative expenses	(X)
Other expenses	(X)
Finance costs	(X)
Profit before tax	X
Income tax expense	(X)
Profit for the year from continuing operations	X
Loss for the year from discontinued operations	(X)
PROFIT FOR THE YEAR	X

XYZ Group – Statement of comprehensive income for the year ended 31 December 20X8

	$'000
Profit for the year	**XX**
Other comprehensive income:	
Available-for-sale financial assets	X
Gains on property revaluation	X
Income tax relating to components of other comprehensive income	X
Other comprehensive income for the year, net of tax	**X**
TOTAL COMPREHENSIVE INCOME FOR THE YEAR	**X**

Note that as an alternative the components of comprehensive income can be presented net of tax. This text will refer to the statement of comprehensive income where the full statement is used and will continue to refer to the income statement where either a two statement approach is used or where there are no entries to be disclosed in the 'other comprehensive income section'.

11.4.3 Information to be presented either in the statement of comprehensive income or in the notes

Certain items must be disclosed either in the statement of comprehensive income or in the notes, if material, including:

(a) write-downs of inventories or property, plant & equipment and reversals of write-downs;
(b) restructurings of the activities and reversals of any related provisions;
(c) disposals of property, plant and equipment;
(d) disposals of investments;
(e) discontinued operations;
(f) litigation settlements;
(g) other reversals of provisions.

An entity should present an *analysis of expenses* using a classification based on either the nature of expenses or their function within the entity.

This analysis can be in the statement of comprehensive income (which is encouraged) or in the notes.

Analysis of expenses – classification, nature of expenses

An analysis based on the *nature of expenses* would, for example, result in classifications for depreciation, purchases, wages and salaries, marketing costs, etc. The expenses would be presented in total for each type of expense. This format is normally adopted by manufacturing entities.

The analysis could look like this:

Revenue		X
Other income		X
Changes in inventories of finished goods and work in progress	X	
Raw materials and consumables used	X	
Employee benefits expense	X	
Depreciation and amortisation expense	X	
Impairment of property, plant and equipment	X	
Other expenses	X	
Total expenses		(X)
Finance costs		(X)
Profit before tax		X

The first item of expense in this format may be slightly confusing – changes in inventories of finished goods and work in progress. The change represents an adjustment to production expenses to reflect the fact that either:

- production has increased inventory levels, or
- sales exceeds production activity resulting in a reduction in inventory levels.

Note that changes in raw materials inventories are not included here. The change in raw materials inventories is in the next expense line and can be calculated as follows:

Opening inventory of raw materials	X
Plus: purchases of raw materials	X
	X
Less: closing inventory of raw materials	(X)
Raw materials and consumables used	X

Analysis of expenses – classification, function of expenses

An analysis based on the *function of the expense* (or cost of sales method) classifies expenses according to their function as part of cost of sales, distribution or administrative activities.

While this presentation can provide more relevant information to users, the allocation of costs to functions can often be arbitrary.

The analysis could look like this:

Revenue	X
Cost of sales	(X)
Gross profit	X
Other income	X
Distribution costs	(X)
Administrative expenses	(X)
Other expenses	(X)
Finance costs	(X)
Profit before tax	X

Entities choosing to classify expenses by function should disclose additional information on the nature of expenses, including depreciation and amortisation expense and employee benefits expense.

The entity should choose the analysis that is reliable and more relevant to the business activities.

 Most examination questions focus on the analysis by function, but occasional questions on analysis by nature of expense may occur.

Dividend disclosures

An entity should disclose either in the statement of changes in equity or in the notes, the amount of dividends recognised as distributions to owners in the period, and the amount of *dividends per share*. An entity must disclose in the notes the amount of dividends proposed or declared but not recognised as a distribution to owners during the period.

11.5 Changes in equity

Changes in an entity's equity between two reporting period ends reflect the *increase or decrease in its net assets* or wealth during the period.

This information is useful to users as changes, excluding changes resulting from transactions with shareholders (e.g. capital injections and dividends) represents the total gains and losses generated by the entity in the period.

IAS 1 requires that certain information relating to equity be presented separately in a *statement of changes in equity.*

An entity must present, as a separate component of its financial statements, a statement showing:

(a) the *total comprehensive income* for the period, showing separately the total amounts attributable to owners of the parent and to minority interest;
(b) for each component of equity the effects of retrospective application or retrospective restatement recognised in accordance with IAS 8.
(c) transactions with owners in their capacity as owners, showing separately contributions by and distributions to owners;
(d) a *reconciliation* between the carrying amount of *each class of contributed equity and each reserve* at the beginning and end of the period, separately disclosing each movement.

The changes made by IAS 1 in 2007 mean that there is now only one format used for the statement of changes in equity. The specimen format provided by IAS 1 is given below.

11.5.1 Format for the statement of changes in equity

Specimen entity statement of changes in equity from IAS 1 (simplified by excluding items that are outside this syllabus).

Statement of changes in equity for the year ended 31 December 20X8

	Share capital $'000	Other reserves* $'000	Retained earnings $'000	Total $'000
Balance at 31 December 20X7	X	X	X	X
Changes in accounting policy			X	X
Restated balance	X	X	X	X
Changes in equity for 20X8				
Total comprehensive income for the period		X	X	X
Dividends			(X)	(X)
Transfer to retained earnings		(X)		X
issue of share capital	X			X
Balance at 31 December 20X8	X	X	X	X

* Other reserves are analysed into their components if materials

The above format provides a reconciliation between the opening and closing balances of each element within shareholders' equity.

11.6 Notes to financial statements

Notes to the financial statements normally include narrative descriptions or more detailed analysis of items in the financial statements, as well as additional information such as contingent liabilities and commitments.

IAS 1 also provides guidance on the structure of the accompanying notes to financial statements, the accounting policies and other required disclosures.

The notes to the financial statements of an entity should:

(a) present information about the *basis of preparation* of the financial statements and the specific *accounting policies* adopted for significant transactions;

(b) disclose the *information required by other IFRSs* that is not presented elsewhere in the financial statements;

(c) provide *additional information* which is not presented elsewhere in financial statements but is relevant to an understanding of any of them.

Notes to the financial statements should be presented in a systematic manner and any item in the financial statements should be *cross-referenced* to any related information in the notes.

Notes are normally provided in the following order, which assists users in understanding the financial statements and comparing them with those of other entities:

(a) statement of compliance with IFRSs;

(b) summary of the significant accounting policies applied;

(c) supporting information for items presented in each financial statement in the order in which each line item and each financial statement is presented;

(d) other disclosures, including:

- contingent liabilities, commitments and unrecognised contractual commitments other financial disclosures;

- non-financial disclosures.

11.6.1 Accounting policies

The summary of significant accounting policies in the notes to the financial statements should describe the following:

(a) the measurement basis (or bases) used in preparing the financial statements; and
(b) each specific accounting policy that is necessary for a proper understanding of the financial statements.

11.7 An illustrative question

Before completing the revision questions, please work through this illustrative question.

As you work through it, refer back to the relevant section of this chapter to see how the formats and disclosure requirements are adopted.

This illustrative question is a past CIMA examination question.

Scenario

The following information relates to V, a manufacturing entity.

Trial balance at 30 September 20X8

	Notes	$'000	$'000
Revenue			430
Inventory at 1 October 20X7		10	
Purchases		102	
Advertising		15	
Administration salaries		14	
Manufacturing wages		57	
Interest paid		14	
Dividends received	(e)		12
Audit fee		7	
Bad debts		10	
Taxation	(d) & (g)	10	
Dividends paid	(e)	120	
Premises (cost)	(b)	450	
Plant (cost)	(c)	280	
Premises (depreciation)			40
Plant (depreciation)			160
Investments (long term)		100	
Trade receivables		23	
Bank		157	
Payables			7
Deferred taxation	(f)		89
Loan notes			140
Share capital			100
Retained earnings at 1 October 20X7			391
		1,369	1,369

Notes

(a) Inventory was worth $13,000 on 30 September 20X8.
(b) Premises consist of land costing $250,000 and buildings costing $200,000. The buildings have an expected useful life of 50 years.

(c) Plant includes an item purchased during the year at a cost of $70,000. These were the only transactions involving non-current assets during the year.

Depreciation of plant is to be charged at 10 per cent per annum on a straight-line basis.

(d) The balance on the tax account is an underprovision for tax brought forward from the year ended 30 September 20X7.

(e) The entity paid $48,000 on 27 November 20X7 as a final dividend for the year ended 30 September 20X8. A dividend of $12,000 was received on 13 January 20X8. The 20X8 interim dividend was paid on 15 April 20X8.

(f) The provision for deferred tax is to be reduced by $17,000.

(g) The directors have estimated that tax of $57,000 will be due on the profits of the year.

(h) The directors have proposed a final dividend for the year of $50,000.

Requirement

Prepare a single statement of comprehensive income (analysing expenses by income) for V for the year ended 30 September 20X8, a statement of changes in equity and a statement of financial position at that date. These should be in a form suitable for presentation to the shareholders in accordance with the requirements of IFRSs and be accompanied by notes to the accounts as far as is possible from the information given above.

You are *not* required to prepare the note relating to accounting policies.   **(25 marks)**

Discussion

This question carries 25 marks. You would therefore have 45 minutes to do it in an examination. You will only build up to that speed with a lot of practice. The question requires the expenses within profit to be disclosed by function, so we need to work out the totals for cost of sales, distribution costs and administrative expense.

Let us go through the question and pause to think about items needing attention. It is useful to begin with the additional information below the trial balance, deciding what to do with them and marking the related items in the trial balance where necessary.

Notes (a) and (b) and (c) are routine adjustments to inventory and non-current tangible assets.

Note (e) tells us about dividends received and paid. Dividends paid on 27 November 2007 relates to dividends from the previous financial year so we ignore the $48000. The dividends received is classed as other income and will go in the statement of comprehensive income after Gross profit.

Note (f) gives us a straightforward movement on deferred tax.

Note (g) gives us the tax charge for the year and note (d) tells us about the underprovision of current tax in the previous year.

Note (h) gives us the proposed final dividend.

Now for the trial balance

- Revenue, put into the profit or loss section of the statement of comprehensive income
- *Inventory at 1 October 20X7*
- *Purchases*
- *Advertising*
- *Administration salaries*
- *Manufacturing wages.*

All these items go into a three-column working to arrive at the three disclosable totals – cost of sales, distribution costs and administrative expenses.

	Cost of sales $'000	Distribution costs $'000	Administrative expenses $'000
Inventory 1.10.X7	10		
Purchases	75		
Advertising		15	
Administrative salaries			14
Manufacturing wages, etc.	57		

For the rest of this working, see the answer below.

Returning to the trial balance, the items given here clearly direct us to the function of expense format for the profit or loss.

- *Interest paid.* There is no complication here. We simply include it as an expense at the correct place in the format. There is another point, not relevant for this question. Always check to confirm that the interest charge is for the full year, to find out whether an adjustment is needed. For example, if the trial balance includes 10 per cent loan notes $100,000 and interest paid is $5,000, clearly an accrual of $5,000 is required, unless the loan notes were issued halfway through the current year.
- *Audit fee.* Include in the expense working.
- *Bad debts.* Include in the expense working.
- *Taxation.* We shall need a working account for taxation (covered in detail in Chapter 6).
- *Dividend.* This is the interim dividend paid explained in note (e). The proposed dividend cannot be accrued, but must be disclosed as a note.

The remaining items are all routine statement of financial position headings.

V – Statement of comprehensive income for the year ended 30 September 20X8

Ref. To Notes		$'000	$'000
	Sales revenue		430
	Cost of sales		(188)
	Gross profit		242
1	Other income		12
	Distribution costs	(25)	
	Administrative expenses	(21)	(46)
			208
	Finance cost		(14)
	Profit before tax		194
2.	Income tax expense		(50)
	Net profit for the period		144
	Other comprehensive income		0
	Total comprehensive income for the year		144

V – Statement of financial position as at 30 September 20X8

Ref. To Notes		$'000	$'000
3.	Assets		
	Non-current assets		
	Property, plant and equipment		498
	Investments		100
			598
	Current assets		
	Inventory	13	
	Trade receivables	23	
	Cash and cash equivalents	157	
			193
	Total Assets		791
	Equity and Liabilities		
	Equity		
	Share capital	100	
	Retained earnings	415	
			515
	Non-current liabilities		
	Loan notes	140	
4.	Deferred tax	72	
			212
5.	*Current liabilities*		
	Trade and other payables	7	
	Current tax	57	
			64
	Total equity and liabilities		791

V – Statement of changes in equity for the year ended 30 September 20X8

	Share capital $'000	Retained earnings $'000	Total $'000
Balance at 30 September 20X7	100	391	491
Total comprehensive income for the period		144	144
Dividend paid		(120)	(120)
Balance at 30 September 20X8	100	415	515

Notes

1. *Profit from operations (required here as expenses are shown by function, see 10.4.3)*

Profit from operations is arrived at after charging:

	$'000
Depreciation	32
Staff costs	74

2. *Taxation (profit or loss)*

	$'000
Taxation estimated for this year	57
Transfer from deferred tax	(17)
	40
Underprovision for previous year	10
Charge to profit or loss	50

3. *Dividends proposed*

A final dividend of $50,000 is proposed for the year.

4. *Tangible non-current assets*

	Land and buildings $'000	*Plant* $'000	*Total* $'000
Cost 1 October 20X7	450	210	660
Additions	0	70	70
	450	280	730
Depreciation 1 October 20X7	(40)	(160)	(200)
Charge for year	(4)	(28)	(32)
	(44)	(188)	(232)
NBV 30 September 20X8	406	92	498
NBV 1 October 20X7	410	50	460

5. *Deferred taxation*

	$'000
Opening balance	89
Decrease in provision	(17)
Closing balance	72

Workings

Analysis of expenses

	Cost of sales $'000	*Distribution costs* $'000	*Administrative expenses* $'000
Opening inventory	10		
Purchases	102		
Advertising		15	
Administration salaries			14
Manufacturing wages	57		
Audit fee			7
Bad debts		10	
Depreciation:			
building	4		
plant	28		
Closing inventory	(13)		
	188	25	21

11.8 Summary

Having completed this chapter, we can now explain the general requirements for the preparation of published financial statements as set out by IAS 1.

We are familiar with the recommended layouts of the main components of financial statements being statement of financial position, statement of comprehensive income and statement of changes in equity (statement of cash flows is covered in Chapter 13) and can adopt these formats in the preparation of financial statements.

Revision Questions

11

In the exam you may have to produce financial statements in a form suitable for publication. Use these examples to build your knowledge of the formats provided by IAS 1. You need to learn them.

Data for Questions 1 and 2

Trade receivables as at 31 December 20X1 were $18,000.

The bad debt provision as at 1 January 20X1 was $900.

During the year, bad debts of $12,000 have been written off to administrative expenses.

After the year-end, but before the accounts had been completed, the entity discovered that a major customer had gone into liquidation and that their outstanding balance of $2,000 was unlikely to be paid.

Furthermore, as a result of the recent bad debt experience, the directors have decided to increase the bad debt provision at 31 December 20X1 to 10 per cent of outstanding trade receivables.

? Question 1

What is the correct balance for trade receivables, net of bad debt provision, as at 31 December 20X1?

(A) $3,600
(B) $5,400
(C) $14,400
(D) $16,200   (2 marks)

? Question 2

What is the correct charge to the statement of comprehensive income for bad debts and bad debt provisions for the year to 31 December 20X1?

(A) $14,000
(B) $14,400
(C) $14,700
(D) $15,600   (2 marks)

Question 3

IAS 1 *Presentation of financial statements* requires some of the items to be disclosed in the financial statements and others to be disclosed in the notes.

  (i) Depreciation
 (ii) Revenue
(iii) Closing inventory
(iv) Finance cost
 (v) Dividends

 Which TWO of the above have to be shown in profit or loss, rather than in the notes:

(A) (i) and (iv)
(B) (iii) and (v)
(C) (ii) and (iii)
(D) (ii) and (iv)   **(2 marks)**

 Question 4

IAS 1 *Presentation of Financial Statements* encourages an analysis of expenses to be presented in a statement of comprehensive income. The analysis of expenses must use a classification based on either the nature of expense, or its function, within the entity such as:

  (i) Raw materials and consumables used
 (ii) Distribution costs
(iii) Employee benefit costs
(iv) Cost of sales
 (v) Depreciation and amortisation expense.

 Which of the above would be disclosed in profit or loss if a manufacturing entity uses analysis based on function?

(A) (i), (iii) and (iv)
(B) (ii) and (iv)
(C) (i) and (v)
(D) (ii), (iii) and (v)   **(2 marks)**

 Question 5

The following is an extract from the trial balance of CE at 31 March 2008:

	$'000	$'000
Administration expenses	260	
Cost of sales	480	
Interest paid	190	
Interest bearing borrowings		2,200
Inventory at 31 March 2008	220	
Property, plant and equipment at cost	1,500	
Property, plant and equipment, depreciation to 31 March 2007		540
Distribution costs	200	
Revenue		2,000

Notes:

(i) Included in the closing inventory at the end of the reporting period was inventory at a cost of $35,000, which was sold during April 2008 for $19,000.

(ii) Depreciation is provided for on property, plant and equipment at 20 per cent per year using the reducing balance method. Depreciation is regarded as cost of sales.

(iii) A member of the public was seriously injured while using one of CE's products on 4 October 2007. Professional legal advice is that CE will probably have to pay $500,000 compensation.

Requirement

Prepare CE's Statement of Comprehensive income for the year ended 31 March 2008 down to the line 'profit before tax'. **(5 marks)**

❓ Question 6

The following information has been extracted from the accounting reports of P:

P – trial balance at 31 March 20X8

	$'000	$'000
Sales revenue		5,300
Cost of sales	1,350	
Dividends received		210
Administrative expenses	490	
Distribution costs	370	
Interest payable	190	
Income tax	25	
Dividends paid	390	
Property, plant and equipment	4,250	
Short-term investments	2,700	
Inventory	114	
Trade receivables	418	
Bank	12	
Trade payables		136
Long-term loans (repayable 20Y1)		1,200
Share capital		1,500
Share premium		800
Accumulated profits		1,163
	10,309	10,309

(a) During the year, P paid a final dividend of $240,000 in respect of the year ended 31 March 20X7. This was in addition to the interim dividend paid on 1 September 20X0 in respect of the year ended 31 March 20X8.

(b) The balance on the taxation account comprises the balance remaining from the settlement of the estimated tax charge for the year ended 31 March 20X7. The tax charge for this year has been estimated at $470,000.

(c) The directors have proposed a final dividend of $270,000.

Requirement

Prepare a statement of comprehensive income and a statement of changes in equity for the year ended 31 March 20X8, and a statement of financial position at that date. These should be in a form suitable for publication.

Your answer should include any notes intended for publication and these should be distinguished from workings.

You are *not* required to provide a note on accounting policies. **(30 marks)**

 # Question 7

Z imports electronic goods and resells these to large retail organisations. It specialises in luxury products such as electronic games and portable audio equipment. Almost half of Z's sales occur during the months of October and November.

Z faces intense competition and attempts to compete by anticipating consumer trends and offering products which are new to the market.

Z's trial balance at 30 September 20X8 is as follows:

	$'000	$'000
Sales revenue		9,800
Purchases	1,300	
Inventory at 30 September 20X7	480	
Warehouse and delivery wages	350	
Sales commissions	180	
Sundry distribution costs	310	
Sundry administrative expenses	85	
Administrative staff salaries	220	
Legal fees and damages	270	
Tax	45	
Dividends paid	1,775	
Warehouse premises – cost	8,500	
Warehouse premises – depreciation		800
Computer network – cost	900	
Computer network – depreciation		200
Delivery vehicles – cost	700	
Delivery vehicles – depreciation		280
Trade receivables	535	
Trade payables		470
Bank	90	
Loan – repayable 20Y3		500
Loan interest	25	
Share capital		1,000
Accumulated profits		2,715
	15,765	15,765

Notes:

(i) The closing inventory was counted on 30 September 20X8 and was valued at $520,000.

(ii) The legal fees and damages were paid in settlement of a claim against Z for a faulty product that had caused injury to a customer. Z has introduced safety checks on new products which will help to prevent any recurrence of this type of accident.

(iii) Depreciation has still to be charged for the year on the following bases:

Warehouse premises	2% of cost
Computer network	25% of book value
Vehicles	25% of book value

(iv) The tax expense for the year has been estimated at $1,900,000.

(v) Z paid a final dividend of $800,000 for the year ended 30 September 20X7 and an interim dividend of $975,000 during the year. The directors propose a final dividend of $1 m.

Requirement

Prepare a statement of comprehensive income and a statement of changes in equity for the year ended 30 September 20X8, and a statement of financial position at that date, together with notes to the financial statements for Z. These should be in a form suitable for publication in so far as is possible given the information provided. You are not required to provide a statement of accounting policies.   **(30 marks)**

Solutions to Revision Questions

 Solution 1

The correct answer is (C). The bad debts already written off have already been deducted from the receivables balance. As the $2,000 is unlikely to be paid, it should be provided for as a bad debt. Deduct this specific bad debt provision first then calculate the 10% provision.

	$
Trade receiveables	18,000
Less bad debt	(2,000)
	16,000
Less 10% provision	(1,600)
	14,400

 Solution 2

The correct answer is (C).

The total charge to statement of comprehensive income will include the amount already written off plus the new bad debt provision plus the increase in the general bad debt provision.

	$	$
Bad debts already written off		12,000
Bad debt at year-end		2,000
		14,000
Increase in provision		
Bad debt provision b/f	900	
Bad debt provision c/f	1,600	
Increase		700
Total		14,700

 Solution 3

The correct answer is (D), see Section 10.4.3.

 Solution 4

The correct answer is (B), see Section 10.4.3.

Solution 5

CE – Statement of comprehensive income for the year ended 31 March 2008

	$'000
Revenue	2,000
Cost of sales	(688)
Gross profit	1,312
Distribution costs	(200)
Administrative expenses	(760)
Profit	352
Finance costs	(190)
Profit before tax	162

Workings:
Cost of sales = 480 + 192 + 16 = 688
Administration = 260 + 500 = 760

 Solution 6

P – Statement of comprehensive income for the year ended 31 March 20X8

	Notes	$'000
Revenue		5,300
Cost of sales		(1,350)
Gross profit		3,950
Other income		210
Distribution costs		(370)
Administrative expenses		(490)
Profit		3,300
Finance cost		(190)
Profit before tax		3,110
Income tax expense	1	(495)
Profit for the year		2,615
Other comprehensive income		0
Total comprehensive income for the year		2,615

P – Statement of financial position at 31 March 20X8

	Notes	$'000	$'000
Assets			
Non-current assets			
Property, plant and equipment			4,250
Current assets			
Inventory		114	
Trade receivables		418	
Investments		2,700	
Cash and cash equivalents		12	
			3,244
Total assets			7,494

Equity and Liabilities

Capital and reserves

Issued capital	1,500	
Share premium	800	
Retained earnings	3,388	
		5,688
Non-current liabilities		
Long-term loans		1,200
Current liabilities		
Trade payables	136	
Taxation	470	
		606
Total equity and liabilities		7,494

P – Statement of changes in equity for the year ended 31 March 20X8

	Share capital $'000	Share premium $'000	Retained earnings $'000	Total $'000
Balance at 31 March 20X7	1,500	800	1,163	3,463
Total comprehensive income for the period			2,615	2,615
Dividends paid			(390)	(390)
Balance at 31 March 20X8	1,500	800	3,388	5,688

Notes to the accounts

1. *Taxation*

	$'000
Tax for the year	470
20X7 underprovision	25
	495

2. *Dividends*

	$'000
Dividends paid:	
Final, year ended 31 March 20X7	240
Interim, year ended 31 March 20X8	150
	390

The directors propose a final dividend of $270,000 for the year ended 31 March 20X8.

Solution 7

Z – Statement of comprehensive income for the year ended 30 September 20X8

	Note	$'000
Revenue		9,800
Cost of sales		(1,430)
Gross profit		8,370
Distribution costs		(945)
Administrative expenses		(750)
Profit	1	6,675
Finance costs		(25)
Profit before tax		6,650
Tax expense	2	(1,945)
Profit for the period		4,705

Z – Statement of financial position at 30 September 20X8

	Note	$'000	$'000
Assets			
Non-current assets			
Property, plant and equipment	4		8,370
Current assets			
Inventory		520	
Receivables		535	
Cash and cash equivalents		90	
			1,145
Total Assets			9,515
Equity and Liabilities			
Capital and reserves			
Issued capital		1,000	
Retained earnings		5,645	
			6,645
Non-current liabilities			
Long-term loan	5		500
Current liabilities	6		
Trade payables		470	
Tax		1,900	
Total Equity and Liabilities			2,370
			9,515

Z – Statement of changes in equity, year ended 30 September 20X8

	Share capital $'000	Retained earnings $'000	Total $'000
Balance at 30 September 20X7	1,000	2,715	3,715
Total comprehensive income for the period		4,705	4,705
Dividends paid:			
Final, year ended 30 September 20X7		(800)	(800)
Interim, year ended 30 September 20X8		(975)	(975)
Balance at 30 September 20X8	1,000	5,645	6,645

Z – notes to the financial statements

1. *Operating profit*
   Operating profit is stated after charging:

	$'000
Depreciation	450
Exceptional item – non-recurring legal fees and damages (see Chapter 12 for treatment)	270
	720

2. *Taxation*

	$'000
Tax charge for the year	1,900
Underprovision from previous years	45
	1,945

3. *Dividends*
   The directors propose a final dividend of $1,000,000 for the year.

4. *Tangible non-current assets*

	Premises $'000	Computer $'000	Delivery vehicles $'000	Total $'000
Cost at 30 September 20X7 and 20X8	8,500	900	700	10,100
Depreciation at 30 September 20X7	800	200	280	1,280
Charge for the year	170	175	105	450
Depreciation at 30 September 20X8	970	375	385	1,730
Net book value at 30 September 20X8	7,530	525	315	8,370
Net book value at 30 September 20X7	7,700	700	420	8,820

5. *Long-term loan*
   This loan is due to be repaid in 5 years.

6. *Current liabilities*

	$'000
Trade payables	470
Tax	1,900
	2,370

Workings

	$'000
Cost of sales	
Opening inventory	480
Purchases	1,300
Closing inventory	(520)
	1,260
Depreciation on premises (2% × 8,500)	170
	1,430

Distribution costs

Warehouse and delivery wages	350
Sales commissions	180
Sundry distribution costs	310
Depreciation on vehicles (25% × 700 − 280)	105
	945

Administrative expenses

Sundry administrative expenses	85
Administrative staff salaries	220
Legal fees and damages	270
Depreciation on computer (25% × 900 − 200)	175
	750

12

Reporting Financial Performance

Reporting Financial Performance 12

LEARNING OUTCOME

After completing this chapter, you should be able to:

▶ apply the accounting rules contained in IFRS's and IAS's dealing with reporting performance.

The syllabus topics covered in this chapter are as follows:

- Reporting performance: recognition of revenue, measurement of profit or loss, prior period items, discontinuing operations and segment reporting (IAS 1 (revised), 8, and 18, IFRS 5 & 8).

12.1 Introduction

In the previous chapter, we studied the requirements (primarily of IAS 1 *Presentation of Financial Statements*) for the presentation of financial statements. This chapter builds on the knowledge gained in Chapter 10, but focuses on the statement of comprehensive income and separate income statement if one is presented.

In this chapter, we are going to consider the recognition of revenue, the measurement of profit, presentation issues regarding unusual items in the statement of comprehensive income or separate income statement and presentation and disclosure requirements regarding segmental information.

The five accounting standards covered in this chapter are all concerned with specific items, transactions and adjustments that appear either in statement of comprehensive income or in the accompanying notes.

Some of the standards give illustrative formats and where these are helpful in understanding the presentation aspects of these items, they will be included in the chapter.

Remember that although we are now looking in more detail at items within the statement of comprehensive income or income statement, if a separate one is presented, the recommended format outlined in Chapter 10 will still apply, if the accounts are to be in a form suitable for publication.

12.2 IAS 18 *Revenue Recognition*

12.2.1 Introduction

IAS 18 defines when revenue may be recognised on the sale of goods, the rendering of services and the receipt of interest, royalties and dividends.

12.2.2 Sale of goods

Revenue from the sale of goods should be recognised when the following five conditions have been met:

1. the significant risks and rewards of ownership of the goods have been transferred to the buyer;
2. the entity selling does not retain any continuing influence or control over the goods;
3. revenue can be measured reliably;
4. it is reasonably certain that the buyer will pay for the goods;
5. the costs to the selling entity can be measured reliably.

12.2.3 Rendering of services

The conditions to be met for services are similar to those for the supply of goods.
Revenue from services should be recognised when:

(a) the amount of revenue can be measured reliably;
(b) it is reasonably certain that the client will pay for the services;
(c) the stage of completion of the transaction can be measured reliably;
(d) the costs to the entity supplying the service can be measured reliably.

Revenue is recognised acccording to the degree of completion.

12.2.4 Interest, royalties and dividends

The prime conditions for interest, royalties and dividends are that the amount of revenue can be measured reliably and their receipt is reasonably certain.
Once those conditions are met, interest and royalties should be recognised on an accruals basis and dividends recognised when the right to receive them is established.

12.2.5 Disclosure requirements

(a) The accounting policies adopted for the recognition of revenue.
(b) The amount of each significant category of revenue recognised (i.e. figures for sale of goods, rendering of services, interest, royalties and dividends, if material).

IAS 18 states that when the selling price includes an amount for subsequent servicing or support, for example, free support and updates for software for a period after purchase, some revenue should not be recognised immediately. Instead, a proportion of the revenue should be deferred and recognised as revenue in the period when the service is provided. The amount deferred should cover expected costs plus a proportion for profit.

12.3 Profit or loss for the period

The objective of *IAS 8 Accounting Policies, Changes in Accounting Estimates and Errors* (2003) is to prescribe the criteria for selecting and changing accounting policies, together with the accounting treatment and disclosure changes in accounting policies, changes in accounting estimates and corrections of errors. The standard is intended to enhance the relevance and reliability of an entity's financial statements, and the comparability of those statements over time and with the financial statements of other entities. The financial information provided by the statement of comprehensive income about the financial performance of an entity is historical; however, users often use this statement as a basis to evaluate the entity's future performance and any information that can assist in this process is relevant.

12.3.1 Extraordinary items

IAS 8 *Accounting Policies, Changes in Accounting Estimates and Errors* replaces IAS 8 *Net Profit or Loss for the Period, Fundamental Errors and Changes in Accounting Policies (revised in 1993). The 1993 version of IAS 8* required that profit or loss for the period, shown in the income statement, be separated into two components:

1. profit or loss from ordinary activities
2. extraordinary items.

The original standard defined *extraordinary items* and included extensive disclosure requirements if extraordinary items were present in the income statement. The new IAS 8 eliminates extraordinary items and as a result you will not be examined on them even although they are referred to in the syllabus. There is no reference in IAS 8 now, it was transferred to IAS 1 *Presentation of Financial Statements.* The revised IAS 1 says that an entity should not present any items of income and expense as extraordinary items, either in the statement of comprehensive income or the separate income statement (if presented) or in the notes.

12.3.2 Profit or loss from ordinary activities

The term 'from ordinary activities' is now redundant as IAS 1 has removed extraordinary items; there is now only one category of profit, which is referred to simply as profit or loss.

There may be items of income or expense that occur within the normal course of business but, because of their size or unusual nature, should be separately disclosed.

Providing information about *large or unusual items* reported within profit will again help users to evaluate the profit or loss that the entity is likely to generate in future periods (from trading activities).

The standard gives some examples of circumstances that may result in the separate disclosure of items. They include:

(a) the write-down of inventories to net realisable value;
(b) the write-down of property, plant and equipment to recoverable amount and reversals of previous write-downs;
(c) restructuring of the activities of an entity and the reversal of any provisions made for the costs of restructuring;
(d) disposals of items of property, plant and equipment;
(e) disposals of long-term investments;

(f) discontinuing operations;
(g) litigation settlements;
(h) other reversals of provisions.

12.4 Definitions – Accounting policies, accounting estimates and errors

- Accounting policies are the specific principles, bases, conventions and practices applied by an entity in preparing their financial statements.
- A change in accounting estimates is an adjustment of the carrying amount of an asset or liability or the periodic charge to the profit or loss arising from the use of an asset that results from a change to the expected future benefits or future obligations associated with the asset or liability. Changes in accounting estimates arise from new information or developments and are not corrections of errors.
- Errors are material omissions or misstatements in the financial statements. Ideally errors should be found and corrected within the same accounting period, but if they are not discovered until a later period they are treated as prior period adjustments.

12.5 Changes in accounting policies

The need for comparability means that, where possible, an entity will adopt the same accounting policies year after year. However, changes are sometimes needed. Possible reasons being:

- a new statutory requirement;
- a new accounting standard;
- the change will result in a more appropriate presentation of events or transactions in the financial statements.

According to IAS 8, when an accounting standard is applied to conditions that differ in substance from the previous situation, it is not to be treated as a change in accounting policy. If an accounting policy is applied to transactions or events that had not previously occurred or was previously immaterial, then it is not a change in accounting policies as there would not be an existing policy to change.

12.5.1 Treatment and disclosure

The required treatment in IAS 8 for changes in accounting policy is for the change to be applied retrospectively. This means that the effect of the change should be reported as an adjustment to the opening balance of retained earnings, with comparative information being restated unless impracticable.

When a change in accounting policy has a material effect on the current period or any prior period presented, or may have a material effect in subsequent periods, an entity should disclose the following:

- the reason for the change;
- the nature of the change;

- a description of transitional provisions, including those that might have an effect on future periods;
- the amount of the adjustment for the current period and for comparative figures for each financial statement line affected; and
- the amount of the adjustment relating to periods prior to those included in the comparative information;
- the fact that comparative information has been restated or that it is impracticable to do so.

Where entities choose to change an accounting policy, as opposed to a change caused by a new standard or interpretation, they should also disclose the reasons why applying the new accounting policy provides reliable and more relevant information.

The following example is amended from the example given in the appendix of IAS 8.

Example 12.A

During 20X2, Gamma changes its accounting policy with respect to the treatment of borrowing costs that are directly attributable to the acquisition of a hydroelectric power station, which is in course of construction (borrowing costs are specifically covered in Chapter 13). In previous periods, Gamma had capitalised such costs (the allowed alternative treatment in IAS 23). Gamma has now decided to treat these costs as an expense, rather than capitalise them (the benchmark treatment).

Gamma capitalised borrowing costs incurred of $2,600 during 20X1 and $5,200 in periods prior to 20X1 . All borrowing costs incurred in previous years were capitalised.

In 20X1, Gamma reported:

Profit before interest and income taxes	$18,000
Interest expense	–
Profit before income taxes	$18,000
Income taxes	($5,400)
Profit	$12,600

20X1 opening retained earnings was $20,000 and closing retained earnings totalled $32,600 ($20,000 plus profit of $12,600). Gamma's tax rate was 30% for 20X2 and 20X1.

The extract from statement of comprehensive income for 20X2 for Gamma, prepared under the benchmark treatment, will be as follows:

	20X2 $	20X1 $ (restated)
Profit before interest and income taxes	30,000	18,000
Interest expense	(3,000)	(2,600)
	27,000	15,400
Income taxes	(8,100)	(4,620)
Profit	18,900	10,780

The Statement of changes in equity for Gamma, prepared under the benchmark treatment, will be as follows:

	20X2 $	20X1 $ (restated)
Opening retained earnings as previously reported	32,600	20,000
Change in accounting policy with respect to the capitalisation of interest (net of income taxes of $2,340 for 20X2 and $1,560 for 20X1) (Note 1)	(5,460)	(3,640)
Opening retained earnings as restated	27,140	16,360
Profit	18,900	10,780
Closing retained earnings	46,040	27,140

Extract from notes to the financial statements
Note 1

During 20X2, Gamma changed its accounting policy with respect to the treatment of borrowing costs that are directly attributable to the acquisition of a hydroelectric power station which is in course of construction. In order to conform with the benchmark treatment in IAS 23, *Borrowing Costs,* the entity now expense rather than capitalise such costs. This change in accounting policy has been accounted for retrospectively. The comparative statements for 20X1 have been restated to conform to the changed policy.

The effect of the change is an increase in interest expense of $3,000 (20X2) and $2,600 (20X1).

Opening retained earnings for 20X1 have been reduced by $3,640, ($5,200 less tax $1,560) which is the amount of the adjustment relating to periods prior to 20X1.

Opening retained earnings for 20X2 are adjusted for $5,460 ($3,640 plus ($2,600 less tax of $780)).

12.6 Changes in accounting estimates

The process of accounting requires estimation in many areas, for example, allowances for doubtful debts, inventory obsolescence or the estimated useful lives of non-current assets. The estimation process involves judgements based on the latest information available, and by their nature accounting estimates can rarely be measured with precision.

Where circumstances change or new information becomes available, the accounting estimate may need to be revised. The effect of the change of an accounting estimate should be reported as a part of the profit or loss for the period in which the change occurs.

It can be difficult to distinguish between a change in accounting policy and a change in an accounting estimate. Where this is the case, the change is treated as a change in an accounting estimate.

> Remember, a change in accounting policy will usually need a prior period adjustment, but a change in accounting estimate must be adjusted in profit or loss for the period and is not allowed to be treated as a prior period adjustment.

12.7 Errors

The 1993 version of IAS 8 referred to fundamental errors. The revised version of IAS 8 refers to material omissions and misstatements and prior period material omissions and misstatements, there is no mention of fundamental errors.

An omission or misstatement is material if individually or collectively they influence economic decisions of users taken on the basis of the financial statements. Materiality depends on the size and nature of the omission or misstatement judged according to its circumstances. An item could therefore be material because of its relative size or because of the nature of the error.

A prior period error is one where the material omissions and misstatements occurred in a previous period as a result of the failure to use or the misuse of reliable information that was available at the time and could reasonably be expected to have been obtained and taken into account when preparing the financial statements.

Such errors could be the result of:

- mathematical mistakes
- mistakes in applying accounting policies
- misinterpretation of facts

- fraud
- oversights.

Financial statements do not comply with IFRSs if they contain either material errors or immaterial errors made intentionally to achieve a particular presentation of the entities financial position, financial performance or cash flows.

12.7.1 Treatment and disclosure

The treatment for the correction of prior period errors is that the opening balance of retained earnings, in the first set of financial statements after the error is discovered, be adjusted by restating the comparative information, unless this is impracticable.

This means that the financial statements for the current period are presented as if the error had been corrected in the period in which the error was made. The financial statements for the current period must, however, disclose:

- the nature of the prior period error;
- the amount of the correction for the current period and for comparative figures presented for each line item affected;
- the amount of the correction relating to periods prior to those included in the comparative information;
- the fact that comparative information has been restated or that it is impracticable to do so.

The following example is amended from the example given in the appendix of IAS 8.

Example 12.B

During 20X2, Beta Co. discovered that certain products that had been sold during 20X1 were incorrectly included in inventory at 31 December 19X1 at $6,500.

Beta's accounting records for 20X2 show sales of $104,000, cost of goods sold of $86,500 (including $6,500 for error in opening inventory), and income taxes of $5,250.

In 20X1, Beta reported:

Sales	73,500
Cost of goods sold	(53,500)
Profit before income taxes	20,000
Income taxes	(6,000)
Profit	14,000

20X1 opening retained earnings was $20,000 and closing retained earnings totalled $34,000 ($20,000 plus profit for 20X1 of $14,000). Beta's income tax rate was 30 per cent for 20X2 and 20X1.

The extract from statement of comprehensive income for 20X2 for Beta, will be as follows:

	20X2 $	20X1 $ (restated)
Sales	104,000	73,500
Cost of goods sold	(80,000)	(60,000)
Profit before income taxes	24,000	13,500
Income taxes	(7,200)	(4,050)
Profit	16,800	9,450

Note: 20X1 closing stock is overstated and therefore 20X1 cost of goods sold is understated by $6,500. Correction of this increases cost of goods sold from $53,500 to $60,000. Income taxes are calculated at 30% of $ 13,500, which is the revised profit.

20X2 cost of goods sold is correctly recorded at $80,000 ($86,500 less the $6,500 overstatement of opening stock charged to cost sales).

The retained earnings for Beta part of the Statement of changes in equity will be as follows:

	20X2 $	20X1 $ (restated)
Opening retained earnings as previously reported	34,000	20,000
Correction of prior year error (net of taxes of $ 1,950) (Note 1)	(4,550)	
Opening retained earnings as restated	29,450	20,000
Profit	16,800	9,450
Closing retained earnings	46,250	29,450

Extract from notes to the financial statements
Note 1

Certain products that had been sold in 20X1 were incorrectly included in inventory at 31 December 20X1 at $6,500. The financial statements of 20X1 have been restated to correct this error. The effect of the restatement on those financial statements is summarised below. There is no effect in 20X2.

		Effect on 20X1 $
statement of comprehensive income	(Increase) in cost of goods sold	(6,500)
	Decrease in income tax expense	1,950
	(Decrease) in profit	(4,550)
Statement of financial position	(Decrease) in inventory	(6,500)
	Decrease in income tax payable	1,950
	(Decrease) in equity	(4,550)

12.8 Discontinuing operations

International Financial Reporting Standard 5 *Non-current Assets Held for Sale* and *Discontinued Operations* (IFRS 5) sets out requirements for the classification, measurement and presentation of non-current assets held for sale and the presentation and disclosure of discontinued operations.

12.8.1 Objective

The objective of IFRS 5 is to specify the accounting for assets held for sale, and the presentation and disclosure of discontinued operations.

IFRS 5 sets principles for reporting information about discontinued operations, to enable users of financial statements to more easily evaluate an entity's future performance and cash flows.

Separate disclosure of results relating to discontinued operations will allow them to evaluate more accurately the likely performance of the operations that will be generating income in future periods.

12.8.2 Definition of a discontinued operation

IFRS 5 defines a discontinued operation as a component of an entity that has been disposed of, or is classified as held for sale and:

(a) is part of a single plan to dispose of a separate major line of business or geographical area of operations; or
(b) that represents a separate major line of business or geographical area of operations; or
(c) is a subsidiary acquired exclusively with a view to resale.

A component of an entity is defined as operations and cash flows that can be clearly distinguished, operationally and for financial reporting purposes, from the rest of the entity.

IFRS 5 introduces the concept of a disposal group, being a group of assets and liabilities directly associated with those assets, to be disposed of, by sale or otherwise, together as a group in a single transaction.

A disposal group may be a group of *cash-generating units,* a single cash-generating unit, or part of a cash-generating unit.

Classification of non-current assets (or disposal groups) as held for sale
Non-current asset (or disposal group) already held by the entity:

1. Classified as held for sale if its carrying amount will be recovered principally through a sale transaction rather than through continuing use. This occurs where:
   (a) The asset (or disposal group) is available for immediate sale in its present condition subject only to terms that are usual and customary for sales of such assets (or disposal groups) and its sale must be highly probable.
   (b) To be highly probable, the appropriate level of management must be committed to a plan to sell the asset (or disposal group), and an active programme to locate a buyer and complete the plan must have been initiated. The asset (or disposal group) must be actively marketed for sale at a price that is reasonable in relation to its current fair value and the sale should be expected to qualify for recognition as a completed sale within 1 year from the date of classification.

Non-current asset (or disposal group) acquired exclusively with a view to its subsequent disposal:

1. Classified as held for sale at the acquisition date only if the one-year requirement is met.

If either categories criteria are met after the reporting period, an entity shall not classify a non-current asset (or disposal group) as held for sale in those financial statements when issued. If the criteria are met after the reporting period but before the authorisation of the financial statements for issue, the entity shall disclose the information in the notes.

Assets classified as non-current in accordance with IAS 1 *Presentation of Financial Statements* (as revised in 2003) cannot be reclassified as current assets until they meet the IFRS 5 criteria to be classified as held for sale.

Assets of a class that an entity would normally regard as non-current that are acquired exclusively with a view to resale cannot be classified as current unless they meet the IFRS 5 criteria to be classified as held for sale.

For example, if a retail entity, Markies, which provides food, clothing and home-wear, decides to withdraw from the food sector, then the related costs of that withdrawal would be recorded within discontinued operations, as long as it was discontinued before the end of the reporting period. The direct costs of abandoning the food division such as redundancy of staff and gain or loss on the sale of assets would be classified under discontinued operations. The costs of restructuring the remaining divisions, even if that restructuring is required as a result of the decision to close the food division, would however be classified as restructuring costs within continuing activities, as the costs relate to clothing and home-wear and these are continuing trading activities.

A decision to withdraw from supplying dairy products would not constitute a discontinued operation as the entity is still operating in the food sector. It is not a withdrawal of a separate major line of business and so the related costs would be shown within continuing operations, probably as restructuring costs.

For the results of the discontinued operation to be separately disclosed, it follows that the related profits, losses, gains, assets and liabilities must be separately identifiable to be included in the financial statements.

12.8.3 Measurement of a non-current asset (or disposal group) held for sale

Non-current assets (or disposal group) classified as held for sale are valued at the lower of:

- The assets carrying amount as measured in accordance with applicable IFRSs.
- Fair value less costs to sell.

Recognition of impairment losses and reversals

When the non-current assets (or disposal group) are measured at fair value on initial recognition as held for sale, an impairment is recognised (in accordance with IAS 36) if the fair value less costs to sell are less than the assets carrying amount.

An entity can recognise a gain for any subsequent increase in fair value less costs to sell of an asset, but not in excess of the cumulative impairment loss that has been recognised either in accordance with this IFRS or previously in accordance with IAS 36 *Impairment of Assets*.

Depreciation

A non-current asset that is classified as held for sale or is part of a disposal group classified as held for sale *must not* be depreciated or amortised.

Interest and other expenses attributable to the liabilities of a disposal group classified as held for sale shall continue to be recognised.

12.8.4 Presentation and disclosure

An entity shall present and disclose information that enables users of the financial statements to evaluate the financial effects of discontinued operations and disposals of non-current assets (or disposal groups).

Presenting discontinued operations

(a) An entity shall disclose in the statement of comprehensive income or the separate income statement:
- a single amount comprising the total of:
  - (i) the post-tax profit or loss of discontinued operations; and
  - (ii) the post-tax gain or loss recognised on the measurement to fair value less costs to sell;
  - (iii) the post-tax gain or loss on disposal of the assets or disposal group(s).

(b) An entity shall disclose in the notes or in the statement of comprehensive income or the separate income statement:
- an analysis of the single amount in (a) above into:
  - (i) the revenue, expenses and pre-tax profit or loss of discontinued operations;
  - (ii) the related income tax expense (as required by IAS 12);
  - (iii) the gain or loss recognised on the measurement to fair value less costs to sell and the related income tax expense;
  - (iv) the gain or loss on the disposal of the assets or disposal group(s) and the related income tax expense.
- If presented in the statement of comprehensive income or the separate income statement, it must be presented in a section identified as relating to discontinued operations, and be kept separate from continuing operations.

An entity shall disclose on the statement of cash flows or in the notes, net cash flows attributable to the operating, investing and financing activities of discontinued operations.

Comparative information for prior periods should be restated based on the classifications established in the current reporting period. For example, if the retail division is classified as a discontinued operation in 20X2 and its results are disclosed as such separately in the financial statements, then the comparative information for 20X1 should be restated (from continuing operations where it was included last year) and included as a direct comparison within discontinued operations.

Example 12.C

Let us consider the retail entity mentioned above. The results of Markies were as follows:

	20X2 $m	20X1 $m
Revenue	140	140
Operating expenses	(120)	(92)
Impairment loss	(10)	(20)
	10	28
Interest expense	(25)	(15)
Profit (loss) before tax	(15)	13
Income tax expense	4	(6)
Profit (loss) after tax	(11)	7

Note: The impairment losses both in 20X1 and 20X2 relate to the food division.

The decision was taken to withdraw from the food sector and a formal plan to abandon food related activities was formulated and implemented during the 20X2 financial year. The food division generated the following revenues and costs during 20X1 and 20X2:

	20X2	20X1
	$m	$m
Revenue	40	50
Operating expenses	(60)	(27)
Impairment loss	(10)	(20)
	(30)	3
Interest expense	(5)	(5)
Profit (loss) before tax	(35)	(2)
Income tax expense	10	1
Profit (loss) after tax	(25)	(1)

The 20X2 operating expenses for the food division includes a $30 million provision for employee terminations as a result of the closure.

When the final accounts are prepared, the 20X2 revenues and costs of the food division are shown separately within discontinued operations.

It was noted above that IFRS 5 requires comparative information for prior periods be restated based on the classifications of this reporting period. This means that the revenues and costs generated by the food division in 20X1 must be removed from the continuing operations total in 20X1 and restated as a direct comparison for the discontinued operations. In effect we can now see what revenues and costs were generated by the food division in 20X2 and what that same division generated the previous year.

IFRS 5 Format illustrating the discontinued information shown in the notes:

	20X2	20X1
Continuing operations	$m	$m
Revenue	100	90
Operating expenses	(60)	(65)
	40	25
Finance costs	(20)	(10)
Profit before tax	20	15
Income tax expense	(6)	(7)
Profit for the period from continuing operations	14	8
Discontinued operations		
Loss for the period from discontinued operations*	(25)	(1)
Profit for the period	(11)	7
* The required analysis would be given in the notes		

Notes:
Discontinued operations

	20X2	20X1
	$m	$m
Revenue	40	50
Operating expenses	(30)	(27)
Impairment loss	(10)	(20)
Provision for employee termination	(30)	–
	(30)	3
Interest expense	(5)	(5)
Loss before tax	(35)	(2)
Income tax expense	10	1
Loss after tax	(25)	(1)

From the statement of comprehensive income above, we can now clearly see the figures generated by the food division in the last 2 years. The amounts generated by continuing operations are now separately disclosed and can be used to evaluate future income streams. (This is one of the aims of IFRS 5 – that relevant information about the components of profit be disclosed in order that users can evaluate future profits, which helps them make investment decisions based on this historic information.)

Note: The provision for employee redundancies of $30 million is likely to be reversed in the following period and offset against the actual expense incurred — remember this is the accruals concept being applied; you provide for an expense and you recognise it in the period when it was incurred; when the operation is discontinued, a provision is made for items that are still outstanding at the end of the reporting period. For example, the actual cost of redundancies within the food division may amount to $36 million in 20X3 less the amount previously provided (in 20X2) of $30 million, which results in an additional charge in 20X3 of $6 million, this will be disclosed separately under discontinued operations in 20X3.

Presentation of a non-current asset or disposal group classified as held for sale

Non-current assets classified as held for sale and the assets of a disposal group classified as held for sale are shown separately from other assets in the statement of financial position, under current assets.

The liabilities of a disposal group classified as held for sale shall be presented separately from other liabilities in the statement of financial position, under current liabilities. Assets and liabilities shall not be offset and presented as a single amount.

The major classes of assets and liabilities classified as held for sale must be separately disclosed either in the statement of financial position or in the notes.

Any cumulative income or expense recognised directly in equity relating to a non-current asset (or disposal group) classified as held for sale must be shown separately under equity.

Prior year balances for non-current assets are not adjusted to take account of the reclassification in the statement of financial position for the latest period.

Example 12.D

At the end of 20X5, an entity decides to dispose of part of its assets (and directly associated liabilities). The disposal, which meets the criteria in IFRS 5 to be classified as held for sale, takes the form of two disposal groups, as follows:

	Carrying amount after classification as held for sale	
	Disposal group I: $'000	Disposal group II: $'000
Property, plant and equipment	4,900	1,700
Financial asset	1,400*	–
Liabilities	(2,400)	(900)
Net carrying amount of disposal group	3,900	800

* An amount of $400,000 relating to these assets has been recognised directly in equity.

The presentation in the entity's statement of financial position of the disposal groups classified as held for sale can be shown as follows:

Statement of financial position	20X5	20X4
ASSETS		
Non-current assets		
Tangible	X	X
Intangible	X	X
	X	X
Current assets		
Inventory	X	X
Receivables	X	X
Cash	X	X
	X	X
Non-current assets classified as held for sale	8,000	–
	X	X
Total assets	X	X

	20X5	20X4
EQUITY AND LIABILITIES		
Equity		
Equity shares	X	X
Reserves	X	X
Amounts recognised directly in equity relating to non-current assets held for sale	400	–
	X	X
Total equity	X	X
Non-current liabilities		
Loans	X	X
Current liabilities		
Payables	X	X
Liabilities directly associated with non-current assets classified as held for sale	3,300	–
	X	X
Total liabilities	X	X
Total equity and liabilities	X	X

The presentation requirements for assets (or disposal groups) classified as held for sale at the end of the reporting period do not apply retrospectively. The comparative statement of financial position for any previous periods are therefore not represented.

Additional disclosures

An entity must disclose the following information in the notes in the period in which a non-current asset (or disposal group) has been either classified as held for sale or sold:

(a) a description of the non-current asset or disposal group;
(b) a description of the facts and circumstances of the sale;
(c) in respect of held for sale items, the facts and circumstances leading to the expected disposal, and the expected timing of that disposal.

12.9 International financial reporting standard 8 *Operating Segments* (IFRS 8)

IFRS 8 *Operating Segments* was issued on October 2006 and replaces IAS 14 *Segment Reporting* which it supersedes. IFRS 8 is mandatory for annual periods beginning on or after 1 January 2009.

12.9.1 IFRS 8 *Operating Segments* – core principle

IFRS 8 *Operating Segments* does not specify an objective as previous IAS's have, instead IFRS 8 has a 'core principle'. The core principle of IFRS 8 is: 'An entity shall disclose information to enable users of its financial statements to evaluate the nature and financial effects of the business activities in which it engages and the economic environments in which it operates.' IFRS 8 sets out requirements for disclosure of information about an entity's operating segments and also about the entity's products and services, the geographical areas in which it operates, and its major customers.

12.9.2 Definition of operating segment

The only definition given in IFRS 8 is that of an operating segment. An operating segment is a component of an entity:

(a) that engages in business activities from which it may earn revenues and incur expenses (including revenues and expenses relating to transactions with other components of the same entity);

(b) whose operating results are regularly reviewed by the entity's chief operating decision maker to make decisions about resources to be allocated to the segment and assess its performance; and

(c) for which discrete financial information is available.

Operating segments can be aggregated where they have similar economic characteristics and are similar in each of the following:

- the nature of the products or services;
- the nature of the production process;
- the type of customer for the products or services;
- the methods used to distribute the products or services;
- the nature of the regulatory environment (banking, insurance, etc.).

12.9.3 Reportable segments

An operating segment is a reportable segment if the operation contributes at least 10 per cent of:

- total sales revenue, including sales to other segments; or
- total profits of all profit-making segments; or
- total losses of all loss-making segments; or
- total assets.

An operating segment that falls below all of the 10 per cent thresholds listed above may still be shown as a reportable segment despite its size, should the management believe that it is necessary for users to fully understand the financial statements.

If it is not included as a separately identified reportable segment, it should be included in an 'all other segments' category.

If the total external revenue attributable to reportable segments amounts to less than 75 per cent of the total revenue, additional segments should be identified as reportable segments, even if they do not meet the 10 per cent thresholds, until at least 75 per cent of the revenue is allocated to reportable segments.

12.9.4 Segment accounting policies

IFRS 8 requires the amount reported for each operating segment to be the measure reported to the chief operating decision maker for the purpose of allocating resources to the segment and assessing its performance.

IFRS 8 also requires an explanation to be given of how segment profit or loss, assets and liabilities are measured.

12.9.5 Disclosure

An entity shall disclose information to enable users of its financial statements to evaluate the nature and financial effects of the business activities in which it engages and the economic environments in which it operates.

An entity shall report a measure of profit or loss and total assets for each reportable segment. An entity shall report a measure of liabilities for each reportable segment if such an amount is regularly provided to the chief operating decision maker. An entity shall also disclose the following about each reportable segment if the specified amounts are included in the measure of segment profit or loss reviewed by the chief operating decision maker, or are otherwise regularly provided to the chief operating decision maker, even if not included in that measure of segment profit or loss:

(a) revenues from external customers;
(b) revenues from transactions with other operating segments of the same entity;
(c) interest revenue;
(d) interest expense;
(e) depreciation and amortisation;
(f) material items of income and expense separately disclosed in the statement of comprehensive income;
(g) the entity's interest in the profit or loss of associates and joint ventures accounted for by the equity method;
(h) income tax expense or income; and
(i) material non-cash items other than depreciation and amortisation.

Extracts from IFRS 8 implementation guidance are given below as illustrations of the likely formats of segmental information

CU = currency units

	Car parts CU	Motor vessels CU	Software CU	Electronics CU	Finance CU	All other CU	Totals CU
Revenues from external customers	3,000	5,000	9,500	12,000	5,000	1,000[a]	35,500
Intersegment revenues	–	–	3,000	1,500	–	–	4,500
Interest revenue	450	800	1,000	1,500	–	–	3,750
Interest expense	350	600	700	1,100	–	–	2,750
Net interest revenue[b]	–	–	–	–	1,000	–	1,000
Depreciation and amortisation	200	100	50	1,500	1,100	–	2,950
Reportable segment profit	200	70	900	2,300	500	100	4,070
Other material non-cash items:							
Impairment of assets	–	200	–	–	–	–	200
Reportable segment assets	2,000	5,000	3,000	12,000	57,000	2,000	81,000
Expenditures for reportable segment non-current assets	300	700	500	800	600	–	2,900
Reportable segment liabilities	1,050	3,000	1,800	8,000	30,000	–	43,850

X

12.9.6 Reconciliations

An entity shall provide reconciliations of all of the following:

(a) the total of the reportable segments' revenues to the entity's revenue.
(b) the total of the reportable segments' measures of profit or loss to the entity's profit or loss before tax expense (tax income) and discontinued operations. However, if an entity allocates to reportable segments items such as tax expense (tax income), the entity may reconcile the total of the segments' measures of profit or loss to the entity's profit or loss after those items.
(c) the total of the reportable segments' assets to the entity's assets.
(d) the total of the reportable segments' liabilities to the entity's liabilities if segment liabilities are reported
(e) the total of the reportable segments' amounts for every other material item of information disclosed to the corresponding amount for the entity.

Although the IFRS does not require assets to be identified by segment the requirement to reconcile reportable segments assets and liabilities to total assets and total liabilities effectively means that assets and liabilities have to be disclosed by segment.

Extracts from IFRS 8 showing reconciliations of reportable segment revenues, profit or loss, assets and liabilities

Revenues	**CU**
Total revenues for reportable segments	39,000
Other revenues	1,000
Elimination of intersegment revenues	(4,500)
Entity's revenues	35,500

Profit or loss	**CU**
Total profit or loss for reportable segments	3,970
Other profit or loss	100
Elimination of intersegment profits	(500)
Unallocated amounts:	
Litigation settlement received	500
Other corporate expenses	(750)
Adjustment to pension expense in consolidation	(250)
Income before income tax expense	3,070

Assets	**CU**
Total assets for reportable segments	79,000
Other assets	2,000
Elimination of receivable from corporate headquarters	(1,000)
Other unallocated amounts	1,500
Entity's assets	81,500

Liabilities	**CU**
Total liabilities for reportable segments	43,850
Unallocated defined benefit pension liabilities	30,000
Entity's liabilities	73,850

Other material items	Reportable segment totals CU	Adjustments CU	Entity totals CU
Interest revenue	3,750	75	3,825
Interest expense	2,750	(50)	2,700
Net interest revenue (finance segment only)	1,000	–	1,000
Expenditures for assets	2,900	1,000	3,900
Depreciation and amortization	2,950	–	2,950
Impairment of assets	200	–	200

Geographical information	Revenues[a] CU	Non-current assets CU
United States	19,000	11,000
Canada	4,200	–
China	3,400	6,500
Japan	2,900	3,500
Other countries	6,000	3,000
Total	35,500	24,000

12.9.7 Information about geographical areas

Although IFRS 8 does not require a full geographical analysis it does require an entity to report the following geographical information, unless the necessary information is not available and the cost to develop it would be excessive:

(a) revenues from external customers:
  (i) attributed to the entity's country of domicile and
  (ii) attributed to all foreign countries in total from which the entity derives revenues. If revenues from external customers attributed to an individual foreign country are material, those revenues shall be disclosed separately.

An entity shall disclose the basis for attributing revenues from external customers to individual countries.

(b) non-current assets other than financial instruments, deferred tax assets, post-employment benefit assets, and rights arising under insurance contracts:
  (i) located in the entity's country of domicile and
  (ii) located in all foreign countries in total in which the entity holds assets. If assets in an individual foreign country are material, those assets shall be disclosed separately.

If the necessary information is not available and the cost to develop it would be excessive, that fact shall be disclosed.

12.9.8 Information about major customers

IFRS 8 requires an entity to provide information about the extent of its reliance on its major customers. If revenues from transactions with a single external customer amount to 10 per cent or more of an entity's revenues, the entity shall disclose:

(a) the percentage of revenue for each such customer
(b) the total amount of revenues from each such customer
(c) the identity of the segment or segments reporting the revenues.

The entity need not disclose the identity of a major customer or the amount of revenues that each segment reports from that customer. IFRS 8 regards a group of entities known to a reporting entity to be under common control as a single customer, and a government (national, state, provincial, territorial, local or foreign) and entities known to the reporting entity to be under the control of that government as a single customer.

12.10 Main differences between IAS 14 *Segment Reporting* and IFRS 8 *Operating Segments*

The main differences between IAS 14 and IFRS 8 are:

- IAS 14 requires identification of two sets of segments – one based on related products and services, and the other on geographical areas. IAS 14 regards one set as primary segments and the other as secondary segments. The requirements of IFRS 8 are based on the information about the components of the entity that management uses to make decisions about operating matters. IFRS 8 requires identification of operating segments on the basis of internal reports that are regularly reviewed by the entity's chief operating decision maker in order to allocate resources to the segment and assess its performance.
- IAS 14 limits reportable segments to those that earn a majority of their revenue from sales to external customers. IFRS 8's definition of an operating segment includes a component of an entity that sells primarily or exclusively to other operating segments of the entity, if the entity is managed in that way.
- IAS 14 requires segment information to be prepared in conformity with the accounting policies adopted for preparing and presenting the financial statements of the consolidated group or entity. IFRS 8 requires the amount reported for each operating segment item to be the measure reported to the chief operating decision maker for the purposes of allocating resources to the segment and assessing its performance.
- IAS 14 defines segment revenue, segment expense, segment result, segment assets and segment liabilities. The IFRS 8 does not define these terms, but requires an explanation of how segment profit or loss, segment assets and segment liabilities are measured for each reportable segment.
- IAS 14 requires the entity to disclose specified items of information about its primary segments. IFRS 8 requires an entity to disclose specified amounts about each reportable segment, if the specified amounts are included in the measure of segment profit or loss and are reviewed by or regularly provided to the chief operating decision maker.
- IAS 14 does not require interest income and expense to be split between segments. IFRS 8 requires an entity to report interest revenue separately from interest expense for each reportable segment unless a majority of the segment's revenues are from interest and the chief operating decision maker relies primarily on net interest revenue to assess the performance of the segment and make decisions about resources to be allocated to the segment.
- IAS 14 requires the disclosure of secondary segment information for either industry or geographical segments, to supplement the information given for the primary segments. IFRS 8 requires an entity, including an entity with a single reportable segment, to disclose information for the entity as a whole about its products and services, geographical areas and major customers. This requirement applies, regardless of the entity's organisation, if the information is not included as a part of the disclosures about segments.

12.11 Summary

Having completed this chapter, we can now explain the recognition criteria for revenue and can apply the correct accounting treatment for large or unusual items in arriving at profit for the period. We can also apply the appropriate treatment for changes in accounting policies, accounting estimates, and prior period errors.

We can define non-current assets held for sale and a discontinued operation and explain the disclosures required for non-current assets held for sale and discontinued operations.

We can identify reportable segments and describe the disclosures required in respect of segment reporting.

Revision Questions

? Question 1

IFRS 8 Operating Segments

 (i) Revenue; from external sources
 (ii) Cost of sales
(iii) Interest expense
(iv) Segment profit/loss
 (v) Depreciation
(vi) Capital employed.

Which of the following are required by IFRS 8 Operating Segments to be analysed by segment and disclosed in an entity's financial statements:

(A) (i), (ii), and (iv)
(B) (i), (iv) and (vi)
(C) (i), (iii), and (v)
(D) (i), (iv), and (vi).   **(2 marks)**

? Question 2

Revenue from the sale of goods should be recognised when certain conditions are met.

 (i) the entity selling does not retain any continuing influence or control over the goods;
 (ii) when the goods are dispatched to the buyer;
(iii) revenue can be measured reliably;
(iv) the supplier is paid for the goods;
 (v) it is reasonably certain that the buyer will pay for the goods;
(vi) the buyer has paid for the goods.

Which of the above are included in IAS 18 *Revenue recognition's* conditions for recognition:

(A) (i), (ii) and (v)
(B) (ii), (iii) and (iv)
(C) (i), (iii) and (v)
(D) (i), (iv) and (vi)   **(2 marks)**

? Question 3

In no more than 15 words, define the IAS 8 meaning of an 'error'. **(2 marks)**

? Question 4

Which ONE of the following would be regarded as a change of accounting policy under IAS 8 *Accounting Policies, Changes in Accounting Estimates and Errors?*

(A) An entity changes its method of depreciation of machinery from straight line to reducing balance
(B) An entity has started capitalising borrowing costs for assets under the alternative treatment allowed by IAS 23 *Borrowing Costs.* The borrowing costs previously had been charged to profit or loss
(C) An entity changes its method of calculating the provision for warranty claims on its products sold
(D) An entity disclosed a contingent liability for a legal claim in the previous year's accounts. In the current year, a provision has been made for the same legal claim

(2 marks)

? Question 5

IAS 18 *Revenue Recognition* defines when revenue may be recognised on the sale of goods.

List FOUR of the five conditions that IAS 18 requires to be met for income to be recognised. **(2 marks)**

? Question 6

On 31 March 2007, DT received an order from a new customer, XX, for products with a sales value of $900,000. XX enclosed a deposit with the order of $90,000.

On 31 March 2007, DT had not completed credit referencing of XX and had not despatched any goods. DT is considering the following possible entries for this transaction in its financial statements for the year ended 31 March 2007:

 (i) include $900,000 in profit or loss revenue for the year;
 (ii) include $90,000 in profit or loss revenue for the year;
(iii) do not include anything in profit or loss revenue for the year;
(iv) create a trade receivable for $810,000;
 (v) create a trade payable for $90,000.

According to IAS 18 *Revenue Recognition*, how should DT record this transaction in its financial statements for the year ended 31 March 2007?

(A) (i) and (iv)
(B) (ii) and (v)
(C) (iii) and (iv)
(D) (iii) and (v) **(2 marks)**

Question 7

While Presario was preparing its financial statements for the year to 30 June 20X2, they discovered that goods with a cost of $70,000, which had been sold during 20X1, had been incorrectly included in inventory at 30 June 20X1.

The draft figures for 20X2 and the actual reported figures for 20X1 are given below:

	20X2 (draft)	20X1
	$'000	$'000
Sales	460	400
Cost of sales	(250)	(220)
Gross profit	210	180
Administrative expenses	(50)	(40)
Distribution costs	(40)	(30)
Profit before tax	120	110
Income tax (at 30%)	(36)	(33)
Profit	84	77

The opening retained earnings at 1 July 20X0 was $120,000 and closing retained earnings at 30 June 20X1 totalled $197,000.

The directors have decided that this amounts to a material misstatement in the reported financial statements and wish this to be corrected immediately.

Requirements

(a) Redraft the 20X2 statement of comprehensive income and restate the 20X1 figures where necessary to take account of this prior period error.   **(6 marks)**

(b) Prepare the statement of changes in equity for inclusion in the published financial statements of Presario for the year ended 30 June 20X2.   **(4 marks)**

(Total marks = 10)

 # Question 8

D is a diversified entity that has operated in four main areas for many years. Each of these activities has usually contributed approximately one-quarter of the entity's annual operating profit. During the year ended 31 December 20X3, the entity disposed of its glass-making division.

The entity's chief accountant has prepared the following summary of revenues and expenses:

D – analysis of costs and revenues, year ended 31 December 20X3

	Glass-making	Other division
	$'000	$'000
Sales revenue	150	820
Operating expenses	(98)	(470)
Losses on disposal of non-current assets	(205)	(61)

The entity also incurred interest charges of $37,000 during the year, all of which relates to continuing activities. The income tax charge for the year has been estimated at $24,000, made up of a $50,000 charge on the continuing activities and a $26,000 refund for discontinued activities. A dividend of $30,000 was paid during the year.

The entity made an issue of 100,000 $1 shares at a premium of 80¢ per share during the year. Shareholders' funds at the beginning of the year were made up as follows:

	$'000
Share capital	250
Share premium account	150
Revaluation reserve	160
Retained earnings	670
	1,230

The balance on the revaluation reserve arose when the entity valued the land occupied by the properties used in its retail division. In view of recent developments, it has been S: decided that this reserve should be reduced to $90,000 to reflect the reduced value of the properties.

Requirements

(a) Explain how the analysis required by IFRS 5 *Non-current Assets Held for Sale and Discontinued Operations* assists in assessing a business's future results and cash flows.

(6 marks)

(b) Prepare the statement of comprehensive income (showing the detail in notes to the statement of comprehensive income) for the year ended 31 December 20X3 for D in a form suitable for publication, complying with the requirements of IAS 1 and IFRS 5.

(8 marks)

(c) Prepare a statement of changes in equity for D in accordance with the requirements of IAS 1.

(5 marks)

(Total marks = 19)

? Question 9

Topaz makes up its accounts regularly to 31 December each year. The entity has operated for some years with four divisions, A, B, C and D, but on 30 July 20X2, Division B was sold for $8 million, realising a profit of $2.5 million.

The trial balance of the entity at 31 December 20X2 included the following balances.

	Division B		Divisions A, C and D combined	
	Dr	Cr	Dr	Cr
	$m	$m	$m	$m
Sales revenue		13		68
Costs of sales	8		41	
Distribution costs (including a bad debt of $1.9 m – Division D)	1		6	
Administrative expenses	2		4	
Profit on sale of Division B		2.5		
Cost of fundamental reorganisation			1.8	
Interest on $10 m 10% loan notes issued 20X2			1	
Income tax			4.8	
Interim dividend paid			6	
Revaluation reserve			10	
Retained earnings 31 December 20X1			50	

The balance on the revaluation reserve relates to the entity's property and arose as follows.

	$m
Balance at 1 January 20X2	6
Revaluation during 20X2	4
Balance at 31 December 20X2 per trial balance	10

The share capital of $100 million has remained unchanged throughout the year. The whole of the interest paid relates to continuing operations. The income tax should be divided as $3.6 million for continuing operations and $1.2 million for discontinued operations.

The costs of fundamental reorganisation of $1.8 million relate to the restructuring of Divisions A, C and D following the sale of Division B.

Requirements

(a) (i) Prepare the statement of comprehensive income of Topaz for the year ended 31 December 20X2, complying as far as possible with the provisions of IAS 1 and IFRS 5, (IFRS 5 requirements should be shown in the statement of comprehensive income)

(ii) Prepare the statement of changes in equity for the year as required by IAS 1.

(16 marks)

(b) Explain why the changes to the statement of comprehensive income introduced by IFRS 5 improve the quality of information available to users of the financial statements.

(4 marks)

(Total marks = 20)

? Question 10

On 1 September 2007, the Directors of EK decided to sell EK's retailing division and concentrate activities entirely on its manufacturing division.

The retailing division was available for immediate sale, but EK had not succeeded in disposing of the operation by 31 October 2007. EK identified a potential buyer for the retailing division, but negotiations were at an early stage. The Directors of EK are certain that the sale will be completed by 31 August 2008.

The retailing division's carrying value at 31 August 2007 was:

	$'000
Non-current tangible assets – property, plant and equipment	300
Non-current tangible assets – goodwill	100
Net current assets	43
Total carrying value	443

The retailing division has been valued at $423,000, comprising:

	$000
Non-current tangible assets – property, plant and equipment	320
Non-current tangible assets – goodwill	60
Net current assets	43
Total carrying value	423

EK's directors have estimated that EK will incur consultancy and legal fees for the disposal of $25,000.

Requirements

(i) Explain whether EK can treat the sale of its retailing division as a 'discontinued operation', as defined by IFRS 5 *Non-current Assets held for Sale and Discontinued Operations*, in its financial statements for the year ended 31 October 2007.

(3 marks)

(ii) Explain how EK should treat the retailing division in its financial statements for the year ended 31 October 2007, assuming the sale of its retailing division meets the classification requirements for a disposal group (IFRS 5). **(2 marks)**

(5 marks)

Solutions to Revision Questions

Solution 1

The correct answer is (C), see Section 12.9.5.

Solution 2

The correct answer is (C), see Section 12.2.2.

Solution 3

Errors are defined by IAS 8 as 'material omissions or misstatements in the financial statements', see Section 12.4.

Solution 4

The correct answer is (B), see Section 12.5.

Solution 5

Any FOUR of the following five conditions would gain the marks available.

1. the significant risks and rewards of ownership of the goods have been transferred to the buyer;
2. the entity selling does not retain any continuing influence or control over the goods;
3. revenue can be measured reliably;
4. it is reasonably certain that the buyer will pay for the goods;
5. the costs to the selling entity can be measured reliably, see Section 12.9.2.

Solution 6

The correct answer is (D), see Section 12.2.2.

REPORTING FINANCIAL PERFORMANCE

 Solution 7

(a) Extract from the statement of comprehensive income for Presario for the year ended 30 June 20X2.

	20X2	20X1 (restated)
	$'000	$'000
Sales	460	400
Cost of sales	(180)	(290)
Gross profit	280	110
Administrative expenses	(50)	(40)
Distribution costs	(40)	(30)
Profit before tax	190	40
Income tax (at 30%)	(57)	(12)
Profit	133	28

Workings

20X1 closing inventory was overstated by $70,000. This resulted in cost of sales being overstated and 20X1 profit and retained earnings being understated. Following the correction, 20X1 cost of sales is restated at $290,000 ($220,000 + $70,000). Profit before tax is now restated at $40,000 and income tax (at 30%) recalculated at $12,000.

The 20X2 cost of sales is correctly recorded at $180,000 ($250,000 less $70,000 overstatement of opening inventory charged to cost of sales in the draft accounts).

(b) The statement of changes in equity for Presario for the year ended 30 June 20X2

	20X2	20X1 (restated)
	$'000	$'000
Opening retained earnings as previously reported	197	120
Correction of error (net of taxes of $70 K × 30% = $21 K)	(49)	—
Opening retained earnings as restated	148	120
Profit	133	28
Closing retained earnings	281	148

Note X

Products with a cost of $70,000, which were sold during 20X1, were incorrectly included in inventory as at 30 June 20X1. The financial statements of 20X1 have been restated to correct this error.

 Solution 8

(a) The information provided in financial statements, while historic, is often used by readers of accounts to evaluate future performance. Any additional information about what makes up profits and cash flows can help in the assessment of what is likely to be generated in future periods.

IFRS 5 requires that the financial information be analysed between results from continuing operations and those from discontinued operations. Discontinued operations can be an entire part of the business operations being sold or terminated. It follows then that a discontinued operation will not generate results in future periods and so should not be included in the users' assessment of future performance. The results of continuing operations are likely to recur in future periods and users can then focus on these results when evaluating what the entity is likely to generate in the future.

The analysis of continuing operations and discontinued operations is required for financial performance, assets and liabilities and cash flows.

(b) D – statement of comprehensive income for the year ended 31 December 20X3

Continuing operations	$'000
Sales revenue	820
Operating expenses	(470)
Operating profit	350
Loss on disposal of fixed assets	(61)
Profit before interest	289
Finance costs	(37)
Profit before tax	252
Income tax expense	(50)
Profit for the period from continuing operations	202
Loss for the period from discontinued operations (Note 1)	(127)
Profit for the period	75
Other comprehensive income:	
Net reduction in value of property	(70)
Total comprehensive income for the period	5

Note 1

Discontinued operations	$'000
Sales revenue	150
Operating expenses	(98)
Operating profit	52
Loss on disposal of fixed assets	(205)
Profit before interest	(153)
Finance costs	—
Profit before tax	(153)
Income tax expense	26
Loss for the period from discontinued operations	(127)

(c) Statement of changes in equity, year ended 31 December 20X3

	Share capital $'000	Share premium $'000	Revaluation reserve $'000	Retained earnings $'000	Total $'000
Balance at 31 December 20X2	250	150	160	670	1,230
Total comprehensive income for the period	(70)	75	5		
Dividends paid				(30)	(30)
Issue of share capital	(ii) 100	(ii) 80			180
Balance at 31 December 20X3	350	230	90	715	1,385

Workings

(i) Revaluation reserve to be reduced from $160,000 to $90,000.

(ii) Share issue, 100,000 shares @ 80¢ premium; per value 100,000 × $1 included in share capital and the (100,000 × 80¢) $80,000 premium included in share premium.

Solution 9

(a) (i) Topaz – statement of comprehensive income for the year ended 31 December 20X2

	Continuing operations $m
Sales revenue	68.0
Cost of sales	(41.0)
Gross profit	27.0
Distribution costs (Note 1)	(6.0)
Administrative expenses	(4.0)
Profit from operations	17.0
Profit on sale of discontinued operations (Note 2)	
Costs of fundamental reorganisation (Note 3)	(1.8)
Profit before interest	15.2
Finance cost	(1.0)
Profit before tax	14.2
Income tax expense	(3.6)
Profit for the period from continuing operations	10.6
Profit for the period from discontinued operations (Note 1)	3.3
Profit for the period	13.9
Other comprehensive income:	
Net gain on revaluation of property	4.0
Total comprehensive income for the period	17.9

Note

1.

Discontinued operations	$m
Sales revenue	13.0
Cost of sales	(8.0)
Gross profit	5.0
Distribution costs (Note 1)	(1.0)
Administrative expenses	(2.0)
Profit from operations	2.0
Profit on sale of discontinued operation (Note 2)	2.5
Profit before tax	4.5
Income tax expense	(1.2)
Profit after tax	3.3

2. *Distribution costs.* Distribution costs include a bad debt of $1.9 million which arose on the continuing operations.

3. *Discontinued operations.* Division B was sold on 30 July 20X2 for $8 million, realising a profit on sale of $2.5 million. The results of Division B for the period to 31 December 20X2 are classified as discontinued operations.

4. *Fundamental reorganisation.* Following the sale of Division B in July 20X2 the entity undertook the restructuring of the remaining divisions at a cost of $1.8 million. (Note, this amount is required to be disclosed separately in the statement of comprehensive income because it is material. The restructuring is as a result of the discontinued operation but the costs are incurred reorganising the remaining divisions and so the amount is included in continuing operations.)

(ii) Topaz – statement of changes in equity, year ended 31 December 20X2

	Share capital $'000	Revaluation reserve $'000	Retained earnings $'000	Total $'000
Balance at 31 December 20X1	100	6	50	156
Total comprehensive income for the period		4	13.9	17.9
Dividends paid			(6)	(6)
Balance at 31 December 20X2	100	10	57.9	167.9

(b) The information provided in financial statements, while historic, is often used by readers of accounts to evaluate future performance. Any additional information about what makes up profits can help in the assessment of what is likely to be generated in future periods.

IFRS 5 requires that revenue, expenses and pre-tax profit be analysed between results from continuing operations and those from discontinued operations. Discontinued operations can be an entire part of the business operations being sold or terminated. It follows then that a discontinued operation will not generate results in future periods and so should not be included in the users' assessment of future performance. The results of continuing operations are likely to recur in future periods and users can then focus on these results when evaluating what the entity is likely to generate in the future.

IFRS 5 also requires that any gain or loss on the disposal of the discontinued operation be disclosed in the financial statements. This enables users to identify one-off profits or losses outwith the trading activities.

The additional information required by IFRS 5 is relevant and useful to users when making their investment decisions and therefore improves the quality of the information provided.

✓ Solution 10

(i) EK can treat the disposal of its retailing division as discontinued if it is a component of EK that has been disposed of, or is classified as held for sale. It must also be the disposal of a major line of business or a geographical area of operations. EK's disposal has not been completed by the balance sheet date, so does not meet that requirement.

IFRS 5 says that non-current assets or a disposal group can be classified as held for sale, where the carrying value will be recovered through a sale transaction, rather than their continuing use. The assets must be available for immediate sale in their present condition and the sale must be 'highly probable'. Highly probable means that the directors are committed to the sale and there is an active programme to locate a buyer and the assets are being actively marketed at a reasonable price. The sale must be expected to be completed within a year.

These terms appear to be met in EK's case and the retail division will be designated as held for sale. This means that they will be treated as discontinued operations in the year to 31 October 2007.

(ii) A disposal group is valued at fair value less cost to sell. If this gives rise to a lower value than the current book value, the assets have become impaired and must be written down. The reduction in value is charged to the statement of comprehensive income.

EK has valued the retail division at $423,000 and cost to sell is estimated at $25,000; this will give a net value of $398,000.

The assets in the disposal group will be recognised at the lower of their book value or fair value less cost to sell as follows:

	$000
Non-current assets, property, plant and equipment	300
Non-current assets, goodwill	55
Net current assets	43
	398

The reduction of $45,000 will be charged to the statement of comprehensive income.

Assets and disposal groups designated as held for sale are shown separately on the statement of financial position and are not depreciated.

13

Statement of Cash Flows

Statement of
Cash Flows

13

LEARNING OUTCOME

After completing this chapter you should be able to:
▶ prepare a complete set of financial statements, in a form suitable for publication for a single company.

The syllabus topic covered in this chapter is as follows:

- Preparation of cash flow statements (IAS 7).

13.1 Introduction

> The statement of cash flows is an important primary statement. The preparation of statement of cash flows is not difficult, provided that you keep a clear head and adopt a systematic approach to the presentation of the statement itself and also the preparation of workings. 'T'-accounts are often the most efficient means of drawing conclusions from the information provided in examination questions. It is not sufficient to be able to prepare a statement of cash flows; it is also necessary to be able to interpret it. Essentially, this involves thinking about the extent to which the business in question actually needs cash.

The fundamental purpose of being in business is to generate profit. Ultimately, it is profit that increases the owners' wealth. Profitability is, however, a long-term objective. In the short term, the business' viability is determined by its ability to generate cash. Even profitable entities will collapse if they do not have access to sufficient cash resources when it becomes necessary to settle a bill. Very few businesses could survive a prolonged outflow of cash.

The profit figure for the year is unlikely to bear any resemblance to the increase or decrease in the entity's bank balance over that period. Several of the entries in the statement of comprehensive income, such as depreciation, do not involve receipts or payments of cash. There are also many types of receipt or payment, such as the proceeds of a share issue or a loan repayment, which have no immediate impact on profit. This means that it would be possible for an entity to be trading at a profit and still run into liquidity problems.

The bank balance can, of course, be obtained from the statement of financial position. Comparing statements of financial position at the beginning and end of the year will even show whether cash has increased or decreased. It is, however, difficult to identify the major causes of changes in the balance from doing so. Shareholders and other readers require a more structured presentation of the cash flows.

The statement of cash flows, therefore, is intended to answer questions such as:

- Why has the bank overdraft increased, despite the entity having had a profitable year?
- Is the entity capable of generating funds, as opposed to profit, from its trading activities?
- What was done with the loan that was taken out during the year?

Note: IAS 7 Cash flow statements was renamed by IAS 1 in 2007. IAS is now Statement of cash flows.

13.2 Objective of IAS 7 *Statement of Cash Flows*

The objective of IAS 7 *Statement of Cash Flows* is to ensure that entities provide information about the historical changes in cash and cash equivalents in a standard format by means of a statement of cash flows.

Information about the cash flows of an entity is useful in providing users of financial statements with a basis to assess the ability of the entity to generate and utilise cash and cash equivalents.

IAS 7 defines cash and cash equivalents as follows:

- Cash comprises cash on hand and demand deposits.
- Cash equivalents are short-term, highly liquid investments that are readily convertible to known amounts of cash and which are subject to an insignificant risk of changes in value.

13.3 Statement of cash flows format

The statement of cash flows should report cash flows during the period classified by operating, investing and financing activities. The detailed format used by an entity should be the one that is most appropriate to its business. IAS 7 contains a standard format that should always be used in answering examination questions. The format is as follows (note, headings that relate to items excluded from the syllabus have been left out):

Indirect Method statement of cash flows

	$	$
Cash flows from operating activities		
Profit before taxation	X	
Adjustments for:		
Depreciation	X	
Investment income	X	X
Interest expense	<u>X</u>	X
	X	
Increase/Decrease in trade and other receivables	X	
Increase/Decrease in inventories	X	
Increase/Decrease in trade payables	<u>X</u>	
Cash generated from operations	X	
Interest paid	X	
Income taxes paid	<u>X</u>	
Net cash from operating activities		X

Cash flows from investing activities		
Purchase of property, plant and equipment	X	
Proceeds from sale of equipment	X	
Interest received	X	
Dividends received	X	
Net cash used in investing activities		X
Cash flows from financing activities		
Proceeds from issue of share capital	X	
Proceeds from long-term borrowings	X	
Payment of finance lease liabilities	X	
Dividends paid*	X	
Net cash used in financing activities		X
Net increase in cash and cash equivalents		X
Cash and cash equivalents at beginning of period		X
Cash and cash equivalents at end of period		X

*This could also be shown as an operating cash flow.

Each of the main headings shown above is discussed in detail below.

13.3.1 Cash flows from operating activities

Cash flows from operating activities are normally those arising from transactions relating to trading activities. It is intended to give an indication of the cash generated from operations.

Cash flows from operating activities can be calculated in two ways, using the direct method or the indirect method.

The direct method

The direct method shows operating cash receipts and payments, for example, cash paid to suppliers and employees and cash received from customers. This is useful to users as it shows the actual sources and uses of cash. However, many entities will not generate this information as a matter of course and so it may prove expensive to produce.

The indirect method

The indirect method instead starts with profit before taxation, adding back items shown elsewhere on the statement of cash flows (e.g. finance cost) and adjusting for non-cash items included in arriving at the operating profit figure. Non-cash items would include the following:

- *Depreciation* This is a book adjustment to reflect the wearing out of an asset; the cash impact of non-current assets is the buying of the asset.
- *Profits/losses on disposal of non-current assets* Profit is not cash – the cash impact of the disposal is the disposal proceeds.
- *Changes in inventories* As operating profit is calculated after charging cost of sales, which has been adjusted for opening and closing inventory we need the figure for total cash spent on materials in the year, not the cost of the goods used in the year.
- *Changes in receivables* The figure included in the profit or loss is the sales revenue – we need the cash received from customers and so we must take account of opening and closing receivables for the year.
- *Changes in payables* For the same reason as above – we need to get to the figure for actual cash paid to suppliers, but the direct method will occasionally be examined.

Entities are required to disclose the calculation using the indirect method as it provides the reconciliation of operating profit to cash flows from operating activities, which is an integral part of the statement of cash flows (it is therefore more likely to be the indirect method that is requested in examinations, but the direct method will occasionally be examined).

For illustration purposes, we now look at the calculations using both of these methods in arriving at cash flow from operations.

Example 13.A

The following financial information relates to Weir for the year ended 30 September 20X1.

Statement of comprehensive income for the year ended 30 September 20X1

	$'000
Revenue	222
Operating expenses	(156)
Operating profit	66
Finance costs	(9)
Profit before tax	57
Income tax expense	(21)
Profit	36

The following operating expenses were incurred in the year:

	$'000
Wages	(36)
Auditor's remuneration	(6)
Depreciation	(42)
Cost of materials used	(111)
Gain on sale of non-current assets	30
Rental income	9
	(156)

The following information is also available:

	30.9.X1 $'000	30.9.X0 $'000
Inventories	21	12
Trade receivables	24	21
Trade payables	(15)	(9)

Solution

(i) Direct method

	Workings	$,000
Receipts from customers	1	219
Rental income		9
Payments to suppliers	2	(114)
Wages		(36)
Auditor's remuneration		(6)
Net cash inflow from operations		72

Workings
1. Receipts from customers

	$'000
Sales revenue for the year	222
Plus opening receivables (would have paid in the year)	21
Less closing receivables (cash is outstanding at the year-end)	(24)
Cash received from customers in the year	219

2. Payments to suppliers

	$'000
Cost of materials used	111
Plus closing inventories	21
Less opening inventories	(12)
Materials purchased in the year	120
Plus opening payables	9
Less closing payables	(15)
Payments made to suppliers in the year	114

(ii) Indirect method

	Note	$'000
Profit before tax		57
Add back finance cost		9
Depreciation	1	42
Gain on disposal of non-current assets	2	(30)
Increase in receivables	3	(3)
Increase in inventories	4	(9)
Increase in payables	5	6
Net cash inflow from operations		72

Notes
1. Depreciation has been deducted in arriving at operating profit. However, it is not a cash item and so must be added back in calculating cash inflow from operating activities.
2. Similarly the gain on disposal has been included in operating profit but does not represent the cash flow associated with the disposal and so must be removed. (The cash flow for the disposal is the disposal proceeds total which will be included in 'cash flows from investing activities' further down the statement of cash flows.)
3. An increase in the balance of year-end receivables means that more cash is outstanding, less has been received than is represented in revenue. This is a net cash outflow and is therefore deducted.
4. Increase in inventories is a utilisation of cash resources and so is also deducted.
5. Increase in payables means that cash has been held back rather than paid to suppliers. This is a cash inflow and is therefore added.

13.3.2 Cash flows from investing activities

Cash payments to purchase property, plant and equipment and receipts from the sale of these items, along with cash payments to acquire equity of other entities, will be included under this heading.

13.3.3 Cash flows from financing activities

Proceeds of issue of shares or loan notes, or cash paid for their redemption, appear here, along with dividends paid. (Dividends paid may be shown as operating cash flows instead.) The repayment of the principal amount of a finance lease in included here.

13.3.4 Increase (or decrease) in cash and cash equivalents during period

This is a net movement from all the cash flows in the period. The opening and closing balances of cash and cash equivalents complete the statement.

STATEMENT OF CASH FLOWS

13.4 A worked example

The following example is intended to demonstrate some of the techniques that might be used in preparing a statement of cash flows. The intention is that you work through it line by line and think about the method. Do not expect every cash flow question to follow exactly the same pattern – you might have to adapt your approach in the exam.

13.4.1 Worked example

Requirements

Prepare Charlie's statement of cash flows for the year ended 31 March 20X1 from the following:

Charlie – Statement of comprehensive income for the year ended 31 March 20X1

	$'000
Sales revenue	1,700
Cost of sales	(900)
Gross profit	800
Distribution costs	(50)
Administrative expenses	(120)
Operating profit	630
Interest received	80
Interest paid	(65)
Profit before tax	645
Income tax expense	(28)
Profit for the financial year	617

Charlie – Statement of financial position as at 31 March

	20X1 $m	20X1 $m	20X0 $m	20X0 $m
Non-current assets				
Tangible assets		1,580		1,000
Current assets				
Inventor		250		130
Receivables		450		360
Prepaid distribution costs		4		2
Cash at bank and in hand		220		144
		2,504		1,636
Capital and reserves				
Issued share capital		120		100
Share premium account		88		49
Revaluation reserve		203		130
Accumulated profits		877		315
		1,288		594
Non-current liabilities				
Loans	800		700	
Deferred tax	10		7	
		810		707
Current liabilities				
Trade payables	374		310	
Accrued administrative expenses	6		3	
Income tax	26		22	
		406		335
		2,504		1,636

Additional information

(a) The entity sold some tangible non-current assets, which had a net book value of $200 million. The cost of sales figure includes a loss of $10 million on this disposal.

(b) Cost of sales is arrived at after charging depreciation on the tangible non-current assets of $42 million.

(c) Dividends paid during the year were $55,000.

> *A word about balancing figures.* The trick to answering this type of question is to make the greatest possible use of the information that has been provided in order to determine the figures that have not been provided directly. For example, the question does not tell us how much has been paid for new tangible non-current assets. The secret is to use working schedules or open a 'T'-account and to insert all of the relevant information related to the book value of these assets. We can infer the cost of new assets purchased during the year by calculating a balancing figure in this account.

For example, we could use a working schedule as follows:

Non-current assets	$m
Balance at 1 April 20X0	1,000
Add revaluation	73
Less disposals	(200)
Less depreciation	(42)
	831
Balance at 31 March 20X1	1,580
Purchases	749

Or we could open a 'T' account as follows:

Non-current assets

		$m			$m
1 Apr. X0	Balance b/d	1,000		Disposals	200
	Revaluation	73		Depreciation	42
Bal. figure	Additions	749	31 Mar. X1	Balance c/d	1,580
		1,822			1,822
1 Apr. X1	Balance b/d	1,580			

The question does not actually tell us that the entity spent $749 m on new non-current assets, but we can derive this figure simply by using a consistent method of working/ account to draw together the various pieces of information that we do have.

> In the exam, there is no guarantee that the information in respect of non-current assets will follow this particular pattern. You might, for example, find yourself drawing up a disposal account in order to derive the proceeds of the sale. Try the working schedule method and the 'T' account method, decide which one you prefer and then always use that method.

13.4.2   Cash flow from operations

For the sake of illustration, we will calculate this figure using both the direct and indirect methods. There is, however, no need to provide the information in both formats when the reconciliation using the indirect method is stated.

Direct method

The question does not state the cash received from customers. We can derive this easily though by preparing our workings. Workings can be prepared using either 'T' accounts or working schedules. First we will consider drawing up a 'T' account:

Receivables

		$m				$m
1 Apr. X0	Balance b/d	360	*Bal. figure*	Cash received		1,610
	Sales	1,700	31 Mar. X1	Balance c/d		450
		2,060				2,060
1 Apr. X1	Balance b/d	450				

We would include all information given in the question in this account, including any details of bad debts written off.

It would not matter if the entity made some sales for cash. Provided that we include the cash sales in the debit to receivables, the balancing figure in respect of cash received will include all receipts, whether from cash sales or credit customers.

Payments to suppliers are slightly more complicated. Cost of sales has two non-cash stages: the goods are purchased on credit and they also spend some time sitting in inventory. This means that we have to determine the figure for purchases and then derive the figure for cash paid to suppliers:

Cost of sales

		$m			$m
1 Apr. X0	Opening inventory	130	31 Mar. X1	Profit or loss (see note)	848
Bal. figure	Purchases	968	31 Mar. X1	Balance c/d	250
		1,098			1,098

Payables

		$m			$m
Bal. figure	Cash paid	904	1 Apr. X0	Balance b/d	310
31 Mar. X1	Balance c/d	374		Purchases	968
		1,278			1,278

Distribution costs

		$m			$m
1 Apr. X0	Prepayments b/d	2	31 Mar. X1	Profit or loss	50
Bal. figure	Cash paid	52	31 Mar. X1	Prepayments c/d	4
		54			54

Administrative expenses

		$m			$m
Bal. figure	Cash paid	117	1 Apr. X0	Accruals b/d	3
31 Max. X1	Accruals c/d	6	31 Mar. X1	Profit or loss	120
		123			123

Note: The figure inserted in the cost of sales account excludes the non-cash items of loss on disposal and depreciation (i.e. $900 - 10 - 42 = 848$).

Now we have sufficient information to determine the cash inflow from operating activities:

Charlie: cash flow from operating activities (direct method)

	$m
Cash received from customers	1,610
Cash paid to suppliers	(904)
Other operating expenses (52 + 117)	(169)
Cash generated from operations	537
Interest paid (see Note 1)	(65)
Income taxes paid (see Note 2)	(21)
Net cash from operating activities	451

Note 1

Interest had been removed in arriving at cash generated from operations. To arrive at 'net cash from operating activities', which is the heading required for the statement of cash flows, we must now deduct interest paid, which is likely to have been incurred as a result of funding general trading activity and so remains within this first heading. The interest element of a finance lease repayment is included here.

Note that interest received is likely to have been earned as a result of a deliberate investing activity and so is reclassified within 'cash flows from investing activities'.

Note 2

The calculation for tax paid must adjust the statement of comprehensive income charge for opening and closing balances on the tax accounts held in the statement of financial position.

	$m
Income tax expense as per statement of comprehensive income	28
Opening payable (paid during the year)	22
Closing payable (outstanding at the year-end)	(26)
	24
Increase in deferred tax provision (a non-cash item that has been included in the income tax expense in the statement of comprehensive income)	(3)
Tax paid in the year	(21)

Alternatively, you could set up a 'T'-account to arrive at the balance paid in the year, as shown below:

Taxation

		$m			$m
Bal. fig.	Cash paid	21	1 Apr. X0	Balance b/d	22
31 Mar. X1	Balance c/d	26	1 Apr. X0	Balance b/d	7
31 Mar. X1	Balance c/d	10	31 Mar. X1	Statement of com/income	28
		57			57

Now we will use working schedules to prepare the same figures:

Receivables

Balance 1 April 20X0	360
Add sales	1,700
	2,060
Less balance at 31 March 20X1	450
Cash received	1,610

Cost of sales

Opening inventory 1 April 20X0	130
Closing inventory 31 March 20X1	250
Increase in inventory	120
Charged to statement of comprehensive income	848
Purchases	968

Payables

Balance 1 April 20X0	310
Add purchases	968
	1,278
Less balance at 31 March 20X1	374
Cash paid	904

Distribution costs

Balance 1 April 20X0 – prepayment	2
Balance at 31 March 20X1 – prepayment	4
Increase in prepayments	2
Charged to statement of comprehensive income	50
Cash paid	52

Administrative expenses

Balance 1 April 20X0 – accruals	3
Balance at 31 March 20X1 – accruals	6
Increase in accruals	(3)
Profit or loss	120
Cash paid	117

Indirect method

The indirect method is required to be disclosed as it provides the reconciliation of operating profit (from the profit or loss) to the net cash flow from operating activities that appears in the statement of cash flows. This calculation should, of course, give the same result as the direct method.

The indirect method reconciliation starts with 'profit before tax'.

Charlie: cash flow from operating activities (indirect method)

	Note	$'000
Profit before taxation		645
Depreciation	1	42
Loss on disposal of non-current assets	2	10
Interest received	3	(80)
Interest paid	3	65
Operating profit before working capital changes		682
Increase in inventories	4	(120)
Increase in receivables	4	(90)
Increase in payables	4	64
Increase in prepaid expenses	5	(2)
Increase in accrued expenses	5	3
Cash generated from operations		537
Interest paid		(65)
Income taxes paid		(21)
Net cash inflow from operating activities		451
(agrees to the total calculated using the direct method)		

Notes

1. Depreciation has been deducted in arriving at operating profit. However, it is not a cash item and so must be added back in calculating cash inflow from operating activities.

2. Similarly, the gain on disposal has been included in operating profit but does not represent the cash flow associated with the disposal and so must be removed. (The cash flow for the disposal is the disposal proceeds total which will be included in 'cash flows from investing activities' further down the statement of cash flows.)

3. Interest received and paid have been included in arriving at profit before tax in the statement of comprehensive income. They are removed to arrive at cash generated from operating activities.

4. The changes in working capital elements are discussed in detail in Section 12.3.1.

5. The adjustments made for prepayments and accruals are made for similar reasons to the changes in working capital – some expenses included in the profit or loss are those that relate to the year but are not necessarily paid in the year. Adjusting for prepayments and accruals will ensure that the actual cash flows associated with the expenses are included.

> The simplest way to proceed through any question involving the preparation of an accounting statement is to have a sheet of paper for the statement itself and another for the workings. This makes it easier to work through the statement in a methodical manner, with plenty of space set aside for the workings.

13.4.3 Cash flows from investing activities

Purchase of tangible assets

This figure will be calculated as a balancing figure (discussed in Section 12.4.1). We will use all of the information we are given about tangible assets and conclude that the difference is the additions in the year.

		Tangible non-current assets			
		$m			$m
1 Apr. X0	Balance b/d	1,000		Disposals	200
	Revaluation	73		Depreciation	42
Bal. fig.	Additions	749	31 Mar. X1	Balance c/d	1,580
		1,822			1,822
1 Apr. X1	Balance b/d	1,580			

The opening balance of $1,000 m and the closing balance (balance carried down at 31 March 20X1) are taken from the statement of financial position information.

The net book value of disposals and the depreciation charge for the year are given in the additional information.

There is a movement on the revaluation reserve of $73 m, this is also included as we attempt to reconcile the opening and closing balances for the net book value of tangible assets with the balancing figure being taken as additions in the year.

Proceeds of sale of plant

We are told in the additional information that cost of sales includes a loss of $10 million in respect of a disposal of tangible non-current assets (we removed this figure in arriving at cash flow from operating activities in Section 13.4.2). We are also told that the net book value of the disposed assets totalled $200 million.

We know that the gain or loss on disposal is calculated by comparing the proceeds with the net book value and so can calculate the proceeds as:

	$m
Net book value	200
Loss on disposal	(10)
Proceeds from disposal	190

Interest received

As noted above, this income is likely to have been earned as a result of a specific investing activity and so is included within this category.

13.4.4 Cash flows from financing activities

Proceeds of share issue

The cash inflow resulting from the share issue is calculated by looking at the movements on the share capital and share premium accounts combined.

	$m
Increase in issued share capital (120 − 100)	20
Increase in share premium (88 − 49)	39
Total proceeds from share issue in the year	59

Proceeds from long-term borrowings

The $100 million cash inflow is arrived at by simply comparing the opening and closing balances on the loans account. It moves from $700 million last year to $800 million this year, resulting in a net cash inflow from loans of $100 million.

13.4.5 The statement of cash flows

Now we put together all of the above elements, using the standard IAS 7 format, the complete answer is as follows:

Charlie – Statement of cash flows for the year 31 March 20X1

	$m	$m
Cash flows from operating activities		
Profit before taxation	645	
Adjustments for		
Depreciation	42	
Loss on sale of plant	10	
Interest received	(80)	
Interest paid	65	

STATEMENT OF CASH FLOWS

Operating profit before working capital changes	682	
Inventory – increase	(120)	
Receivables – increase	(90)	
Payables – increase	64	
Prepayments – increase	(2)	
Accruals – increase	3	
Cash generated from operations	537	
Interest paid	(65)	
Income taxes paid	(21)	
Net cash from operating activities		451
Cash flows from investing activities		
Purchase of tangible non-current assets	(749)	
Proceeds of sale of plant	190	
Interest received	80	
Net cash used in investing activities		(479)
Cash flows from financing activities		
Proceeds of issue of shares	59	
Proceeds from long-term borrowings	100	
Dividends paid	(55)	
Net cash from financing activities		104
Net increase in cash and cash equivalents		76
Cash and cash equivalents at 1 April 20X0		144
Cash and cash equivalents at 31 March 20X1		220

13.5 Interpreting a statement of cash flows

We can see that Charlie managed to generate a net increase in cash during the period in question. Normally that would be desirable, but one can never be too categorical about such matters.

While very few entities can survive a prolonged outflow of cash, some businesses have too much tied up in liquid assets. The shareholders of such businesses would probably benefit from a deliberate disbursement of cash. For example, excess funds could be invested in non-current assets or inventories, or even returned to the shareholders by way of a dividend.

It is also worth bearing in mind that it is not difficult to distort cash balances in the short term. If the finance director delayed the payment of suppliers by a few days just before the year-end, then that could increase bank balances by a month's worth of payments to suppliers. Similarly, delaying the replenishment of inventories or encouraging prompt payment from receivables by means of a discount could artificially increase the bank balance.

The statement of cash flows does not give enough information on its own to enable a reader to tell whether a entity's funds have been well managed. The effects of any net movement can only be measured by looking at the closing statement of financial position and considering whether the relationships between the various components of working capital and long-term finance are acceptable.

Even if a net inflow was necessary, the statement cannot show whether the most appropriate type of finance has been raised or whether it has been obtained from the cheapest source.

13.6 Summary

Having completed this chapter, we can now follow the provisions of IAS 7 *Statement of Cash Flows* in arriving at cash flows from operating activities, using both the direct and indirect methods. We can calculate cash flows from investing and financing activities and prepare a statement of cash flows in a form suitable for publication.

Revision Questions

The preparation and interpretation of statement of cash flows has been a common source of examination questions in the past. This is likely to continue to be the case.

? Question 1

How much interest was paid during the year?

	$'000
Interest accrued b/f	600
Interest charged to statement of comprehensive income	700
Interest accrued c/f	500

(A) $600,000
(B) $700,000
(C) $800,000
(D) $1,300,000   **(2 marks)**

Data for Questions 2–7

For each cash flow listed below, identify the IAS 7 *Statement of Cash Flows* heading where the cash flow would be included. The headings to use are:

(A) cash flows from investing activities;
(B) cash flows from financing activities;
(C) cash and cash equivalents;
(D) cash flow from operating activities.

? Question 2

Profit on disposal of a fixed asset.
(A) (B) (C) (D)   **(2 marks)**

? Question 3

Dividends paid on preferred shares.
(A) (B) (C) (D)   **(2 marks)**

Question 4

Cash paid on redemption of debenture maturing during the year.
(A) (B) (C) (D)   **(2 marks)**

 ## Question 5

Surplus cash used to purchase own shares on the stock exchange.
(A) (B) (C) (D)   **(2 marks)**

 ## Question 6

A 60 day, 5% government bond purchased 1 month before the year-end.
(A) (B) (C) (D)   **(2 marks)**

Question 7

Depreciation of property, plant and equipment.
(A) (B) (C) (D)   **(2 marks)**

Question 8

At 30 September 2005, BY had the following balances, with comparatives:

Statement of financial position extracts: As at 30 September

	2005 $'000	2004 $'000
Non-current tangible assets		
Property, plant and equipment	260	180
Equity and reserves		
Property plant and equipment revaluation reserve	30	10

The statement of comprehensive income for the year ended 30 September 2005 included:
Gain on disposal of an item of equipment $10,000
Depreciation charge for the year $40,000

Notes to the accounts:
Equipment disposed of had cost $90,000. The proceeds received on disposal were $15,000.

Calculate the property, plant and equipment purchases that BY would show in its statement of cash flows for the year ended 30 September 2005, as required by IAS 7 *Statement of Cash Flows*.   **(4 marks)**

 ## Question 9

At 1 October 2004, BK had the following balance:
Accrued interest payable $12,000 credit

During the year ended 30 September 2005, BK charged interest payable of $41,000 to its statement of comprehensive income. The closing balance on accrued interest payable account at 30 September 2005 was $15,000 credit.

How much interest paid should BK show on its statement of cash flows for the year ended 30 September 2005?

(A) $38,000
(B) $41,000
(C) $44,000
(D) $53,000 **(2 marks)**

Question 10

Accrued income tax payable, balance at 31 March 2002 $920,000.

Accrued income tax payable, balance at 31 March 2003 $890,000.

Taxation charge to the statement of comprehensive income for the year to 31 March 2003 $850,000.

Deferred tax balance at 31 March 2002 $200,000.

Deferred tax balance at 31 March 2003 $250,000.

How much should be included in the statement of cash flows for income tax paid in the year?

(A) $800,000
(B) $830,000
(C) $850,000
(D) $880,000 **(4 marks)**

Question 11

Y's statement of comprehensive income for the year ended 31 December 20X3 and statements of financial position at 31 December 20X2 and 31 December 20X3 were as follows:

Y – statement of comprehensive income for the year ended 31 December 20X3

	$'000	$'000
Sales revenue		360
Raw materials consumed	(35)	
Staff costs	(47)	
Depreciation	(59)	
Loss on disposal	(9)	
		(150)
Operating profit		210
Interest payable		(14)
Profit before tax		196
Income tax expense		(62)
Profit after tax		134

Y – Statements of financial position as at 31 December

	20X3		20X2	
	$'000	$'000	$'000	$'000
Non-current assets				
Cost		798		780
Depreciation		(159)		(112)
		639		668
Current assets				
Inventory	12		10	
Trade receivables	33		25	
Bank	24		28	
		69		63
		708		731
Capital and reserves				
Share capital	180		170	
Share premium	18		12	
Retained earnings	358		257	
		556		439
Non-current Liabilities				
Long-term loans		100		250
Current liabilities				
Trade payables	6		3	
Income tax	46		39	
		52		42
		708		731

During the year, the entity paid $45,000 for a new piece of machinery.
A dividend of $33,000 was paid during the year.

Requirement

Prepare a statement of cash flows for Y for the year ended 31 December 20X3 in accordance with the requirements of IAS 7. **(15 marks)**

 # Question 12

It has been suggested that 'cash is king' and that readers of an entity's accounts should pay more attention to information concerning its cash flows and balances than to its profits and other assets. It is argued that cash is more difficult to manipulate than profit and that cash flows are more important.

Requirements

(a) Explain whether you agree with the suggestion that cash flows and balances are more difficult to manipulate than profit and non-cash assets. **(8 marks)**
(b) Explain why it might be dangerous to concentrate on cash to the exclusion of profit when analysing a set of financial statements. **(7 marks)**

(Total marks = 15)

Question 13

The following information relates to Neave for the year ended 31 December 20X3.

Statement of comprehensive income for the year ended 31 December 20X3

	$'000
Sales revenue	16,200
Raw materials consumed	(13,000)
	3,200
Depreciation	(200)
Other operating costs	(2,880)
Investment income	60
Operating profit	180
Gain on sale of investment	600
Interest payable	(40)
Profit before tax	740
Income tax expense	(320)
Profit after tax	420

Statements of financial position as at 31 December 20X3

	20X3 $'000	20X3 $'000	20X2 $'000	20X2 $'000
Non-current assets				
Tangible (NBV)		5,400		5,000
Investments		1,200		1,400
		6,600		6,400
Current assets				
Inventories	1,240		1,020	
Trade receivables	1,000		1,040	
Bank	400		140	
		2,640		2,200
		9,240		8,600
Capital and reserves				
Share capital		2,800		2,600
Share premium		1,600		1,400
Revaluation reserve		800		720
Retained earnings		2,400		2,260
		7,600		6,980
Non-current liabilities				
Long-term loans		400		300
Deferred tax		200		120
Current liabilities				
Trade payables	800		1,000	
Income tax	240		200	
		1,040		1,200
		9,240		8,600

Additional information

1. 200,000 $1 ordinary shares were issued during the year for $2.00 per share for cash.
2. $150,000 was raised by a new long-term loan being arranged during the year. Repayments under the existing loan totalled $50,000 in the year.

3. No investments were acquired in the year.
4. The taxation charge in the statement of comprehensive income is made up of:

	$'000
Income tax	240
Deferred tax	80
	320

5. No tangible non-current assets were sold in the year. However, land was revalued upwards by $80,000.
6. Interim dividends paid in the year amounted to $280,000.

Requirement

Prepare the statement of cash flows for the year ended 31 December 20X3 for Neave.

(20 marks)

? Question 14

The financial statements of CJ for the year to 31 March 2006 were as follows:

Statement of Financial Position at	31 March 2006		31 March 2005	
	$'000	$'000	$'000	$'000
Non-current tangible assets				
Property	19,160		18,000	
Plant and equipment	8,500		10,000	
Available for sale investments	1,500		2,100	
		29,160		30,100
Current assets				
Inventory	2,714		2,500	
Trade receivables	2,106		1,800	
Cash at bank	6,553		0	
Cash in hand	409		320	
		11,782		4,620
Total assets		40,942		34,720
Equity and liabilities				
Ordinary shares $0.50 each	12,000			7,000
Share premium	10,000			5,000
Revaluation reserve	4,200			2,700
Retained profit	3,009			1,510
		29,209		16,210
Non-current liabilities				
Interest bearing borrowings	7,000		13,000	
Provision for deferred tax	999	7,999	800	13,800
Current liabilities				
Bank overdraft	0		1,200	
Trade and other payables	1,820		1,700	
Corporate income tax payable	914		1,810	
		3,734		4,710
		40,942		34,720

Statement of comprehensive income for the Year to 31 March 2006

	$'000
Revenue	31,000
Cost of sales	(19,000)
Gross profit	12,000
Other income	200
Administrative expenses	(3,900)
Distribution costs	(2,600)
	5,700
Finance cost	(1,302)
Profit before tax	4,398
Income tax expense	(2,099)
Profit for the period	2,299

Additional information

1. On 1 April 2005, CJ issued 10,000,000 $0.50 ordinary shares at a premium of 100%.
2. No additional available for sale investments were acquired during the year.
3. On 1 July 2005, CJ repaid $6,000,000 of its interest bearing borrowings.
4. Properties were revalued by $1,500,000 during the year.
5. Plant disposed of in the year had a net book value of $95,000; cash received on disposal was $118,000.
6. Depreciation charged for the year was properties $2,070,000 and plant and equipment $1,985,000.
7. The trade and other payables balance includes interest payable of $650,000 at 31 March 2005 and $350,000 at 31 March 2006.
8. Dividends paid during the year, $800,000 comprised last year's final dividend plus the current year's interim dividend. CJ's accounting policy is not to accrue proposed dividends.
9. Other income comprises:

	$
Dividends received	180,000
Gain on disposal of available for sale investments	20,000
	200,000

Dividends receivable are not accrued.

10. Income tax expense comprises:

	$
Corporate income tax	1,900,000
Deferred tax for sale investments	199,000
	2,099,000

Dividends receivable are not accrued.

Requirement

Prepare CJ's statement of cash flows for the year ended 31 March 2006, in accordance with IAS 7 *Statement of Cash Flows*. **(20 marks)**

Solutions to Revision Questions

☑ Solution 1

The correct answer is (C), see Section 13.4.2.

☑ Solution 2

The correct answer is (A), see Section 13.4.3.
   The profit is adjusted in the reconciliation.

☑ Solution 3

The correct answer is (B), see Section 13.4.4.

☑ Solution 4

The correct answer is (B), see Section 13.4.4.

☑ Solution 5

The correct answer is (B), see Section 13.4.4.

☑ Solution 6

The correct answer is (C), see Section 13.2.

☑ Solution 7

The correct answer is (D), see Section 13.4.2.

Solution 8

	$'000
Balance b/fwd	180
Revaluation (30 − 10)	20
Disposal (15 − 10)	(5)
Depreciation	(40)
	155
Balance c/fwd	(260)
Purchases	105

 # Solution 9

	$'000
Statement of comprehensive income	41
Add balance b/fwd	12
	53
Less balance c/fwd	15
	38

 # Solution 10

The correct answer is (B).

	$
Deferred tax 31 March 02	200,000
Deferred tax 31 March 03	250,000
Increase	50,000
Total tax charged to Statement of comprehensive income	(850,000)
Income tax for year	800,000
Tax balance 31 March 2002	920,000
Income tax charge for the year	800,000
	1,720,000
Outstanding at 31 March 2003	890,000
Corporation tax paid in the year	830,000

 # Solution 11

Y – Statement of cash flows for the year ended 31 December 20X3

	$'000	$'000
Cash flows from operating activities		
Profit before taxation	196	
Adjustments for		
Depreciation	59	
Loss on sale of plant	9	
Interest payable	14	
Operating profit before working capital changes	278	
Inventory – increase	(2)	

Receivables – increase	(8)	
Payables – increase	3	
Cash generated from operations	271	
Interest paid	(14)	
Income taxes paid	(55)	
Net cash from operating activities		202
Cash flows from investing activities		
Purchase of non-current assets	(45)	
Proceeds of sale of plant	6	
Net cash used in investing activities		(39)
Cash flows from financing activities		
Proceeds of issue of shares	16	
Repayments of loans	(150)	
Dividends paid	(33)	
Net cash used in financing activities		(167)
Net increase/decrease in cash and cash equivalents		(4)
Cash and cash equivalents at 1 January 20X3		28
Cash and cash equivalents at 31 December 20X3		24

Working notes

Taxation

	$'000
Balance due at 31 December 20X2	39
Add: tax charge for the year to 31 December 20X3	62
	101
Less: tax liability at 31 December 20X3	(46)
Tax paid during year	55

Non-current assets – cost

	$'000
Balance at 31 December 20X2	780
Add: machinery purchased	45
	825
Less: balance at 31 December 20X3	(798)
Disposal in the year	27

Non-current assets – depreciation

	$'000
Balance at 31 December 20X2	112
Add: charge for the year	59
	171
Less: balance at 31 December 20X3	(159)
Depreciation on disposal	12

Receipts from sales of non-current tangible assets

	$'000
Cost (calculated above)	27
Depreciation (calculated above)	(12)
Written-down value	15
Loss on sale	(9)
Proceeds from sale	6

STATEMENT OF CASH FLOWS

 Solution 12

(a) Cash is the most liquid of assets, and it is also the most tangible. A banknote with a face value of $10 can be held in the hand, and there can be no dispute that maybe it is really $11 or $9. Profits, however, are not tangible or liquid, and it is possible to argue that profit should be restated at a higher (or lower) amount.

With simple income and expenditure accounts, the excess corresponds to an amount of cash, and is therefore difficult to manipulate. But, with accruals accounting, problems of estimation arise (e.g. how much to provide for depreciation and bad debts). In the case of modern, multinational groups of entities, the potential for manipulation of profit is much greater still.

It is possible, however, to manipulate cash flows and balances as well as profits. Cash balances can be boosted at the year-end by withholding payment to suppliers; customers can be given incentives to pay any large balances; loans can be taken out (and repaid immediately after the year-end); and assets can be sold for cash.

The International Accounting Standards Committee has been developing and issuing financial reporting standards which attempt to minimise the opportunities for manipulation of profits, cash flows and balances.

(b) Positive cash flows are extremely important for entities to ensure their survival. Many profitable entities have gone into liquidation simply because of their inability to generate sufficient cash. But in the longer term, entities that are unable to make profits will cease to generate cash, and will also fold. Of the two, the ability to generate profits is the most important for the long-term security of the entity. By focusing purely on increasing cash balances, the managers of an entity might neglect their main task, which is to make a profit for shareholders.

It is also not in the best interests of an entity to habitually hold large cash deposits (unless interest rates are running at an abnormally high rate). It makes more sense for the directors to reinvest available funds in non-current assets, which should increase the entity's profitability. The entity's working capital management policy should ensure that enough cash is held to meet its day-to-day requirements, but no more. In the same way, as an entity gains nothing from carrying large amounts of excess inventory, it is likely that better returns can be found for excess cash by alternative investments.

 Solution 13

Neave – Statement of cash flows for the year ended 31 December 20X3

	Notes	$'000	$'000
Cash flows from operating activities			
Profit before taxation			740
Adjustments for:			
Depreciation	1	200	
Gain on sale of Investments	2	(600)	
Interest paid	3	40	
Investment income Received	4	(60)	
			(420)
Operating profit before working capital changes			320
Inventory – increase	5	(220)	
Receivables – decrease	5	40	
Payables – decrease	5	(200)	
			(380)
			(60)

Cash generated from operations			
Interest paid		(40)	
Income taxes paid	6	(200)	
			(240)
Net Cash from operating activities			(300)
Cash flows from investing activities			
Purchase of non-current assets	7	(520)	
Proceeds from sale of investments	8	800	
Investment income		60	
Net cash generated from investing activities			340
Cash flows from financing activities			
Proceeds of share issue	9	400	
Increase in long-term loans		150	
Repayments of loan		(50)	
Dividends paid		(280)	
Net cash from financing activities			220
Net increase in cash and cash equivalents			260
Cash and cash equivalents at 1 January 20X3	10		140
Cash and cash equivalents at 31 December 20X3	10		400

Notes

1. Depreciation is a non-cash item that has been deducted in arriving at profit before tax, and so is added back in the calculation for cash flow from operations.

2. The gain on sale is calculated by comparing the proceeds and the book value of investments, it is not a cash item and so is deducted. The proceeds of the sale will appear later in the cash flow within investing activities.

3. Interest paid has been deducted in arriving at profit before tax. It is added back to arrive at actual cash generated from operations and then appears later as a deduction in arriving at net cash from operating activities as it is likely to have been incurred in the financing of the business's general trading activities (for format purposes).

4. Investment income is removed in arriving at cash flow from operations as it likely to have been earned as a result of deliberate investment activities. It is included further down the statement of cash flows under 'Cash flows from investing activities'.

5. Changes in working capital must be accounted for as turnover and cost of materials used are not cash items – they do not take account of credit extended to customers and by suppliers. Increase in inventory means more inventory has been purchased and is an outflow of cash. Payables decreasing means that payments are being made, which again is an outflow of cash. Receivables decreasing means that cash is being received faster from customers, and so is a source of cash.

6. Income tax paid is then deducted in arriving at net cash from operating activities as this has been incurred by trading. The actual tax paid must be calculated, as there are two statements of financial position balances and a statement of comprehensive income charge all relating to tax. It is calculated as follows:

	$'000
Opening liability – income tax	200
Opening deferred tax balance	120
Charge for the year	320
Closing liability – income tax	(240)
Closing deferred tax balance	(200)
Cash paid in respect of tax	200

STATEMENT OF CASH FLOWS

7. The purchase of non-current assets appears under investing activities. We are not told the figure for purchases and so must derive it using all the information relating to the non-current assets given in the question. The additions in the year will be the balancing figure. We want to track all the movements in the year in order to reconcile the opening and closing net book value that are in the statement of financial position.

	$'000
Opening net book value (B/S)	5,000
Depreciation charge (decreases book value)	(200)
Revaluation in the year (increases book value)	80
Balancing figure – additions in the year	520
Closing net book value	5,400

This calculation could also be performed with the use of a 'T'-account (you should use whatever you feel most confident with):

Tangible non-current assets

		$'000			$'000
1 Jan. X1	Balance b/d	5,000		Depreciation	200
	Revaluation	80			
Bal. fig.	Additions	520	31 Dec. X1	Balance c/d	5,400
		5,600			5,600
1 Jan. X2	Balance b/d	5,400			

8. The cash proceeds from the sale of investments is also included within investing activities although this is a source of cash. We are not told the proceeds but can easily work them out. We know the gain on disposal (from profit or loss) and we know the book value of the investments (from the statement of financial position). We know that the gain is calculated as proceeds less book value and so gain plus book value must equal proceeds:

	$'000
Gain on sale	600
Decrease in book value of investments in the year (1,400 − 1,200)	200
Proceeds from disposal	800

9. The additional information in the question tells us that the share issue was for cash and so the proceeds of share issue are 200,000 × $2 per share = $400,000 cash inflow. This is a method of financing the business and so is included in the cash flows from financing activities.

The opening and closing bank balances are found in the statement of financial position and the net cash flow in the year should reconcile the opening and closing balances for bank and cash.

 Solution 14

CJ – Statement of cash flows for the year ended 31 March 2006

	$'000	$'000
Cash flows from operating activities		
Profit before taxation	4,398	
Adjustments for:		
Other income	(200)	
Depreciation	4,055	

Finance cost	1,302	
Gain on disposal of plant (W2)	(23)	
	9,532	
Increase in inventory	(214)	
Increase in trade receivables	(306)	
Increase in trade and other payables (W6)	420	
Cash generated from operations	9,432	
Interest paid (W3)	(1,602)	
Income taxes paid (W4)	(1,796)	
Net cash from operating activities		6,034
Cash flows from investing activities		
Purchase of property, plant and equipment (W1)	(2,310)	
Investment income received	180	
Proceeds from sale of equipment	118	
Proceeds from disposal of available for sale investments (W5)	620	
Net cash used in investing activities		(1,392)
Cash flows from financing activities		
Proceeds from issue of share capital (W7)	10,000	
Repayment of interest bearing borrowings	(6,000)	
Equity dividends paid*	(800)	
Net cash from financing activities		3,200
Net increase in cash and cash equivalents		7,842
Cash and cash equivalents at 1 April 2005		1(880)
Cash and cash equivalents at 31 March 2006		6,962

*this could also be shown as an operating cash flow

Workings

(W1)

Net book values	Property	Plant	Available for sale investments
	$'000	$'000	$'000
Balance b/fwd	18,000	10,000	2,100
Revaluation	1,500	0	0
	19,500	10,000	2,100
Disposal	0	(95)	(600)
Depreciation for year	(2,070)	(1,985)	0
	17,430	7,920	1,500
Acquired in year (to balance)	1,730	580	0
Balance c/fwd	19,160	8,500	1,500

(W2)
Gain on disposal of plant

Net book value	95
Cash received	118
	23

(W3)
Interest paid

Balance b/fwd	650
Finance cost in profit or loss	1,302
	1,952
Balance c/fwd	(350)
Interest paid in year	1,602

(W4)

Tax paid

Balance b/fwd – Current tax	1,810	
Deferred tax	800	2,610
Statement of comprehensive income charge		2,099
		4,709
Balance c/fwd – Current tax	1,914	
Deferred tax	999	2,913
Paid in year		1,796

(W5)

Proceeds from disposal of available for sale investments

Disposal per (W1)	600
Add gain on disposal	20
	620

(W6)

Increase in trade payables

Trade and other payables balance b/fwd		1,700
Less: Interest b/fwd		(650)
		1,050
Trade and other payables balance c/fwd	1,820	
Less: Interest c/fwd	350	1,470
Increase in trade payables		420

(W7)

Proceeds from issue of equity share capital

Equity shares	5,000
Share premium	5,000
	10,000

14

Accounting for Investments in Subsidiary's and Associates

Accounting for Investments in Subsidiary's and Associates

14

LEARNING OUTCOME

After completing this chapter, you should be able to:

▶ apply the concepts of fair value at the point of acquisition, identifiability of assets and liabilities, and recognition of goodwill.

14.1 Introduction

This chapter introduces the appropriate accounting for investments in other entities. The extent of the investment will often determine the appropriate accounting treatment and this chapter examines the investments that will be accounted for as:

- Basic investments
- Investments in associates
- Investments in subsidiaries

The focus is mainly on accounting for subsidiaries as the rules and requirements outlined will form the basis of the applications in Chapters 15 and 16.

The accounting for fair values in consolidation and the recognition of goodwill are also covered in this chapter.

14.2 Accounting for investments

Entities will often invest in the equity of other businesses. The extent of the equity shareholding will determine how the investment should be accounted for. The accounting treatment applied for investments is intended to reflect the importance of the investment in the financial statements of the investee and how the future performance and financial position might be affected by these investments. It follows then that the greater the level of investment the more detailed the financial information will be. A significant investment in another entity may require additional financial statements to be produced.

14.3 Investment in associates

If an investor holds, directly or indirectly, 20 per cent of the voting rights of an entity then it is normally considered an associated entity and is accounted for in accordance with IAS 28 *Accounting for Associates*. IAS 28 states that there is a presumption that the investor has significant influence over the entity, unless it can be clearly demonstrated that this is not the case.

The key concept in the definition is 'significant influence'. IAS 28 explains that significant influence is the power to participate in the financial and operating policy decisions of the entity but is not control over those policies. The existence of significant influence by an investor is usually evidenced in one or more of the following ways:

- representation on the board of directors;
- participation in policy-making processes;
- material transactions between the investor and the entity;
- interchange of managerial personnel;
- provision of essential technical information.

The impact of this level of investment on the investing entity is likely to be greater than that of a simple investment. There is greater exposure to the results of the associate and a decline in its value will have a greater negative impact on the statement of financial position of the investing entity. The information provided therefore is a step further than that provided for simple investments.

The investment in the associate is equity accounted (covered in depth in Chapter 6) and the investment shown in the balance sheet will include the investing entity's share of the gains of the associate from the date the investment was made. The investing entity will show the share of realised and recognised gains it is entitled to by virtue of this investment rather than just the dividend received.

14.4 Investment in subsidiaries

It is often the case that businesses conduct part of their operations by making investments in other business entities. For example, a business that aims to expand its market share could opt to purchase one or more of its competitors, rather than taking the slower route of building market share by gradual growth. Another example is where a business purchases an investment in one or more of its suppliers of key goods and services in order to integrate and secure its supply chain.

In order to fulfil the needs of investors and other users, additional information is likely to be required, and therefore the IASB has in issue several accounting standards setting out the principles and practices that must be followed where an investment comprises a significant proportion of the total equity of the investee entity.

14.4.1 The principle of control

This chapter will start to examine the accounting required under IFRS for investments in subsidiaries. The accounting standard that sets out the requirements for recognition of an entity as a subsidiary is IAS 27 *Consolidated and Separate Financial Statements*. This standard was revised in January 2008, but its basic principles have been part of IFRS for many years.

First, some relevant definitions taken from the standard:

A *parent* is an entity that has one or more subsidiaries.

A *subsidiary* is an entity, including an unincorporated entity such as a partnership, which is controlled by another entity (known as the parent).

The key concept in determining whether or not an investment constitutes a subsidiary is that of *control*.

Control is the power to govern the financial and operating policies of an entity so as to obtain benefit from its activities.

There is a presumption that control exists where the investor entity owns over half of the voting power of the other entity. If an investor entity, ABC, owns 55% of the voting share capital of entity DEF, in the absence of any special circumstances, ABC is presumed to be in control of DEF. The maximum investment that could be held by another investor is 45%, and so ABC will always have the capacity to win a vote over the other investor(s). The nature of the relationship between ABC and DEF is that of parent and subsidiary.

In most cases, control can be easily determined by looking at the percentage ownership of the ordinary share capital in the investee entity. Provided ownership is greater than 50% a parent/subsidiary relationship can be assumed. However, there are exceptions. A parent/subsidiary relationship can exist even where the parent owns less than 50% of the voting power of the subsidiary since the key to the relationship is control. IAS 27 supplies the following instances:

When there is:

(a) power over more than half of the voting rights by virtue of an agreement with other investors;

(b) power to govern the financial and operating policies of the entity under a statute or agreement;

(c) power to appoint or remove the majority of the members of the board of directors or equivalent governing body and control of the entity is by that board or body; or

(d) power to cast the majority of votes at meetings of the board of directors or equivalent governing body and control of the entity is by that board or body.

The reason for describing the nature of control in such detail in IAS 27 is that entities have sometimes created ownership structures designed to evade the requirements for accounting for subsidiaries.

In the Financial operations examination, you will only be examined on a subsidiary that is fully controlled by the parent. (100% control).

14.4.2 The requirement to prepare consolidated financial statements

Where a parent/subsidiary relationship exists, IAS 27 requires that the parent should prepare consolidated financial statements. It is important to realise from the outset that this is an additional set of financial statements. The parent and subsidiary continue to prepare their own financial statements. Therefore in a group comprising one parent and one subsidiary, a total of three sets of financial statements are required. Where a group comprises, say, the parent and four subsidiaries, a total of six sets of financial statements are required: one for the parent, one for each of the four subsidiaries and one set of consolidated financial statements.

14.4.3 Exclusion from preparing consolidated accounts

A full set of financial statements in addition to those already prepared is, of course, quite an onerous requirement. IAS 27 includes some exemptions, as follows:

A parent need not present consolidated financial statements if and only if:

(a) the parent is itself a wholly owned subsidiary, or is a partially-owned subsidiary of another entity and its other owners, including those not otherwise entitled to vote, have been informed about, and do not object to, the parent not presenting consolidated financial statements;

(b) the parent's debt or equity instruments are not traded in a public market (a domestic or foreign stock exchange or an over-the-counter market, including local and regional markets).

(c) the parent did not file, nor is it in the process of filing, its financial statements with a securities commission or other regulatory organisation for the purpose of issuing any class of instruments in a public market;

(d) the ultimate or any intermediate parent of the parent produces consolidated financial statements available for public use that comply with IFRS.

These provisions have been spelt out in some detail so as to minimise the risk of entities evading the accounting requirements.

14.4.4 Goodwill

When a controlling investment is made the parent is investing in the net assets of the subsidiary. The value of the assets presented on the statement of financial position is unlikely to be what is paid by the investing entity.

Usually, the owners of a profitable business will expect to receive more in exchange for the investment than its net asset value. This additional amount arises for various reasons. It is quite likely that the assets recognised in the statement of financial position do not represent all the assets of the firm but intangibles such as good reputation and customer loyalty may be worth something to the purchaser. The difference between the cost of investment and the fair value of the net assets acquired is known as **goodwill on acquisition**, and the accounting standard IFRS 3 *Business Combinations* requires its recognition in consolidated financial statements.

14.4.5 IFRS 3 *Business combinations*

IFRS 3 was originally issued in March 2004 replacing an earlier standard. However, it was just the first stage in a longer term IASB project on accounting for business combinations. The next stage culminated in the issue, in January 2008, of the revised version of IFRS 3.

IFRS 3 requires that entities should account for business combinations by applying the **acquisition method of accounting**. This involves recognising and measuring the identifiable assets acquired, the liabilities assumed and any non-controlling interest in the acquiree entity (the recognition and measurement of non-controlling interests will be explained in Chapter 3). Measurement should be at fair value on the date of acquisition. Where 100% of the equity of a subsidiary is acquired, goodwill on acquisition is calculated as follows:

> Goodwill on acquisition is the aggregate of:
> Consideration, measured at fair value
> LESS
> Net assets acquired (the fair value of identifiable assets acquired less liabilities assumed)

This measures goodwill on acquisition which is recognised in the consolidated financial statement of position within non-current assets. Goodwill on acquisition is an asset of the group (not of the individual entities within the group) and is subject to impairment reviews to ensure its value is not overstated. The goodwill arises at the date of acquisition and will not change unless impairment is identified, whereby it will be held net of impairment losses (which should be recognised in accordance with IAS 36 *Impairment of Assets*).

14.4.6 Fair values in acquisition accounting

IFRS 3 requires that whenever a group entity is consolidated for the first time the purchase consideration and the group share of the net assets of the acquired entity are measured at fair values. The difference between these two figures is goodwill. The purpose of a fair-value exercise is to apportion the consideration given by the parent to purchase the shares in the newly acquired entity to the net assets of the newly acquired entity for consolidation purposes. Any difference between the fair value of the consideration given and the fair values of the net assets acquired is goodwill on acquisition.

As far as the net assets of the acquired entity are concerned, the amounts that are initially consolidated should normally be restricted to net assets of the acquired entity that existed at the date of the acquisition. They should be recognised separately as at the date of acquisition if they satisfy IFRS 3's criteria for recognition:

- In the case of an asset other than an intangible asset, it is probable that any associated future economic benefits will flow to the acquirer, and its fair value can be measured reliably.
- In the case of a liability other than a contingent liability, it is probable that an outflow of resources embodying economic benefits will be required to settle the obligation, and its fair value can be measured reliably.
- It is an intangible asset that meets the IAS 38 *Intangible Assets* definition.
- In the case of a contingent liability, its fair value can be measured reliably.

General principles

Fair value is defined in IFRS 3 as:

... the amount for which an asset could be exchanged or a liability settled between knowledgeable, willing parties in an arm's-length transaction.

As a general rule, fair value is market value. More detail regarding the fair valuation of specific assets and liabilities is given below.

The cost of a business combination should represent the fair values of assets given, liabilities incurred or assumed, and equity instruments issued by the acquirer, in exchange for control of the acquiree.

Fair value of consideration

Fair value must be measured at the date of the exchange. In cases where the acquisition is for the asset of cash, measurement of fair value is straightforward. However, in some cases the consideration offered will comprise equity shares, wholly or in part. Where this is the case, the shares must be valued at fair value. The published price at the date of exchange is the best evidence of fair value where the equity instruments are listed on a stock exchange. The only exception to this is if, for some reason, the market value of the relevant instrument at the date of acquisition is unusually high or low (e.g. if world events have resulted in a temporary significant downturn in market values of securities). In such circumstances it would be necessary to consider the market value of the instrument around the date of acquisition to arrive at a representative and realistic figure for fair value.

A special case involves contingent consideration:

Entity A might pay $8 million to acquire the shares of entity B, but the contract may be subject to a clause relating to contingent consideration which stipulates that if certain criteria are met in the first year of ownership (relating perhaps to profitability), a further $1 million will be payable to the former shareholders of B. Where an element of the consideration is contingent on future events, that element should be included in the overall cost of the acquisition if the adjustment is probable and can be measured reliably. Occasionally the terms of the agreement may be such that it is impossible to say whether, and if so how much, additional consideration will be paid, and in such circumstances, the group accounts may have to simply disclose the matter, rather than by making provision. The fair value of the contingent consideration should be based on the present value of future consideration payable.

Any costs incurred in the business combination (legal fees, etc.) will be written off as expenses in the period.

Costs of issuing financial instruments in connection with the acquisition should *not* be included as part of the fair value of consideration. Instead, they are included as part of the initial measurement of the financial instrument, in accordance with IAS 39 (see Chapter 11).

Property, plant and equipment

Fair value should be based on depreciated market value unless (in the case of plant and equipment) there is no evidence of market value because of the specialised nature of the plant and equipment or because it is rarely traded, except as part of a continuing business. In such cases fair value should be based on depreciated replacement cost.

Inventories

Where inventories are replaced by purchases in a ready market, the fair value = market value. However, where, as in the case of manufactured inventories, there is no ready market fair value is the current cost to the acquiring entity of obtaining the same inventories. If no current cost figure is readily available (as may well be the case) it can be approximated by taking inventories at sales values less:

- costs to complete (for work-in-progress inventories)
- incidental costs of disposal
- a realistic allowance for profit.

Listed investments

In most cases, the price quoted at the date of exchange will represent fair value.

Intangible assets

The acquirer should recognise an intangible asset of the acquiree at the date of acquisition provided that it meets the definition of an intangible asset provided by IAS 38 *Intangible Assets*, and that it can be measured reliably. Intangible assets must be separable (i.e. must be capable of being separated and divided from the entity and of being sold) or they must arise from contractual or legal rights.

Monetary assets and liabilities

The fair value should be based on the amounts due to be received or paid. For many monetary assets and liabilities, the fair value will be the amount at which they are stated in the subsidiary undertaking's balance sheet at the date of exchange. However, the fair value of some long-term monetary items may be materially different from book value, for example, where an acquired entity is carrying material amounts of long-term borrowings at fixed rates that are not representative of current interest rates. Where fair value is materially different from book values, fair value should be used. It may be necessary, in respect of unlisted financial instruments, to estimate fair value by discounting to present value amounts expected to be received or paid.

Provisions for restructuring

Only the identifiable assets, liabilities and contingent liabilities of the acquiree that exist at the balance sheet date can be recognised separately by the acquirer as part of allocating the cost of the combination. IFRS 3 states that: 'future losses or other costs expected to be incurred as a result of a combination are not liabilities incurred or assumed by the acquirer in exchange for control of the acquiree, and are not, therefore, included as part of the cost of the combination' (para. 28).

Contingent liabilities

Contingent liabilities, in accordance with IAS 37 *Provisions, Contingent Liabilities and Contingent Assets*, are not recognised in financial statements. However, by contrast, IFRS 3 requires that the contingent liabilities of an acquiree are recognised at fair value at the date of acquisition provided that their fair value can be measured reliably. Therefore, when calculating goodwill on acquisition, it is important to remember to include all measurable contingent liabilities. Note that contingent assets are not recognised by the acquiring entity.

14.5 **Summary**

This chapter has reviewed the accounting for investments and looked at how the different levels of investment warrant different accounting treatment. The introduction to accounting for subsidiaries included a review of the principles of control, how to determine fair values of assets and liabilities acquired and how to recognise goodwill on acquisition. The requirements that have to be met to be excluded from preparing consolidated financial statements were also covered.

This chapter covered some key principles in the consolidation process and you may find that you refer back to it as you progress through Chapters 15 and 16.

Revision Questions

? Question 1

Where the purchase price of an acquisition is less than the aggregate fair value of the net assets acquired, which ONE of the following accounting treatments of the difference is required by IFRS 3 *Business Combinations*?

(A) Deduction from goodwill in the consolidated statement of financial position?
(B) Immediate recognition as a gain in the statement of changes in equity?
(C) Recognition in the statement of comprehensive income over its useful life?
(D) Immediate recognition as a gain in profit or loss.   **(2 marks)**

? Question 2

On 30 September 20X8 GHI purchased 100% of the ordinary share capital of JKL for $1.80 million. The book value of JKL's net assets at the date of acquisition was $1.35 million. A valuation exercise showed that the fair value of JKL's property, plant and equipment at that date was $100,000 greater than book value, and JKL immediately incorporated this revaluation into its own books. JKL's financial statements at 30 September 20X8 contained notes referring to a contingent liability (with a fair value of $200,000).

Calculate goodwill on acquisition, and identify any of the above items that should be excluded from the calculation in accordance with IFRS 3 *Business Combinations*.

(3 marks)

? Question 3

AB purchase 100% of the equity share capital of CD and at the date of acquisition the net assets of CD were reviewed and the following is discovered:

1. The intangible non-current assets of CD at the acquisition date, consist of the estimated value of a brand that is associated with the entity. This estimate has been made by the directors and no reliable external estimate of the market value of the brand is available.
2. Relevant details of tangible non-current assets of CD are:

Description	SOFP carrying value $'000	Market value $'000	Depreciated replacement cost $'000	Recoverable amount $'000
Property	10,000	12,000	Not given	13,500
Plant	10,000	Not given	11,000	14,000

3. Inventories of CD comprise:
   - Obsolete inventory (balance sheet value: $500,000). This inventory has a net realisable value of $300,000.
   - The balance of inventory (statement of financial position value: $3,500,000). This inventory has a net realisable value of $4,200,000. A reasonable profit allowance for the sale of the inventory would be $400,000.
4. The provision of $1 million in the statement of financial position of CD is against the reorganisation costs expected to be incurred in integrating the entity into the Sea group. These costs would not be necessary if CD were to remain outside the group. Although the plan was agreed by the board of directors before the acquisition date, it was not made known to those affected by the plan until after that date.

Requirement
Discuss how each of the above should be treated.   **(5 marks)**

Solutions to Revision Questions

 Solution 1

The correct answer is (D).

 Solution 2

Goodwill on acquisition

	$	$
Investment in JKL		1,800,000
Acquired:		
Net assets at book value	1,350,000	
Revaluation	100,000	
Contingent liability	(200,000)	
		1,250,000
Goodwill on acquisition		550,000

 Solution 3

1. No value should be attached to the intangible asset when determining fair value of net assets acquired since there is no reliable market value.
2. The fair value of the property should be based on the market value of $12,000,000.
3. The obsolete inventories should be included at the NRV of $300,000. The remaining inventories are carried at $3,500,000, however the fair value can be taken as the sales value less realistic allowance for profit. The fair value of these inventories is therefore $3,800,000.
4. No amount should be included for the provision. Although the plan is approved it has not been communicated to those that will be affected (e.g. employees, customers, suppliers, etc.) and so as per IAS 37 no constructive obligation exists. IFRS 3 only allows provisions where there is a constructive obligation.

15

The Consolidated
Statement of
Financial Position

The Consolidated Statement of Financial Position

15

LEARNING OUTCOME

After completing this chapter you should be able to:

▶ prepare the consolidated Statement of financial position for a group of companies in a form suitable for publication for a group of companies comprising directly held interests in one or more fully controlled subsidiary (such interests having been acquired at the beginning of the accounting period).

15.1 Introduction

This chapter builds upon the foundations established in Chapter 14, and applies the principles of full consolidation and prepares a consolidated statement of financial position, firstly for a simple group scenario, including:

- Elimination of the investment on consolidation
- Recognising goodwill on acquisition.

The chapter continues with the preparation of the consolidated statement of financial position, incorporating the more common complexities in group accounting, including:

- Accounting for the effects of transactions between group entities
- Accounting for adjustments to fair values at the date of acquisition

Adjustments may be required to achieve uniform accounting policies between parent and subsidiary, and this is also covered.

15.2 Applying the principles of consolidation: the consolidated statement of financial position

Consolidated financial statements represent the performance and position of the combined group entities as if they were a single economic entity. All the results and the assets and liabilities that are under the control of the parent are combined together to show single totals for each item in the financial statements. This means that the revenue and expenses, assets and liabilities of the entities in the group are added together, line by line. So, if a parent's revenue for the year is $2 m and its only subsidiary has revenue for the year of $1 m, group revenue is reported on a single line in the consolidated income statement at $3 m.

Example 15.A

On 31 December 20X8 A purchased all of the shares of B for $25,000. The statements of financial positions of the individual entities at that date were:

	A $	B $
Non-current assets	60,000	20,000
Property, plant and equipment	25,000	–
Investment	85,000	20,000
	15,000	5,000
Net current assets	100,000	25,000
Equity		
Share capital	50,000	10,000
Retained earningsl	50,000	15,000
	100,000	25,000

Solution

In this introductory example A has paid $25,000 for the investment in 100% of B. B's equity has a book value of $25,000. The objective is to prepare a consolidated statement of financial position that recognises the assets and liabilities over which A now has control. This means combining the asset and liability figures. For example, the consolidated figure for property, plant and equipment is calculated by adding across that line: $60,000 ≤ $20,000 ≤ $80,000.

However, it is important to ensure that assets and liabilities are not double counted. It would be incorrect to include both A's investment in B and the assets and liabilities represented by that investment, and so the investment in B is eliminated. The net asset side of the statement of financial position therefore is as follows:

A Group: consolidated statement of financial position at 31 December 20X8

	$	Comment
Non-current assets		
Property, plant and equipment	80,000	A ≤ B
Investment in B	'''	Eliminated – B's net assets recognised instead
Net current assets	20,000	A ≤ B
	100,000	

The equity side of the consolidated statement of financial position shows the share capital of the parent only. Consolidated retained earnings is the total of:
The retained earnings of the parent
The post-acquisition retained earnings of the subsidiary

	$	Comment
Equity		
Share capital	50,000	A only
Retained earnings	50,000	A ≤ post-acquisition retained earnings of B-$50,000 – $0
	100,000	

Because the investment was bought on the last day of the financial year, post-acquisition earnings in the subsidiary are $0. This will, of course, not usually be the case.

This consolidated statement of financial position shows the effect of a single consolidation adjustment: the investment in B shown in A's statement of financial position has been eliminated against the share capital and retained earnings of B:

DR Share capital and retained earnings of B	25,000
CR Investment in B	25,000

After the initial acquisition, earnings will be made in B. The group share of post-acquisition earnings (in this case 100%) will form part of the total of consolidated retained earnings, balanced by increases in net assets on the other side of the statement of financial position in the future. Example 15.B below demonstrates the preparation of the consolidated statement of financial position one year after the initial acquisition.

Example 15.B

Statement of financial positions at 31 December 20X8

	A $	B $
Non-current assets	65,000	24,000
Property, plant and equipment	25,000	—
Investment	90,000	24,000
	20,000	6,000
Net current assets	110,000	30,000
Equity		
Share capital	50,000	10,000
Retained earningsl	60,000	20,000
	110,000	30,000

Solution

Note that the investment has remained exactly the same in the individual statement of financial position of A. This would normally be the case, unless impairment had taken place.

This means, however, that the elimination of the investment against the equity of B leaves a difference of $5,000 ($25,000 is set against a total of $30,000). This difference is post-acquisition retained earnings which will be reflected as part of consolidated retained earnings.

The same principles as before are following in preparing the consolidated statement of financial position for the A Group:

A Group: consolidated statement of financial position at 31 December 20X8

	$	Comment
Non-current assets		
Property, plant and equipment	89,000	A ≤ B
Investment in B	—	Eliminated – B's net assets recognised instead
Net current assets	26,000	A ≤ B
	115,000	
Equity		
Share capital	50,000	A only
Retained earnings	65,000	A ($60,000 ≤ post-acquisition reserves in of B$50,000)
	115,000	

15.2.1 Goodwill

In Example 15.A a subsidiary with a net asset value of $25,000 was acquired for exactly $25,000. This involved two simplifying assumptions:

(a) the investment in B could be acquired from its owners for exactly the amount of net assets in the statement of financial position; and
(b) the carrying value of net assets was equivalent to its fair value.

It will, in practice, hardly ever be the case that both of these conditions exist. Usually, the owners of a profitable business will expect to receive more in exchange for the investment than its net asset value. This additional amount arises for various reasons. It is quite likely that the assets recognised in the statement of financial position do not represent all the assets of the firm but intangibles such as good reputation and customer loyalty may be worth something to the purchaser. The difference between the cost of investment and the fair value of the net assets acquired is known as goodwill on acquisition. The requirements of IFRS 3 relating to the recognition of goodwill were discussed in Chapter 14.

Where 100% of the equity of a subsidiary is acquired, goodwill on acquisition is calculated as follows:

The aggregate of: consideration, measured at fair value
LESS
Net assets acquired (the fair value of identifiable assets acquired less liabilities assumed)

Example 15.C

C acquired 100% of the equity share capital of D on 31 December 20X8. The statements of financial positions of the two entities at that date were as shown below:

Statement of financial positions at 31 December 20X8

	C $	D $
Non-current assets	100,000	30,000
Property, plant and equipment	50,000	–
Investment	150,000	30,000
	50,000	10,000
Net current assets	200,000	40,000
Equity		
Share capital	50,000	10,000
Retained earnings	150,000	30,000
	200,000	40,000

Note: The fair value of D's net current assets was the same as carrying value at 31 December 20X8. The fair value of the property, plant and equipment was $32,000.

Prepare the consolidated statement of position at 31 December 20X8.

Solution

Working

1. Calculation of goodwill on acquisition

	C $	D $
Consideration		50,000
Net assets acquired, at fair value		
Property, plant and equipment	32,000	
Net current assets	10,000	–
Total identifiable net assets		42,000
Goodwill		8,000

C Group: consolidated statement of financial position at 31 December 20X8

	$	Comment
Non-current assets		
Goodwill	8,000	See working 1
Property, plant and equipment	132,000	100,000 ≤ 30,000 ≤
Investment in D	–	2,000 (Fair value adjustment) Eliminated – D's net assets recognised instead 50,000 ≤ 10,000
Net current assets	60,000	
	200,000	
Equity		
Share capital	50,000	C only
Retained earnings	150,000	Retained earnings of C
	200,000	

Some points to note:
1. The revaluation of D's property, plant and equipment has been accounted for in the calculation of goodwill. No revaluation reserve is required in the consolidated financial statements. The adjustment to fair value has been recognised in the consolidated financial statements in order to comply with IFRS 3. However, it need not necessarily be recognised in D's own financial statements – recognition will depend upon D's accounting policies.
2. The retained earnings at 31 December 20X8 are those of C, the parent, only. This is because the acquisition has taken place on that day. Remember that in subsequent consolidated statements of position consolidated retained earnings will comprise the retained earnings of the parent plus its share of the post-acquisition retained earnings in the subsidiary.
3. An alternative way of calculating goodwill is to deduct the value of equity plus or minus any adjustments in respect of fair value from the consideration:

	$	$
Consideration		50,000
Less:		
Equity acquired	40,000	
Fair value adjustment	2,000	
		42,000
Goodwill		8,000

This method is likely to be quicker than listing all the assets and liabilities acquired.

15.2.2 Bargain purchases

Occasionally, it happens that the amount of consideration paid for an investment in a subsidiary is less than the aggregate of the fair value of net assets acquired. The difference between the two amounts, rather than giving rise to an asset, goodwill, is a credit balance. This difference is sometimes referred to as 'negative goodwill'. Where this occurs, the acquiring entity must reassess the assets and liabilities acquired to ensure that all are included, and that they are appropriately measured. If, after this exercise, there is still a credit balance, IFRS 3 requires that the acquirer should recognise the credit as a gain through profit or loss on the date of acquisition.

15.3 The elimination of intragroup balances

IAS 27 requires that:

> 'Intragroup balances, transactions, income and expenses should be eliminated in full'.

Intra-group balances are likely to arise where the parent and subsidiary entities trade with each other. The consolidated financial statements present the results and position of the parent entity and its subsidiary (or subsidiaries) as if they were a single combined entity. Therefore, where balances appear in both a parent and subsidiary statement of financial position, they must be eliminated against each other on consolidation. If this were not done, elements such as receivables and payables would be overstated.

The balances should be cancelled out against each other as part of the consolidation process. Where there are items in transit (usually cash or inventory) the balances may not cancel entirely. Any surplus must be recognised as an in-transit item in the consolidated statement of financial position.

Example 15.D

The statements of financial positions of A and B as at 31.12.X7 are as follows:

	A		B	
	$	$	$	$
ASSETS				
Non-current assets				
Investment in B (note 1)		15,000		
Property, plant and equipment		30,000		15,000
Current assets				
Inventories	10,000		5,000	
Receivables (note 2)	12,000		6,000	
		22,000		11,000
		67,000		26,000

EQUITY + LIABILITIES

Equity

Issued capital		40,000	10,000
Retained earnings		14,000	8,000
		54,000	18,000
Current liabilities			
Trade payables (note 2)	8,000		4,000
Bank overdraft	5,000		4,000
		13,000	8,000
		67,000	26,000

Notes
1. A bought 100% of the shares in B on 31.12.X4 when the retained earnings of B stood at $4,000. Since that date, there has been no impairment of goodwill on consolidation.
2. The receivables of A include $3,000 in respect of goods supplied to B in the last few months of the year. The payables of B include $2,000 payable to A. You ascertain that on 30.12.X7 B sent a payment of $1,000 to A. This payment was received and recorded by A on 3.1.X8.

Prepare the consolidated statement of financial position as at 31.12.X7.

Solution

Before starting to prepare the consolidated statement of financial position it is worth noting that:
- The intra-group balances differ by $1,000 ($3,000 ''' $2,000). The difference is clearly caused by the cash in transit of $1,000.

We now proceed to prepare the consolidated statement of financial position.

A Group: Consolidated statement of financial position at 31 December 20X7

	$	$	
ASSETS			
Non-current assets			
Goodwill		1,000	See working 2
Property, plant and equipment		45,000	A ≤ B
		46,000	
Current assets			
Inventories	15,000		A ≤ B
Receivables	15,000		A ≤ B − $3,000
Cash in transit	1,000		The reconciling item
		31,000	
		77,000	
EQUITY + LIABILITIES			
Equity			
Issued capital		40,000	A only
Retained earningsl		18,000	See working 3
		58,000	
Current liabilities			
Trade payables	10,000		A ≤ B − $2,000
Bank overdraft	9,000		A ≤ B
		19,000	
		77,000	

Workings

1. *Goodwill*

	$	$
Cost of investment		15,000
Net assets at the date of acquisition		
Issued capital	10,000	
Retained earnings	4,000	–
		14,000
Total goodwill		1,000

2. *Retained earnings*

	$
Retained earnings of A	14,000
100% of post- acquisition retained earnings of B ($8,000 − $4,000)	4,000
	18,000

15.4 Intra-group loans and preference shares

Example 15.D deals with intra-group balances that arise in respect of trading. It is also, however, possible that intra-group balances arise because one group entity holds loans or preference shares in another group entity.

This means that loans and preference shares in practice are likely to be dealt with in the same way. The long-term receivable in one entity corresponds with the long-term payable in another and for group accounting purposes they cancel each other out. (Example 15.D in the next section of this chapter demonstrates how this is done.)

15.5 The treatment of unrealised profits on assets bought from group companies

IAS 27 explains that profits and losses arising from intra-group transactions that are recognised in assets, such as inventory and non-current assets, should be eliminated in full. These are commonly known as unrealised profits because, from a group point of view, the profit on such transactions has not yet been realised. Suppose that an entity D habitually purchases inventory from its parent, A. A makes a profit on the sale which is recognised upon despatch of the goods to D. This is fine for the purposes of entity-level financial statements for A and D. However, the A group accounts present the results and position of the group as if it were a single entity. It would be incorrect to artificially boost the profits of this single entity by including profit made on transfers of inventories or other assets between the constituent entities, and therefore they must be eliminated as part of the consolidation process. Profit on such transactions cannot be recognised until the inventories or other assets are sold outside the group, at which point the profits are realised from a group point of view.

Taking the example of A and D a little further:

Example 15.D

D sells inventories to A at a standard profit margin of 25%. At the group's year end of 31 December, the inventories of A include goods purchased from D at cost to A of $12,500.

Assumption 1: D is a wholly owned subsidiary of A.

What is the amount of the adjustment to eliminate intra-group profits?

Solution

First, the amount of profit made by D must be established. The goods at cost to A are $12,500. D's profit margin is 25% which means that the value in A of $12,500 represents 125% of cost to D.

Profit made by D = 25/125 × $12,500 = $2,500

Inventories in A, from a group accounting perspective, are therefore overstated by $2,500 as is profit in D. The consolidation adjustment required is:

DR Consolidated profits	2,500	
CR Consolidated inventories		2,500

Example 15.E below is a comprehensive example that includes consolidation adjustments in respect of elimination of intra-group payables and receivables, both long term and short term and the elimination of intra-group profits.

Example 15.E

The statements of financial positions of A and B as at 31.12.X7 are as follows:

		C		D	
	$	$		$	$
ASSETS					
Non-current assets					
Property, plant and equipment		145,000			50,000
Investments		53,000			–
		198,000			50,000
Current assets					
Inventories	40,000			30,000	
Trade receivables	45,000			17,600	
Intra-group receivables	–			2,500	
Cash at bank	17,000			9,900	
		102,000			60,000
		300,000			110,000
EQUITY + LIABILITIES					
Equity					
Ordinary ($1) shares		100,000			40,000
Retained earnings		90,000			32,000
		190,000			72,000
Non-current liabilities					
5% borrowings	70,000			20,000	
		70,000			20,000
Current liabilities					
Trade payables (note 2)	39,000			18,000	
Intra-group payables	1,000			–	
		40,000			18,000
		300,000			110,000

Notes
1. The investment by C in D was made many years ago for £53,000
2. A remittance of $1,500, sent by C to D on 30.12.X2, was not recorded in the books of D until 4.1.X3.
3. Goods had been sold at normal selling price by D to C during the year. The total sales of such goods during the year were $80,000. The inventory of C at 31.12.X2 contained goods purchased from D at a selling price of $16,000. D earns 20% profit margin on its sales to H.

Requirement: prepare a consolidated statement of financial position at 31.12.X2.

Solution

The following points are important:
1. C owns 100% of the ordinary shares of D when retained earnings were $12,000.
2. There is a difference on intra-group balances of $1,500 (the receivable of D is $2,500 while the payable of C is $1,000. The difference is due to cash in transit between C and D).
3. The inventory of C contains goods costing C $16,000 that were purchased from D. D made a profit of $3,200 on these goods ($16,000 × 20%). From the group's perspective the profit on these goods will not be realised until the goods are sold outside the group. Therefore an adjustment must be made to the closing consolidated inventory figure to ensure that it is included at cost to the group. There is no need to adjust consolidated inventory for goods that have been sold by one group company to another and that have been then sold on outside the group. As far as the group is concerned, profit on the sale of these inventories has been recognised. The unrealised profit adjustment is made in respect only of inventories sold intra-group that remain in the group at the year end.

The consolidated statement of financial position of the C group as at 31.12.X2 is as follows:

	$	$	*Comments*
ASSETS			
Non-current assets			
Goodwill		1,000	See working 1
Property, plant and equipment		195,000	C + D
		196,000	
Current assets			
Inventories	66,800		$40,000 ≤ $3,000 − $2,000 (see note 3 above)
Trade receivables	62,600		C ≤ D
Cash in transit	1,500		See note 2 above
Cash at bank	26,900		
		157,800	
		353,800	
EQUITY AND LIABILITIES			
Equity			
Share capital		100,000	C only
Consolidated retained earnings		106,800	See working 2
		206,800	
Non-current liabilities			
5% borrowings	90,000		
		90,000	
Current liabilities			
Trade payables		57,000	C D
		353,800	

Workings
1. *Goodwill*

	$	$
Cost of investment in ordinary shares		53,000
Net assets at the date of acquisition:		
Share capital	40,000	
Reserves	12,000	–
		(52,000)
Goodwill		1,000

2. *Consolidated retained earnings*

	$
C	90,000
D (32,000 − 12,000)	20,000
unrealised profit in inventory	
	(3,200)
	106,800

15.6 Adjustments for fair value at the date of acquisition

In Chapter 14 it was noted that goodwill was calculated using fair value measurements for assets and liabilities in the subsidiary at the date of acquisition, in accordance with the requirements of IFRS 3. Example 14.C incorporated a fair value adjustment for property, plant and equipment. For the moment, in this chapter, we will examine the implications of measurement at fair value on the financial statements subsequent to acquisition.

Sometimes the fair values of net assets at the point of acquisition are recognised in the subsidiary at the date of consolidation, where the accounting policy of the entity itself permits this. However, where the subsidiary adopts the cost model of valuation, there will be continuing differences on consolidation arising from the fact that the net assets of the subsidiary are recognised at fair value upon acquisition. In the latter case, consolidation adjustments will be required.

The example below illustrates the adjustments required.

Example 15.F

The statements of financial positions of Star and its subsidiary entity Ark as at 31 December 20X7 were as follows:

	Star $'000	Ark $'000
Property, plant and equipment	120	177
Investment in Ark	160	
Inventory	10	5
Receivables	30	25
Bank	10	5
	330	212

Ordinary share capital	120	75
Retained earnings	144	120
	244	195
Current liabilities	66	17
	330	212

Additional information

1. On 1 January 20X5, when the retained earnings of Ark showed a balance of $60,000, Star purchased 75,000 ordinary shares in Ark for $160,000.
2. Star sold goods to Ark during the year for $10,000 at a mark-up of 25% on cost. At the year-end, half of these goods were still held in inventory by Ark.
3. On 1 January 20X5 the net assets of Ark had a fair value of $155,000. The excess of fair value over the carrying value in the individual financial statements of Ark was due to plant included in property, plant and equipment. This plant had a useful economic life of 5 years from 1 January 20X5. None of the plant that was subject to a fair-value adjustment at 1 January 20X5 had been sold by 31 December 20X7. Property plant and equipment is measured in Ark's own financial statements at depreciated cost.
4. Since acquisition there has been no impairment of goodwill on consolidation.

Prepare the consolidated statement of financial position for the group as at 31.12.X7.

Solution

Before we prepare the consolidated statement of financial position, let us consider the implications of each of the additional pieces of information we have been given (the numbers below correspond with the numbered pieces of information):

1. This tells us that Star owns 100% of the shares of Ark. At the date of acquisition the individual financial statements of Ark showed net assets of $135,000 (share capital $75,000 plus retained earnings $60,000).
2. This tells us that there is unrealised profit in the closing inventory of Ark. The closing inventory of Ark that was bought from Star is $5,000 [(1/2) × $10,000]. The profit element in this inventory is $1,000 [(25/125) × $5,000]. We need to take care when computing this figure – the profit is expressed as a percentage of the group cost, not the intra-group selling price.
3. This tells us that the fair value of the net assets of Ark was $20,000 ($155,000 − $135,000) greater than the carrying value in the individual statement of financial position of Ark at the date of acquisition. Since the excess is due to plant that is being depreciated over 5 years the fair-value adjustment will have an impact on closing net assets as well (the acquisition took place three years ago). The impact on closing net assets is an increase of $8,000 [$20,000 × (2/5)]. We can summarise the effect as:
   - pre-acquisition retained earnings increased by $20,000 to $80,000;
   - closing property, plant and equipment increased by $8,000 to $185,000;
   - closing net assets increased by $8,000 to $203,000;
   - closing retained earnings increased by $8,000 to $128,000.

We now prepare the consolidated statement of financial position:

	$'000	Comments
Goodwill	5	See working 2
Property, plant and equipment	305	120 + 185 – using *adjusted* figure
Inventory	14	10 + 5 – 1 (unrealised profit)
Receivables	55	S + A
Bank	15	S + A
	394	
Share capital	120	Star only
Retained earnings	191	See working 3
	311	
Current liabilities	83	60 + 17
	394	

Workings
1. *Goodwill*

	$'000	$'000
Cost of investment		160
Net assets at the date of acquisition:		
Share capital	75	
Retained earnings – *as amended*	80	
Group share		(155)
Total goodwill		5

2. *Retained earnings*

	$'000
Star	144
Ark using *amended* figures:	
($128,000 − $80,000)	48
Unrealised profit in inventory – made by the *parent*	(1)
	191

15.7 Summary

This chapter introduced the application of the rules for full consolidation. The IFRS 3 requirements for recognition of goodwill were applied and the consolidation was completed for fully owned subsiduary's. The consolidated statement of financial position was prepared.

The chapter also covered several additional complexities involved in the preparation of the consolidated statement of financial position, including intra-group trading and balances, fair value adjustments.

 Students should be sure that they have completely understood the chapter and its examples, and should have worked through the revision questions that follow, before moving on to Chapter 16.

Revision Questions

? Question 1

On 31 December 20X4 AB acquired 100% of the ordinary share capital of its subsidiary, CD for $50,000. The statements of financial positions of the individual entities at that date were:

	AB $	CD $
Non-current assets		
Property, plant and equipment	70,000	30,000
Investment	50,000	–
	120,000	30,000
Net current assets	30,000	15,000
	150,000	45,000
Equity		
Share capital	50,000	20,000
Retained earnings	100,000	25,000
	150,000	45,000

Requirement

Prepare the consolidated statement of financial position for the AB Group at 31 December 20X4.

? Question 2

This question relates to AB and CD (facts of the acquisition as in Question 1) one year on from the acquisition. The statements of financial positions of the two entities at 31 December 20X5 were as follows:

	AB $	CD $
Non-current assets		
Property, plant and equipment	75,000	32,000
Investment	50,000	–
	125,000	32,000
Net current assets	37,000	17,000
	162,000	49,000
Equity		
Share capital	50,000	20,000
Retained earnings	112,000	29,000
	162,000	49,000

Requirement

Prepare the consolidated statement of financial position for the AB Group at 31 December 20X5.

? Question 3

AX acquired all of the 50,000 issued ordinary voting shares of CY on 1 April 20X7, for $90,000. Retained earnings of CY at that date were $25,000. The acquisition was sufficient to give it control over CY's operating and financial policies.

The statements of financial positions of the two entities were as follows on 31 March 20X8:

	AX $	CY $
Non-current assets		
Property, plant and equipment	125,000	50,000
Investment	90,000	–
	215,000	50,000
Net current assets	40,000	30,000
	255,000	80,000
Equity		
Share capital	130,000	50,000
Retained earnings	125,000	30,000
	255,000	80,000

It is the group's policy to value non-controlling interests at its proportionate share of the fair value of the subsidiary's identifiable net assets.

Requirement

Prepare the consolidated statement of financial position for the AX Group at 31 March 20X8.

? Question 4

The statements of financial positions as at 30 June 20X4 of A and its subsidiary entity B is summarised below.

	A $	A $	B $	B $
ASSETS				
Non-current assets				
Property, plant and equipment		9,000		4,800
Investment in subsidiary		10,000		–
		19,000		4,800
Current assets				
Inventories	12,000		18,000	
Trade Receivables	25,000		21,000	
Current account with B	4,000		–	
Bank balance	20,000		–	
		61,000		39,000
		80,000		43,800

EQUITY + LIABILITIES

Equity

Issued capital ($1 each)		40,000	8,000
Retained earnings		24,000	9,800
		64,000	17,800

Current liabilities

Trade payables	16,000		18,000	
Current account with A			2,000	
			6,000	
Bank overdraft	–	16,000		26,000
		80,000		43,800

Notes

1. A acquired all the ordinary shares in B many years ago. The balance on B's retained earnings at the date of acquisition by A was $1,000. Goodwill on consolidation had been written off following an impairment review before the start of the current financial year.
2. On 30 June 20X4 there was cash in transit from B to A of $2,000.

Requirement

Prepare a consolidated statement of financial position for the A group as at 30 June 20X4.

 ## Question 5

The statements of financial positions as at 31 December 20X4 of X and its subsidiary entity Y are summarised below:

	X		Y	
	$	$	$	$
ASSETS				
Non-current assets				
Intangible assets				2,000
Property, plant and equipment		29,000		24,800
Investment in Y		26,000		
		55,000		26,800
Current assets				
Inventories	12,000		18,000	
Trade receivables	24,750		21,000	
Trading account with Y	4,000			
Interest receivable from Y	250			
Bank balance	20,000			
		61,000		39,000
		116,000		65,800
EQUITY + LIABILITIES				
Equity				
Ordinary shares of ($1 each)		45,000		8,000
Retained earningsl		21,000		11,000
		66,000		19,000

Non-current liabilities			
Interest bearing borrowings	30,000		20,000
Current liabilities			
Trade payables	20,000	18,300	
Interest payable		500	
Current account with X		2,000	
Bank overdraft		6,000	26,800
	116,000		65,800

Notes

1. X acquired 8,000 ordinary shares in Y on 1 January 20X1. The price paid was $16,000. The balance on Y's retained earnings at the date of acquisition by X was $5,000. This included an intangible asset of $1,000 (see note 4 below). Goodwill on consolidation is retained at cost in the group statement of financial position. There has been no evidence of impairment since acquisition. X made a long-term loan of $10,000 to Y on the same date.
2. On 31 December 20X4 there was cash in transit from Y to X of $2,000.
3. On 31 December 20X4 the inventory of Y included $4,800 of goods purchased from X. X had invoiced these goods at cost plus 25%.
4. The intangible asset of Y does not satisfy the recognition criteria laid down in IAS 38. IAS 38 is to be followed in preparing the consolidated accounts.

Requirement

Prepare a consolidated statement of financial position for the X group as at 31 December 20X4.

? Question 6

STV owns 100% of the ordinary share capital of its subsidiary TUW. At the group's year end, 28 February 20X7, STV's payables include $3,600 in respect of inventories sold to it by TUW.

TUW's receivables include $6,700 in respect of inventories sold to STV. Two days before the year end STV sent a payment of $3,100 to TUW that was not recorded by the latter until two days after the year end.

The in-transit item should be dealt with as follows in the consolidated statement of financial position at 28 February 20X7:

(A) $2,325 to be included as cash in transit
(B) $3,100 to be added to consolidated payables
(C) $3,100 to be included as inventories in transit
(D) $3,100 to be included as cash in transit

(2 marks)

Question 7

LPD buys goods from its 100% owned subsidiary QPR. QPR earns a mark-up of 25% on such transactions. At the group's year end, 30 June 20X7. LPD had not yet taken delivery of goods, at a sales value of $100,000, which were despatched by QPR on 29 June 20X7.

At what amount would the goods in transit appear in the consolidated statement of financial position of the LPD group at 30 June 20X7?

(A) $60,000
(B) $75,000
(C) $80,000
(D) $100,000   **(2 marks)**

 Solution 1

Working 1: Goodwill

	$
Consideration	50,000
Net assets acquired:	
100% × $45,000	(45,000)
Goodwill	5,000

AB Group: consolidated statement of financial position at 31 December 20X4

	$	Comment
Non-current assets		
Goodwill	5,000	See working 1
Property, plant and equipment	100,000	70,000 + 30,000
Net current assets	45,000	30,000 + 15,000
	150,000	
Equity		
Share capital	50,000	AB only
Retained earnings	100,000	Retained earnings of AB
	150,000	

 Solution 2

Working 1: Retained earnings

Retained earnings for the group = retained earnings of the parent + post-acquisition retained earnings in the subsidiary:

Retained earnings of the parent	112,000
Post-acquisition retained earnings in the subsidiary (29,000 − 25,000)	4,000
	116,000

Tutorial note: goodwill on acquisition is calculated once – upon acquisition.

AB Group: Consolidated statement of financial position at 31 December 20X5

	$	Comment
Non-current assets		
Goodwill	5,000	As in solution 1
Property, plant and equipment	107,000	75,000 + 32,000
Net current assets	54,000	37,000 + 17,000
	166,000	

THE CONSOLIDATED STATEMENT OF FINANCIAL POSITION

Equity

Share capital	50,000	AB only
Retained earnings	116,000	See working 1
	166,000	

 Solution 3

Workings

1. *Goodwill on consolidation*

	$	$
Consideration		90,000
Net assets at date of acquisition:		
Share capital ($1 shares)	50,000	
Retained earnings	25,000	
	75,000	
Group share (100%)		75,000
Goodwill		15,000

2. *Retained earnings*

	$
Retained earnings of AX	125,000
100% of post-acquisition retained earnings of CY:	
($30,000 − $25,000)	5,000
	130,000

AX Group: consolidated statement of financial position at 31 March 20X8

	$	Comment
Non-current assets		
Goodwill	15,000	See working 2
Property, plant and equipment	175,000	125,000 + 50,000
	190,000	
Net current assets	70,000	40,000 + 30,000
	260,000	
Equity attributable to owners of the parent		
Share capital	130,000	AX only
Retained earnings	130,000	See working 3
	228,000	
	260,000	

 Solution 4

A – consolidated statement of financial position as at 30 . 6 . X4

	$	$
ASSETS		
Non-current assets		
Goodwill (W3)		–
Property, plant and equipment		13,800
		13,800
Current assets		
Inventories	30,000	
Trade receivables	46,000	
Cash in transit	2,000	
Bank balance	20,000	

		98,000
		111,800

EQUITY + LIABILITIES		
Equity		
Issued capital		40,000
Retained earnings (W2)		31,800
		71,800
Current liabilities		
Trade payables	34,000	
Bank overdraft	6,000	
		40,000
		111,800

Workings

1. *Goodwill on consolidation (all written off)*
   $10,000 − ($8,000 + $1,000) = $1,000
2. *Consolidated retained earnings*

	$
Retained earnings of A	24,000
100% of post-acquisition retained earnings of B	
($9,800 − $1,000 = $8,800)	8,800
Goodwill written off (W3)	(1,000)
	31,800

☑ Solution 5

X – consolidated statement of financial position as at 31.12 . X4

	$	$
ASSETS		
Non-current assets		
Goodwill on consolidation (W3)		4,000
Property, plant and equipment		53,800
		57,800
Current assets		
Inventories (W2)	29,040	
Trade receivables	45,750	
Cash in transit (W5)	2,000	
Bank balance	20,000	
		96,790
		154,590
EQUITY + LIABILITIES		
Equity		
Ordinary shares of $1		45,000
Retained earnings (W4)		25,040
		70,040
Non-current liabilities		
Interest bearing borrowings (X + Y − 10,000)		40,000
Current liabilities		
Trade payables	38,300	
Interest payable (W6)	250	
Bank overdraft	6,000	
		44,550
		154,590

THE CONSOLIDATED STATEMENT OF FINANCIAL POSITION

Workings

1. *Pre-consolidation adjustment*

   Group policy does not recognise the intangible assets that are in Y's own statement of financial position. This makes the retained earnings of Y at the statement of financial position date $9,000 ($11,000 − $2,000) and the retained earnings of Y at the date of acquisition $4,000 ($5,000 − $1,000).

2. *Unrealised profit in inventory*

   Profit element is 25% of the cost to X, or 25/125 of the selling price charged by X, which is also the cost to Y.

   Therefore the unrealised profit is 25/125 × $4,800 = $960. There is no Non-controlling interest since the profit is made by the parent. Consolidated inventories are reduced by $960.

3. *Goodwill*

Consideration		16,000
Net assets at date of acquisition:		
Share capital ($1 shares)	8,000	
Retained earnings	4,000	
	12,000	
Group share (100%)		12,000
Goodwill		4,000

4. *Consolidated retained earnings*

	$
Retained earnings of X	21,000
100% of post-acquisition retained earnings of Y as adjusted ($9,000 − $4,000)	5,000
Unrealised profit in inventory (W3)	(960)
	25,040

5. *Intra-group balances*

   The intra-group balances (receivables/payables) are cancelled out on consolidation and cash in transit of $2000 represents the difference.

6. *Interest payable*

   Half of the interest payable by Y is due to X as X invested $10,000 in the borrowings of Y. This intercompany amount ($250) is eliminated on consolidation.

 Solution 6

The correct answer is (D).

 Solution 7

The correct answer is (C).

16

The Consolidated Statements
of Comprehensive Income

The Consolidated Statements of Comprehensive Income

16

LEARNING OUTCOMES

After studying this chapter, you should be able to:

► prepare a consolidated statement of comprehensive income;

► apply the concepts of fair value at the point of acquisition.

16.1 Introduction

The previous two chapters introduced some of the basic principles of consolidation accounting and applied them to the preparation of a consolidated statement of financial position. This chapter extends the application of the principles to the preparation of a consolidated statement of comprehensive income.

16.2 Basic principles

We discussed the underlying rationale for consolidated financial statements in Chapter 14. The objective is to present one set of financial statements for all entities under common control. In the context of the income statement, this means presenting the results of all group entities in one statement of comprehensive income.

   The majority of the figures are simple aggregations of the results of the parent entity and all the subsidiaries. Intra-group investment income is eliminated. This is because intra-group investment income is replaced by the underlying profits and losses of the group entities.

Example 16.A

Draft statements of comprehensive income for the year ended 31 December 20X4

	Acquirer $	Swallowed $
Revenue	600,000	300,000
Cost of sales	(420,000)	(230,000)
Gross profit	180,000	70,000
Distribution costs	(50,000)	(25,000)
Administrative expenses	(50,000)	(22,000)
Profit from operations	80,000	23,000
Investment income	4,000	–
Finance cost	(8,000)	(3,000)
Profit before tax	76,000	20,000
Income tax expense	(30,000)	(8,000)
Profit for the year	46,000	12,000

Acquirer purchased all of the 20,000 issued $1 shares in Swallowed on 31 December 20X1 for $33,000. The balance on Swallowed's equity at that date was $35,000 (issued share capital $20,000 plus retained earnings $15,000). There has been no impairment of goodwill since acquisition.

Prepare a consolidated statement of comprehensive income for the year ending 31 December 20X4

Solution

Before we prepare the statement of comprehensive income itself we should note that:

- Acquirer owns all of Swallowed's 20,000 issued $1 shares so this makes Swallowed.

Consolidated statement of comprehensive income

	$	Comments
Revenue	900,000	A + S
Cost of sales	(650,000)	A + S
Gross profit	250,000	
Distribution costs	(75,000)	A + S
Administrative expenses	(72,000)	A + S
Profit from operations	103,000	
Finance cost	(11,000)	A + S: investment income eliminated as inter-group
Profit before tax	92,000	
Income tax expense	(38,000)	A + S
Profit for the period	54,000	

16.3 Intra-group trading

There is no need to worry about cancellation of intra-group balances for the consolidated income statement. This is clearly a statement of financial position issue. Intra-group trading will be of relevance in the consolidated statement of comprehensive income to the extent that one group entity provides goods or services for another group entity. In these circumstances there are clearly income and costs that are wholly intra-group.

Intra-group revenue must be eliminated *in full* from revenue. This is the case whatever has subsequently happened to any goods that are sold by one group entity to another. Unless there is unrealised profit on unsold inventory (see below) then the adjustment to costs is the same as the adjustment to revenue.

We have already seen from our studies of the consolidated statement of financial position (see Chapter 15) that unrealised profit on intra-group revenue must be eliminated from closing inventory and profit. Unrealised profit on intra-group revenue is deducted from gross profit. The adjustment to cost of sales is the difference between the adjustment to revenue and the adjustment to gross profit.

Where there is unrealised profit brought forward then this amount will have been charged against the consolidated reserves of previous years. Therefore the charge to gross profit for the year is the *movement* on the provision for unrealised profit.

Where the unrealised profit is made by a subsidiary in which there is a non-controlling interest then a share of the charge to the consolidated income statement is made against the non-controlling interest.

Example 16.B

Statement of comprehensive income of PQR and its subsidiary XYZ for the year ended 31 December 20X1

	PQR	XYZ
	$'000	$'000
Revenue	125,000	50,000
Cost of sales	(50,000)	(20,000)
Gross profit	75,000	30,000
Distribution costs	(10,000)	(4,000)
Administrative expenses	(8,000)	(3,200)
Profit from operations	57,000	22,800
Investment income	3,180	–
Finance cost	(24,500)	(7,750)
Profit before taxation	35,680	15,050
Income tax	(14,000)	(7,000)
Profit for the period	21,680	8,050

Other information
1. Included in the revenue of XYZ is $5 million in respect of sales to PQR. XYZ earns a profit of 25% on cost. These are sales of components that XYZ has been supplying to PQR on a regular basis for a number of years. The amount included in the inventory of PQR in respect of goods purchased from XYZ at the beginning and end of the year was as follows:

Date	Inventory of components in PQR's books
	$'000
31.12.X1	800
31.12.X0	600

Solution

1. PQR owns 100% of the ordinary shares of XYZ . The investment income in PQR statement of comprehensive income is from XYZ so will be eliminated from the consolidation.
2. Intra-group sales of $5 million will be eliminated from revenue and cost of sales:
   DR Group revenue $5,000,000
   CR Group cost of sales $5,000,000
   There is unrealised profit on both opening and closing inventory:
   - Unrealised profit on closing inventory = $160,000 (25/125 × $800,000)
   - Unrealised profit on opening inventory = $120,000 (25/125 × $600,000)
     So the movement on unrealised profit and the deduction from gross profit for the year is $40,000.
   - DR Group cost of sales $40,000
   - CR Provision for unrealised profit $40,000

Consolidated income statement of the PQR Group for the year ended 31 December 20X1

	$'000	Comments
Revenue	170,000	PQR + XYZ − $5 million
Cost of sales	(65,040)	PQR + XYZ − $5 million + $40,000
Gross profit	104,960	
Distribution costs	(14,000)	PQR + XYZ
Administrative expenses	(11,200)	PQR + XYZ
Finance costs	(32,250)	PQR + XYZ
Profit before tax	47,510	
Income tax	(21,000)	PQR + XYZ
Profit for the period	26,510	

16.4 Summary

This chapter has explained various aspects involved in preparing a consolidated statement of comprehensive income. Students will have noted that the treatment of these items is consistent with their treatment in the consolidated statement of financial position.

This examination may contain long questions (20 or 25 marks) that require the preparation of statement of comprehensive income and a Statement of financial statement.

Revision Questions

Question 1

Draft statements of comprehensive income of H and its subsidiary S for the year ended 31 December 20X4

	H	S
	$'000	$'000
Revenue	2,100	1,200
Cost of sales	(1,850)	(1,066)
Gross profit	250	134
Distribution costs	(50)	(20)
Administrative expenses	(30)	(14)
Investment income	16	–
Profit before tax	186	100
Income tax expense	(80)	(40)
Profit for the period	106	60

H purchased 100% of the shares in S when S's equity (share capital plus retained earnings) was $40,000. Goodwill of $12,000 was fully written off to consolidated retained earnings at 31.12 . X3, following an impairment review.

Requirement

Prepare the consolidated statement of comprehensive income of the H group for the year ended 31 December 20X4.

Question 2

Draft statement of comprehensive income of Hope and its subsidiary Despair for the year ended 30 June 20X7

	Hope	Despair
	$	$
Revenue	159,800	108,400
Cost of sales	(79,200)	(61,600)
Gross profit	80,600	46,800
Administrative expenses	(27,000)	(16,000)
Investment income:		
Ordinary dividend	9,000	–
Loan interest	1,000	1,500
Finance cost	(6,000)	(4,000)
Profit before tax	57,600	28,300
Income tax expense	(29,400)	(14,800)
Profit for the period	28,200	13,500

Other information

1. Hope acquired its interest in Despair as follows:
   All of the $1 ordinary shares on 30 June 20X3 when the equity of Despair was $35,000 (ordinary shares $10,000 plus retained earnings $25,000).
2. Hope has not provided Despair with any of its loan capital.
3. The revenue of Hope includes $19,000 in respect of goods sold to Despair at a price that yielded a profit of 20% on selling price. $8,000 of these goods were in the inventory of Despair at 30 June 20X7. Inventories of such goods at 30 June 20X6 amounted to $6,000.

Requirements

 (a) produce the consolidated statement of comprehensive income.
 (b) explain the treatment of the intra-group sales between Hope and Despair.

？ Question 3

GPT regularly sells goods to its subsidiary in which it owns 100% of the ordinary share capital. During the group's financial year ended 31 August 20X7. GPT sold goods to its subsidiary valued at $100,000 (selling price) upon which it makes a margin of 20%. By the group's year end all of the goods had been sold to parties outside the group.

   What is the correct consolidation adjustment in respect of these sales for the year ended 31 August 20X7?

(A) No adjustment required.
(B) DR Revenue $60,000; CR Cost of sales $60,000.
 C) DR Revenue $80,000; CR Cost of sales $80,000.
(D) DR Revenue $100,000; CR Cost of sales $100,000.   **(2 marks)**

Solutions to Revision Questions

 Solution 1

Consolidated statement of comprehensive income

	$'000
Revenue (H + S)	3,300
Cost of sales (H + S)	(2,916)
Gross profit	384
Distribution costs (H + S)	(70)
Administrative expenses (H + S)	(44)
Income tax expense	(120)
Profit for the period	150

 Solution 2

(a) **Hope Group: Consolidated statement of comprehensive income for the year ended 30 June 20X7**

	$
Revenue (H + D − $19,000 [W1])	249,200
Cots of sales (balancing figure)	(122,200)
Gross profit (H + D − $400 [W1])	127,000
Administrative expenses (H + D)	(43,000)
Investment income (external only) W2	2,500
Finance cost (H + D)	(10,000)
Profit before taxation	76,500
Income tax expense (H + D)	(44,200)
Profit for the period	32,300

1. Intra-group sales of $19 million are adjusted in the consolidated income statement. The adjustment at gross profit level is the movement in the provision for unrealised profit:
   - Unrealised profit on closing inventory is 20% × $8,000 = $1,600
   - Unrealised profit on opening inventory is 20% × $6,000 = $1,200
   So, the movement is $1,600 − $1,200 = $400.
2. The cancellation of investment income is of the intra-group element only (the dividend received by Hope from Despair). The interest income of both entities is not intra-group and so it remains in the consolidated income statement: $1,000 + $1,500 = $2,500.

(b) The correct treatment of the intra-group sale is to eliminate it in full from revenue in the consolidated income statement. Where the goods have not been sold on outside the group at the year end then it is necessary to eliminate any profit made on those goods by the supplying entity (Hope in this case). Where the profit elimination is required at the beginning and end of the year then a net adjustment is required in the consolidated income statement, since the opening provision for unrealised profit will be reversed in the year, assuming that the goods are sold on outside the group.

 Solution 3

The correct answer is (D).

17

Associates

Associates

17

LEARNING OUTCOME

After studying this chapter students should be able to:

▸ prepare a consolidated statement of financial position and statement of comprehensive income for a group of companies with an associate.

17.1 Introduction

In Chapter 14 we discussed how cost information about investments and investment income is sometimes insufficient to give the investors appropriate information does not just hold good in situations where the investor has control. Where the investor has a degree of influence over the operations of the investment, but not outright control, then there is an argument for saying that the 'normal' method of accounting for investments is inappropriate.

In this chapter we consider the effect on an investor's financial position and performance of its interest in a specific kind of investments – associates. In this case, the investor can exercise a degree of influence over the affairs of the investment but cannot direct its operating and financial policies (as is the case with subsidiaries). In these circumstances one of forms of consolidation may well be appropriate in the consolidated financial statements of the investor. The form used is the *equity method of consolidation*.

Section 17.2 looks at accounting for associates and the detailed application of equity accounting.

17.2 Accounting for associates

An associate is defined as:

> An entity, including an unincorporated entity such as a partnership, over which the investor has significant influence and that is neither a subsidiary nor an interest in a joint venture. The key concept in the definition is 'significant influence'. It is regarded that significant influence is the power to participate in the financial and operating policy decisions of the entity but is not control over those policies. The existence of significant influence by an investor is usually evidenced in one or more of the following ways:
>
> - representation on the board of directors;
> - participation in policy-making processes;
> - material transactions between the investor and the entity;
> - interchange of managerial personnel;
> - provision of essential technical information.

If an investor holds, directly or indirectly, 20 per cent of the voting rights of an entity, then there is a presumption that the investor has significant influence over the entity, unless it can be clearly demonstrated that this is not the case.

17.2.1 Equity accounting

Associates are accounted for using equity accounting. This is not a method of consolidation, the assets and liabilities of the associate are not aggregated on a line by line basis in the group accounts. Instead, only selected items are included in the consolidated financial statement:

The consolidated statement of comprehensive income

- The investor will include **its share of the results of the associate for the period** in its consolidated statement of comprehensive income (or income statement depending on how the statements have been prepared).
- The share of results is based on the associate's profit after tax, but is included in the consolidated profit before tax in the group accounts.
- The investor will also include its share of any other comprehensive income of the associate in the 'other comprehensive income' section of the income statement.

The consolidated statement of financial position

- The investor will include one figure within non-current assets in the consolidated statement of financial position, entitled **Investment in associate**. The balance to be included under this heading is calculated as follows:

Investment at cost; plus
Share of profits or losses since acquisition; plus
Share of any other changes to shareholders' funds e.g., other comprehensive income (maybe from revaluation of non-current assets); less
Impairment of goodwill; less
Dividends received.

This calculation makes sense if we think about the value of the investment to the investor; the investment increases in value as profits are generated and as other gains are recognised, but reduces in value if an impairment is required. Dividends received from an associate reduce the value of the associate by the amount of the distribution but this is balanced by an increase to cash in the books of the investor.

Goodwill on acquisition

Note that the starting point for this calculation is cost of investment. This means the value of any goodwill on acquisition is already included. Goodwill is part of the value of investment. It may have to be calculated if any impairment is to be recorded, however it will not appear under the heading of goodwill in the group statement of financial position. The impairment will simply be deducted from the value of the investment.

Example 17.A

On 1 May 20X6 AB purchased 40% of the share capital of GH for $375,000. The retained earnings of GH at that date were $400,000.

The consolidated financial statements of AB are presented below together with the accounts of GH for the year to 31 May 20X8.

Income statements for the year ended 31 May 20X8	AB	GH
	$000	$000
Profit from operations	1,270	290
Interest paid	(130)	(40)
Profit before tax	1,140	250
Income tax	(140)	(50)
Profit for the period	1,000	200

Statements of financial positions as at 31 May 20X8	AB	GH
	$000	$000
Assets		
Non-current assets		
Investment in GH	375	
Other assets	2,100	900
	2,475	900
Capital and liabilities		
Share capital	500	250
Retained earnings	1,875	550
	2,375	800
Liabilities	100	100
	2,475	900

Additional information:
1. Goodwill is impaired by 20% in the year. No impairment was considered necessary in previous years.

Required

Prepare the consolidated statement of financial position and consolidated income statement for the AB group for the year ended 31 May 20X8.

Solution

Consolidated income statement for the year ended 31 May 20X8	AB
	$000
Profit from operations ($1,270 − W1 $23)	1,247
Interest paid	(130)
	1,077
Share of profit of associate (W2)	80
Profit before tax	1,157
Income tax	(140)
Profit for the period	1,017

Consolidated statement of financial position as at 31 May 20X8	AB
	$000
Assets	
Non-current assets	
Investment in associate (W3)	412
Other assets	2,100
	2,512
Capital and liabilities	
Share capital	500
Retained earnings (W4)	1,912
Liabilities	100
	2,512

Workings

1. *Impairment of goodwill*

   the impairment is given as a percentage so we will have to calculate goodwill to determine the impairment. Goodwill on acquisition:

Consideration paid		$375
Net assets acquired:		
Share capital	$250	
Retained earnings at acquisition	$400	
40% acquired		260
Goodwill on acquisition		115

   Impairment of goodwill is therefore 20% × £115,000 = $23,000. This will be charged to the group income statement in the year and will reduce the value of the investment:

Dr	Profit from operations	$23,000	
	Cr Investment in associate		$23,000

   Being the impairment of goodwill on associate

2. *Share of profit of associate*

   AB is entitled to 40% of the profit after tax of GH, 40% × $200,000 = $80,000.

3. *Investment in associate*

	$000
Cost of investment	375
Plus share of post-acquisition profits	
40% × ($550,000 − $400,000)	60
Less impairment	(23)
Investment in associate	412

4. *Retained earnings*

	Group $000	GH $000
Retained earnings of AB	1,875	
Retained earnings of GH		550
RE of GH at acquisition		(400)
		150
40% group share of GH	60	
Impairment of goodwill	(23)	
	1,912	

17.3 Fair values and accounting policies

Where, at the date of acquisition, the fair value of the net assets of an investment that is equity accounted or proportionally consolidated is significantly different from their carrying values in the financial statements of the acquired entity, the initial consolidated carrying values should be based on fair values.

In addition, wherever possible the financial statements of the investee entity should be prepared to the same date, and using the same accounting policies, as the rest of the group. If the financial statements are not prepared to the same date, the difference between the dates should be no more than 3 months.

17.4 Summary

This chapter has reviewed the methods of accounting that are appropriate where an investor does not have complete control over an investee's activities. Generally, it is appropriate to use the equity method of accounting for associates. As a general rule of thumb, associate status is often indicated where an investor holds between 20 and 50 per cent of the equity capital of the investee entity.

Revision Questions

Question 1

The following statements refer to a situation where an investing entity (D) seeks to exert control or influence over another entity (E). Assume that D is required to prepare consolidated accounts because of other investments.

 (i) if D owns more than 20% but less than 50% of the equity shares in E, then E is bound to be an associate of D.
 (ii) if D controls the operating and financial policies of E, then E cannot be an associate of D.
 (iii) if E is an associate of D, then any amounts payable by E to D are not eliminated when preparing the consolidated statement of financial position of D.

Which of the statements are true?

(A) (i) and (ii) only
(B) (ii) only
(C) (ii) and (iii) only
(D) (i) and (iii) only. **(2 marks)**

Question 2

You are the accountant responsible for training at Develop, an entity with a number of investments throughout the world. A key financial reporting task is to prepare consolidated financial statements and this forms an important aspect of the training of new accountants.

A recently employed trainee has sent you this memorandum.

I have just attended my first training course and have learned the mechanics of how to treat subsidiaries and associates in the consolidated accounts. I'm reasonably comfortable with the numbers, but the concepts baffle me. Why does the exercise of adding together the statement of financial position of our entity with those of our subsidiaries give our shareholders useful financial information? Why do we treat associates differently – I find the concept of adding together all the net assets and showing our share as one amount particularly confusing?

Requirement

Draft a reply to your trainee that explains the principles underpinning the preparation of consolidated financial statements. You should clearly explain why subsidiaries and associates are treated differently and why the information is of benefit to the shareholders of the investor. **(10 marks)**

Solutions to Revision Questions

☑ Solution 1

The first statement is not true; a simple ownership test does not categorically determine the nature of the relationship between an investor and investee entity. However, the second and third statements are correct, so the correct answer is (C).

☑ Solution 2

Consolidated financial statements show the resources deployed by a single economic entity and the return generated by those resources. The boundary of the single economic entity is determined by common control. Control is essentially the ability to direct the operating and financial policies of an entity. IAS 27 *Consolidated and Separate Financial Statements* – defines a subsidiary in terms of the ability of the parent to exercise control. That is why a group consists of a parent undertaking and its subsidiary undertakings. Because this single economic entity (comprising more than one separate legal entities) is under common control, it is logical to show one statement of financial position containing 100% of the controlled resources and one income statement containing 100% of the returns earned by those resources. However, a further function of financial statements is to show the interests of the investors in the resources under common control, so the ownership interests section of the statement of financial position needs to separately identify the interests of the parent undertaking's shareholders from those of other 'non-controlling interests' in the economic entity.

It is inappropriate to treat associates and trade investments the way we treat subsidiaries because they are outside the boundary of control. However, associates do qualify for special treatment. Although the parent undertaking cannot control the deployment of resources, it is in a position to exercise a significant degree of influence over their deployment. If they actively exercise this significant influence, then mere inclusion of the amount invested, plus the amounts that happen to be received as dividends, is unlikely to adequately reflect the extent of the investor's interest. Therefore, although full consolidation is inappropriate, because control is not present, a special form of treatment is needed. This treatment, known as the equity method of consolidation, shows the investor's share of the net assets of the associate and its share of the profits.

18

Non-current
Tangible Asset
Standards

Non-current Tangible Asset Standards

18

LEARNING OUTCOME

After completing this chapter you should be able to:

▶ apply the accounting rues contained in IFRS's and IAS's dealing with non-current assets including their impairment.

The syllabus topics covered in this chapter are as follows:

- Property, plant and equipment (IAS 16): the calculation of depreciation and the effect of revaluations, changes to economic useful life, repairs, improvements and disposals.
- Related financing costs (IAS 23).

You will have studied the basic accounting for tangible non-current assets in Financial Accounting Fundamentals or the course giving you exemption from it. If required, refresh your knowledge by revisiting your previous text.

18.1 IAS 16 *Property, Plant and Equipment*

18.1.1 Objective

The objective of IAS 16 is to prescribe the accounting treatment for property, plant and equipment so that users of the financial statements have information about the entity's investment in its property, plant and equipment and changes in that investment. The main issues being the recognition of the assets, determining their carrying amounts and associated depreciation charges.

18.2 Revision of some definitions in IAS 16

 You should know these definitions from your earlier studies. You need to ensure that you know all of the following definitions for your examination.

345

18.2.1 Property, plant and equipment

Property, plant and equipment are tangible items that are held for use in the production or supply of goods or services, for rental to others, or for administrative purposes.

18.2.2 Carrying amount

The amount at which an asset is recognised, after deducting any accumulated depreciation and impairment losses. Also referred to as book value.

18.2.3 Cost

The amount paid and the fair value of other consideration given to acquire an asset at the time of its acquisition or construction. See Section 18.3.1.

18.2.4 Depreciable amount

The cost or valuation of an asset less its residual value.

18.2.5 Depreciation

The systematic allocation of the depreciable amount of an asset over its useful life.

18.2.6 Fair value

The amount for which an asset can be exchanged between knowledgeable, willing parties in an arm's length transaction.

18.2.7 Impairment loss

The amount by which the carrying amount exceeds its recoverable amount.

18.2.8 Recoverable amount

The higher of an asset's net realisable value and its value in use.

18.2.9 Residual value

The residual value of an asset is the amount that the entity would currently obtain from disposal of the asset, after deducting the estimated costs of disposal, assuming that the asset was already at the point where it would be disposed of (using the age and condition that would be assumed to apply at the time of disposal).

18.2.10 Useful life

IAS 16 defines useful life as the period over which the asset is expected to be available for use by the entity or the volume of output expected from the asset.

18.3   Recognition

IAS 16 requires that an item of property, plant or equipment should be recognised as an asset when:

- it is probable that future economic benefits associated with the asset will flow to the entity;
- the cost of the item can be measured reliably.

The first point is based on the principle that the item should only be recognised as an asset and included in the financial statements when it reaches its location and condition necessary for it to be capable of operating in the manner intended by management.

The second point deals with cost. If the asset has been purchased, then the asset is initially recognised at its original cost.

18.3.1   Elements of cost

The cost of an item of property, plant or equipment can include any of the following:

- Invoice price, including any import duties and non-refundable purchase taxes;
- Any costs directly attributable to bringing the asset to the location and condition necessary for it to be capable of operating in the manner intended. Directly attributable costs can include:
  –site preparation
  –initial delivery and handling costs
  –installation and assembly costs
  –testing and initial set up costs
  –professional fees.
  Note: Administration expenses and general overhead costs cannot be included.
- The initial estimate of dismantling and removing the item and restoring the site on which it is located. This will involve creating a provision which is dealt with in Chapter 23.

18.3.2   Self-constructed assets

Where the entity constructs the asset itself for its own use, then the cost is determined using the same principles as for an acquired asset. Attributable costs are likely to include the cost of materials and labour and other inputs used in the construction and will exclude any profit element.

18.3.3   Recognising parts of an asset as separate assets

IAS 16 allows significant parts of an asset to be recorded separately if each part has a different useful economic life. For example, a furnace may require relining after a specified number of hours of use, or aircraft interiors such as seats and galleys may require replacement several times during the life of the airframe.

18.4   Measurement

IAS 16 requires that an entity must choose between the cost model or the revaluation model as its accounting policy and apply that policy to an entire class of property, plant and equipment.

18.4.1 Cost model

Once recognised as an asset, the item should be carried at its cost less any accumulated depreciation and any accumulated impairment losses.

18.4.2 Revaluation model

Once recognised as an asset, an asset whose fair value can be measured reliably, can be held at a revalued amount less any subsequent accumulated depreciation and impairment losses. The revalued amount being its fair value at the date of revaluation. Revaluation should be undertaken regularly to ensure that value of the asset does not vary significantly from its fair value. The fair value of land and buildings will usually be market value determined by a professional valuer. The fair value of plant and equipment is usually current market value. If the asset is of a specialised type that is rarely sold, an entity may have to estimate fair value using depreciated replacement cost.

18.5 Subsequent expenditure

IAS 16 requires the recognition principle to be applied to the subsequent expenditure, in other words:

- it is probable that future economic benefits associated with the asset (i.e. the additional expenditure) will flow to the entity;
- the cost of the item (additional expenditure) can be measured reliably.

If the recognition criteria are met, an entity recognises in the carrying amount of an item of property, plant and equipment the cost of replacing part of such an item when that cost is incurred. The carrying amount of those parts that are replaced is derecognised in accordance with the derecognition provisions. If a part of an item of property, plant and equipment is depreciated separately, when it is replaced, it will be treated as a disposal. The part replaced will be derecognised and the new part treated as an acquisition.

A condition of continuing to operate an item of property, plant and equipment (e.g. an aircraft) may be performing regular major inspections for faults regardless of whether parts of the item are replaced. When each major inspection is performed, its cost is recognised in the carrying amount of the item of property, plant and equipment as a replacement if the recognition criteria are satisfied. Any remaining carrying amount of the cost of the previous inspection (as distinct from physical parts) is derecognised. This occurs regardless of whether the cost of the previous inspection was identified in the transaction in which the item was acquired or constructed.

18.6 Accounting for depreciation

All assets with a limited useful life must be depreciated. Land has an unlimited useful life (unless it is a mine, quarry, etc.) and is not depreciated. Depreciation should be allocated on a systematic basis over the asset's economic useful life and charged as an expense to profit or loss, unless it is included in the carrying amount of another asset. For example, depreciation of assets used in development work may be included in the carrying amount of intangible assets recognised under IAS 38 *Intangible Assets* (see Chapter 21 for details).

IAS 16 requires that each part of an item of property, plant and equipment with a cost that is significant in relation to the total cost of the item shall be depreciated separately. The initial cost of the asset will need to be allocated to its significant parts, for example, the airframe and engines of an aircraft would need to be treated separately as they have different useful lives. If the significant parts have the same useful lives, they can be grouped together for depreciation purposes.

IAS 16 also requires the assets residual value and useful life to be reviewed at every year-end. If changes are made to either, it will count as a change in accounting estimate and be dealt with using IAS 8, as previously discussed in Chapter 11.

IAS 16 specifically states that repair and maintenance of an asset does not remove the need to provide for depreciation. The residual value of an asset may increase to an amount equal to or greater than its carrying value, if this happens depreciation will be zero.

Depreciation commences when the asset reaches the location and condition necessary for it to be capable of operating in the manner intended by management and only ceases when it is fully depreciated or when it is derecognised.

Example 18.A

A machine was purchased on 1 January 2003 for $50,000. The asset is used from the date of acquisition and its estimated economic useful life is 5 years. The following entry will be recorded in respect of depreciation in the year ended 31 December 2003:

		$	$
Debit	Depreciation expense	10,000	
Credit	Accumulated depreciation		10,000
Being the depreciation expense for the year			

The machine will be included in the statement of financial position as at 31 December 2003 at $40,000 (cost $50,000 less accumulated depreciation of $10,000).

18.6.1 Review of useful life

The useful life of the asset and its residual value should be reviewed periodically (at least at each financial year-end), and if there are significant changes then future depreciation charges should be adjusted. The useful life of an asset to an entity may be less than its total economic life as an entity may have a policy to replace each type of asset after a fixed period of time or after a fixed amount of usage.

Example 18.B

A machine was purchased on 1 January 2000 for $50,000. The asset is used from the date of acquisition and its estimated economic useful life is 10 years. After 3 years of use, the asset's useful life is reviewed. The machine is expected to last only a further 5 years from the date of review.

The depreciation charge will now be calculated based on the carrying value of $35,000 (cost less 3 years' depreciation) and a remaining useful life of 5 years. The charge for the next 5 years will be $7,000.

The higher charge to statement of comprehensive income will ensure the original cost of the asset is expensed to the statement of comprehensive income over its total revised life of 8 years – 3 years of $5,000 and 5 years of $7,000.

18.6.2 Depreciation method

IAS 16 requires that the depreciation method used should reflect the actual pattern in which the assets' future economic benefits are expected to be consumed by the entity. The depreciation method should also be reviewed at the end of each year and if there is a change in the pattern of usage, the method should be changed to reflect the new consumption of economic benefits. Any change in depreciation method will be treated as a change in accounting estimate under IAS 8.

> A variety of depreciation methods can be used to allocate the depreciable amount of an asset over its useful life. The most common in examinations are the straight-line method and the reducing balance method. You should have covered depreciation methods in your foundation studies, you may find it useful to revise the different methods of depreciation.

Example 18.C

Depreciation methods revision

A machine is purchased on 1 January 2000 for $100,000. It has a useful economic life of 5 years and at the end of that time it is expected to have a residual value of $10,000.

Calculate depreciation for each year using:
(a) straight-line depreciation
(b) reducing balance depreciation at 35%

Straight-line depreciation

The depreciable amount is $100,000 − $10,000 = $90,000. This will be depreciated over 5 years, therefore each years depreciation is $90,000/5 = $18,000.

Reducing balance depreciation

When calculating reducing balance depreciation, ignore the residual value and apply the depreciation rate to the carrying amount. In year 1, the carrying amount is the cost $100,000 × 35% = $35,000.

In year 2, deduct the first years depreciation from the cost to give the carrying amount, $100,000 − $35,000 =$65,000. This is then multiplied by the depreciation rate to give the annual depreciation charge, $65,000 × 35% = $22,750.

In year 3, deduct the second years depreciation, $65,000 − $22,750 = $42,250. The third years' depreciation is then $42,250 × 35% = $14,788.

And so on:
Year 4 = $42,250 − $14,788 = $27,462 × 35% = $9,612
Year 5 = $27,462 − $9,612 = $17,850 × 35% = $6,248

Carrying value at end of year 5 is $17,850 − $6,248 = $11,602, a little over the $10,000 estimated.

18.7 Retirements and disposals

The carrying amount of an asset should be derecognised on disposal of that asset or when there is no future economic benefit expected from its continued use or disposal. Derecognition means removing the asset from the statement of financial position. **Gains or losses on disposal** are calculated by comparing the net disposal proceeds and the carrying value of the asset at the date of disposal. Gains or losses should be recognised in profit or loss as income or expense, but IAS 16 specifies that they cannot be included as revenue.

Example 18.D

A machine was purchased on 1 January 2001 for $50,000. The asset is used from the date of acquisition and its estimated economic useful life is 5 years. The asset is sold on 1 March 2004 for $24,000. The entity policy is to charge a full year's depreciation in the year of acquisition and none in the year of disposal.

The gain on disposal is the difference between the proceeds of $24,000 and the carrying value of the asset, $20,000 (cost of $50,000 less 3 years' depreciation).

The disposal will be recorded as:

		$	$
Debit	Bank	24,000	
Debit	Accumulated depreciation	30,000	
Credit	Cost of asset		50,000
Credit	Gain on disposal profit or loss		4,000

Being the disposal of the asset and recognition of the gain.

18.8   Revaluation of assets

Property is often revalued as it better reflects the fair value of the asset, due to changes in property valuations. The valuations are usually performed by professional valuers and if valuation fluctuations are frequent, it may be necessary to revalue annually; if not, every 3 or 5 years is sufficient.

If an item of property, plant or equipment is revalued, that entire class of property, plant or equipment must be revalued. A class is a grouping of assets of a similar nature, for example:

- land
- buildings
- machinery
- motor vehicles
- office equipment
- furniture and fittings.

18.8.1   Revaluation surplus

When an asset is revalued, the asset's carrying value is increased and the increase recognised in other comprehensive income and accumulated in equity under the heading *revaluation reserve*.

Example 18.E

An asset was purchased on 1 January 2001 for $500,000. The asset is used from the date of acquisition and its estimated economic useful life is 50 years. After 3 years of use, the asset is revalued on 1 January 2004 at $540,000. The revaluation surplus is the difference between the revalued amount and the carrying value of the asset which is $70,000, $540,000 less $470,000. The revaluation is recorded as follows:

		$	$
Debit	Accumulated depreciation	30,000	
Debit	Cost of asset	40,000	
Credit	Revaluation reserve		70,000

Being the revaluation of the asset at 1 January 2004.

Accumulated depreciation on the asset is **eliminated** and the balance of the surplus is debited to the cost of the asset. The asset will now be **held at valuation less any subsequent accumulated depreciation**, calculated on the revalued amount over the asset's remaining useful life.

18.8.2 Revaluation deficits

If future revaluations result in a fair value that is less than the carrying value, then the decrease is recognised in other comprehensive income to the extent that there is a credit balance in the revaluation reserve for that asset. The decrease recognised in other comprehensive income reduces the amount accumulated in equity under revaluation reserve. If there is an insufficient amount in the revaluation reserve in respect of the asset, then the balance of the deficit will be charged to profit or loss.

The effect of taxes on income resulting from revaluations must be recognised and disclosed in accordance with IAS 12, this will usually mean an increase in asset value will give rise to an increase in deferred tax. Tax effects are shown in the same section of the statement of comprehensive income as the item giving rise to them, so an increase in deferred tax arising from an asset revaluation will be shown under other comprehensive income.

Example 18.F

If the asset in Example 18.E was revalued again 5 years after purchase at $500,000, the calculations would be as follows:

	$	$
Original cost	500,000	
3 years depreciation (3/50)	(30,000)	
Net book value	470,000	
Revaluation to	540,000	
Gain on revaluation		70,000
2 years depreciation (2/47 × 540,000)	22,978	
Net book value	517,022	
Revalued to	500,000	
Loss on revaluation, charged to revaluation reserve		17,022
Balance on revaluation reserve		52,978

Example 18.G

If the asset in Example 18.E was revalued to $440,000 after 3 years, a deficit of $30,000 would arise. This would be calculated as follows:

	$
Original cost	500,000
3 years depreciation (3/50)	(30,000)
Net book value	470,000
Revaluation to	440,000
Loss on revaluation	30,000

In this example, the asset has not previously been revalued, the loss must be charged to profit or loss.

18.8.3 Disposal of a revalued asset

When a previously revalued asset is disposed of, the gain on disposal is measured as the difference between the carrying value at the date of disposal and the proceeds received.

Example 18.H

Continue with Example 18.E, an asset was purchased on 1 January 2001 for $500,000. The asset is used from the date of acquisition and its estimated economic useful life is 50 years. After 3 years of use, the asset is revalued on 1 January 2004 at $540,000. Depreciation is charged on a monthly basis.

If the asset is sold on 30 June 2004 for $550,000, how much profit should be recognised in the statement of comprehensive income.

	$	$
Original cost	500,000	
3 years depreciation (3/50)	(30,000)	
Net book value	470,000	
Revaluation to	540,000	
Gain on revaluation		70,000
Depreciation (6/12 × 540,000/47)	5,745	
Net book value at date of disposal	534,255	
Proceeds	550,000	
Gain on disposal, recognised in the profit or loss		15,745

When this asset is disposed of, the revaluation surplus included in equity in respect of an item of property, plant and equipment may be transferred directly to retained earnings. This may involve transferring the whole of the surplus when the asset is retired or disposed of. IAS 16 specifically says that transfers from revaluation surplus to retained earnings are not made through profit or loss. The transfer will be shown in the statement of changes in equity.

IAS 16 also allows some of the revaluation surplus to be transferred as the asset is used by an entity. In such a case, the amount of the surplus transferred would be the difference between depreciation based on the revalued carrying amount of the asset and depreciation based on the asset's original cost. This amount can be transferred to retained earnings each year.

Example 18.I

In Example 18.H, the disposal takes place within the following period, so the whole of the revaluation surplus can be transferred to retained earnings. The amount transferred is $70,000.

Example 18.J

Using the data and answer to Example 18.F:

	$	$	$
Original cost	500,000		
3 years depreciation (3/50)	(30,000)		
Net book value	470,000		
Revaluation to	540,000		
Gain on revaluation			70,000
2 years depreciation (2/47 × 540,000)	22,978	22,978	
2 years depreciation based on cost is		20,000	
Transfer to retained earnings from revaluation reserve (1,489 each year)			(2,978)
Net book value	517,022		
Revalued to	500,000		
Loss on revaluation, charged to revaluation reserve			(17,022)
Balance on revaluation reserve			50,000
Depreciation (500,000/45)		11,111	
Depreciation based on cost		10,000	
Transfer to retained earnings from revaluation reserve			(1,111)
Balance on revaluation reserve			48,889

18.9 Disclosure requirements

IAS 16 has extensive disclosure requirements:

(a) measurement bases used (e.g. cost or valuation);
(b) depreciation methods used;
(c) useful lives or depreciation rates used;
(d) gross carrying amount and accumulated depreciation at the beginning and end of the period;
(e) reconciliation of opening and closing figures with details of additions, disposals, revaluations, impairments and depreciation;
(f) details of any pledging of items of property, plant and equipment as security for liabilities;
(g) commitments for future capital expenditure;
(h) if the asset has been revalued:
    (i) basis of valuation
    (ii) date of valuation
    (iii) whether an independent valuer was used
    (iv) the carrying value of the asset if no revaluation had taken place
    (v) the revaluation surplus.

18.10 IAS 23 *Borrowing Costs* (revised 2007)

18.10.1 Introduction

IAS 23 deals with the accounting treatment of interest, etc., including the extent to which it may be capitalised as a part of the cost of a non-current asset.

18.10.2 Borrowing costs – accounting treatment

IAS 23 was revised in 2007. The new IAS 23 requires that borrowing costs are capitalised if they are directly attributable to the acquisition, construction or production of a qualifying asset (one that takes a long time to get ready for use or sale). The borrowing costs that are directly attributable to the acquisition, construction or production of a qualifying asset are those borrowing costs that would have been avoided if the expenditure on the qualifying asset had not been made.

Debit	Asset
Credit	Bank

18.10.3 Interest rate

For specific borrowings, the actual interest cost will be used. For general borrowings, the weighted average cost will be used.

18.10.4 Period of capitalisation

Capitalisation will commence when expenditure on the asset and borrowing costs are being incurred, and must cease when substantially all the activities necessary to prepare the asset for sale or use are complete. If development work is interrupted for any extended period, capitalisation of borrowing costs should be suspended for that period.

18.10.5 Disclosure

The financial statements must disclose:

(a) borrowing costs capitalised in the period
(b) the capitalisation rate used.

18.11 Available for sale financial assets

You do not need to know the detail of IAS 32 – *Financial Instruments: Disclosure and Presentation* or IAS 39 – *Financial Instruments: Recognition and Measurement* as the only part of these standards in the syllabus relates to share capital which is dealt with in Chapter 17. However, the asset headings defined in IAS 32 and IAS 39 have to be used in the statement of financial position, so you need to understand what the headings mean.

IAS 32 defines financial assets, the definition includes equity instruments in other entities.

IAS 39 categorises financial assets into four categories, the only category effecting this syllabus is 'available for sale investments'. These are investments in equity and other types of shares in other entities. They appear on the statement of financial position under the non-current asset heading as financial assets. They are measured at fair value and revalued to fair value on each end of the reporting period.

Note that being classified as available for sale does not mean that there is any intention to sell them.

18.12 Summary

Having completed this chapter, we can now account for and disclose the amounts relating to property, plant and equipment, including depreciation, changes in useful life, disposal and the effects of revaluation.

Finally, we can explain how to treat and disclose amounts relating to borrowing costs.

Revision Questions

? Question 1

A building contractor decides to build an office building, to be occupied by his own staff. Tangible non-current assets are initially measured at cost. Which of the following expenses incurred by the building contractor cannot be included as a part of the cost of the office building?

(A) Interest incurred on a specific loan taken out to pay for the construction of the new offices
(B) Direct building labour costs
(C) A proportion of the contractor's general administration costs
(D) Hire of plant and machinery for use on the office building site.   **(2 marks)**

? Question 2

The purpose of depreciation is to:

(A) Allocate the cost less residual value on a systematic basis over the asset's useful economic life
(B) Write the asset down to its market value each period
(C) Charge profits for the use of the asset
(D) Recognise that assets lose value over time.   **(2 marks)**

? Question 3

Which of the following tangible non-current assets are NOT usually depreciated:

(A) Machinery purchased through a finance lease
(B) Land
(C) Buildings with a life in excess of 30 years
(D) Vehicles.   **(2 marks)**

Question 4

IAS 16 *Property, Plant and Equipment* requires an asset to be measured at cost on its original recognition in the financial statements.

EW used its own staff, assisted by contractors when required, to construct a new warehouse for its own use.

Which ONE of the following costs would NOT be included in attributable costs of the non-current asset?

(A) Clearance of the site prior to work commencing.
(B) Professional surveyors' fees for managing the construction work.
(C) EW's own staff wages for time spent working on the construction.
(D) An allocation of EW's administration costs, based on EW staff time spent on the construction as a percentage of the total staff time.   **(2 marks)**

Question 5

AB purchased a specialised machine for $20,000 on 1 April 2000. The machine had an expected useful life of 10 years and was depreciated using the straight-line method. Residual value was assumed to be zero.

Due to a worldwide shortage of specialised parts for manufacturing new machines of this type, the price of new machines of a similar type more than doubled by 31 March 2003. AB decided to revalue their machine on 31 March 2003 to market value. The market value of a two-year old machine was $35,000.

AB ceased the production of a product line and no longer required the machine. They sold the machine for $32,000 on 31 March 2004.

On disposal of the machine AB should:

 (i) Transfer $21,000 from revaluation reserve to retained earnings
 (ii) Credit a gain on disposal of $2,000 to the statement of comprehensive income
(iii) Debit loss on disposal of $1,000 to the statement of comprehensive income
(iv) Transfer $15,000 from revaluation reserve to retained earnings
 (v) Credit gain on disposal of $23,000 to statement of comprehensive income.

Which of the following are the correct entries to record the gain/loss on disposal?

(A) (i) and (iv)
(B) (iii) and (iv)
(C) (v) only
(D) (i) and (ii)   **(4 marks)**

Question 6

Plant and machinery, costing $50,000, was purchased on 1 April 20X0. This was depreciated for 2 years at 20 per cent using the reducing balance method. On 1 April 20X2, the machinery (original cost $25,000) was sold for $12,000. Replacement machines were acquired on the same date for $34,000. What was the net book value of plant and machinery at 1 April 20X3?

(A) $39,800
(B) $43,200
(C) $40,800
(D) $40,000 **(4 marks)**

? **Question 7**

Roming purchased property costing $440,000 on 1 January 2000. The property is being depreciated over 50 years on a straight-line basis.

The property was revalued on 1 January 2004 at $520,000. The useful life was also reviewed at that date and is estimated to be a further 40 years.

Requirement

Prepare the accounting entries to record the revaluation and calculate the depreciation charge that will apply from 1 January 2004. **(5 marks)**

? **Question 8**

The financial statements are being prepared for Diska and the accountant has asked you how the borrowing costs of $30 million should be treated in the accounts. Of the $30 million, $7 million relates specifically to the construction of the entity's new manufacturing plant (at a total cost of $60 million).

Requirement

Discuss the appropriate accounting treatment for the above costs, explaining what options are available and the disclosures that would be required. **(4 marks)**

? **Question 9**

CI purchased equipment on 1 April 2002 for $100,000. The equipment was depreciated using the reducing balance method at 25% per year. CI's period end is 31 March.

Depreciation was charged up to and including 31 March 2006. At that date, the recoverable amount was $28,000.

Calculate the impairment loss on the equipment according to IAS 36 *Impairment of Assets*. **(3 marks)**

? **Question 10**

Which ONE of the following items would CM recognise as subsequent expenditure on a non-current asset and capitalise it as required by IAS 16 *Property, Plant and Equipment?*

(A) CM purchased a furnace five years ago, when the furnace lining was separately identified in the accounting records. The furnace now requires relining at a cost of $200,000. When the furnace is relined, it will be used in CM's business for a further 5 years
(B) CM's office building has been badly damaged by a fire. CM intends to restore the building to its original condition at a cost of $250,000

(C) CM's delivery vehicle broke down. When it was inspected by the repairers, it was discovered that it needed a new engine. The engine and associated labour costs are estimated to be $5,000

(D) CM closes its factory for 2 weeks every year. During this time, all plant and equipment has its routine annual maintenance check and any necessary repairs are carried out. The cost of the current year's maintenance check and repairs was $75,000

(2 marks)

? Question 11

A property was purchased on 1 January 1998 for $800,000. The asset is used from the date of acquisition and its estimated economic useful life is 50 years. After 5 years of use, the asset is revalued on 1 January 2003 at $830,000.

A subsequent valuation was completed 1 year later, as the property valuations in that area were experiencing significant fluctuations, and the property valuation was $750,000.

Requirements

(a) Explain the treatment and prepare the accounting entries to record the revaluation on 1 January 2003. **(4 marks)**

(b) Explain the treatment and prepare the accounting entries to record the revaluation on 1 January 2004. **(6 marks)**

(Total marks = 10)

? Question 12

AD owns three hotels. The entity has employed C and J, a firm of chartered surveyors, to revalue its properties during the past year. The directors have decided that the valuations should be incorporated into the entity's financial statements.

This is the first time that such a revaluation has taken place and the clerk responsible for the preparation of the non-current asset note in the statement of financial position is unsure of the correct treatment of the amounts involved. The entity's year-end is 30 September 20X3.

The clerk has extracted the following table from the report prepared by C and J:

	Original cost	Depreciation to 30.9.X2	Market value at 1.1.X3	Estimated useful life 1.1.X3
	$'000	$'000	$'000	Years
Hotel G	400	96	650	50
Hotel H	350	56	420	30
Hotel K	250	35	160	40

Depreciation for the first 3 months of the year is to be based on the entity's original depreciation policy of writing off 2 per cent of cost per annum. Depreciation for the remainder of the year is to be based on the estimated asset lives stated in the surveyors' report.

Requirements

(a) Prepare the non-current asset note, which would appear as a part of A's published accounts, assuming that A owns no non-current assets apart from the three hotels listed above.

(You are *not* required to prepare the description of accounting policies which would appear in respect of non-current assets.) **(8 marks)**

(b) Answer the following queries posed by the accounts clerk:

   (i) The book value of Hotel K has fallen as a result of the revaluation. How should this decrease be reflected in the financial statements? **(4 marks)**

   (ii) Does all of the depreciation based on the revalued amounts for Hotels G and H have to be charged to profit or loss or can a proportion be offset against the revaluation reserve instead? **(2 marks)**

(Total marks = 14)

Solutions to Revision Questions

 Solution 1

The correct answer is (C), see Section 18.3.1.

Only specific costs incurred directly on the asset can be included. Finance costs can be included. Direct labour costs are also specific, as are the hire costs.

 Solution 2

The correct answer is (A), see Section 18.5.

 Solution 3

The correct answer is (B), see Section 18.5.

All tangible fixed assets, with finite useful lives are usually depreciated.

 Solution 4

The correct answer is (D), see Section 18.3.

Solution 5

The correct answer is (D), see Sections 18.6 and 18.7.

	$
Original cost	20,000
3 years depreciation	(6,000)
	14,000
Revaluation, transfer to reserve	21,000
	35,000
Depreciation (1/7)	(5,000)
	30,000
Less cash on disposal	32,000
Gain on disposal	2,000
Reversal of revaluation gain to retained earnings	21,000

Solution 6

The answer is (D), see Section 18.5.

	$	$
Cost		50,000
20% depreciation		(10,000)
		40,000
20% depreciation		(8,000)
		32,000
Less disposal, net book value		
Cost	25,000	
Depreciation, 2 years	9,000	
		(16,000)
		16,000
Add acquisition		34,000
NBV 1 April 20X2		50,000
Less 20% depreciation		10,000
NBV 1 April 20X3		40,000

 # Solution 7

The annual charge for depreciation was $440,000/50 years = $8,800.

The asset had been used and depreciated for 4 years (2000 to 2003).

The carrying value of the asset at the date of valuation was therefore $404,800 (cost of $440,000 – accumulated depreciation of $35,200).

The revaluation surplus is calculated as the valuation amount of $520,000 less the carrying value of the asset of $404,800. The surplus is therefore $115,200.

The revaluation at 1 January 2004 will be recorded as:

		$	$
Debit	Accumulated depreciation	35,200	
Debit	Cost of asset	80,000	
Credit	Revaluation surplus		115,200

Being the revaluation of the asset at 1 January 2004.

The depreciation charge for 2004 and beyond will be based on the asset's valuation over the remaining useful life of the property. The useful life has also been revised to 40 years, so the depreciation will now be $13,000, being value of $520,000 over 40 years, see Section 18.8.

 # Solution 8

IAS 23 *Borrowing Costs* requires that borrowing costs be capitalised if they are directly attributable to the acquisition, construction or production of a qualifying asset.

Diska should charge $23 m to the statement of comprehensive income and $7 million would be capitalised and included in the cost of constructing the plant.

The financial statements would disclose:

- the accounting policy adopted;
- the amount of borrowing costs capitalised in the period, see Section 18.10.

 ## Solution 9

	$
Cost	100,000
Depreciation 2002/03	(25,000)
	75,000
Depreciation 2003/04	(18,750)
	56,250
Depreciation 2004/05	(14,063)
	42,187
Depreciation 2005/06	(10,547)
	31,640
Impaired value	(28,000)
Reduction	3,640

See Section 18.8.2.

 ## Solution 10

The correct answer is (A), see Section 18.5.

 ## Solution 11

At 1 January 2003

The annual charge for depreciation was $800,000/50 years = $16,000.

The asset had been used and depreciated for 5 years (1998–2002).

The carrying value of the asset at the date of valuation was therefore $720,000 (cost of $800,000 – accumulated depreciation of $80,000).

The revaluation surplus is calculated as the valuation amount of $830,000 less the carrying value of the asset of $720,000. The surplus is therefore $110,000.

The revaluation at 1 January 2003 will be recorded as:

		$	$
Debit	Accumulated depreciation	80,000	
Debit	Cost of asset	30,000	
Credit	Revaluation surplus		110,000

Being the revaluation of the asset at 1 January 2003.

At 1 January 2004

The annual charge for depreciation is now $830,000/45 years (the remaining useful life of the asset) = $18,444.

The asset had been used and depreciated one further year: 2003.

The carrying value of the asset at the date of the second valuation was therefore $811,556 (valuation of $830,000 – accumulated depreciation of $18,444).

The revaluation effect is calculated as the new valuation amount of $750,000 less the carrying value of the asset of $811,556. This results in a deficit on revaluation of $61,556.

The deficit will first be charged against any surplus relating to this asset's previous revaluations, with any balance of the deficit being charged in profit or loss.

There are sufficient amounts in the revaluation reserve, in this case to absorb the deficit at 1 January 2004, and so the revaluation at 1 January 2004 will be recorded as:

		$	$
Debit	Revaluation surplus	61,556	
Credit	Carrying value of the asset		61,556

Being the revaluation of the asset at 1 January 2004, resulting in an impairment deficit.

See Section 18.8.

Solution 12

(a) Tangible non-current assets

	$'000
Land and buildings at cost or valuation	
At 1 October 20X2 (400 + 350 + 250)	1,000
Revaluation gain (To Balance)	230
At 30 September 20X3 (650 + 420 + 160)	1,230
Depreciation	
At 1 October 20X2 (96 + 56 + 35)	187
Revaluation adjustment (187 + 5)	(192)
Charge for year (workings)	28
At 30 September 20X3 (for 9 months)	23
Net book value	
At 1 October 20X2	813
At 30 September 20X3	1,207

Land and buildings (hotels) were revalued at 1 January 20X3 on an open-market basis.

Depreciation	$'000
Charge for first 3 months (400 + 350 + 250) × 2% × 3/12	5
Charge for the last 9 months	
((650/50) + (420/30) + (160/40)) × 9/12	23
	28

(b) IAS 16 requires that any revaluation loss which is caused by a clear consumption of economic benefit should be recognised as an expense in profit or loss. It is unlikely that this would apply to a hotel, where increased occupancy is unlikely to have any real effect on wear and tear on the fabric of the building.

If the building has previously been revalued, then the loss would be shown in other comprehensive income and decrease revaluation surplus to the extent that any credit balance existed in the revaluation reserve for that asset. When all the previous revaluation gain has been eliminated, the balance will be written off to statement of comprehensive income.

19

Accounting for
Leases

Accounting for Leases

19

LEARNING OUTCOME

After completing this chapter, you should be able to:

▸ apply the accounting rules contained in IAS's dealing with leases (lessee only)

The syllabus topics covered in this chapter are as follows:

● Leases (IAS 17) – Distinguishing operating from finance leases and the concept of substance over form (from the framework); accounting for leases in the books of the lessee.

19.1 Introduction

The IASB defines an asset as '... a resource controlled by the entity as a result of past events and from which economic benefits are expected to flow to the entity'.

In general terms, we normally consider assets to be items that we own. The definition above, however, is based on an entity having 'control' over an asset and determining how that asset will be used in order to generate revenues. The accounting treatment for leasing transactions is based on the essence of this definition.

The recognition of assets and liabilities should reflect the commercial reality of business transactions.

Most entities want to have a strong statement of financial position and, historically, many abused the accounting rules in order to enhance their financial position. One of the most common ways was to sell the assets that were necessary to the business and then lease them back. The assets, and more importantly, any associated liability for the financing of the assets, were removed and replaced with a simple annual leasing charge.

The commercial reality was, of course, that the entity still determined how the assets were to be used; in substance, they retained control over the assets. The fact that legal title had transferred was irrelevant in accounting terms. The accounting treatment for leases now ensures that the entity controlling the assets, irrespective of ownership, recognises the assets and associated liability in order to show a true and fair view of their financial position.

Note: The paper 7 syllabus only requires a knowledge of the treatment of leases in the lessee's financial statements. Accounting by the lessor is outside the syllabus.

19.2 Key definitions

The following definitions are given in the standard and help to explain terms used later in this chapter.

> A *lease* is an agreement whereby the lessor conveys to the lessee in return for a payment or series of payments the right to use an asset for an agreed period of time. (This definition includes hire purchase agreements.)

A *finance lease* is a lease that transfers substantially all the risks and rewards incidental to ownership of an asset. Title may or may not be eventually transferred.

An *operating lease* is a lease other than a finance lease.

The *lease term* is the non-cancellable period for which the lessee has contracted to lease the asset. Where the lessee has the option to continue to lease the asset for further terms, with or without further payment, and it is reasonably certain at the inception of the lease that this right will be exercised, then the lease term can be taken to include this further period.

19.3 Characteristics of leases

19.3.1 Finance leases

The classification of leases is based on the definitions of operating and finance leases given above; however, in practice, deciding on the classification can be extremely complex. IAS 17 does not provide a quantifiable test for deciding the classification; instead, we should consider all the features within the lease agreement, focusing on which party has the significant rights and rewards normally associated with ownership.

> For the purposes of this syllabus, you will be expected to identify and discuss the main characteristics of leases and arrive at a decision as to how the lease should be classified and then accounted for. When asked to decide on or evaluate the classification of a lease, refer to the list given below.

A lease is classified as a finance lease if it transfers substantially all the risks and rewards incidental to ownership from the lessor to lessee. The classification is based on the substance of the transaction rather than the legal form, so greater weight should be given to those features that have a commercial effect in practice. The standard gives some situations that could indicate that transfer of ownership has taken place:

- legal title is transferred to the lessee at the end of the lease;
- the lease term is for the majority of the asset's economic useful life, irrespective of title transfer;

- at the inception of the lease, the present value of the minimum lease payment amounts to at least substantially all of the fair value of the leased asset;
- the lessee has the option to purchase the asset for a price sufficiently below the fair value of the asset at the date this option can be exercised;
- the leased assets are of a specialised nature and as such can only be used by the lessee unless modifications are made;
- where the lessee can cancel the lease but has to bear any losses associated with the cancellation;
- the lessee has the ability to continue the lease for a secondary period at a rate substantially below the market rent;
- gains or losses from the fluctuation in the fair value of the residual value of the asset fall to the lessee.

In answering a question, these *badges of ownership* should always form the basis of your justification for the classification of a lease.

Example 19.A

On 1 January 2003, Dixon Doors leased a new machine from EK Finance. The capital cost of the machine is $25,000. Six half-yearly payments of $5,000 are payable in advance, the first instalment being due on 1 January 2003. A secondary term of 3 years is being offered by EK Finance for $100 per annum. Dixon Doors have not yet decided if they will use the secondary term.

The estimated economic useful life of the asset is 5 years with a nil residual value. After 3 years (primary lease term), the asset is expected to have a residual value of $5,000. Under the lease agreement, Dixon Doors is entitled to 95 per cent of the proceeds should the asset be sold.

Explain, with justifications, how this lease should be classified.

Solution

From the information given, we can calculate that the minimum lease payments (six payments of $5,000 × $30,000) are greater than the fair value of the asset (capital cost $25,000). The difference is the finance cost associated with the lease.

The primary lease term is in this case 3 years (Dixon Doors has not yet decided on taking a secondary term), which is for the majority of the assets economic useful life.

The lessee has the option to lease the asset for a secondary term at a substantially reduced rate ($100 p.a. for an asset worth $5,000 at the inception of the secondary term).

And finally the fact that Dixon Doors are entitled to 95 per cent of the proceeds should the asset be sold at the end of the primary lease term.

These are all badges of ownership which indicate that the risks and rewards normally associated with owning an asset are transferred to the lessee, Dixon Doors. This lease would therefore be classified as a finance lease.

19.3.2 Operating leases

If the information given does not point to the lease being a finance lease, that is, there are no clear indicators that ownership has transferred to the lessee, then the lease should be classified as an operating lease.

19.3.3 Leases of land and buildings

The land and buildings elements of a lease of property should be considered separately, unless the land element is immaterial. To achieve this, the minimum lease payments need to be allocated between the land and buildings element in proportion to the relative fair values of the leasehold interests in the land element and the buildings element. The land is normally classified as an operating lease, unless title is expected to pass to the lessee at the end of the lease term, then it will be a finance lease. The buildings element will need to be classified as either an operating lease or a finance lease based on the criteria in 14.3.1. If it is not possible to allocate the minimum lease payments reliably between the land element and the building element, the entire lease should be classified as a finance lease, unless it is clear that both elements are operating leases.

Where the amount of land to be separately recognised is immaterial, the lease of land and buildings can be treated as a single unit in determining the classification of the lease.

19.4 Accounting for operating leases

Operating lease rentals are viewed as an annual expense of the business and should be charged to the statement of comprehensive income on a systematic basis (normally straight-line basis) over the term of the lease.

The accounting policies will normally state this.

Rentals payable under operating leases are charged to statement of comprehensive income as incurred.

Example 19.B

Buyer Products has a non-cancellable five-year operating lease costing $2,000 per annum for 5 years. The machine has an estimated useful life of 20 years. The annual charge in respect of this operating lease will be recorded as follows:

		$	$
Debit	Operating lease charges	2,000	
Credit	Bank		2,000

Being the payment of the operating lease charge.

Property leases often give incentives to lessees to encourage uptake of leases, such as rent-free periods and reverse premiums. Although no specific reference is made to these in the standard, the principle to be applied is straightforward, and that is to charge the profit or loss on a straight-line basis over the term of the lease. This ensures that the expense is charged and matched against the income that the asset generates while leased. Consider the two basic examples below.

19.4.1 Rent-free period

Example 19.C

Buyer Products enters into a second non-cancellable five-year operating lease. Under the terms of the lease, $5,000 is payable for 4 years commencing in year 2. The machine has an estimated useful life of 20 years.

Buyer Products will use the asset to help generate income for the next 5 years and so should charge the profit or loss with an expense in respect of leasing this asset. The annual charge should be $4,000 ($5,000 × 4 years = $20,000. $20,000 over 5 years = $4,000 per annum.)

The charge in respect of this operating lease in year 1 will be recorded as follows:

		$	$
Debit	Operating lease charges	4,000	
Credit	Accrued lease charges		4,000

Being the recording of the operating lease charge in year 1.

The charge in respect of this operating lease in years 2–5 will be recorded as follows:

		$	$
Debit	Operating lease charges	4,000	
Debit	Accrued lease charges	1,000	
Credit	Bank		5,000

Being the recording of the operating lease charge in years 2–5.

19.4.2 Cashback incentives

The recording of the operating lease charge where a cashback incentive has been granted, relies on the matching principle and requires that the total payable under the operating lease be allocated over the full term of the lease.

Example 19.D

Buyer Products enters into a third non-cancellable five-year operating lease. Under the terms of the lease, $4,000 is payable for 5 years; however, there is a cashback incentive of $2,500 paid at the start of the lease. The machine has an estimated useful life of 20 years.

Buyer Products will use the asset to help generate income for the next 5 years and so should charge the statement of comprehensive income with an expense in respect of leasing this asset. The annual charge should be $3,500 ($4,000 × 5 years = $20,000. $20,000 − $2,500 = $17,500 over 5 years = $3,500 per annum).

The recording of the cashback in year 1 will be recorded as follows:

		$	$
Debit	Bank	2,500	
Credit	Deferred income		2,500

Being the recording of the cashback in year 1.

The charge in respect of this operating lease in years 1–5 will be recorded as follows:

		$	$
Debit	Operating lease charges	3,500	
Debit	Deferred income ($2,500/5 years)	500	
Credit	Bank		4,000

Being the recording of the operating lease charge in years 2–5.

Note: The cashback of $2,500 is released to the profit or loss over the lease term at $500 per annum.

19.5 Disclosures for operating leases

A note to the financial statements should show:

- Lease payments recognised as an expense in the period
- A general description of the entity's significant lease arrangements
- The total of future minimum lease payments under non-cancellable operating leases for each of the following periods:
  - not later than 1 year
  - later than 1 year and not later than 5 years
  - later than 5 years.

An example will help us understand this disclosure requirement.

Example 19.E

Snowyday Boots have three non-cancellable operating leases as at 31 December 2002. The details for the leases are as follows:

Lease 1	$10,000 per annum	Expires 31 December 2003
Lease 2	$20,000 per annum	Expires 31 December 2005
Lease 3	$30,000 per annum	Expires 31 December 2009

This disclosure is intended to show the cash commitment that the business has underoperating leases in future periods. Remember that operating leases are an expense item, there is no asset or liability on the statement of financial position of the lessee. The leases are, however, non-cancellable and so the business must disclose this commitment somewhere in the financial statements to provide a true and fair view. The note will be as follows:

Snowyday Boots – extract from the notes to the accounts

Lease commitments
  Operating leases
  The following charges arise from non-cancellable operating leases:

Minimum lease payments	$
Not later than 1 year	60,000
Later than 1 year and not later than 5 years	160,000
Later than 5 years	60,000
	280,000

Workings

The total of the minimum lease payments is $280,000 calculated from the annual lease payment multiplied by the remaining lease term as at 31 December 2002:

	Years remaining	Due less than 1 year $	Due in 2–5 years $	Due in more than 5 years $
Lease 1	1	10,000	0	0
Lease 2	3	20,000	40,000 (20K × 2 yrs)	0
Lease 3	7	30,000	120,000 (30K × 4 yrs)	60,000 (30K × 2 yrs)
Total		60,000	160,000	60,000

19.6 Accounting for finance leases

Before we consider the treatment of finance leases, let us remind ourselves of the business reasons for entering into such an arrangement.

There are a number of ways that a business can acquire an asset:

• it can purchase the asset outright

Non Current Asset	Fixed asset
Credit	Bank

Being the purchase of a fixed asset for cash.

• it can take a loan and then purchase the asset

Debit	Bank
Credit	Bank loan

Being the receipt of the loan.

Non Current Asset	Fixed asset
Credit	Bank

Being the purchase of a fixed asset using the loaned cash.

- it can lease the asset

Non Current Asset	Fixed asset
Credit	Finance lease creditor

Being the leasing of the asset and the recognition of the associated liability.

A finance lease allows the lessee the use of the asset as if it were his/her own and creates a liability to the lessor for the capital amount to be repaid. This is effectively like a loan from the lessor – it just cuts out the bank as a middle man.

Similarly to the bank, the lessor will charge the lessee finance costs or interest for financing the acquisition of the fixed asset, and just as we do with a bank loan we have to allocate the repayments between those amounts that relate to interest and those that reduce the liability. (The difference with an asset acquired using a finance lease is that legal title is not transferred.)

The accounting for these transactions is straightforward:

Non Current Asset	Fixed asset
Credit	Finance lease creditor

Being the acquisition of the asset and the recognition of the associated liability.

Debit	Finance lease creditor
Debit	Interest expense
Credit	Bank

Being the repayments made to the lessor allocated between interest and capital.

Debit	Depreciation expense
Credit	Accumulated depreciation

Being the depreciation of the leased asset by the lessee.

These entries result in the asset being held at book value in the accounts of the lessee and the asset is depreciated by the lessee, ensuring that the expense associated with the asset, depreciation, is matched against the income that the asset is helping to generate.

This treatment ensures that the business reality of the transaction and not its legal form prevails. The leased asset is included in the total assets of the business and the liability associated with funding the acquisition of the leased asset is disclosed on the statement of financial position. Business ratios, for example, gearing and return on capital employed, are more meaningful with the leased assets included.

Do not lose sight of the basic accounting entries. The recording of finance lease transactions is straightforward and must not be overshadowed by the calculation of implied interest, which is what we are about to look at.

With many loan agreements the bank will simply calculate the interest due based on the interest rate to be applied and the outstanding liability at that date. Under finance lease agreements, it is generally the total rentals payable that is stated. We then must compare this with the fair value (usually the cost) of the fixed asset to establish the total amount of interest that is to be paid over the term of the lease. The main calculation then is how best to allocate the interest expense to profit or loss.

19.7 Calculating the implied interest on finance leases

The standard requires that finance lease interest allocated to periods should be calculated so as to produce a constant periodic rate of interest on the outstanding balance of the liability for each period. This is then charged as a finance expense.

There are three methods of allocating the finance charges in a finance lease:

1. the straight-line method
2. the sum-of-digits method
3. the actuarial method.

The method which gives the constant periodic rate of interest on the outstanding liability is the actuarial rate. This rate can be computer generated. The standard, however, permits the use of some approximation to the rate in order to simplify the calculation.

The sum of digits (also known as the 'rule of 78') gives a suitable approximation to the actuarial method. The straight-line method is the easiest to calculate but does not provide us with a constant rate of interest.

You will be expected to apply all three methods within this syllabus. Remember that this calculation is just for calculating the interest. Once this calculation is completed we can then record the lease repayments, allocating the payment between interest and reduction of capital.

Let us work through an example of a finance lease in the books of a lessee. We will use one set of information and calculate the interest allocation using all three methods. We will then select one of these methods and record the accounting entries and draft the relevant extracts and disclosures.

Example 19.F Shanks and Ward – lease information

- The accounting year-end is 31 December.
- The cost of the leased asset is $280,000.
- The estimated economic useful life is eight years.
- The asset has a nil residual value.
- The lease commences 1 January 2003.
- The primary lease term is 7 years.
- The lease repayments are $50,000 per annum in advance.
- Residual value at the end of the primary lease term is $35,000.
- Lessee is entitled to 95 per cent of the residual value at the end of the primary term.

Step 1. Confirm that the lease is to be treated as a finance lease. This lease is a finance lease. The total rentals exceed the fair value of the asset at the inception of the lease. The lease term is for the majority of the asset's economic useful life. The lessee is entitled to the majority of the proceeds should the asset be sold at the end of the primary lease term. These are clear indicators that the benefits of ownership of the asset has transferred to the lessee.

Step 2. Calculate the total finance charge. The total finance charge is calculated by comparing the total rentals payable and the fair value (cost) of the asset. In this case the total finance charge is $70,000, being total rentals of $350,000 ($50,000 for 7 years) less the cost of the asset $280,000.

Step 3. Establish the basis for allocating the total finance charge. Decide (or follow requirement in any exam question) on the method of allocation from one of the three methods. Establish the total number of periods being financed.

It is vitally important for your calculations that you correctly identify the number of periods over which you want to charge interest. The clue is in the repayment details.

If the repayments are to be made in advance, then your first payment will reduce your capital immediately before you start receiving funding, and when you make the final instalment, your final period of use of the asset will be with no outstanding liability. To calculate the finance periods for repayments in advance, take the total number of repayments and deduct 1.

If the repayments are in arrears, then you will not have extinguished the lease liability until the end of the primary lease term. The finance periods will equal the number of repayments.

Let us look at a quick illustration of this calculation before we continue.

The date of the inception of the lease is 1 January 2001. If the lease term is 3 years and the repayments are half-yearly in arrears, then the total finance periods over which you will allocate any interest is six (twice a year for 3 years).

The first instalment is made on 30 June 2001 and the last instalment you make under this lease will be on 31 December 2003. A lease liability exists until the end of the lease term and is not extinguished until 31 December 2003 when the final instalment is made. It follows then that if the lessor was providing you with funding for the full six periods then you will allocate interest over the six periods.

However, if the repayments are in advance then the first instalment will be made on 1 January 2001, at the inception of the lease. The final instalment will be made on 1 July 2003. For the period from 1 July 2003 to 31 December 2003, you will use the asset; however, you have extinguished the lease liability at the start of the period.

You are not receiving funding for the final six months and therefore should not be allocating interest for this final period. The total finance periods are then five (half-yearly for 3 years less one) which results in us allocating interest from 1 January 2001 until 30 June 2003.

Step 4. Calculate the interest to be charged to each period. Use one of the three methods mentioned above. We will use all three in this example for illustration purposes.

Step 5. Record the relevant accounting entries for the year. Capitalise and depreciate the leased assets, create the lease creditor and record the repayments allocating the payments between interest and capital based on the calculations in step 4.

Let us now calculate the interest using the three methods based on the lease information for Shanks and Ward. The first three steps are the same for each of the three methods.

- Step 1. Confirm the lease is a finance lease – justification is given above in Section 14.7.1 Step 1.
- Step 2. Calculate the total interest to be allocated – completed above – $70,000.
- Step 3. Establish the basis for allocation – the number of finance periods. The repayments are annual in advance and the lease term is 7 years. Total finance periods = (7 − 1) = 6.
- Step 4. Calculate the interest to be allocated to each period.

Straight-line method

$$\frac{\text{Total finance cost to be allocated}}{\text{Number of finance periods}} = \frac{\$70,000}{6} = 11,667 \text{ per period}$$

This is the most straightforward method to use as it simply allocates the same amount of interest to each finance period. It may not reflect the commercial reality of the transaction as the liability is reducing each period and therefore the interest incurred is also reducing.

Step 5. Record the relevant accounting entries for the year.

		$	$
Non Current Asset	Fixed asset	280,000	
Credit	Finance lease creditor		280,000
Being the capitalisation of the leased asset on 1 January 2003.			
Debit	Finance lease creditor	38,333	
Debit	Finance lease interest	11,667	
Credit	Bank		50,000
Being the repayment made on 1 January 2003.			

(The total repaid is $50,000. We calculated implied interest of $11,667 using the straight-line method. The difference is the amount of the repayment that reduces the liability.)

		$	$
Debit	Depreciation charge for the year	35,250	
Credit	Accumulated depreciation		35,250

Being the depreciation of the leased asset for the year to 31 December 2003.

(Total cost of asset $280,000, less the residual value that Shanks and Ward is entitled to at the end of the primary lease term: 95% × $35,000 = $33,250.)

$$\frac{\$280,000 - 33,250}{7 \text{ Years}} = 32,250 \text{ per annum}$$

Remember, the amount you want to depreciate is the net cost of the asset to the lessee. There is no indication that a secondary lease term will be used and so we depreciate over the primary lease term of 7 years.

Let us look at how the liability would be extinguished over the period of the lease using this method.

Period	Liability at start of period $	Rental paid $	Liability during period $	Allocated interest $	Liability at end of period $
1 Jan. 2003	280,000	(50,000)	230,000	11,667	241,667
1 Jan. 2004	241,667	(50,000)	191,667	11,667	203,334
1 Jan. 2005	203,334	(50,000)	153,334	11,667	165,001
1 Jan. 2006	165,001	(50,000)	115,001	11,667	126,668
1 Jan. 2007	126,668	(50,000)	76,668	11,666	88,334
1 Jan. 2008	88,334	(50,000)	38,334	11,666	50,000
1 Jan. 2009	50,000	(50,000)	–	–	–
Totals		(350,000)		70,000	

Let us have a look at the information this table provides:

- compare the opening and closing liabilities each year – it reduces by the amount of the repayment which represents capital $38,333 ($50,000 − $11,667);
- the total rentals paid is $350,000;
- the total interest allocated is $70,000 – which is what we calculated above;
- the interest has been allocated over six finance periods;
- the final instalments made on 1 January 2009 extinguishes the lease liability – remember, the repayments were in advance.

Let us now complete steps 4 and 5 using the sum-of-digits method of allocating interest.

Sum-of-digits method

The sum of digits can be calculated using a simple formula:

$$\frac{n(n + 1)}{2}$$

where *n* is the number of finance periods.

In this example, the sum of digits is 21, being (6 × 7)/2. We calculated the number of finance periods in step 3 above.

The total interest of $70,000 (calculated in step 2 above) is allocated by multiplying it by the 'relevant digit' divided by the sum of digits. The relevant digit will be the number of finance periods remaining at the date the repayment is made. In this example, the first instalment made on 1 January 2003 will be digit 6, as there are six finance periods remaining when this repayment is made. The relevant digit then reduces by one each period as the number of funding periods remaining decreases.

Let us recreate our table to see the whole repayment plan using the sum-of-digits method.

Period	Liability at start of period $	Rental paid $	Liability during the period $	Interest calculation	Allocated interest $	Liability at end of period $
1 Jan. 2003	280,000	(50,000)	230,000	6/21 × $70,000	20,000	250,000
1 Jan. 2004	250,000	(50,000)	200,000	5/21 × $70,000	16,667	216,667
1 Jan. 2005	216,667	(50,000)	166,667	4/21 × $70,000	13,333	180,000
1 Jan. 2006	180,000	(50,000)	130,000	3/21 × $70,000	10,000	140,000
1 Jan. 2007	140,000	(50,000)	90,000	2/21 × $70,000	6,667	96,667
1 Jan. 2008	96,667	(50,000)	46,667	1/21 × $70,000	3,333	50,000
1 Jan. 2009	50,000	(50,000)	–		–	–
Totals		(350,000)			70,000	

Let us have a look at the information this table provides:

- compare the opening and closing liabilities each year – it reduces by the amount of the repayment which represents capital

  - $30,000 ($50,000 – $20,000) in year 1
  - $33,333 ($50,000 – 16,667) in year 2 and so on;
- the total rentals paid is $350,000;
- the total interest allocated is still $70,000 – it is just allocated on a different basis;
- the interest has again been allocated over six finance periods;
- the final instalment made on 1 January 2009 extinguishes the lease liability – remember, the repayments were in advance.

Step 5. Record the entries for the year-end 31 December 2003

		$	$
Debit	Fixed asset	280,000	
Credit	Finance lease creditor		280,000

Being the capitalisation of the leased asset at 1 January 2003.

		$	$
Debit	Finance lease creditor	30,000	
Debit	Finance lease interest	20,000	
Credit	Bank		50,000

Being the repayment made on 1 January 2003.

(The total repaid is $50,000. We calculated implied interest of $20,000 using the sum-of-digits method. The difference is the amount paid towards reducing the liability.)

		$	$
Debit	Depreciation charge for the year	35,250	
Credit	Accumulated depreciation		35,250

Being the depreciation of the leased asset for the year to 31 December 2003 (as calculated earlier during the straight-line method).

Note that the accounting entries are the same as those for the straight-line method – the only difference is the amount of the repayment that has been allocated to interest and capital, respectively.

Actuarial method

The constant rate of interest can only be computer-generated or by a long process of trial 2and error.

> If you are asked to use this method in an examination, an interest rate will be provided. If an interest rate is provided, then the examiner wants you to use the actuarial method of allocation. If an interest rate is not given, use the sum-of-digits method.

For the Shanks and Ward example, the approximate rate of interest (rounded to two decimal places) is 8.16 per cent. This rate is applied to the outstanding liability at the start of the period to give the interest expense to be charged for the period.

We will recreate our table to see the full effect:

Period	Liability at start of period $	Rental paid $	Liability during period $	Interest at 8.16% applied to liability during period	Liability at end of period $
1 Jan. 2003	280,000	(50,000)	230,000	18,768	248,768
1 Jan. 2004	248,768	(50,000)	198,768	16,219	214,987
1 Jan. 2005	214,987	(50,000)	164,987	13,463	178,450
1 Jan. 2006	178,450	(50,000)	128,450	10,482	138,932
1 Jan. 2007	138,932	(50,000)	88,932	7,257	96,189
1 Jan. 2008	96,189	(50,000)	46,189	3,811*	50,000
1 Jan. 2009	50,000	(50,000)	–	–	–
Totals		(350,000)		70,000	

* This amount includes $42 rounding as the rate used is the closest approximation rounded to two decimal places.

Let us have a look at the information this table provides:

- compare the opening and closing liabilities each year – it reduces by the amount of the repayment which represents capital:
  - $31,232 ($50,000 – $18,768) in year 1
  - $33,781 ($50,000 – $16,219) in year 2 and so on;
- the total rental paid is $350,000;
- the total interest allocated is still $70,000 – it is just allocated on a different basis;
- the interest has again been allocated over six finance periods;
- the final instalment made on 1 January 2006 extinguishes the lease liability – remember, the repayments were in advance.

Step 5. Record the entries for the year to 31 December 2000.

The accounting entries for step 5 are once again those for the other methods, the only difference being the amount of the repayment allocated to interest and capital.

We have now calculated the allocated interest using the three permitted methods. The results can be summarised as follows:

Year ended 31 December	Interest calculated using straight line $	Interest calculated using sum of digits $	Interest calculated using actuarial $
2003	11,667	20,000	18,768
2004	11,667	16,667	16,219
2005	11,667	13,333	13,463
2006	11,667	10,000	10,482
2007	11,666	6,667	7,257
2008	11,666	3,333	3,811
2009	–	–	–
Totals	70,000	70,000	70,000

The sum-of-digits method gives a close approximation to the actuarial method. The straight-line method, while being the simplest to calculate, provides a somewhat arbitrary allocation.

19.7.1 In advance/in arrears

The tables and calculations we have performed in this example are based on a lease agreement with repayments in advance. Note that if the repayments were to be in arrears, then the total finance periods would be seven and not six. The lease liability would not be extinguished until the final instalment was made on 31 December 2009 and as a result there would be interest charged in this period. For completeness, let us consider the same lease as above but with repayments in arrears, the interest being apportioned using the sum-of-digits basis.

Example 19.G

We will use the example in 19.F above.

The sum of digits is calculated as:

$$\frac{n(n + 1)}{2}$$

where *n* is the number of finance periods.

In this example, the sum of digits is 28, being $(7 \times 8)/2$. The finance periods now total seven as the repayments are in arrears and the lessee is receiving funding until the end of the lease term.

The total interest of $70,000 (calculated in step 2 above) is allocated by multiplying it by the 'relevant digit' divided by the sum of digits. The relevant digit will be the number of finance periods remaining at the date the repayment is made.

In this example, the first instalment made on 31 December 2003 will be digit 7, as there are seven finance periods remaining when this repayment is made. The relevant digit then reduces by one each period as the number of funding periods remaining decreases.

Let us recreate our table to see the whole repayment plan, using sum of digits for *repayments in arrears*.

Period	Liability at start of period $	Interest calculation	Allocated interest $	Rental paid $	Liability of end of period $
1 Jan. 2003	280,000	7/28 × $70,000	17,500	(50,000)	247,500
1 Jan. 2004	247,500	6/28 × $70,000	15,000	(50,000)	212,500
1 Jan. 2005	212,500	5/28 × $70,000	12,500	(50,000)	175,000
1 Jan. 2006	175,000	4/28 × $70,000	10,000	(50,000)	135,000
1 Jan. 2007	135,000	3/28 × $70,000	7,500	(50,000)	92,500
1 Jan. 2008	92,500	2/28 × $70,000	5,000	(50,000)	47,500
1 Jan. 2009	47,500	1/28 × $70,000	2,500	(50,000)	–
Totals			70,000	350,000	

Let us have a look at the information this table provides:

- compare the opening and closing liabilities each year – it reduces by the amount of the repayment which represents capital ($50,000 − $17,500 = $32,500 in year 1);
- there is no column for 'capital during the period' as the repayment is made at the end of the period and therefore the entire amount is outstanding for the period;
- the total rentals paid is $350,000;
- the total interest allocated is still $70,000 – it is just allocated on a different basis;
- the interest has been allocated over seven finance periods;
- the final instalment made on 31 December 2009 extinguishes the lease liability – remember, the repayments were in arrears.

19.8 Disclosures for finance leases

From the accounting entries we processed in the above examples, we can draft any relevant extracts from the financial statements, using the sum-of-digits figures from Example 19.F above:

Shanks and Ward – extracts from the financial statements for the year ended 31 December 2003.

Statement of comprehensive income

	$
Operating expenses	
Depreciation charge for the year	35,250
Finance lease interest (sum of digits)	20,000

Statement of financial position

Non-current assets
Property, plant and equipment
(cost $280,000 less $35,250)   244,750
Current liabilities
Finance lease creditor   33,333
Non-current liabilities
Finance lease creditor   216,667

To understand how the creditor figures are calculated, refer back to Example 19.F. The creditor within current liabilities will represent the amount of next year's repayment that will be allocated to capital, that is $50,000 less interest of $16,667.

The non-current liability creditor is the outstanding balance at the end of the following year or it can be calculated by taking the closing liability at the end of the reporting period ($250,000) and deducting the amount that is due within 1 year (just calculated above) of $33,333.

It is not necessary to complete the full schedule of repayments, unless it is asked for. In order to calculate the creditor due within 1 year and greater than 1 year, however, you will have to calculate the interest to be allocated for the following period – remember that next year's repayment less interest allocated to next year leaves the amount which is due to be repaid to capital next year.

Lessees are required to make the following disclosures in respect of finance leases:

- for each class of asset, the net carrying amount at the end of the reporting period;
- a reconciliation between the total of future minimum lease payments at the end of the reporting period and their present value analysed between:
  - not later than 1 year
  - later than 1 year and not later than 5 years
  - later than 5 years.

The disclosure note for the Shanks and Ward example would be as follows:
Obligations under finance leases as at 31 December 2003
The minimum lease payments payable under finance leases are as follows:

	$
Not later than 1 year	50,000
Later than one year and not later than 5 years	250,000
Later than 5 years	–
	300,000
Less finance charges allocated to future periods	
(70,000 − 20,000, see Example 14.F)	(50,000)
Present value of lease payments	250,000

You can check this present value calculation – it should equal the total of the creditors due within and greater than 1 year that is recorded in the statement of financial position (see extracts above). $33,333 + $216,667 which equals $250,000.

19.9 Summary

Having completed this chapter, we can now correctly classify operating and finance leases, using the badges of ownership to justify our treatment. We can prepare the accounting entries to record an operating lease and draft the relevant extracts and additional disclosures for incorporation into the financial statements.

In accounting for finance leases, we can use the three acceptable methods of calculating the implied rate of interest on the lease, namely straight line, sum of digits and actuarial. Once the finance costs are calculated, we can prepare the accounting entries that correctly allocate revenue and capital elements of lease repayments. The relevant extracts and notes to the accounts can also be drafted.

Revision Questions

? Question 1

A finance lease runs for 5 years, with annual payments in arrears of $25,000. The fair value of the asset was $90,000. Using the sum-of-digits method, what would the outstanding lease creditor be at the end of year 2?

(A) $47,000
(B) $61,000
(C) $64,500
(D) $40,000   (2 marks)

? Question 2

An operating lease is:

(A) a lease that is not a finance lease
(B) a lease that transfers substantially all risks and rewards to the lessor
(C) a lease that is for virtually all the estimated useful life of the asset
(D) a lease where the lessee is responsible for repairs, insurance and other running costs.
                                                        (2 marks)

? Question 3

L leases a delivery vehicle to D on an operating lease. The terms of the lease are:

- term 3 years
- special introductory discount in year one, rental reduced to $2,000
- annual rentals of $5,000 per year for years two and three.

How much should D recognise as an expense in its profit or loss for the first year of the lease?

(A) $2,000
(B) $4,000
(C) $5,000
(D) $12,000   (2 marks)

Question 4

Logan's Locks are preparing financial statements for the year ended 31 December 2003. During the year, Logan's entered into two operating lease agreements which are detailed below.

(a) On 1 August 2003, the entity entered into an operating lease for plant and machinery. The lease term is 3 years and quarterly rentals of $9,000 are payable in arrears.

(b) The entity entered into a second agreement on 1 October 2003 for the lease of motor vehicles. This agreement was again for 3 years. Under the terms of the contract, Logan has paid an initial rental of $75,000, this will be followed by quarterly rentals of $4,000. The rentals are payable in advance and commence on 1 April 2004.

Requirement

Prepare the accounting entries to account for the operating leases above in the financial statements for Logan's Locks for the year ended 31 December 2003 and draft the relevant extracts and disclosure notes. **(5 marks)**

 Question 5

An item of machinery leased under a five-year finance lease on 1 October 2003 had a fair value of $51,900 at date of purchase.

The lease payments were $12,000 per year, payable in arrears.

If the sum-of-digits method is used to apportion interest to accounting periods, calculate the finance cost for the year ended 30 September 2005. **(3 marks)**

Data for Questions 6 and 7

CS acquired a machine, using a finance lease, on 1 January 2004. The machine had an expected useful life of 12,000 operating hours, after which it would have no residual value.

The finance lease was for a five-year term with rentals of $20,000 per year payable in arrears. The cost price of the machine was $80,000 and the implied interest rate is $7 \times 93\%$ per year. CS used the machine for 2,600 hours in 2004 and 2,350 hours in 2005.

 Question 6

Using the actuarial method, calculate the non-current liability and current liability figures required by IAS 17 *Leases* to be shown in CS's Statement of financial position at 31 December 2005. **(3 marks)**

 Question 7

Calculate the non-current asset – property, plant and equipment net book value that would be shown in CS's Statement of financial position at 31 December 2005. Calculate the depreciation charge using the machine hours method. **(2 marks)**

? Question 8

On 1 April 2005, DX acquired plant and machinery with a fair value of $900,000 on a finance lease. The lease is for five years with the annual lease payments of $228,000 being paid in advance on 1 April each year. The interest rate implicit in the lease is 13.44%. The first payment was made on 1 April 2005.

Requirements

(i) Calculate the finance charge in respect of the lease that will be shown in DX's statement of comprehensive income for the year ended 31 March 2007.

(ii) Calculate the amount to be shown as a current liability and a non-current liability in DX's statement of financial position at 31 March 2007.

(All workings should be to the nearest $'000.) **(5 marks)**

? Question 9

On 1 January 2003, Caps leased a new machine from ITC Finance. The cost of the machine is $100,000. The asset has an estimated useful life of 5 years and has a nil residual value.

Under the terms of the three-year lease, six half-yearly payments of $20,000 each are payable in advance, commencing 1 January 2003. There is a secondary two-year term available to Caps for $200 per annum. Caps have not yet decided whether or not they will take advantage of this offer.

At the end of the primary term of the lease, the asset has an estimated residual value of $20,000. Caps are entitled to 95 per cent of this should the asset be sold.

Requirements

(a) Explain, with reasons, why the above lease should be classified as an operating or finance lease. **(4 marks)**

(b) Using the sum-of-digits method of calculating implied finance charges on the lease, prepare all the relevant accounting entries to record this transaction in the financial statements of Caps Incorporated for the year ended 31 December 2003. **(10 marks)**

(c) Draft extracts from the accounts for the following account categories:
- non-current assets
- current liabilities
- non-current liabilities. **(6 marks)**

(Total marks = 20)

? Question 10

Campbells Framing leased a new machine from Greenan Finance on 1 October 2002. The capital cost of the machine is $180,000. Under the terms of the finance lease agreement, six annual payments of $40,000 are payable in arrears with the first payment due on 30 September 2003.

There is an indefinite secondary term to the lease for a nominal fee and Campbells are anticipating taking advantage of this term. The asset has an estimated useful life of 10 years with an estimated residual value at the end of its life of nil. The residual value at the end of six years is $40,000 and Campbells have a 90 per cent interest in this value.

Requirements

(a) Using the sum-of-digits method of allocating interest, calculate the finance charge to be included in the statement of comprehensive income for the year ended 30 September 2003 and draft all relevant accounting entries for this period for incorporation into the accounts. **(10 marks)**

(b) Draft the relevant extracts from statement of comprehensive income and the statement of financial position for the year ended 30 September 2003. **(6 marks)**

(Total marks = 16)

Solutions to Revision Questions

 Solution 1

The correct answer is (B) see Example 19.F $61,000 calculated as follows:

	$
Payments (5 × $25,000) =	125,000
Fair value	90,000
Finance charge	35,000
no. of finance periods =	5
N(*n* + 1)/2 = (5 × 6)/2 =	15
Interest charges	
Year 1–5/15 * 35K =	11,667
Year 2–4/15 * 35K =	9,333
Lease creditor	
Initial balance	90,000
Interest	11,667
Payment 1	(25,000)
Interest	9,333
Payment 2	(25,000)
Balance	61,000

 Solution 2

The correct answer is (A), see Section 19.2.

Solution 3

The correct answer is (B), see Section 19.4.

IAS 17 requires interest expense to be recognised evenly over the life of the lease.

Total expense $2,000 + $5,000 + $5,000 = $12,000 divided by 3 years is $4,000 a year.

Solution 4

(a) The lease agreement commences 1 August 2003 and the reporting year-end is 31 December 2003. The lease payments are made quarterly in arrears and so the first payment made is on 31 October 2003, recorded as:

		$	$
Debit	Operating lease charges	9,000	
Credit	Bank		9,000

Being the payment and recording of the lease repayment on 31 October.

We must also account for the operating lease charges for November and December, although the payment will not be made until January. It will therefore be accrued by recording:

		$	$
Debit	Operating lease charges	6,000	
Credit	Accrued charges		6,000

Being the accrued operating lease charges for November and December.

(b) The total amount payable under this lease should be allocated to match against the period of use irrespective of the cash flow.

The total payable can be calculated as follows:

	$
Initial payment	75,000
Ten payments of $4,000	40,000
Total payable over 3 years	115,000

$$\left(\frac{\$115,000}{36 \text{ months}} \right) \times \text{months} = \$9,583$$

The accounting entries for the year end 31 December 2003 will be:

		$	$
Debit	Deferred lease charges	75,000	
Credit	Bank		75,000

Being the initial payment of $75,000 paid on 1 October 2003.

		$	$
Debit	Operating lease charges	9,583	
Credit	Deferred lease charges		9,583

Being the lease charges recognised for the 3 months to 31 December 2003.

Logan's Locks – financial statement extracts for the year ended 31 December 2003.

Statement of comprehensive income

	$
Operating expenses	
Operating lease charges ($9,000 + $6,000 + $9,583)	24,583

Notes to the accounts

Commitments under non-cancellable operating leases

At 31 December 2003, the entity were committed to making the following payments in respect of non-cancellable operating leases:

	$
Not later than 1 year	48,000
Later than 1 and not later than 5 years	91,000
Later than 5 years	–

Workings for the note

	Contract (a)	Contract (b)	Total
Payable in 2004	4 × $9,000 = $36,000 (first payment: 1 April)	3 × $4,000 = $12,000	$48,000
Payable beyond 2004	12 payments in total, one made in 2003 and four in 2004. The remainder will be paid beyond 2004: $9,000 × 7 = $63,000.	10 repayments of $4,000 will be made, three in 2004 and the remainder in the periods beyond 2004. 7 × $4,000 = $28,000.	$91,000

See Section 19.4

 ## Solution 5

	$
Lease payments (5 × 12)	60,000
Fair value	51,900
Finance cost	8,100
Sum of digits (5 × 6)/2 =	15
Year 2 digit =	4
Finance charge = 8,100 × 4/15 = 2,160	

See Section 19.7.

 ## Solution 6

Interest rate 7.93%

	Bal b/fwd	Interest	Payment	Balance c/fwd
2004	80,000	6,344	−20,000	66,344
2005	66,344	5,261	−20,000	51,605
2006	51,605	4,092	−20,000	35,697
2007	35,697	2,831	−20,000	18,528
2008	18,528	1,472	−20,000	0

Note: Only the first three rows needed to be calculated to answer the question.

Answer – Non-current liability	$35,697
Current liability (51,605 − 35,697) =	$15,908

See Section 19.7.

Solution 7

	$
Cost	80,000
Depreciation	33,000
	47,000

See Section 19.7.

 ## Solution 8

Finance lease – finance cost

Interest

Year ended 31 March	13.44% Bal b/fwd	Payment	Subtotal	Interest	Bal c/fwd
	$'000	$'000	$'000	$'000	$'000
2006	900	−228	672	90	762
2007	762	−228	534	72	606
2008	606	−228	378	51	429
2009	429	−228	201	27	228
2010	228	−228	0	0	0

(i) Finance charge for year ended 31 March 2007 = $72,000

(ii)

		$'000
Current liability	(606 − 378) =	228
Non-current liability		378

 ## Solution 9

(a) This lease should be classified as a finance lease. There are clear indicators that the rights normally associated with ownership have been transferred from the lessor to the lessee:

- The minimum lease payments ($20,000 × 6) totalling $120,000 exceed the capital cost of the asset ($100,000).
- The lease term is 3 years and the useful life is estimated at 5 years, so the lease agreement is for the majority of the asset's useful life.
- Should the asset be sold, 95 per cent of the proceeds would accrue to the lessee.
- A secondary term has been offered at a nominal rate below the market rate for leasing the asset.

  Remind yourself of the steps we used when dealing with a finance lease question. Refer back to the chapter text if necessary.

(b) *Step 1:* Confirm classification as a finance lease – done in part (a).

Step 2: Calculate the total finance charge:

	$
Total repayments (6 × $20,000)	120,000
Capital cost of the asset	100,000
Total interest to be allocated	20,000

Step 3: Establish the number of finance periods over which to allocate interest. There are six repayments but they are payable in advance, so the last finance period has no outstanding liability as the final instalment payable on 1 July 2005 extinguishes the creditor balance. The lease term then continues to 31 December 2005. The finance periods total $6 - 1 = 5$.

Step 4: Calculate the interest to be charged to the periods. The question requires the use of the sum-of-digits method of allocating interest.

Sum of digits $= n(n + 1)/2$, where n is the number of finance periods

Sum of digits $= (5 \times 6)/2 = 15$

Period	Capital at start	Payment	Outstanding during period	Interest to be allocated	Capital at end
	$	$	$	$	$
1/1/03	100,000	(20,000)	80,000	$20,000 \times 5/15 = 6,667$	86,667
1/7/03	86,667	(20,000)	66,667	$20,000 \times 4/15 = 5,333$	72,000
1/1/04	72,000	(20,000)	52,000	$20,000 \times 3/15 = 4,000$	56,000
1/7/04	56,000	(20,000)	36,000	$20,000 \times 2/15 = 2,667$	38,667
1/1/05	38,667	(20,000)	18,667	$20,000 \times 1/15 = 1,333$	20,000
1/7/05	20,000	(20,000)	–		–
		(120,000)		(20,000)	

Note: The full allocation is given above for illustration purposes only. In order to answer this question, the calculation need only go as far as 1/7/04 – that is, to calculate the entries for 2003 and the creditor due within 1 year (i.e. payable in 2004) for part (c).

The accounting entries for the year to 31 December 2003 are as follows:

		$	$
Debit	Asset	100,000	
Credit	Lease creditor		100,000

Being the acquisition of the asset under finance lease on 1 January.

		$	$
Debit	Finance lease creditor	28,000	
Debit	Finance lease interest	12,000	
Credit	Bank		40,000

Being the lease repayments on 1 January and 1 July allocated between interest and capital.

		$	$
Debit	Depreciation	27,000	
Credit	Accumulated depreciation		27,000

Being the depreciation charge for the asset for the year ($100,000 – residual value
$19,000 ($20,000 × 95%) = $81,000; $81,000/3 years = $27,000.)

(c) Extracts from accounts: Caps Statement of financial position at 31 December 2003

	$
Non-current assets	
Plant and machinery ($100,000 − $27,000)	73,000
Current liabilities	
Finance lease creditor ($40,000 − $6,667)	33,333
Non-current liabilities	
Finance lease creditor ($72,000 − $33,333)	38,667

Solution 10

(a) *Step 1:* Confirm classification as a finance lease – given in question.

Step 2: Calculate the total finance charge:

	$
Total repayments 6 × $40,000	240,000
Capital cost of the asset	180,000
Total interest to be allocated	60,000

Step 3: Establish the number of finance periods over which to allocate interest.

There are six repayments and they are payable in arrears. The final payment is due on 30 September 2008, which is the end of the lease term. The lessee is therefore getting funding for the entire lease term and so the interest should be allocated over all six periods. Finance periods total six.

Step 4: Calculate the interest to be charged to the periods.

The question requires the use of the sum-of-digits method of allocating interest.

Sum of digits $= n(n + 1)/2 = (6 × 7)/2 = 21$

Period	Capital at start	Interest to be allocated	Payment	Capital at end
	$	$	$	$
30/09/03	180,000	$60,000 × 6/21 =17,143	(40,000)	157,143
30/09/04	157,143	$60,000 × 5/21 =14,286	(40,000)	131,429
30/09/05	131,429	$60,000 × 4/21 =11,429	(40,000)	102,858
30/09/06	102,858	$60,000 × 3/21 = 8,571	(40,000)	71,429
30/09/07	1,429	$60,000 × 2/21 = 5,714	(40,000)	37,143
30/09/08	37,143	$60,000 × 1/21 = 2,857	(40,000)	–
		60,000	240,000	

Note: The full allocation is given above for illustration purposes only. In order to answer this question, the calculation need only go as far as 30/09/04, that is, to calculate the entries for the year ended 30 September 2003 and the creditor due within 1 year which can only be calculated by calculating the interest allocated to 2004.

The accounting entries for the year to 30 September 2003 are as follows:

		$	$
Debit	Asset	180,000	
Credit	Lease creditor		180,000

Being the acquisition of the asset under finance lease on 1 October 2002.

		$	$
Debit	Finance lease creditor	22,857	
Debit	Finance lease interest	17,143	
Credit	Bank		40,000

Being the lease repayment on 30 September 2003 allocated between interest and capital.

		$	$
Debit	Depreciation	18,000	
Credit	Accumulated depreciation		18,000

Being the depreciation charge for the asset for the year ($180,000/10 years – Campbells expect to use the asset for its entire useful life by exercising the secondary lease term.)

(b) Campbells: financial statements for the year ended 30 September 2003 (extracts)

Statement of comprehensive income

	$
Operating expenses	
Depreciation charge	18,000
Finance lease interest	17,143

Statement of financial position

Non-current assets	
Plant and machinery ($180,000 − $18,000)	162,000
Current liabilities	
Finance lease creditor ($40,000 − $14,286)	25,714
Non-current liabilities	
Finance lease creditor ($157,143 − $25,714)	131,429

20

Inventories and
Construction
Contracts

Inventories and Construction Contracts

20

LEARNING OUTCOME

After completing this chapter you should be able to:

▸ apply the accounting rules contained in IFRS's and IAS's dealing with inventories and construction contracts.

The syllabus topics covered in this chapter are as follows:

- Inventories (IAS 2)
- Construction contracts and related financing costs (IAS 11 and 23): determination of cost, net realisable value, the inclusion of overheads and the measurement of profit on uncompleted contracts.

20.1 Introduction

This chapter will cover two specific areas: inventories and construction costs. They are dealt with in separate accounting standards.

We will look first at IAS 2 *Inventories*, which prescribes the accounting treatment for inventories. The standard provides guidance on the amount of cost to be recognised as an asset and carried forward until the related revenues are generated. The standard also gives guidance on what constitutes cost and how to write down the asset to net realisable value.

IAS 11 *Construction Contracts* prescribes the accounting treatment of revenue and costs associated with construction contracts. The standard gives guidance on how to recognise contract revenues and associated costs and how these amounts should be recorded and disclosed.

20.2 IAS 2 *Inventories*

20.2.1 Definition of inventories

The standard defines inventories as assets:

- held *for sale* in the ordinary course of business (like items of clothing in a retail clothing business);
- in the *process of production* for such sale (like cloth in a clothing manufacturing business); or
- in the form of materials or *supplies to be consumed* in the production process or in the rendering of services (like thread and buttons in a clothing manufacturing business).

20.2.2 Measurement

The underlying principle of IAS 2 is that inventories should be measured at the lower of cost and net realisable value.

- *Net realisable value* is the estimated selling price (in the normal course of business) less the estimated costs of completion and the estimated costs of making the sale.

  Inventories are usually written down to net realisable value, item by item or groups of similar items where it is not practical to evaluate separate items.
- *Cost* should comprise all costs of purchase, costs of conversion (if manufacturing) and other costs incurred in bringing the inventories to their present location and condition.

20.2.3 Determining cost

- *Costs of purchase* include the purchase price, import duties and other taxes (to the extent that they are not recoverable from the tax authority), handling costs and other costs directly attributable to the acquisition.
- *Costs of conversion* include costs directly related to the units being produced, for example, direct labour costs. The costs also include an allocation of fixed and variable overhead that are incurred, in converting materials into finished goods.
- *Variable production overheads* are those indirect costs of production that vary directly with the volume being produced, for example indirect materials and indirect labour.
- *Fixed production overheads* are those indirect costs of production that remain constant irrespective of the numbers of units produced, for example, depreciation of factory buildings and equipment and the cost of factory management and administration.
- *Financing costs*, if the requirements of IAS 23 are satisfied, financing costs can be included (see Section 20.10).

20.2.4 Costs not included in cost of inventory

Examples of costs excluded from the cost of inventories and recognised as expenses in the period in which they are incurred are:

(a) abnormal amounts of wasted materials, labour or other production costs;
(b) storage costs, unless those costs are necessary in the production process before a further production stage;
(c) administrative overheads that do not contribute to bringing inventories to their present location and condition;
(d) selling and distribution costs.

20.2.5 Allocation of overheads

The allocation of fixed production overheads to the cost of production is based on the normal capacity of the business. Any abnormal production problems that occur during the period should be charged to that period's statement of comprehensive income.

Example 20.A

The following costs have been included in the month of July:

	$
Cost of raw materials	20,000
Cost of related consumables	10,000
Direct wages	4,000
Indirect production costs	6,000
Power	1,000
Administration – production	1,200
Administration – general	1,100
Selling and marketing costs	2,300
Depreciation	3,950

Additional information

1. All administration and 40 per cent of indirect production costs are fixed.
2. Depreciation figure above includes $1,850, which relates to the production equipment.
3. 95 per cent of the power relates to the production of goods.
4. There was a breakdown during the month and 10 per cent of the month's production was lost.
5. During July, 250,000 units were produced.

Calculate the unit cost of the goods.

Solution

The costs that can be charged to the cost of the goods are as follows:

	$
Raw material costs	20,000
Cost of related consumables	10,000
Direct wages	4,000
Variable indirect production costs (60% – remaining 40% is a fixed cost)	3,600
Power (95%)	950
Depreciation	1,850
	40,400
Fixed indirect production costs (normal activity of 90% × 40% fixed element × 6,000)	2,160
Fixed production administration (90% × $1,200)	1,080
Total cost	43,640
Cost per unit	17.5¢

Note that fixed costs are allocated based on the normal level of activity – the question tells us that 10 per cent of production is lost due to a breakdown. The costs associated with this are not included in the cost of inventory but instead charged to statement of comprehensive income in the period in which the loss occurred.

Other costs can be included in the cost of inventories if they have been incurred to bring the goods to their present location or condition, for example, the design costs of specific goods.

20.2.6 Calculation of costs

Inventory should be valued at either cost itself or reasonably close approximations to actual cost, the most common methods of valuation are:

(a) Actual unit cost.
(b) *First in first out (FIFO).* The inventory is assumed to consist of the latest purchases made which cover the quantity in inventory and is priced accordingly.
(c) *Average cost.* The weighted average cost at which an inventory item has been purchased during the period is taken.
(d) *Standard cost.* This is acceptable, provided that the standard costs are reviewed frequently to ensure that they bear a reasonable relationship to actual costs during the period.
(e) *Selling price less gross profit margin.* This method is acceptable only if it can be demonstrated that it gives a reasonable approximation of the actual cost.

The same basis must be used for all inventories that are similar in nature or use. Inventories of a different nature or use can be valued on a different basis.

20.2.7 Allowed alternative method

When IAS 2 was revised in 2003, the allowed alternative method of last in first out was removed. IAS 2 now has no allowed alternative treatment.

20.2.8 Disclosures for inventories

The financial statements should disclose:

(a) the accounting policies adopted in measuring inventories including the cost formula used;
(b) the total amount of inventories in classifications appropriate to the business;
(c) the carrying amount of inventories carried at net realisable value.

20.3 IAS 11 *Construction Contracts*

20.3.1 General principle

A construction contract is a contract for the construction of a single asset or a combination of assets that are related. Contracts can often span more than one accounting period and this creates additional accounting problems:

- How much revenue should be included in profit or loss?
- How much should be charged for related costs?
- How much profit should be recognised in the period in respect of this contract?

Normally revenues and profits are only recognised in statement of comprehensive income once they are realised. However, the nature of construction contracts can mean that the contract is only invoiced and revenues realised on completion of the contract. The statement of comprehensive income must show a fair representation of the activities of the entity for the period. Here the prudence concept and the matching concept are head to head.

The matching concept wins, and for the sake of the financial statements showing a fair presentation of the activities of the entity and providing useful and relevant information to users, we include an appropriate part of revenue and profits of the contract in the period in which the activity has taken place.

Each contract must be accounted for separately and then the totals aggregated and included in the financial statements.

20.3.2 Accounting treatment

When the outcome of a contract can be assessed with reasonable certainty, IAS 11 provides that contract revenues and costs can be recognised according to the stage of completion of the contract. The stage of completion is usually assessed and then certified by a professional surveyor.

The treatment required by IAS 11 results in our accounting entries being based, to a great extent, on judgement rather than on actual transactions.

The economic reality with a construction contract is that it may span more than one accounting period and the related invoice may not be raised until the contract is completed. However, the contractor will not wish to bear the full cost of financing the project throughout its duration, so the customer will often pay for stages of work completed on the contract. These interim payments are known as *progress payments* and are usually paid once a piece of work completed has been certified by a surveyor or other professional.

As progress payments are not for the completed project, they are not credited directly to sales or turnover, as would happen with a completed sale, but are recorded for each invoice raised during the course of the contract.

The recording for invoices raised for construction contracts is:

- We raise an invoice

Debit	Receivables
Credit	Progress payments

- We receive payment

Debit	Bank
Credit	Receivables

This is fine for the invoice-raising, but when is the sales revenue recorded?

Well, as we noted above, we must include an appropriate part of total revenue and profits of the contract in the accounting period where there is activity on the contract. However, since no final transaction has taken place, it is the preparer who must decide how much should be included for revenue, related costs and profit.

The standard gives guidance as to how these figures should be arrived at (discussed below). However, the recording is as follows:

- We record sales revenue

Debit	Progress payments
Credit	Sales revenue

- We match related costs

Debit	Cost of sales
Credit	Contract costs

Note

- When revenue is recorded, the debit entry is to progress payments – this could be considered to be like a contract account, recording all customer monies received during the contract and recording any revenues recognised. Remember that the trade receivables account is only affected by the raising of an invoice – in the entry seen above.
- Any contract costs not yet transferred to cost of sales (may have purchased all the materials for the contract at the start of the contract to secure discount) will be included within assets in the statement of financial position. As the costs are incurred, however, they are held within a contract cost account, there is one for each contract (because each contract must be accounted for separately) and then the balances are aggregated in the financial statements.

Accounting for construction costs affects a number of headings in the statement of comprehensive income and statement of financial position:

1. Sales value of work completed is included in 'revenue' in statement of comprehensive income. Related costs of the work completed are included in 'cost of sales' in statement of comprehensive income.
2. If the contract is expected to be profitable overall, then an appropriate part of that profit is recognised within profit or loss by the above entries.
3. If the contract is expected to make a loss overall, then all of the loss must be recognised as soon as it is anticipated, by adding the expected loss for future periods on to the cost of sales.
4. If the outcome of the contract cannot be measured with reasonable certainty (e.g. if the contract is at an early stage of completion), then revenue recognised must be made to equal contract costs in order to create no profit or loss in the period.
5. Any contract costs incurred but not yet transferred to cost of sales should be included within contract costs under the heading 'gross amounts due from customers for contract work' in the statement of financial position.
6. Where sales revenue recognised exceeds the progress payments received, the balance should be included in 'gross amounts due from customers for contract work' within assets.
7. Where sales revenue recognised is less than the progress payments received, the balance should be included as a separate item within 'payables', as 'gross amounts due to customers for contract work'.

For the last two points, remember that the preparer decides the level of revenue to be included in profit or loss at the end of the accounting period based on the stage of completion. However, this may not be the same as the work that has been completed and certified, so the figures for revenue and progress payments received are unlikely to match unless a certification takes place at the end of the reporting period.

We are now going to look at the detailed accounting for construction contracts using examples wherever possible to reinforce a practical understanding of the procedure.

20.3.3 Sales revenue

In order to estimate an appropriate part of contract revenue to be included in statement of comprehensive income, we must first establish the stage of completion of each contract.

There is no set rule on how to determine turnover, but the two main methods used in practice are:

- *By reference to the proportion of work done.* Established either by certification of work by the surveyor, or by comparing the costs incurred to date to the total contract costs anticipated to give an estimate of work completed so far.
- *By identifying specific points in the contract where the work completed has separately ascertainable sales values.* For example, a contract for residential property development could have a sales value for the building of a house, and separate values for the construction of a garage, swimming pool, stables, etc.

Sales revenue should be recognised based on the activity on the contract in the period, regardless of the profit that is likely.

Remember that items included in statement of comprehensive income are recorded only once, so for a contract that spans, say, 4 years, we must deduct any contract revenues previously recognised. The calculations will be:

Year 1   (Total contract revenue × % stage of completion) = sales revenue for year 1
Year 2   (Total contract revenue × % stage of completion) − revenue recognised in year 1 = sales revenue for year 2
Year 3   (Total contract revenue × % stage of completion) − revenue recognised in year 1 and 2 = sales revenue for year 3

Example 20.B

Moby has the following contract details for a contract that started in 20X2:

	20X2	20X3	20X4
Total contract sales value	$10m	$11m	$11.5m
Estimated % completion	40%	75%	100%

Note that the total contract value has changed over the duration of the contract – this can only be included in the revenue calculations if these amendments have been agreed with the customer. This is a common occurrence as the costs associated with labour and materials during the course of the contract may change, an unforeseen obstacle may occur which is beyond the control of the contractor, or the customer specifications may change.

The revenue to be recognised is as follows:

	20X2 $m	20X3 $m	20X4 $m
Revenues recognisable to date:			
20X2: 40% × $10m	4.00		
20X3: 75% × $11m		8.25	
20X4: 100% × $11.5m			11.50
Less revenues recognised in prior periods		(4.00)	(8.25)
Revenue for the period	4.00	4.25	3.25

20.3.4 Recognisable contract profits

The recognition of contract profit is usually based on the percentage of work completed on the contract.

The amount of revenue and profit to be included are both calculated (based on work done) and the cost of sales figure is the balancing figure.

Example 20.C

Plusman contract A commenced in 20X2 and has the following details for the year ended 31 December 20X3:

Total contract value	$80m
Costs incurred to date	$50m
Estimated costs to complete	$7m
Completion	80%
Profit recognised in 20X2	$11m

The first step to calculate the total estimated profit on the contract:

	$m	$m
Total sales value of the contract		80
Less: contract costs incurred to date	(50)	
estimated costs to completion	(7)	
Total estimated contract costs		(57)
Total estimated contract profit		23

The second step is to establish the stage of completion of the contract and calculate the profit recognisable to date:

Total estimated contract profit × % completion of the contract
= recognisable profit to date $23m × 80% completion = $18.4m

The third step is to calculate the profit reportable for this accounting period:

	$m
Recognisable profit to date	18.4
Less cumulative profit recognised in prior periods	(11.0)
Profit recognisable in this period	7.4

In this case, turnover and cost of sales will be recognised to give the $7.4m profit in statement of comprehensive income for the period.

20.3.5 Expected contract losses

Whenever an overall contract loss is expected, the loss must be recognised as soon as it is anticipated.

The first step, calculating the overall profit or loss on the contract, would still be performed. However, if the overall contract is loss-making, the full amount of the loss will be recognised immediately.

Example 20.D

Plusman's contract B commenced during 20X3 and will complete in 20X4. It has the following details for the year ended 31 December 20X3:

Total contract value	$70m
Costs incurred to date	$40m
Estimated costs to complete	$39m
Completion	50%

The first step is to calculate the overall outcome for this contract:

	$m	$m
Total sales value of the contract		70
Less contract costs incurred to date	(40)	
estimated costs to completion	(39)	
Total estimated contract costs		(79)
Total estimated contract loss		(9)

Contact B is 50 per cent complete and revenue recognised must reflect this activity in the period, so the fact that the contract is loss-making does not remove the need to recognise sales revenue.

If we follow the previous example, the revenues and costs will occur as follows (50 per cent of revenue and 50 per cent of costs, resulting in 50 per cent of loss in the period. This would leave the same again to be recognised next year).

Statement of comprehensive income (extract)

	2003 $m	2004 $m
Sales revenue (50% in each of the 2 years)	35.0	35.0
Cost of sales	(39.5)	(39.5)
Loss on contract	(4.5)	(4.5)

IAS 11 and prudence require that we recognise the whole of the loss as soon as it is anticipated and so the $4.5 million loss expected to occur in 20X4 is pulled back and charged to 20X3's profit or loss through cost of sales. What it does mean is that cost of sales must be charged with an amount that results in the full contract loss of $9 million being recognised immediately. The income statement extract now shows:

Statement of comprehensive income (extract)

	2003 $m	2004 $m
Sales revenue (50% in each of the two years)	35	35
Cost of sales (39.5 + 4.5)	(44)	(35)
Profit/(loss) on contract	(9)	–

We know that cost of sales must be charged with $44 million to ensure that the full contact loss of $9 million is recognised in the first year (i.e. as soon as it is anticipated).

In this case the cost of sales charge is made up of two elements:

1. 50 per cent of total contract costs of $79m = $39.5 million;
2. the remaining amount of the loss that is expected to occur next year, which is $4.5 million.

20.3.6 Uncertain outcome

If the outcome of the contract cannot be estimated with reasonable certainty, then no profit should be recognised. However, profit or loss must still reflect the activity in the period and so an appropriate part of revenue and cost of sales must be recognised.

Example 20.E

Plusman's contract C commenced in 20X3 and has the following details for the year ended 31 December 20X3:

Total contract value	$40m
Costs incurred to date	$3m
Estimated costs to complete	$30m
Completion	10%

Plusman has only just commenced work on this contract and cannot be certain of its outcome at the year-end date. The overall contract is expected to be profit-making. However, the contract has only just started (10 per cent complete) and so the outcome cannot be measured with reasonable certainty. In this case, prudence dictates that no profit should be recognised in the year ended December 20X3.

Revenue would normally include 10 per cent of revenue and cost of sales would be made to match the revenue to create a nil profit:

Statement of comprehensive income (extract)

	$m
Sales revenue (10% × $40m)	4
Cost of sales	(4)
Profit/loss on contract	–

However, in this case we cannot transfer $4 million to cost of sales as we have only incurred costs of $3 million to date. Where costs to date are less than the required cost of sales charge, we instead restrict the revenue figure to the level of costs incurred to date. The income statement for 20X3 would therefore include the following for contract C:

Statement of comprehensive income
(extract)

	$m
Sales revenue	3
Cost of sales	(3)
Profit/loss on contract	–

20.3.7 Inventories

Any contract costs incurred but not yet transferred to cost of sales should be included within contract costs under the heading 'gross amounts due from customers for contract work' in the statement of financial performance.

Remember that each contract is accounted for separately, so some contracts may have inventories, some may not. Each contract is calculated and then the total from each contract is aggregated in the statement of financial performance.

Example 20.F

Let us look at Plusman's contract A again.
Plusman's contract A commenced in 20X2 and has the following details for the year ended 31 December 20X3:

Total contract value	$80m
Costs incurred to date	$50m
Estimated costs to complete	$7m
Completion	80%
Profit recognised in 20X2	$11m

Solution

Costs incurred to date total $50m:

		$m	$m
Debit	Contract costs	50	
Credit	Bank/payables		50

The amount we will have charged to cost of sales to date (20X2 and 20X3) is based on the percentage completion × the total contract costs (80% × $57 million) × $45.6 million. Over the 2 years of the contract we will have recorded:

Transfer to cost of sales:

		$m	$m
Debit	Cost of sales	45.6	
Credit	Contract costs		45.6

There is therefore a balance remaining on contract costs at 31 December 20X3 of $4.4m ($50m − $45.6m). This amount represents contract costs incurred that relate to a future activity and is therefore recognised as an asset and will be included in 'gross amounts due from customers'.

20.3.8 Receivables

Let us stay with this example and look at the impact on receivables in the balance sheet. Where sales revenue recognised to date exceeds the progress payments received, the balance should be included in the statement of financial position as an asset and referred to as 'unbilled contract revenue' within the heading 'gross amounts due from customers for contract work'.

The progress payments received to date at 31 December 20X3 for Contract A totalled $60 million:

		$m	$m
Debit	Bank	60	
Credit	Progress payments		60

The total sales revenue recognised to date at 31 December 20X3 is $64 million (80% × $80 million).

		$m	$m
Debit	Progress payments	64	
Credit	Sales revenue		64

This results in a $4 million receivable in respect of this contract. We have calculated (based on percentage completion) that sales and therefore amounts due from customers to date totals $64 million and the customer has paid $60 million to date. The remaining $4 million is therefore a receivable and is referred to as 'unbilled contract revenue' within 'gross amounts due from customers for contract work'.

IAS 11 specifies that an entity should present the gross amount due from customers for contract work as an asset. Note that it does not specify where the asset should be recorded.

 In an examination question, gross amounts due from customers should be treated as a current asset.

20.3.9 Payables

Where sales revenue recognised to date is less than the progress payments received, the balance should be included as a separate item within payables, and referred to as 'gross amounts due to customers for contract work'

Let us assume that for Contract A the progress payments received at 31 December 2003 totalled $70 million.

		$m	$m
Debit	Bank	70	
Credit	Progress payments		70

The total sales revenue recognised to date at 31 December 20X3 is $64 million (80% × $80 m).

		$m	$m
Debit	Progress payments	64	
Credit	Sales revenue		64

In this case, we have calculated that $64 million is due on this contract and the customer has already paid $70 million. We have received customer monies that have not yet been earned and so the balance of $6 million is included within payables as 'gross amounts due to customers for contract work' (included as a liability until the money has been earned through next year's activity on the contract).

IAS 11 specifies that an entity should present the gross amount due to customers for contract work as a liability. It does not state how the liability should be included.

> In an examination question, gross amounts due to customers should be included as a current liability.

20.3.10 Provisions for foreseeable losses

Whenever a loss is provided for, it is charged to profit or loss and the corresponding credit entry is made in the statement of financial position. IAS 11 permits foreseeable losses to be deducted from 'gross amounts due from customers for contract work' on a contract-by-contract basis, in some cases this will turn an amount due from the customer into an amount due to the customer, see Section 15.3.13. Forseeable losses charged to cost of sales are therefore recorded as:

Debit	Cost of sales
Credit	Contract costs/unbilled contract revenue

20.3.11 Disclosure requirements

An entity should disclose the following for construction contracts:

(a) contract revenue recognised;
(b) methods used to determine contract revenue recognised;
(c) methods used to determine stage of completion of contracts;
(d) for work-in-progress:
　　(i) costs incurred and profits less losses to date;
　　(ii) advances received (i.e. payments from customers before the related work is performed);
　　(iii) retentions (i.e. progress billings not paid until satisfaction of conditions in contract or until defects are rectified).

20.3.12 Illustrations from IAS 11

IAS 11 also contains illustrations showing the procedure. They are given below and you should work through them once you have fully understood the procedure described above.

Illustration 1

A contractor has a fixed-price contract for $9,000 to build a bridge. The initial amount of revenue agreed in the contract is $9,000. The contractor's initial estimate of contract costs is $8,000. It will take 3 years to build the bridge.

By the end of year 1, the contractor's estimate of contract costs has increased to $8,050.

In year 2, the customer approves a variation resulting in an increase in contract revenue of $200 and estimated additional contract costs of $150. At the end of year 2, costs incurred include $100 for standard materials stored at the site to be used in year 3 to complete the project.

The contractor determines the stage of completion of the contract by comparing the proportion of contract costs incurred for work performed to date with the latest estimated total contract costs. A summary of the financial data during the construction period is as follows:

	Year 1 $	Year 2 $	Year 3 $
Initial amount of revenue agreed in contract	9,000	9,000	9,000
Variation	–	200	200
Total contract revenue	9,000	9,200	9,200
Contract costs incurred to date	2,093	6,168	8,200
Contract costs to complete	5,957	2,032	–
Total estimated contract costs	8,050	8,200	8,200
Estimated profit	950	1,000	1,000
Stage of completion	26%	74%	100%

The stage of completion for year 2 (74 per cent) is determined by excluding from contract costs incurred for work performed to date the $100 of standard materials stored at the site for use in year 3.

The amounts of revenue, expenses and profit recognised in profit or loss in the 3 years are as follows:

		To date $	Recognised in prior year $	Recognised in current year $
Year 1	Revenue (9,000 × .26)	2,340		2,340
	Expenses (8,050 × .26)	2,093	___	2,093
	Profit	247	___	247
Year 2	Revenue (9,200 × .74)	6,808	2,340	4,468
	Expenses (8,200 × .74)	6,068	2,093	3,975
	Profit	740	247	493
Year 3	Revenue (9,200 × 1.00)	9,200	6,808	2,392
	Expenses	8,200	6,068	2,132
	Profit	1,000	740	260

Illustration 2

A contractor has reached the end of its first year of operation. All its contract costs incurred have been paid for in cash and all its progress billings and advances have been received in cash. Contract costs incurred for contracts B, C and E include the costs of materials that have been purchased for the contract but which have not been used in contract performance to date. For contracts B, C and E, the customers have made advances to the contractor for work not yet performed.

The status of its five contracts in progress at the end of year 1 is as follows:

			Contract			
	A	B	C	D	E	Total
	$'000	$'000	$'000	$'000	$'000	$'000
Contract revenue recognised	145	520	380	200	55	1,300
Contract expenses recognised	110	450	350	250	55	1,215
Expected losses recognised	–	–	–	40	30	70
Recognised profits less recognised losses	35	70	30	(90)	(30)	15
Contract costs incurred in the period	110	510	450	250	100	1,420
Contract costs incurred recognised as contract expenses	110	450	350	250	55	1,215
Contract costs that relate to future activity recognised as an asset	–	60	100	–	45	205
Contract revenue (see above)	145	520	380	200	55	1,300
Progress billings	100	520	380	180	55	1,235
Unbilled contract revenue	45	–	–	20	–	65
Advances	–	80	20	–	25	125

Let us examine this information step by step.

The first section shows us the information required for profit or loss:

			Contract			
	A	B	C	D	E	Total
	$'000	$'000	$'000	$'000	$'000	$'000
Contract revenue recognised	145	520	380	200	55	1,300
Contract expenses recognised	110	450	350	250	55	1,215
Expected losses recognised	–	–	–	40	30	70
Recognised profits less recognised losses	35	70	30	(90)	(30)	15

The totals provide us with the detail we need to complete profit or loss:

Income statement (extract)	$'000	$'000
Contract revenue		1,300
Contract expenses	1,215	
Expected losses	70	1,285
Profit		15

The middle section provides information on the contract costs incurred and those recognised as contract expenses in the period and transferred to cost of sales:

			Contract			
	A	B	C	D	E	Total
	$'000	$'000	$'000	$'000	$'000	$'000
Contract costs incurred in the period	110	510	450	250	100	1,420
Contract costs incurred recognised as contract expenses	110	450	350	250	55	1,215
Contract costs that relate to future activity recognised as an asset	–	60	100	–	45	205

The third section provides information on the revenue recognised in the period and the progress billings:

| | | | Contract | | | |
	A	B	C	D	E	Total
	$'000	$'000	$'000	$'000	$'000	$'000
Contract revenue (see above)	145	520	380	200	55	1,300
Progress billings	100	520	380	180	55	1,235
Unbilled contract revenue	45	–	–	20	–	65

From the above we can now calculate the 'gross amounts due from/to customers for contract work'. This is calculated as the contract costs that relate to future activities plus the unbilled contract revenue less provisions for losses.

| | | | Contract | | | |
	A	B	C	D	E	Total
	$'000	$'000	$'000	$'000	$'000	$'000
Contract costs that relate to future activity recognised as an asset	0	60	100	0	45	205
Unbilled contract revenue	45	0	0	20	0	65
Expected losses recognised	0	0	0	(40)	(30)	(70)
'gross amounts due from customers for contract work'	45	60	100	0	15	220
'gross amounts due to customers for contract work'	0	0	0	(20)	0	(20)

Note that contract D has unbilled contract revenue of $20,000, but with the expected loss this is turned in to an amount due to the customer and is treated as a liability in the statement of financial position.

Payments received in advance from customers are shown separately as liabilities:

| | | | Contract | | | |
	A	B	C	D	E	Total
	$'000	$'000	$'000	$'000	$'000	$'000
Payments in advance shown as a liability	–	80	20	–	25	125

In summary, the statement of financial position entries for the five contracts would be:

	$'000
Payments due from customers for contract work, shown as an asset	220
Payments due to customers for contract work, shown as a liability	(20)
Payments in advance, shown as a current liability	(125)

IAS 11 also requires the following amounts to be disclosed:

	$'000
Contract revenue recognised as revenue in the period	1,300
Contract costs incurred and recognised profits (less recognised losses) to date	1,435
Advances received, presented as a current liability	(125)
Gross amount due from customers for contract work – presented as an asset	220
Gross amount due to customers for contract work – presented as a liability	(20)

The above figures can also be arrived at as follows:

	A $'000	B $'000	C $'000	Contract D $'000	E $'000	Total $'000
Contract costs incurred	110	510	450	250	100	1,420
Recognised profits less recognised losses	35	70	30	(90)	(30)	15
	145	580	480	160	70	1,435
Progress billings	(100)	(520)	(380)	(180)	(55)	(1,235)
Due from customers	45	60	100		15	220
Due to customers				(20)		(20)

20.3.13 A comprehensive example

This worked example includes all of the headings discussed above.

Example 20.G

Crave has three contracts in progress during the year and the following details are available for the year ended 31 December 2003:

Contract	Alpha	Beta	Gamma
Commenced	June 20X2	Jan 20X3	Nov 20X3
Total contract value	$90m	$60m	$100m
Costs incurred to date	$70m	$45m	$15m
Estimated costs to complete	$10m	$23m	$70m
Completion	80%	60%	10%
Progress payments received	$65m	$32m	$20m

Additional information
- Contract Alpha commenced during 20X2 and at 31 December 20X2 was 50 per cent complete; accordingly appropriate amounts for revenue and profit were included in the 20X2 profit or loss.
- Crave has a policy of recognising profit on contracts once the contracts have reached a minimum of 30 per cent completion, to ensure that their outcome can be assessed with reasonable certainty.

Solution

	Sales revenue		
	Alpha $m	Beta $m	Gamma $m
Revenues recognisable to date			
Alpha (80% × $90m)	72		
Beta (60% × $60m)		36	
Gamma (10% × $100m)			10
Revenues previously recognised			
Alpha (50% × $90m)	(45)		
Revenues recognisable in the period	27	36	10

Total sales revenue that is recognisable and will be included in profit or loss for the year ended 31 December 20X3 is $73 million (27 + 36 + 10).

Contract profits and losses

	Alpha $m	Beta $m	Gamma $m
Overall contract position			
Total contract value	90	60	100
Total contract costs (incurred to date plus costs to complete)	(80)	(68)	(85)
Contract profit/(loss)	10	(8)	15
Profits/losses recognisable to date			
Alpha (80% × $10m)	(8)		
Beta (100% × (loss of $8m))		(8)	
Gamma (Nil – only 10% complete)			–
Amounts previously recognised			
Alpha (50% × $10m)	(5)		
Profits/(losses) in the period	3	(8)	–

Using the revenues and profits calculated above, we can now draft profit or loss extract for Crave for December 20X3:

Income statement (extract)

	Alpha $m	Beta $m	Gamma $m	Total $m
Sales revenue	27	36	10	73
Cost of sales	(24)	(44)	(10)	78
Contract profits/(losses)	3	(8)	–	(5)

Note
- Alpha – we must remember to deduct the revenues and profits previously recognised.
- Beta – the overall contract is expected to make a loss of $8 million and the entire loss must be recognised immediately. The cost of sales figure therefore includes cost of sales for 20X3 of $40.8 million (60% × total contract costs of $68m) plus anticipated loss for 20X4 of $3.2 million (40% X $8m); rounded to $41 million and $3 million.
- Gamma – the contract is only 10 per cent complete and so 10 per cent of revenue can be recognised but no profit must be recognised as the contract outcome cannot be assessed with reasonable certainty. Cost of sales is therefore charged with an amount to match revenue (provided that there is sufficient in contract costs from this contract to transfer to cost of sales).

Inventories

	Alpha $m	Beta $m	Gamma $m	Total $m
Contract costs incurred to date	70	45	15	
Transferred to cost of sales to date	(64)	(41)	(10)	
Balance contract costs that relate to future activities	6	4	5	15

Note: Alpha is 80 per cent complete to date and has therefore transferred 80 per cent of total contract costs to cost of sales over 20X2 and 20X3.

Receivables and payables

	Alpha $m	Beta $m	Gamma $m	Total $m
Progress payments received	65	32	20	
Sales revenue recognised to date	72	36	10	
Receivables – unbilled contract revenue	7	4		11
Payables – progress payments received			(10)	(10)

Summary

	Alpha $m	Beta $m	Gamma $m	Total $m
Inventories, contract costs that relate to future activities	6	4	5	15
Receivables – unbilled contract revenue	7	4	0	11
Expected loss recognised	0	(3)	0	(3)
Payments due from customers for contract work	13	5	5	23
Payments due to customers for contract work	0	0	(10)	(10)

20.4 Summary

Having completed this chapter, we can now define and account for inventories, including the determination of cost and net realisable value. We can also explain the disclosures required by IAS 2 *Inventories.*

In addition, we can explain the principle of revenue recognition with regard to construction contracts. We can correctly account for construction contracts, including the treatment of losses, and explain the required disclosures required by IAS 11 *Construction Contracts.*

Revision Questions

? Question 1

Item code ZYX321 had 320 items in inventory at 31 March, the entity year-end. The original cost of the inventory, according to the inventory control system, was $5,000. Alternative valuations were obtained at 31 March for this inventory item. Which value should be used in the accounts at 31 March?

(A) Net realisable value $4,750
(B) Original cost $5,000
(C) Replacement cost $5,500
(D) Selling price $6,000   **(2 marks)**

Data for Questions 2–4

Details of contract AB1375 are:

	$'000	$'000
Certified work completed		300
Costs incurred to date:		
Attributable to work completed	345	
Further costs attributable to partly completed work	50	
		395
Progress payments received		320
Expected further loss on completion		40

Using the above data, identify the correct entries for contract AB1375 items in Questions 2–4.

? Question 2

The revenue and cost of sales figure should be:

	Revenue	Cost of sales
	$'000	$'000
(A)	340	395
(B)	320	395
(C)	300	385
(D)	300	435

(2 marks)

Question 3

The liability shown in the statement of financial position for 'progress payments received in advance' should be:

(A) $5,000
(B) $10,000
(C) $20,000
(D) $30,000   **(2 marks)**

 Question 4

The asset shown in the statement of financial position for 'gross amounts due from customers for contract work' should be:

(A) $0
(B) $10,000
(C) $50,000
(D) $395,000   **(2 marks)**

 Question 5

	$'000
Total contract value	370
Certified work completed	320
Costs to date – attributable to work completed	360
Progress payments received	300
Expected further costs to completion	50

The amounts shown in the profit or loss for Revenue and Cost of Sales should be:

	Revenue	Cost of Sales
	$'000	$'000
(A)	320	360
(B)	320	400
(C)	370	360
(D)	370	410

(2 marks)

 Question 6

BL started a contract on 1 November 2004. The contract was scheduled to run for 2 years and has a sales value of $40 million. At 31 October 2005, the following details were obtained from BL's records:

	$m
Costs incurred to date	16
Estimated costs to completion	18
Percentage complete at 31 October 2005	45%

Applying IAS 11 *Construction Contracts*, how much revenue and profit should BL recognise in Statement of comprehensive income for the year ended 31 October 2005.

(2 marks)

? Question 7

Details from DV's long-term contract, which commenced on 1 May 2006, at 30 April 2007 were:

	$'000
Invoiced to client for work done	2,000
Costs incurred to date:	
Attributable to work completed	1,500
Inventory purchased, but not yet used	250
Progress payment received from client	900
Expected further costs to complete project	400
Total contract value	3,000

DV uses the percentage of costs incurred to total costs to calculate attributable profit.

Calculate the amount that DV should recognise in its statement of comprehensive income for the year ended 30 April 2007 for revenue, cost of sales and attributable profits on this contract according to IAS 11 *Construction Contracts*. **(4 marks)**

? Question 8

(a) IAS 2 *Inventories* requires inventories of raw materials and finished goods to be valued in financial statements at lower cost and net realisable value.

Requirements

(i) Describe the three methods of arriving at the cost of inventory which are benchmark treatments in IAS 2. **(4 marks)**

(ii) Explain how the cost of an inventory of finished goods held by a manufacturer would normally be arrived at when obtaining the figure for the financial statements. **(3 marks)**

(b) Sampi is a manufacturer of garden furniture. The entity has consistently used FIFO (first in first out) in valuing inventory, but it is interested to know the effect on its inventory valuation of using weighted average cost instead of FIFO.

At 28 February 20X8, the entity had a inventory of 4,000 standard plastic tables, and has computed its value on each of the two bases as:

Basis	Unit cost	Total value
	$	$
FIFO	16	64,000
Weighted average	13	52,000

During March 20X8, the movements on the inventory of tables were as follows:

Received from factory

Date	Number of units	Production cost per unit
		$
8 March	3,800	15
22 March	6,000	18

Sales

Date	Number of units
12 March	5,000
18 March	2,000
24 March	3,000
28 March	2,000

On a FIFO basis, the inventory at 31 March 20X8 was $32,400.

Requirements

Compute what the value of the inventory at 31 March 20X8 would be using weighted average cost. **(5 marks)**

In arriving at the total inventory values you should make calculations to two decimal places (where necessary) and deal with each inventory movement in date order.

(Total marks 12)

Data for Questions 9 and 10

CN started a three-year contract to build a new university campus on 1 April 2004. The contract had a fixed price of $90 million.

CN incurred costs to 31 March 2006 of $77 million and estimated that a further $33 million would need to be spent to complete the contract.

CN uses the percentage of cost incurred to date to total cost method to calculate stage of completion of the contract.

Question 9

Calculate revenue earned on the contract to 31 March 2006, according to IAS 11 *Construction Contracts*. **(2 marks)**

Question 10

State how much gross profit/loss CN should recognise in its statement of comprehensive income for the year ended 31 March 2006, according to IAS 11 *Construction Contracts*.

(2 marks)

? **Question 11**

Basset, a construction entity, prepares its accounts to 31 December 2001. During the year, the entity undertook five contracts all of which commenced in the period and will require more than 12 months to complete.

The position of each contract at 31 December 2001 is as follows:

Contract	1001	1002	1003	1004	1005
	$'000	$'000	$'000	$'000	$'000
Contract value	1,800	390	260	4,800	2,000
Certified work to date	1,010	240	200	1,500	1,700
Progress payments received	1,300	200	200	1,900	1,400
Costs to be transferred to cost of sales	1,010	240	200	1,200	1,300
Costs incurred to date	1,310	240	200	1,450	1,400

In addition to the amounts transferred to cost of sales, foreseeable losses are anticipated on two contracts: contract 1001 a loss of $50,000 and contract 1002 a loss of $80,000.

Basset recognises turnover based on the value of work certified at the end of the reporting period.

Requirement

Prepare a summary statement showing profits and losses on all five contracts and the related statement of financial position totals for each. **(20 marks)**

Solutions to Revision Questions 20

✓ Solution 1

The correct answer is (A), see Section 20.2.2.

IAS 2 requires inventory to be valued at cost or net realisable value whichever is the lower.

✓ Solution 2

The correct answer is (C), see Section 20.3.5.

The cost of sales must include the full provision for expected future losses:
345 + 40 = 385.

✓ Solution 3

The correct answer is (C), see Section 20.3.9.

The excess payments received in advance from customers is 320 − 300 = 20.

✓ Solution 4

The correct answer is (B), see Section 20.3.7.

The provision for future losses is subtracted from further costs attributable to partly completed work, 50 − 40 = 10.

✓ Solution 5

The correct answer is (A), see Section 20.3.5.

	$'000
Total contract:	
Contract price	370
Costs (360 + 50)	410
Loss	(40)
To date:	
Revenue	320
Cost of sales	360
Loss	(40)

$40,000 loss is recognised, there is no need for a provision.

Solution 6

	$m
Total revenue	40
Total cost 16 + 18 =	34
Profit	6

Recognise – Revenue 40 × 45% = £18 million
          – Profit 6 × 45% = £2 × 7 million

See Section 20.3.3 and 20.3.4.

 Solution 7

	$'000
Total cost	
Cost incurred on attributable work	1,500
Inventory not yet used	250
Expected further costs	400
	2,150

Cost incurred on attributable work 1,500
% complete 1,500/2, 150 = 69.76% (round to 70%)

Total contract revenue	3,000
Total cost	2,150
Total profit	850

Income statement figures for contract	
Revenue (3,000 × 70%)	2,100
Cost of sales	1,500
Profit	600

Solution 8

(a) (i) 1. *First in first out.* Under FIFO, inventory is valued at the price of the most recent purchases, whether or not it is composed of these particular items.
   2. *Unit cost.* Inventory is valued at the price paid for each inventory item held.
   3. *Average cost.* Inventory is priced at the weighted average price at which each item has been purchased during the year.

   All these methods represent actual cost (method 2) or a reasonably close approximation to actual cost (methods 1 and 3).

(ii) The cost of an inventory of finished goods would be arrived at by taking the cost of the labour and materials used in their manufacture plus an allocation of overheads. In allocating overheads, a normal level of production must be assumed, and selling and general administrative overheads excluded.

(b) Closing inventory is therefore:

Value of inventory using weighted average

	Units	Weighted average cost $	Value of closing inventory $
Opening inventory	4,000	13.00	
8 March	3,800	15.00	
Balance	7,800	13.97	
12 March	(5,000)		
	2,800	13.97	
18 March	(2,000)		
	800	13.97	
22 March	6,000	18.00	
	6,800	17.53	
24 March	(3,000)		
	3,800	17.53	
28 March	(2,000)		
	1,800	17.53	31,554

Summary

		$
Inventory value:	FIFO	32,400
	Weighted average	31,554

See Section 20.2.6.

 ## Solution 9

	$m
Revenue earned	63

See Section 20.3.3.

 ## Solution 10

Statement of comprehensive income for year ended 31 March 2006

	$m
Gross loss	(20)

See Section 20.3.4.

 ## Solution 11

Statement of comprehensive income figures for 2001

Contract	1001 $'000	1002 $'000	1003 $'000	1004 $'000	1005 $'000	Total $'000
Certified work to date	1,010	240	200	1,500	1,700	4,650
Costs to be transferred to cost of sales	(1,010)	(240)	(200)	(1,200)	(1,300)	(3,950)
Less foreseeable losses on contracts	50	80	–	–	–	(130)
Profit/(loss) on contracts	(50)	(80)	–	300	400	570

Inventories

Inventories are calculated by comparing the costs incurred to date with amounts transferred to cost of sales. Any balance remaining is included in 'gross amounts due from customers for contract work'.

Contract	1001	1002	1003	1004	1005	Total
	$'000	$'000	$'000	$'000	$'000	$'000
Costs incurred to date	1,310	240	200	1,450	1,400	4,600
Costs to be transferred to cost of sales	(1,010)	(240)	(200)	(1,200)	(1,300)	3,950
Contract costs that relate to future activity	300	–	–	250	100	650

Receivable/payables

To establish amounts to be included in either receivables or payables we compare the sales revenue recognised to date with the progress payments received to date.

Contract	1001	1002	1003	1004	1005	Total
	$'000	$'000	$'000	$'000	$'000	$'000
Costs work to date	1,010	240	200	1,500	1,700	4,650
Progress payments received	(1,300)	(200)	(200)	(1,900)	(1,400)	5,000
Receivables – unbilled contract revenue		40	–	–	300	340
Excess progress payments received	(290)			(400)		(690)

Contract	1001	1002	1003	1004	1005	Total
	$'000	$'000	$'000	$'000	$'000	$'000
Contract costs that relate to future activity	300	–	–	250	100	650
Unbilled contract revenue	–	40	–		300	340
Foreseeable losses on contracts	(50)	(80)	–	–	–	(130)
Gross amounts due from customers for contract work	250		0	250	400	860
Gross amounts due to customers for contract work		(40)				(40)

Statement of financial position extract	$'000
Gross amounts due from customers for contract work, treated as an asset	860
Gross amounts due to customers for contract work, treat as a liability	(40)
Progress payments received in advance, treated as a current liability	(690)

See Section 20.3.13.

21

Non-current Intangible Assets

Non-current
Intangible Assets

21

LEARNING OUTCOME

After completing this chapter, you should be able to:

▸ apply the accounting rules contained in IFRS's and IAS's dealing with non-current assets including impairment.

The syllabus topics covered in this chapter are as follows:

- research and development costs (IAS 38): criteria for capitalisation;
- intangible assets (IAS 38) and goodwill (excluding that arising on consolidation): recognition, valuation and amortisation;
- impairment of assets (IAS 36) and its effect on the above.

21.1   Introduction

In Chapter 18, we examined non-current tangible assets. In this chapter, we will consider non-current intangible assets and goodwill and then the impairment of non-current assets (tangible and intangible). Non-current intangible assets are covered by IAS 38 *Intangible Assets*, goodwill is dealt with by IFRS 3 *Business Combinations* and impairment of assets is IAS 36 *Impairment of Assets*.

21.1.1   Objective of IAS 38 *Intangible Assets*

An intangible asset is an identifiable non-monetary asset without physical substance held for use in the business. Entities often use resources to acquire or develop intangibles such as scientific or technical knowledge, design and implementation of a new process or system, licences, trademarks and intellectual property. If it is probable that this investment in the intangible will result in future economic benefits flowing to the entity, then the cost can be recognised as an asset instead of an expense.

21.1.2 Recognition and initial measurement

The recognition of a purchased intangible asset requires an entity to demonstrate that the item meets the definition and recognition criteria set out in IAS 38: an intangible asset should be recognised if and only if:

- it is probable that the future economic benefits from the asset will flow to the entity;
- the cost of the asset can be measured reliably.

An intangible asset purchased separately from a business should be capitalised at cost.

Where an intangible asset is acquired when a business is bought, it should be capitalised separately from purchased goodwill, provided that it can be measured reliably on initial recognition. Cost being the fair value of the asset.

If the fair value of an intangible asset purchased as a part of the acquisition of a business cannot be measured reliably, it should not be recognised and will be included within goodwill.

The cost of an intangible asset is measured in the same way as a tangible non-current asset. The cost of an intangible asset comprises:

(a) its purchase price, including import duties and non-refundable purchase taxes, after deducting trade discounts and rebates;
(b) any directly attributable cost of preparing the asset for its intended use.

Examples of directly attributable costs are:

(a) costs of employee benefits arising directly from bringing the asset to its working condition;
(b) professional fees.

Examples of costs that are not a cost of an intangible asset are:

(a) costs of introducing a new product or service (including costs of advertising and promotional activities);
(b) costs of conducting business in a new location or with a new class of customer (including costs of staff training);
(c) administration and other general overhead costs.

In Section 8.3.4, we considered the 'Framework' and its definition of an asset: 'an asset is a resource controlled by the entity as a result of past events and from which future economic benefits are expected to flow to the entity'. To be recognised as an intangible asset, expenditure must give access to future economic benefits.

The management of the entity must consider the economic conditions that exist and are likely to exist over the useful life of the asset, and then assess the probability of future economic benefits. The assessment should be management's best estimate using all the evidence available, giving greater weight to external evidence. The asset should be measured initially at cost and amortised over its useful life.

21.1.3 Internally generated goodwill

Some expenditure may be incurred with the aim of generating future revenues but does not result in an intangible asset being recognised in the accounts. For example, money spent on developing customer relationships may help generate future revenues but won't result in an identifiable asset that could be sold separately from the business activities. This expenditure is often referred to as contributing to internally generated goodwill.

Internally generated goodwill is not recognised as an asset, as it is not an identifiable resource that can be measured reliably. Where the market value of an entity exceeds the carrying value of the net assets, this could be an indication that internally generated goodwill exists but it is not reliable enough to allow an intangible asset to be included in the accounts. This expenditure is written off to the statement of comprehensive income as it is incurred.

21.1.4 Internally generated intangible asset

For an internally generated intangible asset to be recognised in the financial statements, the item must first meet the detailed criteria set out in IAS 38. The creation of the asset must be separated into:

- a research phase
- a development phase.

If the entity is unable to distinguish between the research and development phases, then the entire expenditure must be recorded as research phase expense.

The accounting treatment for internally generated intangibles is determined first by how research and development activities are defined:

- *Research.* Original and planned investigation undertaken with the prospect of gaining new scientific or technical knowledge and understanding.
- *Development.* The application of research findings or other knowledge to a plan or design for the production of new or substantially improved materials, devices, products, processes, systems or services prior to the commencement of commercial production or use.

Research phase

Expenditure on research should be recognised in the statement of comprehensive income as an expense when it is incurred. It is unlikely that entities could be certain that research expenditure would ultimately create an asset that would generate revenues, capitalisation of research expenditure is not allowed. Only when expenditure creates an asset that can directly be sold or used to make goods that will be sold will recognition be allowable.

Development phase

In the development phase of a project, an entity may be able to identify an intangible asset and demonstrate that it will generate probable future economic benefits. Development activities could include:

- the design and construction of tools involving new technology;
- the design, construction and testing of a chosen alternative for new or improved materials, products, processes or services;
- the design, construction and operation of a pilot plant that is not big enough for commercial production.

An intangible asset should be recognised if, and only if, an entity can demonstrate *all* of the following:

(a) the technical feasibility of completing the intangible asset so that it can be used or sold;

(b) the intention to complete the asset to use it or sell it;

(c) the ability to use or sell the asset;

(d) that the asset will in fact generate probable future economic benefit – does a market exist for the asset if it is to be sold, or can the asset's usefulness be proven if the asset is to be used internally;

(e) that it has the technical, financial and other resources to complete the project to make and use or sell the asset;

(f) that it can measure the expenditure on the development of the asset reliably in order to incorporate the amount in the financial statements.

A detailed business or project plan could be used to illustrate the availability of the entity's resources (point (e) above).

The *cost* of an internally generated intangible asset (point (f) above) can include expenditure such as:

- materials and services used or consumed in generating the intangible asset;
- cost of employee benefits arising from the generation of the intangible asset (wages and salaries);
- other direct costs like patents and licences;
- overheads that were incurred to generate the asset like depreciation on plant, property and equipment used in the process;
- interest charges, as specified in IAS 23 *Borrowing Costs* (see Chapter 18).

Selling and administrative expenses and costs of staff training to use the new product or process are not to be included in establishing the cost of the intangible. Costs can include expenditure incurred from the date that the asset meets all of the above criteria, but cannot include expenditure previously included as an expense in prior years' accounts.

Internally generated brands, mastheads, publishing titles, customer lists and items similar in nature *should not be recognised* as intangibles, as it is unlikely that expenditure on developing such items can be distinguished from expenditure on developing the business as a whole.

Entities may incur other items of expenditure designed to provide future benefits, such as start-up costs (legal costs and product launches), training activities, advertising and promotions; however, no separable item is created and no asset would be recognised. The expenditure would be charged to profit or loss as it was incurred.

21.1.5 Subsequent expenditure

The nature of intangible assets is such that, in many cases, there are no additions to an asset or replacements of part of an asset. Accordingly, most subsequent expenditures are likely to maintain the future economic benefits embodied in an existing intangible asset rather than meet the definition of an intangible asset and the recognition criteria set out in IAS 38. In addition, it is often difficult to attribute subsequent expenditure directly to a particular intangible asset rather than to the business as a whole. Therefore, only rarely will subsequent expenditure – expenditure incurred after the initial recognition of a purchased intangible asset or after completion of an internally generated intangible asset – be recognised in the carrying amount of an asset.

After initial recognition at cost, intangible assets should be carried at cost less any accumulated amortisation or impairment losses.

21.1.6 Subsequent measurement

IAS 38 allows intangible non-current assets to be carried at amortised cost or at revalued amount, being its fair value at the date of the revaluation less any subsequent accumulated amortisation and any subsequent accumulated impairment losses. For the purpose of revaluations under IAS 38, fair value should be determined by reference to an active market. IAS 38 suggests that there will not usually be an active market in an intangible asset, therefore the revaluation model will not be used. Revaluations should be made with sufficient regularity such that the carrying amount does not differ materially from that which would be determined using fair value at the end of the reporting period.

If an intangible asset is revalued, all the other assets in its class should also be revalued, unless there is no active market for those assets. If an intangible asset in a class of revalued intangible assets cannot be revalued because there is no active market for this asset, the asset should be carried at its cost less any accumulated amortisation and impairment losses.

If the fair value of a revalued intangible asset can no longer be determined by reference to an active market, the carrying amount of the asset should be its revalued amount at the date of the last revaluation by reference to the active market less any subsequent accumulated amortisation and any subsequent accumulated impairment losses.

If an intangible asset's carrying amount is increased as a result of a revaluation, the increase shall be recognised in other comprehensive income and accumulated in equity under the heading of revaluation surplus. However, the increase shall be recognised in profit or loss to the extent that it reverses a revaluation decrease of the same asset previously recognised in profit or loss.

If an intangible asset's carrying amount is decreased as a result of a revaluation, the decrease is recognised in profit or loss unless the intangible asset has previously been revalued. If an intangible non-current asset has previously been revalued upwards, any decrease in value can be recognised in other comprehensive income and deducted from the heading of revaluation surplus in equity, to the extent of any credit balance existing in the revaluation surplus in respect of that asset. The decrease recognised in comprehensive income reduces the amount accumulated in equity under the heading of revaluation surplus.

The cumulative revaluation surplus included in equity may be transferred directly to retained earnings when the surplus is realised. The whole surplus may be realised on the retirement or disposal of the asset. However, some of the surplus may be realised as the asset is used by the entity; each year, the amount of the surplus realised is the difference between amortisation based on the revalued carrying amount of the asset and amortisation that would have been recognised based on the asset's historical cost. The transfer from revaluation surplus to retained earnings is made through the statement of changes in equity.

21.1.7 Amortisation

The depreciable amount of an intangible asset should be allocated on a systematic basis over the best estimate of its useful life. Amortisation should start from the date the asset is available for use.

As with tangible assets, the most difficult decision for management is determining the useful life of the asset. The useful life of an intangible asset should take account of such things as:

- the expected usage of the asset;
- possible obsolescence and expected actions by competitors;
- the stability of the industry;
- market demand for the products and services that the asset is generating.

The method of amortising the asset should reflect the pattern in which the assets' economic benefits are expected to be consumed by the entity. If that proves difficult to determine, then the straight-line method is acceptable. The residual value of the intangible should be assumed to be zero unless there is a commitment from a third party to purchase the asset or the entity intends to sell the asset and a readily available active market exists. The annual amortisation amount will be charged to profit or loss as an expense.

The useful life and method of amortisation should be reviewed at least at each financial year-end. Changes to useful life or method of amortisation should be effective as soon as they are identified and should be accounted for as changes in accounting estimates (IAS 8), by adjusting the amortisation charge for the current and future periods.

21.1.8 Impairment losses

The treatment for impairment of assets is dealt with by IAS 36, *Impairment of Assets*. In addition to the requirements of IAS 36 (discussed in Section 21.3), an entity should estimate the recoverable amount of intangibles at least at every year-end, including assets that are not yet available for use.

21.1.9 Retirements and disposals

An intangible asset should be removed from the statement of financial position on disposal or when no future economic benefits are expected from its use or future disposal. Any gains or losses from disposal (the difference between the net proceeds and the carrying value of the asset) should be recognised as income or expense in the statement of comprehensive income. Amortisation ceases when the asset is derecognised or is designated as 'held for sale' in accordance with IFRS 5.

21.1.10 Disclosure

The financial statements should disclose the following for each class of intangible assets, distinguishing between internally generated intangible assets and other intangible assets:

(a) the useful lives or amortisation rates used;
(b) the amortisation methods used;
(c) the gross carrying amount and the accumulated amortisation (together with accumulated impairment losses) at the beginning and end of the period;
(d) the amount of amortisation charged to the statement of comprehensive income;
(e) a reconciliation of the carrying amount at the beginning and the end of the period showing:
  - additions (internally developed assets and acquisitions);
  - retirements and disposals;

- changes to the intangible assets due to revaluations, impairment losses and other changes;
- impairment losses recognised and reversed in profit or loss;
- amortisation recognised during the period.

In addition, an entity must disclose details of any intangible given an indefinite useful life and any individual intangible that is material to the financial statements as a whole.

If intangible assets are carried at revalued amounts, the following should be disclosed:

(a) by class of intangible assets:

     (i) the effective date of the revaluation;

     (ii) the carrying amount of revalued intangible assets;

(b) the amount of the revaluation surplus that relates to intangible assets at the beginning and end of the period, indicating the changes during the period and any restrictions on the distribution of the balance to shareholders;

(c) the methods and significant assumptions applied in estimating the assets' fair values.

21.2 Purchased goodwill

IFRS 3 Business combinations regulates the treatment of purchased goodwill.

Goodwill arises on the acquisition of an entity or an entity's assets or assets and liabilities. IFRS 3 defines purchased goodwill as *future economic benefits arising from assets that are not capable of being individually and separately recognised.'* Purchased goodwill is calculated as *'excess of the cost of acquisition over the acquirer's interest in the fair value of the identifiable net assets and liabilities acquired as at the date of the transaction.'* The excess payment is made in anticipation of future economic benefits arising from the acquisition.

The IFRS 3 definition can give rise to 'positive goodwill' where the purchase consideration exceeds the fair value of the net assets, or negative goodwill where the fair value of the net assets exceeds the purchase consideration.

IFRS 3 requires positive goodwill to be recognised as an asset and recorded on the statement of financial position as an asset.

21.2.1 Purchased goodwill – recognition and measurement

Positive goodwill should be recognised as an asset and carried at cost less any accumulated impairment losses (IFRS 3).

IFRS 3 requires that the entity carries out annual assessments of the recoverable amount of the goodwill to identify any impairment losses arising each year. These impairment losses are recognised instead of amortisation.

21.2.2 Negative purchased goodwill

Negative purchased goodwill is conceptually the equivalent of a discount on the purchase price. When negative goodwill arises, IFRS 3 emphasises the need to check that the correct fair values of the assets and liabilities acquired have been used in the calculation of the goodwill figure.

Negative goodwill is credited to the statement of comprehensive income in the year of acquisition.

21.3 IAS 36 *Impairment of Assets*

21.3.1 Introduction

Your syllabus requires only knowledge of the principles of IAS 36.

The object of IAS 36 is to ensure that an entity does not carry its assets at a value above their recoverable amount. (Recoverable amount means the higher of an asset's net selling price and its value in use.)

21.3.2 Procedures to check for impairment

At the end of each reporting period an entity should assess whether there are internal or external indications that the value of any asset is impaired.

In assessing whether there is any indication that an asset may be impaired, an entity shall consider, as a minimum, the following indications:

External sources of information:

(a) during the period, an asset's market value has declined significantly more than would be expected as a result of the passage of time or normal use;
(b) significant changes with an adverse effect on the entity have taken place during the period, or will take place in the near future, in the technological, market, economic or legal environment in which the entity operates or in the market to which an asset is dedicated;
(c) market interest rates or other market rates of return on investments have increased during the period, and those increases are likely to affect the discount rate used in calculating an asset's value in use and decrease the asset's recoverable amount materially;
(d) the carrying amount of the net assets of the reporting entity is more than its market capitalisation.

Internal sources of information:

(a) evidence is available of obsolescence or physical damage of an asset;
(b) significant changes with an adverse effect on the entity have taken place during the period, or are expected to take place in the near future, in the extent to which, or manner in which, an asset is used or is expected to be used. These changes include the asset becoming idle, plans to discontinue or restructure the operation to which an asset belongs, and plans to dispose of an asset before the previously expected date;
(c) evidence is available from internal reporting that indicates that the economic performance of an asset is, or will be, worse than expected.

21.3.3 Recognition and measurement of an impairment loss

An impairment review follows the long-established principle that an asset's statement of financial position carrying value should not exceed its recoverable amount, which is measured by reference to the future cash flows that can be generated from its continued use or disposal. An asset is impaired when the carrying amount of the asset exceeds its recoverable amount.

If any of the indications listed in Section 21.3.2 are present, an entity is required to make a formal estimate of recoverable amount. If no indication of a potential impairment loss is present, there is no requirement to make a formal estimate of recoverable amount.

If the carrying value of an asset is in fact less than the recoverable amount, the shortfall (an impairment loss) must be recognised in the statement of comprehensive income as an expense. The only exception to this is that an impairment loss on an asset that has previously been revalued may be recognised in other comprehensive income, up to the amount of the surplus relating to that asset, any additional impairment is then recognised in the statement of comprehensive income.

An asset's recoverable amount is defined in IAS 36 as the higher of an asset's net selling price and value in use. Net selling price is the asset's market price less the costs of disposal. Calculating the asset's value in use involves the following steps:

(a) estimating the future cash inflows and outflows to be derived from continuing use of the asset and from its ultimate disposal;
(b) applying the appropriate discount rate to these future cash flows.

It is not always necessary to determine both an asset's net selling price and its value in use. For example, if either of these amounts exceeds the asset's carrying amount, the asset is not impaired and it is not necessary to estimate the other amount. It may be possible to determine net selling price, even if an asset is not traded in an active market. However, sometimes it will not be possible to determine net selling price because there is no basis for making a reliable estimate of the amount obtainable from the sale of the asset in an arm's length transaction between knowledgeable and willing parties. In this case, the recoverable amount of the asset may be taken to be its value in use.

If there is no reason to believe that an asset's value in use materially exceeds its net selling price, the asset's recoverable amount may be taken to be its net selling price.

Recoverable amount is determined for an individual asset, unless the asset does not generate cash inflows from continuing use that are largely independent of those from other assets or groups of assets. If this is the case, recoverable amount is determined for the cash-generating unit to which the asset belongs.

The carrying amount of a cash-generating unit:

(a) includes the carrying amount of only those assets that can be attributed directly, or allocated on a reasonable and consistent basis, to the cash-generating unit and that will generate the future cash inflows estimated in determining the cash-generating unit's value in use. It is important to include in the cash-generating unit all assets that generate the relevant stream of cash inflows from continuing use. In some cases, certain assets contribute to the estimated future cash flows of a cash-generating unit, need to be allocated to the cash-generating unit on a reasonable and consistent basis. This might be the case for goodwill or corporate assets such as head office assets;
(b) does not include the carrying amount of any recognised liability, unless the recoverable amount of the cash-generating unit cannot be determined without consideration of this liability.

In outline, the stages of an impairment review are:

- identifying separate cash-generating units;
- establishing a statement of financial position for each cash-generating unit, comprising the net tangible and intangible assets plus allocated purchased goodwill for each cash-generating unit;

- forecasting the future cash flows of the cash-generating unit and discounting them to present value using the rate of return the market would expect for an equally risky investment;
- comparing the present value of the cash flows with the net assets of each cash-generating unit and recognising any shortfall as an impairment loss;
- allocating any impairment loss to write down the assets of the cash-generating unit. Any impairment is allocated first, to goodwill allocated to the cash-generating unit (if any); and then, to the other assets of the unit on a pro-rata basis based on the carrying amount of each asset in the unit.

In allocating an impairment loss, the carrying amount of an asset should not be reduced below the highest of:

(a) its net selling price (if determinable)
(b) its value in use (if determinable)
(c) zero.

Example 21.A

An asset costing $100,000 when purchased on 1 January 2001 has an estimated useful life of 10 years. On 1 January 2004, the asset is estimated to have a recoverable amount of $50,000.

The assets carrying value on 1 January 2004 is cost $100,000 less accumulated depreciation of $30,000 ($10,000 × 3 years).

The $20,000 impairment in value will be charged as an expense to statement of comprehensive income.

		$	$
Debit	Profit or loss – impairment loss	20,000	
Credit	Net book value of asset		20,000

Being impairment loss reducing asset value from $70,000 to $50,000.

Future depreciation expense will be based on the new value of $50,000 – note, however, the estimated useful life of the asset has not changed, so the depreciation will be calculated as $50,000 over the remaining seven years = $7,143.

Example 21.B

Using the same asset as in Example 21.A, let us assume the asset was revalued to $110,000 on 1 January 2003. This created a revaluation surplus of $30,000, being $110,000 less the carrying value of the asset ($100,000 − $20,000).

If on 1 January 2004 the asset is estimated to have a recoverable amount of $90,000, then the impairment loss of $9,000 (recoverable amount ($110,000 − $11,000 = $99,000 − $90,000 = $9,000)) will be recognised in other comprehensive income and deducted from the revaluation reserve, reducing the amount in respect of this asset.

		$	$
Debit	Revaluation reserve	9,000	
Credit	Net book value of asset	9,000	

Being the recording of the impairment loss.

If the revaluation surplus did not have sufficient amounts relating to this specific asset, then the balance of the impairment loss would be charged to profit or loss.

21.4 Disclosure of impairments

For each class of assets, the financial statements should disclose:

(a) the amount of impairment losses recognised in the statement of comprehensive income during the period and the line item(s) of the statement of comprehensive income in which those impairment losses are included;

(b) the amount of reversals of impairment losses recognised in the statement of comprehensive income during the period and the line item(s) of the statement of comprehensive income in which those impairment losses are reversed;

(c) the amount of impairment losses recognised in other comprehensive income during the period;

(d) the amount of reversals of impairment losses recognised in other comprehensive income during the period.

21.5 Summary

Having completed this chapter, we can discuss the recognition and valuation of intangible assets, including purchased goodwill, internally generated goodwill and research and development costs. We can explain the requirement to amortise goodwill and can discuss the criteria for the capitalisation of development costs. We can also explain the main disclosure requirements in respect of intangible assets.

We can explain the principle of impairment of assets and can record the effect of impairment losses on assets.

Revision Questions

21

? Question 1

When can internally developed intangible assets be capitalised? (*max. 35 words*)

(2 marks)

? Question 2

When should a full impairment review be carried out?

(A) When circumstances indicate that an impairment may have occurred
(B) When the directors want to reduce the value of their assets
(C) When the book value of assets seems too high
(D) Every 5 years

(2 marks)

? Question 3

Purchased goodwill is defined by IAS 38 as:

(A) The amount paid for intangible assets
(B) The difference between the statement of financial position value and the amount paid for the business
(C) The difference between the fair value of the tangible non-current assets acquired and the amount paid
(D) The difference between the cost of the acquisition and the fair values of the net assets acquired

(2 marks)

? Question 4

Which of the following can be capitalised and carried forward in the statement of financial position as an asset:

(A) a payment of $10,000 to XY University for original research
(B) $50,000 spent on applied research to develop a new discovery into a possible new product
(C) $22,000 being the cost of developing a new product for final launch on the market. The product is expected to be profitable
(D) $17,000 the cost of developing a product that was then found to be non-viable

(2 marks)

Question 5

IAS 38 specifies criteria that must be met before development expenditure can be deferred:

1. the technical feasibility of completing the project so that the asset can be used;
2. the project has a useful economic life of more than 1 year;
3. the ability to use the asset;
4. total deferred expenditure is less than 10% of turnover;
5. financial resources are sufficient to complete the project and use the asset;
6. adequate resources exist to complete the project and make use of the asset.

Which of the above criteria are included in IAS 36 requirements to defer development expenditure?

(A) 1, 2, 3 and 4
(B) 1, 2, 4 and 5
(C) 1, 3, 5 and 6
(D) 2, 3, 4 and 6   (**2 marks**)

 Question 6

The following measures relate to a non-current asset:

(i) Net book value $20,000
(ii) Net realisable value $18,000
(iii) Value in use $22,000
(iv) Replacement cost $50,000

The recoverable amount of the asset is

(A) $18,000
(B) $20,000
(C) $22,000
(D) $50,000   (**2 marks**)

 Question 7

BI owns a building which it uses as its offices, warehouse and garage. The land is carried as a separate non-current tangible asset in the statement of financial position.

BI has a policy of regularly revaluing its non-current tangible assets. The original cost of the building in October 2002 was $1,000,000; it was assumed to have a remaining useful life of 20 years at that date, with no residual value. The building was revalued on 30 September 2004 by a professional valuer at $1,800,000.

BI also owns a brand name which it acquired 1 October 2000 for $500,000. The brand name is being amortised over 10 years.

The economic climate had deteriorated during 2005, causing BI to carry out an impairment review of its assets at 30 September 2005. BI's building was valued at a market value of $1,500,000 on 30 September 2005 by an independent valuer. A brand specialist valued BI's brand name at market value of $200,000 on the same date.

BI's management accountant calculated that the brand name's value in use at 30 September 2005 was $150,000.

Requirement

Explain how BI should report the events described above and quantify any amounts required to be included in its financial statements for the year ended 30 September 2005.

(5 marks)

 **Question 8**

CD is a manufacturing entity that runs a number of operations including a bottling plant that bottles carbonated soft drinks. CD has been developing a new bottling process that will allow the bottles to be filled and sealed more efficiently.

The new process took a year to develop. At the start of development, CD estimated that the new process would increase output by 15% with no additional cost (other than the extra bottles and their contents). Development work commenced on 1 May 2005 and was completed on 20 April 2006. Testing at the end of the development confirmed CD's original estimates.

CD incurred an expenditure of $180,000 on the above development in 2005/06.

CD plans to install the new process in its bottling plant and start operating the new process from 1 May 2006.

The end of CD's reporting period is 30 April.

Requirements

(i) Explain the requirements of IAS 38 *Intangible Assets* for the treatment of development costs **(3 marks)**

(ii) Explain how CD should treat its development costs in its financial statements for the year ended 30 April 2006. **(2 marks)**

(Total = 5 marks)

Scenario for Questions 9 and 10

T manufactures radar equipment for military and civil aircraft. The entity's latest trial balance as at 31 December 20X1 is as follows:

	$'000	$'000
Administrative costs	800	
Bank overdraft		700
Receivables	2,000	
Factory – cost	18,000	
Factory – depreciation		1,800
Factory running costs	1,200	
Loan interest	1,680	
Long-term loans		12,000
Machinery – cost	13,000	
Machinery – depreciation		8,000
Manufacturing wages	1,300	
Opening inventory – parts and materials	400	
Opening inventory – work in progress	900	
Retained earnings		380
Purchases – parts and materials	2,300	
Research and development	5,300	
Sales revenue		1,000
Sales salaries	600	
Share capital		15,000
Trade payables		600
Trade fair costs	1,000	
	48,480	48,480

(i) The inventory was counted at 31 December 20X1. Closing inventories of parts and materials were valued at $520,000 and closing inventories of work in progress were valued at $710,000. There are no inventories of finished goods because all production is for specific customer orders and goods are usually shipped as soon as they are completed.

(ii) No depreciation has been charged for the year ended 31 December 20X1. The entity depreciates the factory at 2 per cent of cost per annum and all machinery at 25 per cent per annum on the reducing balance basis.

(iii) The balance on the research and development account is made up as follows:

	$
Opening balance (development costs brought forward)	2,100,000
Calibrating equipment purchased for laboratory	600,000
Long-range radar project	900,000
Wide-angle microwave project	1,700,000
	5,300,000

The opening balance comprises expenditure on new products which have just been introduced to the market. The entity has decided that these costs should be written off over 10 years, starting with the year ended 31 December 20X1. T has a policy of capitalising all development costs which meet the criteria laid down by IAS 38.

The new calibrating equipment is used in the entity's research laboratory. It is used to ensure that the measurement devices used during experiments are properly adjusted.

The long-range radar project is intended to adapt existing military radar technology for civilian air traffic control purposes. The entity has built a successful prototype and has had strong expressions of interest from a number of potential customers. It is almost certain that the entity will start to sell this product early in the year 20X3 and that it will make a profit.

The wide-angle microwave project is an attempt to apply some theoretical concepts to create a new radar system for use in fighter aircraft. Initial experiments have been promising, but there is little immediate prospect of a saleable product because the transmitter is far too large and heavy to install in an aeroplane.

(iv) During the year the entity spent $1,000,000 in order to exhibit its product range at a major trade fair. This was the first time that T had attended such an event. No orders have been received as a direct result of this fair, although the sales director has argued that contacts were made, which will generate sales over the next few years.

(v) T has made losses for tax purposes for several years. It does not expect to pay any tax for the year ended 31 December 20X1.

The directors do not plan to pay any dividends for the year ended 31 December 20X1.

? Question 9

(a) Prepare T's statement of comprehensive income for the year ended 31 December 20X1 and its statement of financial position at that date. These should be in a form suitable for publication.

Do *not* prepare notes to the accounts except for those required in part (b).

Do *not* prepare a statement of accounting policies or a statement of changes in equity.

(b) Prepare the following notes to T's accounts:
  (i) Intangible non-current assets
  (ii) Tangible non-current assets

(20 marks)

? Question 10

(a) Explain how each of the following items should be treated in T's financial statements:
  Research and development
  (i) New calibrating equipment purchased for laboratory **(3 marks)**
  (ii) Long-range radar project **(4 marks)**
  (iii) Wide-angle microwave project **(4 marks)**
(b) Explain how the costs associated with the trade fair should be treated in T's financial statements. **(4 marks)**
(c) The directors of T have read that the calculation of an entity's profit figure involves a great deal of subjective judgement and that some entities increase or decrease their profits by biasing the subjective decisions which are associated with accounting. Explain how T's chief accountant should respond if the directors ask for the financial statements to be restated in a manner which makes the entity appear to be more profitable than it actually is. **(5 marks)**
(Total marks = 20)

? Question 11

Z acquired the business and assets of Q, a sole trader, on 31 October 2002.
  The fair value of the assets acquired from Q were:

	$'000
Non-current intangible assets	
Brand X – brand name	220
Non-current tangible assets	
Plant and equipment	268
Inventory	5
	493
Cash paid to Q	523

Z spent the following amounts creating and promoting the Brand Z brand name:

Year to 31 October 2000	$100,000
Year to 31 October 2001	$90,000
Year to 31 October 2002	$80,000

Z's accounting policy on recognised non-current intangible assets in that brand names are amortised over 10 years.
  On 31 October 2003, Z's brand names were valued by an independent valuer as follows:

Brand X at $250,000
Brand Z at $300,000

The directors of Z have been very impressed with the increase in profits from Q's former business. They are certain that the goodwill has increased since they acquired Q's business. Z's directors have estimated that the goodwill is worth $45,000 at 31 October 2003.

Requirements

Explain how Z should treat:

(i) the brand names;   **(9 marks)**
(ii) goodwill;   **(6 marks)**
 in its financial statements for the years ended 31 October 2002 and 2003. Your explanation should include reference to relevant International Accounting Standards.

(Total marks = 15)

Solutions to Revision Questions

☑ Solution 1

Internally developed intangible assets can be capitalised if during the development the entity is able to identify that the development expenditure will enable the generation of probable future economic benefits.

☑ Solution 2

The correct answer is (A), see Section 21.3.2.

☑ Solution 3

The correct answer is (D), see Section 21.2.

☑ Solution 4

The correct answer is (C), see Section 21.1.4.

This specification could meet the requirements of IAS 38 to enable development expenditure to be carried forward to future periods.

☑ Solution 5

The correct answer is (C), see Section 21.1.4.

☑ Solution 6

The correct answer is (C), see Section 21.3.3.

 **Solution 7**

Workings

	$
October 2002 Original cost 1,000,000	
Depreciation 2002/03 (1,000,000/20)	(50,000)
	950,000
Depreciation 2003/04	(50,000)
	900,000
Revalued 30 September 2004, gain	900,000
	1,800,000
Depreciation 2004/05 (1,800,000/18)	(100,000)
	1,700,000
Revalued 30 September 2005	1,500,000
Loss on revaluation	200,000

IAS 16 *Property, Plant and Equipment* requires the $200,000 loss on revaluation shown in the statement of comprehensive income and deducted from the revaluation reserve. It does not go to profit or loss as the building has been previously revalued and the gain is more than the current loss. The buildings will be shown in the statement of financial position at $1,500,000 and be depreciated over the remaining 17 years.

The brand name acquired for $500,000 5 years ago. Net book value at 30 September 2005 is $500,000 × 5/10 = $250,000. The brand name's market value is $200,000 and its value in use is $150,000.

A non-current asset is valued at the higher of its market value or value in use (IAS 36 *Impairment of Assets*). Therefore, the brand names carrying amount should be adjusted to $200,000 and $50,000 written off to the statement of comprehensive income for the year to 30 September 2005, see Section 21.3.3.

 Solution 8

(i) Development expenditure could be regarded as an intangible asset. IAS 38 only allows an intangible asset to be recognised if, and only if, an entity can demonstrate all of the following:

- the technical feasibility of completing the intangible asset so that it can be used or sold;
- the intention to complete the asset to use it or sell it;
- the ability to use or sell the asset;
- that the asset will in fact generate probable future economic benefit – does a market exist for the asset if it is to be sold, or can the asset's usefulness be proven if the asset is to be used internally;
- that it has the technical, financial and other resources to complete the project to make and use or sell the asset;
- that it can measure the expenditure on the development of the asset reliably in order to incorporate the amount in the financial statements.

(ii) All of the above criteria seem to have been met by CD's new process:

- it is technically feasible, it has been tested and is about to be implemented;
- it has been completed and CD intends to use it;

- the new process is estimated to increase output by 15% with no additional costs other than direct material costs;
- the expenditure can be measured as the figures have been given.

CD will treat the $180,000 development cost as an intangible non-current asset in its statement of financial position at 30 April 2006. Amortisation will start from 1 May 2006 when the new process starts operation, see Section 21.1.4.2.

Solution 9

(a) **T – statement of comprehensive income for the year ended 31 December 20X1**

	Notes	$'000
Sales revenue		10,000
Cost of sales		(8,540)
Gross profit		1,460
Selling and distribution costs		(1,600)
Administrative expenses		(800)
Loss from operations	1	(940)
Finance cost		(1,680)
Retained Loss for the year		(2,620)
Other comprehensive income		0
Total comprehensive income for the year		(2,620)

T – statement of financial position at 31 December 20X1

	Notes	$'000	$'000
Non-current assets			
Intangible non-current assets	2		2,790
Tangible non-current assets	3		20,040
			22,830
Current assets			
Inventory	4	1,230	
Receivables		2,000	
			3,230
			26,060
Share Capital and reserves			
Issued capital			15,000
Retained earnings			(2,240)
			12,760
Non-current liabilities			
Long-term loans			12,000
Current liabilities			
Bank overdraft		700	
Trade payables		600	
			1,300
			26,060

NON-CURRENT INTANGIBLE ASSETS

(b) *T – notes to the financial statements*
Intangible non-current assets

	Cost $'000	Amortisation $'000	Net book value $'000
Development expenditure			
At 1 January 20X1	2,100	–	2,100
Additions	900	–	900
Amortised in the year	–	(210)	(210)
At 31 December 20X1	3,000	(210)	2,790

T has capitalised these development costs in order to match them with anticipated revenue. Development costs of $2,100,000 are being written off over 10 years. The balance of costs are not yet being amortised, as commercial production has not yet commenced.

Tangible non-current assets

	Land and buildings $'000	Plant and machinery $'000	Total $'000
Cost at 1.1.20X1	18,000	13,000	31,000
Additions	–	600	600
Cost at 31.12.20X1	18,000	13,600	31,600
Depreciation at 1.1.20X1	1,800	8,000	9,800
Charge for the year	360	1,400	1,760
Depreciation at 31.12.20X1	2,160	9,400	11,560
Net book value at 31.12.20X1	15,840	4,200	20,040
Net book value at 1.1.20X1	16,200	5,000	21,200

Workings

	$'000
Cost of sales	
Opening inventory – parts and materials	400
Opening inventory – work in progress	900
Purchases	2,300
	3,600
Closing inventory – parts and materials	(520)
Closing inventory – work in progress	(710)
	2,370
Depreciation – factory (18,000 × 2%)	360
Depreciation – machinery ((13,000 + 600 − 8,000) × 25%)	1,400
Factory running costs	1,200
Manufacturing wages	1,300
Research costs written off	1,700
Amortisation of development costs (2,100 × 10%)	210
	8,540

	$'000
Selling and distribution costs	
Sales salaries	600
Trade fair costs	1,000
	1,600

☑ Solution 10

(a) (i) The cost of assets acquired to provide facilities for research and development (R&D) should be capitalised and depreciated over their useful lives, and included as part of the R&D expense. Where an asset is used in development activities, the depreciation can be included as development costs and capitalised. The new calibrating equipment purchased for the laboratory is an asset which will be used on various projects, not solely R&D projects. Because the various projects on which it will be used cannot be identified, the machine should be classed as a tangible non-current asset. It should be depreciated in the same way as T's existing machinery.

(ii) The long-range radar project satisfies the criteria stated in IAS 38, which requires R&D expenditure to be deferred to future periods. The project is clearly defined, and its related expenditure is separately identifiable. The outcome of the project has been assessed as technically feasible and commercially viable, and is expected to make a profit. The costs should therefore be included in the statement of financial position as an intangible non-current asset, and amortised when commercial production commences.

(iii) The outcome of the wide-angle microwave project is much less certain. The project may be commercially successful, but it is too early to be sure. IAS 38 does not allow expenditure of this kind to be deferred to future periods. The costs must be written off in statement of comprehensive income as they are incurred. This is because certain expenditure can be regarded as part of the continuing operation required to maintain a entity's business and competitive position. It is also in accordance with the fundamental accounting concept of prudence.

(b) Given that there are no specific accounting standards governing the accounting treatment of the trade fair, T should turn to the IASB Framework. If the costs are carried forward, they need to meet the definition of an asset set out in the Framework. An asset must have future economic benefit to the entity. Since there is no indication of any increase in future sales revenue, the trade fair cost does not seem to have any future economic benefit. It should therefore be treated as an expense not an asset.

Because the cost is significant, and not a normal part of selling and distribution, it should be disclosed separately in a note to the statement of comprehensive income.

(c) Financial statements must be prepared in accordance with accounting standards. It is sometimes possible for an entity to adhere to the *letter* of the law while failing to comply with the *spirit* of the law. The most important requirement is that the accounts show a true and fair view. Thus, even if the directors of T have come up with a creative accounting scheme which does not appear to break any accounting rules or legislation, the chief accountant should explain to the directors that the financial statements must be adjusted to show a true and fair view of the entity's profitability.

The accountant could perhaps ask for the support of T's external auditor, who could explain that any material distortion of the accounts would inevitably lead to a qualified audit report.

Solution 11

(i) Brand names

Purchase of Brand X brand name

A brand *name* is an intangible non-current asset. Intangible non-current assets are covered by IAS 38 *Intangible Assets.*

IAS 38 allows purchased intangible non-current assets to be recognised in the financial statements, if it is probable that future economic benefits will flow from the assets and if their value can be measured reliably at the date of purchase. As a value has been given for the brand X, it is reasonable to assume that its value can be measured reliably. The brand name 'Brand X' should be recognised in the statement of financial position at $220,000 at 31 October 2002 and amortised over its useful economic life of 10 years. $22,000 per year will be charged to the statement of comprehensive income.

The entity must carry out an impairment review at the end of the first financial year after the acquisition, and consider whether the performance of the entity, after the acquisition of the brand, has improved in line with expectations.

Internally generated brand names. Brand Z is an internally generated brand name. Some types of internally generated intangible non-current assets can be recognised in the statement of financial position if they meet specific criteria; however, IAS 38 specifically states that internally generated brand names should not be recognised as assets under any circumstances.

All expenditure will be charged to profit or loss in the year it was incurred.

(ii) *Goodwill*

Purchased goodwill from Q. Purchased goodwill is the price paid over and above the fair value of the assets acquired.

	$'000
Assets acquired (including brand)	493
Cash paid	523
Goodwill	30

Positive purchased goodwill of $30,000 will be recognised in the statement of financial position at cost at 31 October 2002. Annual impairment reviews will be carried out as required by IFRS 3 *Business Combinations* but no amortisation will be provided.

Increase in value of purchased goodwill. IFRS 3 does not allow goodwill to be revalued upwards, so no action should be taken on the directors' valuation. Purchased goodwill will gradually be replaced by self-generated goodwill, so the increase in the valuation is due to internally generated goodwill arising since the acquisition. IFRS 3 specifically forbids the capitalisation of internally generated goodwill.

22

Share Capital
Transactions

Share Capital Transactions

22

LEARNING OUTCOME

After completing this chapter, you should be able to:

▶ explain the accounting rules contained in IFRS's and IAS's governing share capital transactions.

The syllabus topics covered in this chapter are as follows:

• Issue and redemption of shares, including treatment of share issue and redemption costs (IAS 32 and IAS 39), the share premium account, the accounting for maintenance of capital arising from the purchase by a entity of its own shares.

22.1 Introduction

This chapter deals with the accounting entries in respect of the issue and redemption of shares. You could view this as a series of journal entries which have to be learned by rote. This would, however, make the topic much more difficult and certainly far less interesting than it can be. Try to understand the principles involved, you will then be able to work out the journals required, rather than try to memorise them.

This topic is usually governed by local legal requirements that relate to the entity together with IFRS requirements. Countries differ in their legislation governing the issue and redemption of shares. From an international standpoint, it is thus possible only to consider the general principles and the requirements of international accounting standards. IAS 32 *Financial Instruments: Disclosure and Presentation* and IAS 39 *Financial Instruments: Recognition and Measurement* both deal with share and debt classification, presentation, measurement and treatment in the financial statements. These two standards are very long and complex standards that cover a wide range of possibilities relating to financial instruments. As part of your syllabus, you are only required to have a knowledge of the accounting rules governing share capital transactions, the rules relating to debt are outside the syllabus.

22.2 IAS 1 requirements

22.2.1 Interests of shareholders

The notes to an entity's financial statements contain a detailed note about the entity's share capital. This is hardly surprising given that the shareholders are regarded as the primary audience for the published accounts. They are the owners of the entity and need to be able to see how their ownership interests are reflected in the statement of financial position. They need to know how their interests might be affected by the issue of new shares.

A new issue will raise funds which will increase the value of their existing shares if the proceeds are invested wisely. This will, however, dilute their control. They also need to know about the interests of the other shareholders. In particular, they need to know how the existence of different classes of shares might affect their interests.

22.2.2 Disclosures

We studied the requirements of IAS 1 *Presentation of Financial Statements* in detail in Chapter 7. The following disclosures are required by the standard in respect of share capital.

IAS 1 requires that, issued capital and reserves attributable to owners must be shown in the statement of financial position. In addition, IAS 1 requires that, in the statement of financial position or in the notes, equity capital and reserves are analysed showing separately the various classes of paid-in capital, share premium and reserves.

IAS 1 also requires that the following information on share capital and reserves be made available either in the statement of financial position or in the notes:

(a) for each class of share capital:
- the number of shares authorised;
- the number of shares issued and fully paid, and issued but not fully paid;
- par value per share, or that the shares have no par value;
- a reconciliation of the number of shares outstanding at the beginning and at the end of the year;
- the rights, preferences and restrictions attaching to that class including restrictions on the distribution of dividends and the repayment of capital;
- shares in the entity held by the entity itself; and
- shares reserved for issuance under options and sales contracts, including the terms and amounts.

(b) a description of the nature and purpose of each reserve within equity.

IAS 1 requires the following to be disclosed in the notes:
(a) the amount of dividends proposed or declared before the financial statements were authorised for issue, but not recognised as a distribution to owners during the period, and the related amount per share;
(b) the amount of any cumulative preference dividends not recognised.

Example 22.A

Some extracts from the annual report of an imaginary entity quoted on the local stock exchange are shown below.

You are required to read through the extracts and answer the following questions.

1. How many additional shares of each class can the entity's directors issue?
2. What was the selling price of the new shares issued by the entity?
3. What differences are there likely to be between the preference and ordinary shares?

Statement of financial position

	Notes	20X7 $m	20X6 $m
Issued share capital*	23	1,353.7	1,345.2
Share premium account		320.0	310.0
Reserves		2,200.0	2,050.0
		3,873.7	3,705.2

Notes
* Issued share capital

	20X7 $m	20X6 $m
Authorised		
6,000,000,000 ordinary shares of 25¢ each	1,500.0	1,500.0
700,000 7.0% cumulative preference shares of $1 each	0.7	0.7
2,000,000 4.9% cumulative preference shares of $1 each	2.0	2.0
	1,502.7	1,502.7
Issued and fully paid		
5,400,000,000 ordinary shares of 25¢ each	1,350.0	1,342.5
700,000 7.0% cumulative preference shares of $1 each	0.7	0.7
2,000,000 4.9% cumulative preference shares of $1 each	2.0	2.0
	1,353.7	1,345.2

Solution

During the year, the entity issued 30,000,000 ordinary shares with a nominal value of $7,500,000. The aggregate consideration raised was $17,500,000.

The entity has three classes of shares. The directors are authorised to issue up to 6 billion ordinary shares, 700,000 7.0 per cent preference shares and 2 million 4.9 per cent preference shares. They can, therefore, issue a further 0.6 billion ordinary shares without seeking the permission of the shareholders. They can ask the shareholders to increase this limit by changing the internal regulations. The two types of preference shares are at their authorised limits and so the internal regulations would have to be changed before any further issues could be made.

The entity raised $17.5 million from a sale of 30 million shares. The shares must have been sold for 58.3 cents each. The shares have a nominal value of 25 cents each, although their value on the stock market is determined by the market's expectations of the entity's future profitability. In this case, the directors have been able to sell the shares at a premium of 58.3 − 25 = 33.3¢.

22.3   Different classes of shares

There are several different dimensions that can be used to describe and classify share capital. These include:

- authorised versus issued
- nominal value versus issue price
- specific classes of shares, as described in the entity's internal regulations
- equity versus non-equity.

The precise rights attached to each class of shares is a matter for the entity's internal regulations. The usual differences can be summed up as follows:

	Ordinary shares	Preference shares
Voting rights	Ordinary shareholders almost always have the right to vote at general meetings, although some entities issue both voting and non-voting ordinary shares	Preference shareholders would not normally have any voting rights
Rewards	The ordinary dividend is decided by the directors. The ordinary shareholders are entitled to all of the profits after all other claims have been met. Any profits which are not distributed as a dividend will increase the ordinary shareholders' equity	The preference dividend is usually fixed (e.g. 7.0 per cent of nominal value). The directors may, however, be able to suspend the preference dividend if the entity could not afford to pay it. In this case, the directors will probably be required to suspend the ordinary dividend. If the preference shares are 'cumulative', then any unpaid preference dividend will be paid once the entity's circumstances permit, before the ordinary shareholders can receive any dividend
Risks	The ordinary shareholders are the last to be paid if the entity fails. In practice, this means that they may lose everything they have invested	The preference shareholders will not be paid until after all of the entity's debts have been repaid

Preference shares have become unpopular. From the shareholder's point of view, they carry a higher risk than making a loan and they do not have the potential for unlimited dividends offered by ordinary shares. This means that they have to carry a high rate of dividend to make them attractive.

From the entity's point of view, preference dividends cannot be charged as expenses for tax purposes and so they are a very expensive source of finance. There was, however, a brief period when unusual types of preference and other shares became popular as a result of a surge of interest in 'new financial instruments'. These were a means of raising finance which could be treated as share capital in the statement of financial position (thereby reducing the gearing ratio) but which gave the buyer the same rights as debt (thereby making them a cheap source of funds). Now IAS 32 and IAS 39 require these types of shares to be treated as debt in the financial statements (see below).

The disclosure requirements in respect of shares are illustrated quite fully in Exercise 22.A. Entities are required to disclose the authorised share capital and the numbers and nominal value of each class of share which has been allotted. The effects of any allotment which took place during the year should be stated. The entity also has to disclose any options which have been granted to subscribers, stating the numbers of shares involved, the period during which this right can be exercised and the price to be paid. Details also have to be given of any redeemable shares, including the terms on which redemption will take place and the dates when this may occur.

22.4 IAS 32 *Financial Instruments – Presentation*

IAS 32 was introduced to ensure that 'financial instruments' (briefly shares and loan notes) were shown in the financial statements according to their true nature. This means that there must be a clear distinction between equity (e.g. ordinary shares) and liabilities (e.g. loan notes).

The distinction must be made according to the true substance of the financial instrument. In most cases this is not too difficult. To help sort things out, IAS 32 contains several definitions:

Financial instrument: Any contract that gives rise to both a financial asset of one entity and a financial liability or equity instrument of another entity.

Equity instrument: Defined in IAS 32 as any contract that evidences a residual interest in the assets of an entity after deducting all of its liabilities, e.g. ordinary shares.

Financial liability: Any liability that is a contractual obligation to make one or more payments in the future, e.g. bonds and bank loans.

If we apply these definitions to the main elements of the long-term capital in a statement of financial position, we arrive at these conclusions:

(a) *ordinary shares* are clearly equity instruments and will always be classified as such;

(b) *loan notes and bonds* are financial liabilities and will appear as such on the statement of financial position;

(c) *preference shares* are not so easily classified. IAS 32 requires the particular rights attaching to a preference share to be analysed to determine whether it exhibits the fundamental characteristic of a financial liability. For example, if the terms of issue provide for mandatory redemption for cash, they qualify as liabilities as there is an obligation to transfer financial assets to the holder of the share. If the preference shares are non-redeemable, the appropriate classification is based on an assessment of the substance of the contractual arrangements and the definitions of a financial liability and equity instrument. For example, if the payment of a dividend is at the discretion of the issuer they are equity shares. The classification as equity is not affected by the previous history of making dividend payments or the intention of the entity to make payments in the future. If the substance of a preference share is determined to be a liability, the preference share will be treated as debt in the statement of financial position and will be shown under non-current liabilities. The dividend paid on preference shares treated as debt must be treated as finance cost in statement of comprehensive income.

22.5 Issue of shares

22.5.1 Process

The bookkeeping entries in respect of the issue of shares are not complicated. The exact legal requirements may vary from one country to another and there may be additional requirements specified for entities quoted on the local stock exchange. In general, the procedures required to issue a share will follow a similar sequence of events. The accounting entries will follow the chronology of the share issue itself, for example:

1. The entity announces the availability of the shares and their selling price, usually in a formal document.
2. Applicants for shares submit formal requests for part of the issue. These applications will be accompanied by a proportion of the asking price, as requested by the entity in its announcement.

3. If the issue is oversubscribed, then the entity has to decide how the shares should be allocated to the applicants. Any unsuccessful applicants will have their application money returned.
4. The entity will 'allot' or formally issue the shares. The new shareholders will be asked to pay for a further proportion of the total asking price or the full balance outstanding.
5. The entity will make further 'calls' of cash until the shares have been paid for in full. The timing of these calls will be determined by the entity's needs for long-term finance.

The selling price of the shares will be set so as to make the offer attractive to potential investors, but not so attractive that the shares are significantly underpriced. If the shares are sold too cheaply, then the existing shareholders will have their investment diluted. The price is, therefore, likely to be set just below the current market price. If this exceeds the nominal value of the shares, then the difference is called the 'share premium'.

Entities usually take precautions to ensure that the issue is fully sold. If there is a risk that some shares will be left over, then the entity can pay a financial institution to under-write the offer. In return for a premium, the underwriter will agree to buy any unpaid shares left at the closing date of the offer.

If a shareholder does not pay the amounts due on the allotment or calls, then there will usually be provisions included in the issue documents that specify that the shares will be forfeited if payment is not made when due. The entity will be entitled to sell the forfeited shares for any amount that it can get, provided the total amount paid by the original share-holder and the new owner exceeds the nominal value of the shares.

22.5.2 Accounting for the issue of shares

The simplest way to organise the bookkeeping in respect of share capital is to have one account for the nominal value of the shares which have been issued and another for the premium, if any, created when those shares were issued. The balance on these accounts increases as soon as any allotment is made or any call is requested.

The cash received on application is recorded in an 'application and allotment' account. This is like a suspense account with the balance representing the amount paid to the entity in anticipation of either the receipt of some shares or the return of the payment. Once the shares have been allotted, the cash paid on application becomes the property of the entity and the shares transferred to the new shareholders discharge the entity's commitment to them. The entries on application are:

1. Debit   Bank
   Credit   Application and allotment account
   Being recording of monies received on applications for new shares.

2. Debit   Application and allotment account
   Credit   Bank
   Being return of monies to unsuccessful applicants.

3. Debit   Application and allotment account
   Credit   Share capital
   Credit   Share premium
   Being transfer of application monies to share capital and share premium (if shares issued at a premium) on allotment of shares.

Application and allotment

1. Cash received with applications	2. Cash returns to unsuccessful applicants
	3. Balance transferred to share capital

The allotment account is then clear and can be used to record the amount due from shareholders in respect of the entity's request for any further payments. This is recorded by crediting share capital and share premium with the amount requested and debiting the allotment account. Cash received is debited to bank and credited to allotment. The entries on allotment are:

4. Debit   Application and allotment account
    Credit   Share capital
    Credit   Share premium
    Being amounts due on allotment.

5. Debit   Bank
    Credit   Application and allotment account
    Being allotment monies received.

6. Debit   Investment in own shares
    Credit   Application and allotment account
    Being transfer of balance of allotment monies due but not received.

Application and allotment

4. Amount requested on allotment	5. Cash received
	6. Balance transferred to Investment – own shares

If further calls are required, a similar set of entries will be made. The amount requested will be debited to a call account and credited to share capital. Cash will be credited to the call account as it is received. If there is any balance left on the allotment or call accounts once the final deadline for receipt of payments has passed, then the shares will be forfeited. The balance on the account will be transferred to an 'investment in own shares' account. These shares will normally be reissued. Any amount received in excess of the original shareholder's default will be credited to share premium. The entries are:

10. Debit   Bank
     Credit   Investment in own shares
     Being amounts received on reissue of forfeited shares.

11. Debit   Investment in own shares
     Credit   Share premium
     Being transfer of balance to share premium.

Investment own shares

6. Balance transferred from application and allotment	9. Balance transferred from call
10. Cash received from new shareholder	11. Balance transferred to share premium

---

Example 22.B

Randall had a balance on its share capital account of $2 million and a balance on share premium of $600,000. The directors decided to issue a further 500,000 $1 shares for $1.40 each.

The issue was announced and all applicants were asked to send a cheque for 10¢ for every share applied for. A total of 1,100,000 shares were applied for on the due date.

The directors decided to reject the smaller applications and returned application monies for a total of 100,000 shares. The remaining applicants were allotted one share for every two applied for, and were deemed to have paid 20¢ per share.

Applicants were asked to pay a further 90¢ per share, this being deemed to include the share premium associated with the issue. All allotment monies were received by the due date.

A final call of 30¢ per share was made. Payments were received in respect of 495,000 shares. The holder of 5,000 shares defaulted on this call and his shares were forfeited.

The forfeited shares were reissued for 50¢ each.

You are required to prepare the following accounts and enter the transactions described above.

- share capital;
- share premium;
- application and allotment;
- call;
- investment in own shares.

Solution

The entries required to record this series of transactions are as follows:

			$	$
1.	Debit	Bank	110,000	
	Credit	Application and allotment account	110,000	
	Being application monies received.			
2.	Debit	Application and allotment account	10,000	
	Credit	Bank	10,000	
	Being return of application monies.			
3.	Debit	Application and allotment account	100,000	
	Credit	Share capital		100,000
	Being allocation of shares (500,000 shares × 20¢ per share).			
4.	Debit	Bank	450,000	
	Credit	Application and allotment		450,000
	Being further monies received (500,000 shares × 90¢ per share).			
5.	Debit	Application and allotment	450,000	
	Credit	Share capital		250,000
	Credit	Share premium		200,000
	Being allocation of shares including premium of 40¢ per share.			
6.	Debit	Call account	150,000	
	Credit	Share capital	150,000	
	Being amounts due on call (500,000 shares × 30¢).			
7.	Debit	Bank	148,500	
	Credit	Call account		148,500
	Being amounts received on call (495,000 shares × 30¢).			
8.	Debit	Investment in own shares	1,500	
	Credit	Call account		1,500
	Being transfer of call monies due but not received.			

9. Debit	Bank	2,500	
Credit	Investment in own shares		2,500

Being amounts received on reissue of shares (5,000 shares × 50¢ per share).

10. Debit	Investment in own shares	1,000	
Credit	Share premium		1,000

Being transfer of balance to share premium account (5,000 shares reissued at further premium of 20¢, i.e. 50¢ − 30¢).

Share capital

	$		$
		Balance b/d	2,000,000
		3. Application and allotment	100,000
		5. Application and allotment	250,000
Balance c/d	2,500,000	6. Call	150,000
	2,500,000		2,500,000
		Balance b/d	2,500,000

Share premium

	$		$
		Balance b/d	600,000
		5. Application and allotment	200,000
Balance c/d	801,000	10. Investment – own share	1,000
	801,000		801,000
		Balance b/d	801,000

Application and allotment

	$		$
2. Bank	10,000	1. Bank	110,000
3. Share capital	100,000		
	110,000		110,000
5. Share capital	250,000	4. Bank	450,000
5. Share premium	200,000		
	450,000		450,000

Call

	$		$
6. Share capital	150,000	7. Bank	148,500
		8. Investment – own share	1,500
	150,000		150,000

Investment in own shares

	$		$
8. Call	1,500	9. Bank	2,500
10. Share premium	1,000		
	2,500		2,500

Bank			
	$		$
1. Application and allotment	110,000	2. Application and allotment	10,000
4. Application and allotment	450,000		
7. Call account	148,500		
8. Investment in own shares	2,500	Balance c/d	
			701,000
	711,000		711,000

Randall has raised a net total of $701,000 from the issue of shares (495,000 issued at $1.40 and 5,000 issued at $1.60).

22.5.3 Share issue costs, redemption costs and dividends

IAS 39 requires:

(i) interest, dividends, gains and losses relating to a financial liability to be recognised as an expense in the statement of comprehensive income or separate profit or loss (if presented).

This means that:

- dividends on preference shares classified as debt will be treated as an expense in the statement of comprehensive income or separate profit or loss (if presented) and included under finance cost.
- any gains/losses on redemption of a preference share classified as debt will be taken to the statement of comprehensive income or separate profit and loss (if presented) and

(ii) transaction costs of any equity transaction must be recognised in other comprehensive income.

This means that cost of issuing equity shares must be deducted from a reserve and not recognised in profit or loss. Issue costs are usually deducted from share premium, if one exists, or any other reserve. Equity dividends paid are shown in the statement of changes in equity.

IAS 1 requires that equity dividends must be declared before the end of the reporting period if they are to be recognised in the financial statements. Dividends declared after the end of the reporting period cannot be recognised in the financial statements.

22.5.4 Redeemable shares

Any shares that are redeemable for cash are defined as a financial liability. Financial liabilities finance costs are charged to profit or loss on an annual basis. IAS 32 and IAS 39 require that the total finance cost of a financial liability (from issue to redemption) be charged to profit or loss over the life of the shares in such a way as to give a constant annual rate of interest on the outstanding balance of the liability.

The total cost will include:

(i) Any issue costs less any premiums payable on issue
(ii) Annual dividends
(iii) Any redemption costs plus any premium payable on redemption.

The initial amount used to calculate the constant rate of interest is the amount of cash raised, that is, the issue price less any costs. Each year the amount of dividend paid is debited to the reserve and the finance charge (debited to profit or loss) is credited.

See Section 22.9 for a discussion on the treatment of a redemption of shares.

Example 22.C

An entity issued 1,000,000 $1 redeemable 4% preference shares at par on 1 April 2002, which was redeemable on 31 March 2006 at a 10% premium. The issue costs were $100,000.
   The constant annual rate of interest is approximately 9.283%. Ignore all tax implications.
   Calculate the total finance cost, and the annual finance charge to the statement of comprehensive income.

Solution

The total finance cost is:

Issue costs	$100,000
Redemption costs ($1,000,000 × 10%)	$100,000
Annual dividends at 4% ($40,000 × 4 years)	$1,600,000
	$1,800,000

Year	Opening balance	Interest at 9.283%	Dividend at 4%	Closing balance
2002/3	900,000	83,547	40,000	943,547
2003/4	943,547	87,589	40,000	991,136
2004/5	991,136	92,007	40,000	1,043,144
2005/6	1,043,144	96,856	40,000	1,100,000

The annual finance cost is that shown under the column headed 'interest at 9.283%'

22.5.5 Convertible debt

A convertible debt must be examined to establish if it is a debt instrument, an equity instrument or both (a compound instrument).

Compound instruments must be split into its two elements, debt and equity. Each element is then accounted for separately. The value of the debt is calculated as the fair value of a similar debt instrument without the equity element. The value of the equity element is the difference between the fair value of the total instrument and the fair value of the debt element. For example, the debt element of a 10 per cent bond convertible into equity shares on a two-for-one basis after 5 years would be valued by calculating the value of a similar 10 per cent bond without the conversion. This would be deducted from the value of the bond to give the value of the equity element.

22.6 Bonus issues

22.6.1 Process

An entity can convert part of its reserves into shares. These shares can then be given to the existing shareholders in proportion to their holdings at the time of the issue. These 'free shares' are often called bonus shares but may be given other names in some countries.

For example, X might give its shareholders one fully paid $1 ordinary share for every two that they had previously held. If the entity had 1,000,000 ordinary shares outstanding before the issue, then share capital would increase to 1,500,000 shares of $1, or $1,500,000. This credit to share capital would have a corresponding debit of $500,000 to reserves.

Example 22.D

How would a bonus issue affect:

- the market price of shares? (up or down);
- distributable profits? (up or down).

Common sense suggests that the share price would fall in proportion to the size of the issue. Thus a market price of $2.40 before a two-for-one issue would fall to $1.60 immediately after. Two shares before the issue would have been worth $4.80, the same as three shares held afterwards. It is, however, *possible* that the stock market will react positively to the announcement of the bonus because there is a tendency for entities to increase dividend payments after making these issues. Of course, this price change would be because of the expected increase in dividends rather than the increase in the number of shares.

If the reserve account which was debited with the value of the bonus is part of distributable profits, then this will reduce the maximum dividend. This might, therefore, provide lenders with a measure of protection because a greater proportion of the entity's equity is being locked in'. The buffer effect referred to earlier will, therefore, be enhanced. Of course, it is highly unlikely that the entity would make a bonus issue if doing so would severely limit its ability to pay dividends. Thus, the size of a bonus issue is likely to be small in relation to total reserves.

22.6.2 Accounting for a bonus issue

Example 22.E

The directors of A have decided to make a bonus issue of one share for every three previously held. The entity's statement of financial position just before the issue was as follows:

A – statement of financial position as at 31 December 20X2

	$m
Non-current assets	14
Current assets	4
	18
Share capital	9
Retained earnings	4
	13
Liabilities	5
	18

You are required to redraft A's statement of financial position to take the bonus issue into account. Show the journal entry required to bring about your change.

Solution

The share capital will increase by one-third. This means that share capital will increase and the retained earnings decrease by $3 million. This can be shown as a journal entry:

		$m	$m
Debit	Retained earnings	3	
Credit	Share capital		3

The statement of financial position would, therefore, become:

A – statement of financial position as at 31 December 20X2

	$m
Non-current assets	14
Working capital	4
	18
Share capital	12
Accumulated profits	1
	13
Liabilities	5
	18

22.7 Accounting for a rights issue

If an entity issues new shares for cash, it is often required to first offer them to its existing ordinary shareholders in proportion to their shareholdings. This is called a rights issue.

Example 22.F

Using the information provided above in Example 22.E and assuming that the share capital consists of 9 million $1 shares, let us assume the directors of A decide to make a rights issue instead of a bonus issue. The terms of the rights issue are one for every three shares held at $1.20.

Assuming that all the shareholders take up the rights, the transaction would be recorded as follows:

		$m	$m
Debit	Cash	3.6	
Credit	Share capital		3.0
Credit	Share premium		0.6

The rights issue would generate new funds. At a one-for-three rights issue, 3 million new shares would be issued and the balance raised would be credited to share premium.

The new statement of financial position would be:

A – statement of financial position as at 31 December 20X2

	$m
Non-current assets	14.0
Working capital	7.6
	21.6
Share capital	12.0
Share premium	0.6
Accumulated profits	4.0
	16.6
Liabilities	5.0
	21.6

22.8 Accounting for treasury shares

Where an entity acquires its own equity shares, and at the end of the reporting period has not cancelled them, they are referred to as treasury shares.

IAS 32 states that any change in equity resulting from the purchase, sale, issue and cancellation of the entity's own shares should not result in any gain or loss being recognised in profit or loss. Where an entity reacquires its own shares, it should be recorded as a change in equity and the reacquired shares should be reclassified as treasury shares and shown as a deduction from equity. This should be shown in the statement of financial position or in the notes to the financial statements. The transaction would then be included within the statement of changes in equity.

Example 22.G

Murray has 1 million $1 ordinary shares in issue at 31 December 20 × 1. The equity and reserves included the following:

Equity and reserves	$'000
Share capital, $1 shares, fully paid	1,000
Share premium	600
Retained earnings	500
	2,100

In the year to 31 December 20X2, the entity reacquired 300,000 of its shares for $1.30 each. Retained profit for 20X2 was $60,000.

IAS 32 requires that no gain or loss be recorded on the reacquisition of an entity's own shares. Instead, the full amount of issued capital will remain on the statement of financial position and the shares reacquired and held by the entity (and reclassified as treasury shares) will be shown as a deduction from equity. The presentation of this is reasonably flexible. The simplest presentation is to show the total cost of redemption as a deduction from total equity. This could be presented as follows:

Equity and reserves	$'000
Share capital, $1 shares, fully paid	1,000
Share premium	600
	1,600
Treasury shares	(390)
	1,210
Retained earnings	560
Total equity and reserves	1,770

Alternative presentations include showing the deduction for the nominal value of treasury shares against share capital and the premium paid on redemption against share premium.

22.9 The purchase and redemption of shares

One of the basic principles followed in most countries is that the equity capital invested by the shareholders cannot normally be repaid or distributed to the shareholders unless the entity is wound up.

Dividends payments are normally restricted to being paid out of 'distributable' reserves which are, at least essentially, equivalent to retained earnings. This protects the lenders and creditors from the possibility that the entity could use an excessive dividend to reduce the equity base and leave the liabilities uncovered by assets.

While these regulations have a very clear purpose, they may prove unduly restrictive. If an entity is not quoted on a stock market, then it would be difficult for shareholders to sell their investments. It might be preferable for a small entity to be able to buy out individual shareholders rather than have them sell their shares to an outsider. There is, therefore, often some scope in the local legal regulations for the reduction of share capital, subject to some stringent safeguards.

The basic principle almost universally applied is that the equity capital has a 'permanent' component which can never be repaid unless the entity is wound up. Entities can either purchase or redeem their shares, but must normally do so in such a way that this 'permanent' capital is preserved. There are few exceptions to this general rule.

22.9.1 Purchases out of distributable profits

In the simplest possible case an entity can buy back its shares. It is usually required to ensure that equity capital is maintained. This can be achieved by making a transfer from distributable reserves to a reserve that is usually legally classified as non-distributable. This reserve could be called a 'capital redemption reserve' or a capital reserve. This is best illustrated by an example:

Example 22.H

Peters: statement of financial position as at 30 September 20X5

	$'000
Net assets	4,000
Share capital – $1 shares, fully paid	2,000
Share premium	500
Permanent capital	2,500
Distributable profit	1,500
	4,000

The entity is owned by the Peters family, one of whose members wants to sell her shares and retire. The other shareholders are keen to keep all of the entity's shares in the family, but none can afford to buy the retiring shareholder's equity. It has, therefore, been decided that the entity will purchase 100,000 shares for $180,000. This requires two journal entries:

	$	$
Debit Share capital	100,000	
Premium on purchase	80,000	
Credit Bank		180,000
Debit Distributable profits	180,000	
Credit Premium on purchase		80,000
Capital redemption reserve		100,000

The first journal reduces both bank and share capital by the appropriate amounts. The premium on purchase account is used to maintain double entry. The balance on this account will be cancelled by the next step.

The second journal is required to make a transfer from distributable profits which is equal to the amount paid for the purchase of the shares. The corresponding credits go to premium on purchase and capital redemption reserve. These transactions and adjustments would have the following effect on Peters's statement of financial position.

Peters: statement of financial position as at 30 September 20X5

	$'000
Net assets	3,820
Share capital $1 shares, fully paid	1,900
Share premium	500
Capital redemption reserve	100
Permanent capital	2,500
Distributable profit	1,320
	3,820

 Exercise

Look back at the above example. How has the transfer to the capital redemption reserve protected Peters's creditors?

Solution

Clearly, both the entity's capital and net assets have been reduced by $180,000. The transfer to capital redemption reserve has, however, used part of the entity's distributable profits to replace the permanent capital which was used to make the repurchase. The lenders' security will have been affected by the outflow of cash and the reduction of equity. This could, however, have happened anyway if the directors had decided to pay a dividend of $180,000.

It is never going to be in the lenders' interests for the entity to return equity to the shareholders, whether this is accomplished by either dividend or the repurchase of shares. There is, however, some protection from the fact that distributable profits place an upper limit on such payments. Entities can also purchase their own shares from the proceeds of a new share issue. This could be done to repay redeemable shares when they are due for repayment; to 'tidy' up the statement of financial position, that is, redeem separate classes of shares and issue one new class, or to reduce the amount of committed dividends that are required to be paid by redeeming high dividend preference shares and replacing them with lower dividend preference shares or equity. For example:

Example 22.I

ABC: statement of financial position as at 30 September 20X5

	$'000
Net assets	4,000
Share capital $1 equity shares, fully paid	1,500
10% Preference shares (redeemable)	1,000
Permanent capital	2,500
Retained earnings	1,500
	4,000

ABC need to redeem their redeemable preference shares. The preference shares are redeemable for $1.50 per share.

ABC are raising the cash required for the purchase by an issue of 750 $1 equity shares at $2.00 per share.

Prepare ABC's statement of financial position after the redemption of the preference shares.

Solution

Cost of redemption is 1,000 shares at $1.50 equals $1,500. $1,000 is debited to preference share capital and the balance, $500, will be debited to retained earnings.

The issue will raise 750 times $2, $1,500 in cash. This will be allocated to equity: share capital $750 and share premium $750.

The cash raised will be used to redeem the preference shares: debit bank $1,500 and credit bank $1,500.

The statement of financial position after the transactions have taken place will be:

ABC: statement of financial position as at 30 September 20X5

	$'000
Net assets	4,000
Share capital – $1 equity shares, fully paid (1,500 + 750)	2,250
10% Preference shares (redeemable)	0
Share premium	750
Permanent capital	3,000
Retained earnings (1,500 − 500)	1,000
	4,000

Note that in this case the permanent capital is maintained and there is no requirement to make a transfer from retained earnings to a capital reserve. There are often quite complex regulations regarding share redemptions and how much must be transferred to a capital reserve. There are also variations in the treatment of cash raised by a new issue. In some cases, the full amount of the issue proceeds are counted and in others only the equity element is counted.

> If you are not told otherwise in the question, in exam questions you should assume that the nominal amount of the share capital will be maintained and if it is not covered by a new issue it must be appropriated from retained earnings.

22.10 Summary

Having completed this chapter, we can now explain the disclosure requirements of both IAS 1 and IAS 32, and we can discuss the main characteristics of equity and non-equity share capital.

We can account for the issue of shares, including a bonus issue and a rights issue, and can account for the purchase and redemption of shares.

Revision Questions

? Question 1

ZZ redeemed their redeemable preference shares with a cash payment, paying a premium of 20 per cent.

Nominal value of shares redeemed	$70,000
Cash paid on redemption	$84,000

How much should be transferred to the capital redemption reserve (CRR) and how much should be charged to distributable reserves?

	CRR	Distributable reserves
(A)	$70,000	$14,000
(B)	$84,000	$84,000
(C)	$70,000	$84,000
(D)	$84,000	$70,000

(2 marks)

? Question 2

Ordinary shares are usually classified as:

(A) Equity shares
(B) Non-equity shares
(C) Loans
(D) Deferred shares

(2 marks)

? Question 3

Which type of financial instrument has the following characteristics?
– they do not normally have any voting rights;
– they usually have a fixed rate of return;
– they are ranked after unsecured creditors;
– the return can be suspended by directors, but will have to be paid in later years.

(A) Convertible stock
(B) Ordinary shares
(C) Preference shares
(D) Cumulative preference shares

(2 marks)

Question 4

BN is a listed entity and has the following balances included on its opening statement of financial position:

	$'000
Equity and reserves:	
Equity shares, $1 shares, fully paid	750
Share premium	250
Retained earnings	500
	1,500

BN reacquired 100,000 of its shares and classified them as 'treasury shares'. BN still held the treasury shares at the year end.

How should BN classify the treasury shares on its closing statement of financial position in accordance with IAS 32 *Financial Instruments – Disclosure and Presentation?*

(A) As a non-current asset investment.
(B) As a deduction from equity.
(C) As a current asset investment.
(D) As a non-current liability.   **(2 marks)**

 Question 5

Treasury shares are defined as:

(A) equity shares sold by an entity in the period.
(B) equity shares repurchased by the issuing entity, not cancelled before the period end.
(C) non-equity shares sold by an entity in the period.
(D) equity shares repurchased by the issuing entity and cancelled before the period end.
                                                   (2 marks)

 Question 6

The directors of Alpha have decided to make a bonus issue of one for every five shares held by existing shareholders. The statement of financial position of Alpha immediately before the issue was as follows:

Alpha: statement of financial position as at 31 December 20X9

	$'000
Non-current assets	10,500
Working capital	4,800
	15,300
Share capital	10,000
Retained earnings	2,300
	12,300
Liabilities	3,000
	15,300

Share capital consists of 20 million 50¢ ordinary shares.

Requirement

Prepare the accounting entry that records the bonus issue and redraft the statement of financial position immediately after the bonus issue takes place. **(5 marks)**

 ## Question 7

The directors of Beta have decided to make a rights issue of two for every five shares held by existing shareholders at $1.15. All the existing shareholders have chosen to take up this offer. The statement of financial position of Beta immediately before the issue was as follows:

Beta: statement of financial position as at 31 December 20X9

	$'000
Non-current assets	15,500
Current assets	8,800
	24,300
Share capital	15,000
Retained earnings	4,300
	19,300
Liabilities	5,000
	24,300

Share capital consists of 15 million $1 ordinary shares.

Requirement

Prepare the accounting entry that records the rights issue and redraft the statement of financial position immediately after the rights issue takes place. **(5 marks)**

 ## Question 8

CR issued 200,000 $10 redeemable 5% preference shares at par on 1 April 2005. The shares were redeemable on 31 March 2010 at a premium of 15%. Issue costs amounted to $192,800.

Requirements

(a) Calculate the total finance cost over the life of the preference share. **(2 marks)**
(b) Calculate the annual charge to profit or loss for finance expense, as required by IAS 39 *Financial Instruments: Recognition and Measurement*, for each of the five years 2006 to 2010. Assume the constant annual rate of interest as 10%. **(3 marks)**

(Total marks = 5)

Question 9

Optima issued 500,000 $1 ordinary shares for $1.30 on 1 August 20X2. At the end of the reporting period, 31 December 20X2 all the shares issued were fully paid. Costs related to this issue totalled $60,000 and the financial accountant has charged this amount to finance costs in profit or loss. The retained profit for the year as per the draft accounts is $210,000. The equity and reserves of Optima at 31 December 20X1 was as follows:

	$'000
Equity and reserves	
Share capital, $1 shares, fully paid	3,500
Share premium	600
Revaluation reserves	400
Retained earnings	940
	5,440

Requirement

Prepare the accounting adjustments required to ensure that the costs of this share issue are recorded correctly and draft the equity and reserves section of the statement of financial position for inclusion in the financial statements for the year ended 31 December 20X2.

(10 marks)

Solutions to Revision Questions

 Solution 1

The correct answer is (C), see Section 22.9.

Nominal share capital has reduced by $70,000, therefore CRR is credited with $70,000. The cash paid, including the premium, is $84,000, and this needs to be charged to distributable reserves.

 Solution 2

The correct answer is (A), see Section 22.3.

 Solution 3

The correct answer is (D), see Section 22.3.

 Solution 4

The correct answer is (B), see Section 22.8.

 Solution 5

The correct answer is (B), see Section 22.8.

 Solution 6

Share capital will increase by one-fifth. Share capital will increase by $2 million and accumulated profits will reduce by $2 million. The transaction would be recorded as follows:

		$m	$m
Debit	Accumulated profits	2m	
Credit	Share capital		2m

The new statement of financial position would be as follows:

Alpha: statement of financial position as at 31 December 20X9

	$'000
Non-current assets	10,500
Working capital	4,800
	15,300
Share capital	12,000
Accumulated profits	300
	12,300
Liabilities	3,000
	15,300

See Section 22.6.2.

 ## Solution 7

Assuming that all the shareholders take up the rights, then 6 million new shares are created. The transaction would be recorded as follows:

		$m	$m
Debit	Cash	6.9	
Credit	Share capital		6.0
Credit	Share premium		0.9

The rights issue would generate new funds. At a two-for-five rights issue, 6 million new shares would be issued and the balance raised would be credited to share premium.

The new statement of financial position would be as follows:

Beta: statement of financial position as at 31 December 20X9

	$'000
Non-current assets	15,500
Working capital	15,700
	31,200
Share capital	21,000
Share premium	900
Retained earnings	4,300
	26,200
Liabilities	5,000
	31,200

See Section 22.7.

 ## Solution 8

(a) The total finance cost is:

	$
Issue costs	192,800
Annual dividend (200,000 × $10 × 5%) × 5	500,000
Redemption cost (200,000 × $10 × 15%)	300,000
	992,800

(b)

	Balance b/fwd	Finance cost 10%	Dividend paid	Redemption	Balance c/fwd
	$	$	$	$	$
2005/06	1,807,200	180,720	−100,000		1,887,920
2006/07	1,887,920	188,792	−100,000		1,976,712
2007/08	1,976,712	197,671	−100,000		2,074,383
2008/09	2,074,383	207,438	−100,000		2,181,821
2009/10	2,181,821	218,179	−100,000		2,300,000
31/10/2010	2,300,000			−2,300,000	0

Note: Finance cost in 2009/10 includes a rounding adjustment of −$3, See Section 22.5.4.

 ## Solution 9

The financial accountant has recorded the issue costs as:

Dr	Finance costs	$60,000
Cr	Bank	$60,000

Being the recording of the share issue costs.

The standard requires that costs relating to a new issue of equity should be offset against share premium rather than being charged to the statement of comprehensive income. The entry that should have been recorded by the accountant was:

Dr	Share premium	$60,000
Cr	Bank	$60,000

Being the recording of the share issue costs.

The bank entry that has been posted is correct. The charge to finance costs, however, should be reversed and the costs debited against share premium in accordance with the standard. The correcting entry is:

Dr	Share premium	$60,000
Cr	Finance costs	$60,000

Being the correcting entry to record the share issue costs.

Extract from the statement of financial position of Optima as at 31 December 20X2

Equity and reserves	$'000
Share capital, $1 shares, fully paid	4,000
Share premium (see workings)	690
Revaluation reserves	400
Retained earnings (see workings)	1,210
	6,300

Workings

Share premium	$'000
As at 31/12/X1	600
Premium on issue in 20X1	150
(500K shares × 30 cents)	
Less issue costs	(60)
As at 31/12/X2	690

Retained earnings	$'000
As at 31/12/X1	940
Profit per draft accounts	210
Plus the add back of the issue costs incorrectly charged within finance costs in arriving at profit	60
As at 31/12/X2	1,210

23

Recognition and Disclosure of Other Significant Accounting Transactions

Recognition and Disclosure of Other Significant Accounting Transactions

23

LEARNING OUTCOME

After completing this chapter, you should be able to:

▶ apply the accounting rules contained in IFRS's and IAS's dealing with disclosure of related parties to a business, events after the reporting period and provisions and contingencies.

The syllabus topics covered in this chapter are as follows:

- events after the reporting period (IAS 10)
- provisions and contingencies (IAS 37)
- the disclosure of related parties to a business (IAS 24).

23.1 Introduction

In this chapter, we cover three IASs which deal with various aspects of recognition and disclosure of other significant transactions. They are:

- IAS 10 *Events After the Reporting Period*
- IAS 37 *Provisions, Contingent Liabilities and Contingent Assets*
- IAS 24 *Related Party Disclosures*.

23.2 IAS 10 *Events After the Reporting Period*

23.2.1 Introduction

It is a fundamental principle of accounting that regard must be had to all available information when preparing financial statements. This must include relevant events occurring after the reporting period, up to the date on which the financial statements are authorised for issue. The objective of IAS 10 is to:

- define the extent to which different types of events after the reporting period are to be reflected in financial statements;
- define when an entity should adjust its financial statements for events after the reporting period;
- set out the disclosures that the entity should provide about the date the statement of financial position was authorised;
- specify disclosures required about events arising after the end of the reporting period.

23.2.2 Definitions

IAS 10 defines an event after the end of the reporting period as 'events after the end of the reporting period are those events, favourable and unfavourable, that occur between the end of the reporting period and the date when the financial statements are authorised for issue.'

IAS 10 identifies two main types of events after the reporting period: adjusting events and non-adjusting events.

23.2.3 Adjusting events

These are 'events which provide evidence of conditions that existed at the end of the reporting period'. They require changes in amounts to be included in financial statements, because financial statements should reflect all available evidence as to conditions existing at the end of the reporting period.

Examples of *adjusting events* are:

1. *Non-current assets.* The subsequent determination of the purchase price or of the proceeds of sale of assets purchased or sold before the year-end.
2. *Property.* A valuation which provides evidence of a permanent diminution in value.
3. *Investments.* The receipt of a copy of the financial statements or other information in respect of an unlisted entity which provides evidence of a permanent diminution in the value of a long-term investment.
4. *Inventories and work in progress.*
   - The receipt of proceeds of sales after the end of the reporting period or other evidence concerning the net realisable value of inventories.
   - The receipt of evidence that the previous estimate of accrued profit on a long-term construction contract was materially inaccurate.
5. *Receivables.* The renegotiation of amounts owing by customers, or the insolvency of a customer.
6. *Taxation.* The receipt of information regarding rates of taxation.
7. *Claims.* Amounts received or receivable in respect of insurance claims, which were in the course of negotiation at the end of the reporting period.

8. *Obligations.* The settlement after the end of the reporting period of a court case that confirms that the entity had a present obligation at the end of the reporting period.
9. *Discoveries.* The discovery of errors or frauds which show that the financial statements were incorrect.

23.2.4 Non-adjusting events

Non-adjusting events are events that are indicative of conditions that arose after the end of the reporting period. Consequently, they do not result in changes in amounts in financial statements.

Although non-adjusting events do not lead to changes in amounts in financial statements, they should still be disclosed by note, if material.

Examples of *non-adjusting events* are:

1. issues of shares and loan notes;
2. purchases and sales of non-current assets and investments;
3. losses of fixed assets or inventories as a result of a catastrophe, such as fire or flood;
4. opening new trading activities or extending existing trading activities;
5. closing a significant part of the trading activities if this was not anticipated at the year end;
6. decline in the value of property and investments held as non-current assets, if it can be demonstrated that the decline occurred after the year-end;
7. government action, such as nationalisation;
8. strikes and other labour disputes.

23.3 Proposed dividends

IAS 10 was revised in 1999 and 2003, an important change made in 1999 and reinforced in 2003 was to prevent proposed equity dividends being recognised as liabilities unless they are declared before the end of the reporting period. Declared means that the dividend is appropriately authorised, and is no longer at the discretion of the entity.

> IAS 1 requires the disclosure by note to the financial statements of the amounts of dividends proposed or declared before the financial statements were authorised for issue but not recognised as a distribution to owners during the period. It is, of course, unusual for entities to propose or declare a final dividend before the end of the reporting period.

23.4 Going concern

If management determines after the end of the reporting period that it is necessary to liquidate the entity or cease trading, or that it has no realistic alternative but to do so, the financial statements should not be prepared on a going-concern basis.

RECOGNITION AND DISCLOSURE OF OTHER SIGNIFICANT ACCOUNTING TRANSACTIONS

23.5 Disclosure requirements of IAS 10

(a) *Events after the end of the reporting period requiring changes to the financial statements.* A material adjusting event after the end of the reporting period requires changes to the financial statements.

(b) *Events after the end of the reporting period requiring disclosure by note.* A material event after the end of the reporting period should be disclosed [by note] where it is a non-adjusting event of such importance that its non-disclosure would affect the ability of users of financial statements to reach a proper understanding of the financial position.

   The note should disclose the nature of the event and an estimate of the financial effect, or a statement that it is not practicable to make such an estimate. The estimate should be made before taking account of taxation, with an explanation of the taxation implications where necessary for a proper understanding of the financial position.

(c) *Date directors approve financial statements.* The date on which the financial statements are authorised for issue should be disclosed.

23.6 IAS 37 Provisions, Contingent Liabilities and Contingent Assets

23.6.1 Introduction

IAS 37 *Provisions, Contingent Liabilities and Contingent Assets* regulates the recognition and disclosure of provisions and contingencies. For your examination, you need to understand the principles relating to provisions, contingent liabilities and contingent assets and be able to apply those principles.

23.6.2 Provisions

The term 'provision' is defined in IAS 37 as 'a liability of uncertain timing or amount'. The main objectives of IAS 37 in this area are to ensure that entities make provisions for all such liabilities and do not make excessive provisions.

   A provision should be recognised when, and only when:

(a) an entity has a present obligation (legal or constructive) as a result of a past event;
(b) it is probable (i.e. more likely than not) that an outflow of resources embodying economic benefits will be required to settle the obligation; and
(c) a reliable estimate can be made of the amount of the obligation.

(a) *An entity has a present obligation (legal or constructive) arising from a past event:*
   • There is a present obligation if it is more likely than not that an obligation exists at the end of the reporting period.
   • A legal obligation could arise from a contract, legislation or other legal requirement.
   • A constructive obligation derives from the entity's actions:
      ○ by an established pattern of past practice, published policies or a sufficiently specific current statement, the entity has indicated to current parties that it will accept certain responsibilities; and
      ○ as a result, the entity has created a valid expectation on the part of those other parties that it will discharge those responsibilities.

(b) *It is probable (i.e. more likely than not) that an outflow of resources embodying economic benefits will be required to settle the obligation:*

- A transfer of economic benefits is regarded as probable if it is more likely than not to occur.
- Where there are a number of similar obligations the probability that a transfer will be required is determined by considering the class of obligations as a whole, for example, warranties.

(c) *A reliable estimate can be made of the amount:*

- If it is not possible to make a reliable estimate, a provision cannot be made. The item must be disclosed as a contingent liability. IAS 37 notes that it is only in extremely rare cases that a reliable estimate will not be possible.

A reimbursement from a third party, to pay for part or all of the expenditure provided as a provision should only be recognised if it is reasonably certain that it will be received. If it is recognised, it should be treated as a separate asset, rather than set off against the provision.

23.6.3 Measurement of provisions

The amount recognised should be the best estimate of expenditure required to settle the obligation at the end of the reporting period.

- if the obligation is one item, the most likely outcome is the best estimate
- if the provision involves a large number of items, the estimate should be made using expected values, see Section 23.6.5.

23.6.4 Provision for decommissioning costs

When a facility such as an oil well or a mine is authorised by the government, the licence normally includes a legal obligation for the entity to decommission the facility at the end of its useful life. IAS 37 requires a provision for decommissioning costs to be recognised immediately after the facility commences operation. The provision will be debited to the cost of the asset and credited to provisions. Where the decommissioning cost occurs several years in the future and is material, the amount should be discounted to present value and the discounted amount provided for. The discount must be recalculated each year. The unwinding of the discount is charged to statement of comprehensive income under the heading of finance cost and credited to the provision.

23.6.5 Provision for warranties

If an entity sells goods and provides a warranty against faults occurring after sale, a provision needs to be created for the future warranty claims. The process is known as *expected values* and uses estimates of the likely cost and the probability of it occurring.

Example 23.1

An entity provides a one-year warranty on its goods. The entity estimates that at the year-end if all goods needed minor repairs, the cost would be $4 million and if all goods needed major repairs, the cost would be $15 million. The probability of goods needing no repair 90% minor repair 8% and major repair 2%.
Calculate the provision for warranty claims.

Solution

The amount, using expected values is ($4m × 0.08) + ($15m × 0.02) = $620,000

For each class of provision, the financial statements should disclose, if material:

(a) the opening and closing balance
(b) additional provisions made in the period
(c) amounts used (i.e. incurred and charged against the provision)
(d) details of the nature of the obligation provided for, including expected timing and any uncertainties relating to the obligation.

A provision once created, can only be used for expenditures for which the provision was originally recognised. Any unused provision is credited to the statement of comprehensive income when it is no longer required.

23.7 Contingent liabilities and contingent assets

A contingent liability is:

(i) a possible obligation that arises from past events and whose existence will be confirmed only by the occurrence of one or more uncertain future events not wholly within the control of the entity; or
(ii) a present obligation that arises from past events but is not recognised because it is not probable that a transfer of economic benefits will be required to settle the obligation; or the amount of the obligation cannot be measured with sufficient reliability.

A contingent asset is:

A possible asset that arises from past events and whose existence will be confirmed only by the occurrence or non-occurrence of one or more uncertain future events not wholly within the control of the entity.

The accounting treatment of contingent liabilities and contingent assets depends upon the degree of probability. The following table shows the requirements.

Likelihood of occurrence	Material contingent asset	Material contingent liability
Remote	No disclosure allowed*	No disclosure
Possible	No disclosure allowed*	Disclose by note
Probable	Disclose by note	In these two categories the contingent
Virtually certain	Accrual	liability requires a provision

* Note that disclosure is not allowed for 'remote' or 'possible' contingent gains. The prudence concept dictates that contingent gains are treated with more caution than contigent losses.

When a contingency is disclosed by note, the following information should be given:

(i) the nature of the contingency;
(ii) an estimate of the financial effect.

The following extract illustrates these disclosure requirements, as it describes the nature of the contingency and the financial effect of it.

Extract from the consolidated accounts of the Nestlé Group for the year ended 31 December 2005

Notes to the accounts

35. Contingent assets and liabilities

The Group is exposed to contingent liabilities amounting to CHF 870 million (2004: CHF 690 million) representing various potential litigations (CHF 784 million) and other items (CHF 86 million). Contingent assets for litigation claims in favour of the Group amount to CHF 258 million (2004: CHF 170 million).

23.8 Problems with IAS 37 as regards contingencies

(a) *Determining level of probability.* It must be a matter of judgement in many cases to determine the appropriate level of probability of an event, and hence the appropriate accounting treatment of it. Opinion is bound to differ both as to the percentage probability of an event and as to the category a given percentage should be placed into. *UK GAAP,* an authoritative work on accounting standards and practice in the UK, suggests an answer to the second of these uncertainties by proposing the following:

Likelihood of outcome	Level of probability
Remote	0–5%
Possible	5–50%
Probable	50–95%
Virtually certain	95–100%

(b) *Disclosure of information* about a claim which may prejudice the settlement of that claim. Entities will typically attempt to limit damage to their cause by including in the disclosure note a statement declaring that the claims will be strenuously resisted.

(c) *Counterclaims.* An entity may have a contingent liability for a claim against it which is matched by a counterclaim or a claim by the entity against a third party. The likelihood of success, and the probable amounts of the claim and the counterclaim, should be separately assessed and disclosed where appropriate. For example, an entity might have an action brought against it which it could in turn bring against a subcontractor. If the subcontractor had no material assets, the claim would, if successful, fall upon the entity, with no practical recourse to the subcontractor.

23.9 Related party disclosures

IAS 24 *Related Party Disclosures* was issued in March 1984, reformatted in 1994 and updated in 2003. The objective of the standard is to ensure that financial statements disclose to shareholders the effect of the existence of related parties, any material transactions with them and any outstanding balances.

In the absence of information to the contrary, we assume that an organisation has independent discretionary power over its transactions and resources, and pursues its activities independently of the interests of its owners, managers and others. We presume that transactions have been undertaken 'at arm's length'.

These assumptions may not be justified when related party relationships exist, because the requisite conditions for competitive, free-market dealings may not be present. The parties themselves may endeavour to trade at arm's length, but the very nature of the relationship may preclude this. Even when trading does take place at arm's length, it is still useful to report on the nature of the relationship.

23.10 Definitions

IAS 24 includes the following definitions:
Related party: A party is related to an entity if:

(a) directly, or indirectly through one or more intermediaries, the party:
  (i) controls, is controlled by, or is under common control with the entity (this includes parents, subsidiaries and fellow subsidiaries);
  (ii) has an interest in the entity that gives it significant influence over the entity; or
  (iii) has joint control over the entity;
(b) the party is an associate (as defined in IAS 28 Investments in Associates) of the entity;
(c) the party is a joint venture in which the entity is a venturer (see IAS 31 *Interests in Joint Ventures*);
(d) the party is a member of the key management personnel of the entity or its parent;
(e) the party is a close member of the family of any individual referred to in (a) or (d);
(f) the party is an entity that is controlled, jointly controlled or significantly influenced by, or for which significant voting power in such entity resides with, directly or indirectly, any individual referred to in (d) or (e); or
(g) the party is a post-employment benefit plan for the benefit of employees of the entity, or of any entity that is a related party of the entity.

Note: Parents, subsidiaries, associates, joint ventures and post-retirement benefits are all outside the scope of your syllabus.

Related party transaction: A transfer of resources or obligations between related parties, regardless of whether a price is charged.

You can see from the above definition that 'related parties' include entities in the same group as the reporting entity, associated entities, directors and their close families, and pension funds for the benefit of employees of the reporting entity. In addition, key managers and those controlling 20 per cent or more of the voting rights are presumed to be related parties unless it can be demonstrated that neither party has influenced the financial and operating policies of the other in such a way as to inhibit the pursuit of separate interests.

23.10.1 Exclusions

In the context of this standard, the following are not necessarily related parties:

(a) two entities simply because they have a director or other member of key management personnel in common, notwithstanding (d) and (f) in the definition of 'related party'.
(b) two venturers simply because they share joint control over a joint venture.
(c) (i) providers of finance;
  (ii) trade unions;
  (iii) public utilities; and

(iv) government departments and agencies.

Simply by virtue of their normal dealings with an entity (even though they may affect the freedom of action of an entity or participate in its decision-making process); and

(d) a customer, supplier, franchisor, distributor or general agent with whom an entity transacts a significant volume of business, merely by virtue of the resulting economic dependence.

23.11 Disclosure

The standard concerns the disclosure of related party transactions in order to make readers of financial statements aware of the position and to ensure that the financial statements show a true and fair view.

23.11.1 Disclosure of control

Related party relationships where control exists should be disclosed irrespective of whether any transactions took place.

23.11.2 Disclosure of transactions and balances

If there have been transactions between related parties, an entity shall disclose the nature of the related party relationship as well as information about the transactions and outstanding balances necessary for an understanding of the potential effect of the relationship on the financial statements.

Disclosures that related party transactions were made on terms equivalent to those that prevail in arm's length transactions are made only if such terms can be substantiated.

At a minimum, disclosures shall include:

(a) the amount of the transactions;
(b) the amount of outstanding balances:
   (i) their terms and conditions, including whether they are secured, and the nature of the consideration to be provided in settlement;
   (ii) details of any guarantees given or received;
(c) provisions for doubtful debts related to the amount of outstanding balances;
(d) the expense recognised during the period in respect of bad or doubtful debts due from related parties.

In addition, IAS 24 requires an entity to disclose key management personnel compensation in total and for each of the following categories:

(a) short-term employee benefits
(b) post-employment benefits
(c) other long-term benefits
(d) termination benefits
(e) equity compensation benefits.

23.11.3 Examples of related party transactions

- purchases or sales of goods;
- purchases or sales of property and other assets;
- rendering or receipt of services;
- agency arrangements;
- leasing arrangements;
- management contracts;
- any of these or similar transactions would require to be disclosed if material;
- transfers of research and development;
- transfers under licence agreements;
- transfers under finance arrangements (including loans and equity contributions in cash or in kind);
- provision of guarantees or collateral;
- settlement of liabilities on behalf of the entity or by the entity on behalf of another party.

23.12 Summary

Having completed this chapter, we can now account for adjusting and non-adjusting events occurring after the end of the reporting period and can discuss the principles of recognising provisions and can define and account for contingencies.

We can define related parties and related party transactions and can explain the disclosures required by IAS 24 *Related Party Disclosures*.

Revision Questions

? Question 1

Which of the following could be classified as an adjusting event occurring after the end of the reporting period:

(A) A serious fire, occurring 1 month after the year-end, that damaged the sole production facility, causing production to cease for 3 months.

(B) One month after the year-end, a notification was received advising that the large balance on a receivable would not be paid as the customer was being wound up. No payments are expected from the customer.

(C) A large quantity of parts for a discontinued production line was discovered at the back of the warehouse during the year-end inventory count. The parts have no value except a nominal scrap value and need to be written off.

(D) The entity took delivery of a new machine from the USA in the last week of the financial year. It was discovered almost immediately afterwards that the entity supplying the machine had filed for bankruptcy and would not be able to honour the warranties and repair contract on the new machine. Because the machine was so advanced, it was unlikely that any local entity could provide maintenance cover. **(2 marks)**

? Question 2

X is currently defending two legal actions:

(i) An employee, who suffered severe acid burns as a result of an accident in X's factory, is suing for $20,000, claiming that the directors failed to provide adequate safety equipment. X's lawyers are contesting the claim, but have advised the directors that they will probably lose.

(ii) A customer is suing for $50,000, claiming that X's hair-care products damaged her hair. X's lawyers are contesting this claim, and have advised that the claim is unlikely to succeed.

How much should X provide for these legal claims in its financial statements?

(A) $0
(B) $20,000
(C) $50,000
(D) $70,000 **(2 marks)**

? Question 3

Which of the following could be regarded as a related party of X:

(A) P is X's main customer, taking 50 per cent of their turnover.
(B) S is X's main supplier, supplying approximately 40 per cent of X's purchases.
(C) A is the managing director of X and is the largest single shareholder, holding 35 per cent of the equity.
(D) B is X's banker and has provided X with an overdraft facility and a short-term loan.

(2 marks)

? Question 4

Which ONE of the following would be regarded as a related party of BS:

(A) BX, a customer of BS.
(B) The president of the BS Board, who is also the chief executive officer of another entity, BU, that supplies goods to BS.
(C) BQ, a supplier of BS.
(D) BY, BS's main banker.

(2 marks)

? Question 5

Which ONE of the following would require a provision to be created by BW at the end of it's reporting period, 31 October 2005:

(A) The government introduced new laws on data protection which come into force on 1 January 2006. BW's directors have agreed that this will require a large number of staff to be retrained. At 31 October 2005, the directors were waiting on a report they had commissioned that would identify the actual training requirements.
(B) At the end of the reporting period, BW is negotiating with its insurance provider about the amount of an insurance claim that it had filed. On 20 November 2005, the insurance provider agreed to pay $200,000.
(C) BW makes refunds to customers for any goods returned within 30 days of sale, and has done so for many years.
(D) A customer is suing BW for damages alleged to have been caused by BW's product. BW is contesting the claim and, at 31 October 2005, the directors have been advised by BW's legal advisers it is unlikely to lose the case. **(2 marks)**

? Question 6

DH has the following two legal claims outstanding:

- A legal action against DH claiming compensation of $700,000, filed in February 2007. DH has been advised that it is probable that the liability will materialise.
- A legal action taken by DH against another entity, claiming damages of $300,000, started in March 2004. DH has been advised that it is probable that it will win the case.

How should DH report these legal actions in its financial statements for the year ended 30 April 2007?

	Legal action against DH	Legal action taken by DH	
(A)	Disclose by a note to the accounts	No disclosure	
(B)	Make a provision	No disclosure	
(C)	Make a provision	Disclose as a note	
(D)	Make a provision	Accrue the income	**(2 marks)**

 ## Question 7

EP sells refrigerators and freezers and provides a 1 year warranty against faults occurring after sale.

EP estimates that if all goods with an outstanding warranty at the balance sheet date need minor repairs the total cost would be $3 million. If all the products under warranty needed major repairs the total cost would be $12 million.

Based on previous years' experience, EP estimates that 85% of the products will require no repairs; 14% will require minor repairs and 1% will require major repairs.

Calculate the expected value of the cost of the repair of goods with an outstanding warranty at the statement of financial position. **(3 marks)**

 ## Question 8

The objective of IAS 24 *Related Party Disclosures* is to ensure that financial statements disclose the effect of the existence of related parties.

Requirement

With reference to *IAS 24*, explain the meaning of the terms 'related party' and 'related party transaction'. **(5 marks)**

 ## Question 9

BJ is an entity that provides a range of facilities for holidaymakers and travellers.

At 1 October 2004 these included:

- a short haul airline operating within Europe; and
- a travel agency specialising in arranging holidays to more exotic destinations, such as Hawaii and Fiji.

BJ's airline operation has made significant losses for the last 2 years. On 31 January 2005, the directors of BJ decided that, due to a significant increase in competition on short haul flights within Europe, BJ would close all of its airline operations and dispose of its fleet of aircraft. All flights for holiday makers and travellers who had already booked seats would be provided by third party airlines. All operations ceased on 31 May 2005.

On 31 July 2005, BJ sold its fleet of aircraft and associated non-current assets for $500 million, the carrying value at that date was $750 million.

At the end of the reporting period, BJ were still in negotiation with some employees regarding severance payments. BJ has estimated that in the financial period October 2005 to September 2006, they will agree a settlement of $20 million compensation.

The closure of the airline operation caused BJ to carry out a major restructuring of the entire entity. The restructuring has been agreed by the directors and active steps have been taken to implement it. The cost of restructuring to be incurred in year 2005/2006 is estimated at $10 million.

Requirement

Explain how BJ should report the events described above and quantify any amounts required to be included in its financial statements for the year ended 30 September 2005. (Detailed disclosure notes are not required.) **(5 marks)**

? Question 10

CB is an entity specialising in importing a wide range of non-food items and selling them to retailers. George is CB's president and founder and owns 40% of CB's equity shares:

- CB's largest customer, XC accounts for 35% of CB's revenue. XC has just completed negotiations with CB for a special 5% discount on all sales.
- During the accounting period, George purchased a property from CB for $500,000. CB had previously declared the property surplus to its requirements and had valued it at $750,000.
- George's son, Arnold is a director in a financial institution, FC. During the accounting period, FC advanced $2 million to CB as an unsecured loan at a favourable rate of interest.

Requirement

Explain, with reasons, the extent to which each of the above transactions should be classified and disclosed in accordance with IAS 24 *Related Party Disclosures* in CB's financial statements for the period. **(5 marks)**

? Question 11

Timber Products is a timber supplies wholesale entity. The end of the reporting period is 31 December. On turnover of $83.5 million, the entity has pre-tax earnings of $31.6 million (last year $40.3 million on sales revenue of $91.2 million).

Timber Products has a small number of customers of which one, Homestead, represents 75 per cent of the sales revenue of Timber Products. Homestead has direct online access to Timber Products' order book and inventory records. Whenever Homestead requires a delivery, it accesses Timber Products' inventory records and order book.

Requirements

Explain whether Homestead is a related party:

(a) if, when there is insufficient quantity of the item it requires in inventory or on order, Homestead asks Timber Products to place an order with its supplier; **(4 marks)**

(b) if, when there is insufficient quantity of the item it requires in inventory or on order, Homestead generates an order from Timber Products to its suppliers. **(4 marks)**

(Total marks = 8)

? Question 12

Holiday Refreshments runs a brewing business. In February 2004, the accounts for the year ended 31 December 2003 are being finalised. The following issues remain outstanding:

1. A customer bought a glass of Holiday Best Beer in his local bar during October 2003 and became ill. He is suing the bar and Holiday Refreshments. The case has not yet come to court and although the entity's solicitors believe they will win the case, the directors offered an out-of-court settlement of $10,000 as a goodwill gesture. Under the terms of the offer, each side would meet their own costs which in the case of Holiday Refreshments are $1,500 up to December 2003. All of this amount had been paid by the year-end. The customer has not yet formally accepted the offer.
2. A consignment of hops costing $95,000 was delivered to the brewery on 20 December 2003. The supplier has not yet issued an invoice.
3. Bottles for the entity's beers are supplied by Bottlebank. Five years ago, in order to secure supplies, Holiday gave a guarantee over a $3,000,000 10-year bank loan taken out by Bottlebank. The guarantee is still in force. Bottlebank's latest accounts indicate net assets of $6.8 million and it has not breached any of the terms and conditions of the loan.
4. Due to a faulty valve, a batch of beer was inadvertently discharged into a river instead of into the bottling plant in March 2003. The entity paid a fine of $20,000 in July 2003 for an illegal discharge. It is also responsible for rectifying any environmental damage. To 31 December 2003, $200,000 had been paid. The extent of further expenditure is uncertain although it is estimated to be between $100,000 and $140,000.

Requirement

Explain how each of the above items should be treated in the accounts of Holiday Refreshments for the year to 31 December 2003. **(10 marks)**

Solutions to Revision Questions

23

 Solution 1

The correct answer is (B), see Section 23.2.3.

Further information is now available that throws more light on the prevailing position at the year end.

(A) is a non-adjusting event occurring after the end of the reporting period.

(C) is an adjusting event but was discovered at the year-end inventory count. It is therefore an adjusting event but is not after the end of the reporting period.

(D) if the lack of maintenance cover is material, it could be treated as a non-adjusting event occurring after the end of the reporting period.

 Solution 2

The correct answer is (B), see Section 23.6.2.

The directors need to create a provision for $20,000 as the employee's claim is probably going to succeed but the customer's claim is not. Provisions have to be created when it is probable that the organisation will have to transfer economic benefit. Probability is usually taken as more than 50 per cent likely.

 Solution 3

The correct answer is (C), see Sections 23.10 and 23.10.1.

IAS 24 presumes directors and shareholders who can exercise significant influence to be related parties. The largest single shareholder is certain to have significant influence.

(A) and (B) are incorrect because IAS 24 does not require parties with whom the reporting entity transacts a significant volume of business to be treated as a related party.

(D) is incorrect because IAS 24 does not require providers of finance in the ordinary course of business to be treated as a related party.

 Solution 4

The correct answer is (B), see Section 23.10.1.

Solution 5

The correct answer is (C), see Section 23.6.5.

Solution 6

The correct answer is (C), see Section 23.6.

Solution 7

Warranty cost provision = ($3 m × 0.14) + ($12 m × 0.01) = $540,000, see Section 23.6.5.

Solution 8

IAS 24 – A party is related to an entity if:

(a) directly, or indirectly the party:
  (i) controls, is controlled by, or is under common control with, the entity;
  (ii) has an interest in the entity that gives it significant influence over the entity; or
  (iii) has joint control over the entity.
(b) the party is an associate;
(c) the party is a joint venture in which the entity is a venturer;
(d) the party is a member of the key management personnel of the entity or its parent,
(e) the party is a close member of the family of any individual referred to in (a) or (d);
(f) the party is an entity that is controlled, jointly controlled or significantly influenced by, or for which significant voting power in such entity resides with, directly or indirectly, any individual referred to in (d) or (e); or
(g) the party is a post-employment benefit plan for the benefit of employees of the entity, or of any entity that is a related party of the entity.

Related party transaction: Transfer of resources, services or obligations between related parties, regardless of whether a price is charged.

The transfer of resources or obligations can include any transaction, including purchases or sales of goods, property or other assets and rendering of receipt of services.

Solution 9

IFRS 5 defines a discontinued operation as a component of an entity that has been disposed of and that represents a separate major line of business. A component of an entity is defined as operations and cash flows that can be clearly distinguished, operationally and for financial reporting purposes, from the rest of the entity. The disposal of the airline business represents a separate major line of business, which can be clearly distinguished and it was disposed of during the year.

Conclusion

The closure of the airline business should be treated as a discontinued operation and separately disclosed.

The revenue and profit must be separately disclosed in the income statement.

The $250 million loss on disposal of the aircraft fleet is material and must be shown on the face of the income statement.

Employee severance payments are committed as a result of a past event (the disposal of the airline), they will have to be paid (they are certain to be paid) but the exact timing and amount are not yet known as they are still being negotiated. IAS 37 *Provisions, contingent liabilities and contingent assets* requires a provision to be made, using the best estimate which is $20 million.

The costs of restructuring the remaining division, even although that restructuring is required as a result of the decision to close the airline business, should be classified as restructuring costs within continuing activities, as the costs relate to the travel agency business and this is continuing activities (IAS 37). As the restructuring has been published and the entity is committed to it the liability of $10 million should be provided for. The cost should be reported in the income statement under continuing activities.
see Section 23.6.2.

 ## Solution 10

According to IAS 24 *Related Party Disclosures,* a customer with whom an entity transacts a significant volume of business is not a related party merely by virtue of the resulting economic dependence. XC is not a related party and the negotiated discount does not need to be disclosed.

A party is related to an entity if it has an interest in the entity that gives it significant influence over the entity. The party is related to an entity if they are a member of the key management personnel of the entity.

As founder member and major shareholder holding 40% of the equity, George is able to exert significant influence and is a related party of CB.

George is also a related party as he is CB's president. He is a member of the key management personnel of CB.

The sale of the property for $500,000 will need to be disclosed, along with its valuation as a related party transaction.

Providers of finance are not related parties simply because of their normal dealings with the entity. However, if a party is a close member of the family of any individual categorised as a related party, they are also a related party. As Arnold is George's son and George is a related party, Arnold is also a related party. The loan from FC will need to be disclosed along with the details of Arnold and his involvement in the arrangements, see Section 23.10.

 ## Solution 11

(a) It could be argued that a related party relationship exists because, as a result of Homestead representing 75 per cent of the sales of Timber Products, Homestead has influence over the financial and operating policies of Timber Products to an extent that Timber Products might be inhibited from pursuing at all times its own separate interests. However, paragraph 6(c) of IAS 24 states that no disclosure is required of a relationship that exists simply as a result of a party being a customer of the reporting entity with whom it transacts a significant volume of business.

(b) A related party relationship exists because Homestead has effectively, as a result of its having direct control over the purchase ordering system of Timber Products, influence over the financial and operating policies of Timber Products to an extent that Timber Products might be inhibited from pursuing at all times its own separate interests, see Section 23.10.

 Solution 12

1. *Court case.* An offer has been made but not yet accepted. It is uncertain whether it must be accepted or whether the customer will pursue his case. The offer arose out of a past event (supply of beer in October) and there is a present obligation as an offer has been made. A provision of $10,000 should be made and brief details disclosed, see Section 23.6.2.

2. *Hops.* This is a straightforward accrual. An obligation arises from a past event and there is no significant uncertainty.

3. *Guarantee.* No present obligation exists as Bottlebank has net assets and met the terms of the loan. There is a possibility that the guarantee will be called in during the next 5 years and therefore the granting of the guarantee (a past event) may give rise to a possible obligation. This is a contingent liability which should be disclosed in the notes to the accounts but not provided for in the accounts, see Section 23.7.

4. *Environmental discharge.* The damage occurred as a result of a past event – the discharge of beer. The fine and $200,000 rectification costs will already be included in the accounts. There is an obligation to make good further environmental damage. There is uncertainty concerning the amount. A provision should be made of, say $120,000, with an explanation of the range of possible payments, see Section 23.6.2.

Preparing for the Examination

Preparing for the Examination

This chapter is intended for use when you are ready to start revising for your examination. It contains:

- a summary of useful revision techniques;
- details of the format of the examination;
- a bank of examination-standard revision questions and suggested solutions. These solutions are of a length and level of detail that a competent student might be expected to produce in an examination;
- a complete past examination paper. This should be attempted when you consider yourself to be ready for the examination, and you should emulate examination conditions when you sit for it.

Revision technique

Planning

The first thing to say about revision is that it is an addition to your initial studies, not a substitute for them. In other words, don't coast along early in your course in the hope of catching up during the revision phase. On the contrary, you should be studying and revising concurrently from the outset. At the end of each week, and at the end of each month, get into the habit of summarising the material you have covered to refresh your memory of it.

As with your initial studies, planning is important to maximise the value of your revision work. You need to balance the demands for study, professional work, family life and other commitments. To make this work, you will need to think carefully about how to make best use of your time.

Begin as before by comparing the estimated hours you will need to devote to revision with the hours available to you in the weeks leading up to the examination. Preparing a written schedule setting out the areas you intend to cover during particular weeks, and break that down further into topics for each day's revision. To help focus on the key areas try to establish:

- which areas you are weakest on, so that you can concentrate on the topics where effort is particularly needed,
- which areas are especially significant for the examination – the topics that are tested frequently.

Don't forget the need for relaxation, and for family commitments. Sustained intellectual effort is only possible for limited periods, and must be broken up at intervals by lighter activities. And don't continue your revision timetable right up to the moment when you enter the exam hall: you should aim to stop work a day or even two days before the exam.

Beyond this point the most you should attempt is an occasional brief look at your notes to refresh your memory.

Getting down to work

By the time you begin your revision, you should already have settled into a fixed work pattern: a regular time of day for doing the work, a particular location where you sit, particular equipment that you assemble before you begin and so on. If this is not already a matter of routine for you, think carefully about it now in the last vital weeks before the exam.

You should have notes summarising the main points of each topic you have covered. Begin each session by reading through the relevant notes and trying to commit the important points to memory.

Usually this will be just your starting point. Unless the area is one where you already feel very confident, you will need to track back from your notes to the relevant chapter(s) in the *Learning System*. This will refresh your memory on points not covered by your notes and fill in the detail that inevitably gets lost in the process of summarisation.

When you think you have understood and memorised the main principles and techniques, attempt an exam-standard question. At this stage of your studies, you should normally be expecting to complete such questions in something close to the actual time allocation allowed in the exam. After completing your effort, check the solution provided and add to your notes any extra points it reveals.

Tips for the final revision phase

As the exam approaches, consider the following list of techniques and make use of those that work for you:

- Summarise your notes into more concise form, perhaps on index cards that you can carry with you for revision on the way into work.
- Go through your notes with a highlighter pen, marking key concepts and definitions.
- Summarise the main points in a key area by producing a wordlist, mind map or other mnemonic device.
- On areas that you find difficult, rework questions that you have already attempted, and compare your answers in detail with those provided in the *Study System*.
- Rework questions you attempted earlier in your studies with a view to producing more 'polished' answers (better layout and presentation may earn marks in the exam) and to completing them within the time limits.
- Stay alert for practical examples, incidents, situations and events that illustrate the material you are studying. If you can refer in the exam to real-life topical illustrations, you will impress the examiner and may earn extra marks.

Exam Q & As

At the time of publication there are no exam Q & As available for the 2010 syllabus. However, the latest specimen exam papers are available on the CIMA website. Actual exam Q & As will be available free of charge to CIMA students on the CIMA website from summer 2010 onwards.

Index

Index